CONTROVERSIES
in
MEDIA ETHICS
Second Edition

A. David Gordon
University of Wisconsin–Eau Claire

John Michael Kittross
K\E\G Associates

Overview and Commentary by John C. Merrill
University of Missouri–Columbia

Contributions by Carol Reuss
University of North Carolina at Chapel Hill

 **LONGMAN**

An imprint of Addison Wesley Longman, Inc.

New York • Reading, Massachusetts • Menlo Park, California • Harlow, England
Don Mills, Ontario • Sydney • Mexico City • Madrid • Amsterdam

Editor-in-Chief: Priscilla McGeehon
Editor: Donna Erickson
Project Coordination and Text Design: York Production Services
Cover Designer: Keithley and Associates, Inc.
Cover Design Manager: Nancy Danahy
Full Service Production Manager: Rich Ausburn
Publishing Services Manager: Al Dorsey
Print Buyer: Denise Sandler
Electronic Page Makeup: York Production Services
Printer and Binder: The Maple-Vail Book Manufacturing Group
Cover Printer: Coral Graphic Services, Inc.

Library of Congress Cataloging-in-Publication Data

Gordon, David, 1935–
    Controversies in media ethics/A. David Gordon, John Michael Kittross; overview and
commentary by John C. Merrill; contributions by Carol Reuss.—2nd ed.
        p. cm.
    Includes bibliographical references and index.
    ISBN 0-8013-3025-4
    1. Mass media—Moral and ethical aspects. I. Kittross, John Michael, 1929– .
II. Merrill, John Calhoun, 1924– . III. Reuss, Carol. IV. Title.
P94.G67   1998
175—dc21   98–19950
                                                                                         CIP

ISBN 0-8013-3025-4

1234567890—MA—00999897

*To those who helped, mentored, and supported us along this way . . .
and those who create the horrible examples for us to consider.*

C O N T E N T S

Preface   *ix*

Note to Instructors   *xiii*

OVERVIEW   **Foundations for Media Ethics (Merrill)**   1

CHAPTER 1   **Ethics and Freedom: Mass Media Accountability**   26

Freedom of expression must be zealously guarded regardless of whether that freedom is exercised ethically by the mass media (*Gordon*)   26

Freedom of expression should not be allowed to become an excuse for irresponsible media conduct (*Reuss*)   32

Commentary (*Merrill*)   38

CHAPTER 2   **Individual Autonomy and Ethical Decisions**   40

The values of individual mass media practitioners shape their ethical decision making and the contents of the mass media (*Reuss*)   40

Social, economic, and political forces severely constrain the ethical decisions of individual media practitioners (*Gordon*)   46

Commentary (*Merrill*)   52

CHAPTER 3   **Codes of Ethics**   56

Media codes of ethics are impotent, and too often they are facades that imply ethical behavior (*Reuss*)   57

Media codes of ethics are useful and necessary to the mass media and to society (*Gordon*)   61

Commentary (*Merrill*)   68

CHAPTER 4   **Manipulation by the Media: Truth, Fairness, and Objectivity**   72

Truth precludes any need for further ethical concerns in journalism and public relations (*Gordon*)   73

The social value of journalism and public relations requires high-quality practices reflecting ethical considerations that go beyond truth and objectivity to accuracy and fairness (*Kittross*)   80

Commentary (*Merrill*)   89

CHAPTER 5   **Influences on Media Content:**
           The Public Relations Factor   **92**

The mass media cannot ignore individuals and groups
    seeking to manipulate media content, nor should
    they ignore such sources of news and information
    (*Reuss*)   92

The mass media should ignore material submitted by sources
    who want to manipulate their content (*Gordon*)   98

Commentary (*Merrill*)   105

CHAPTER 6   **Accessing the Media:**
           Information Equity Versus Apartheid   **109**

The mass media must guard against practices that isolate
    some groups in society from access to information they
    need (*Gordon*)   110

Market forces are sufficient safeguards against any groups in
    society being deprived of access to necessary information
    (*Reuss*)   115

Commentary (*Merrill*)   119

CHAPTER 7   **The Ethics of "Correctness" and "Inclusiveness":**
           Culture, Race, and Gender in the Mass Media   **124**

The mass media must make special efforts to deal with
    concerns about race, gender, culture, and ethnicity
    in both their news and entertainment functions
    (*Gordon*)   124

No special efforts are required on the part of the mass
    media to deal "correctly" with race, gender, culture,
    religion, and ethnicity (*Kittross*)   134

Commentary (*Merrill*)   144

CHAPTER 8   **Private Lives, Public Interests**   **148**

The news and entertainment media should be the sole
    judges of how their activities impinge on individual
    rights of privacy (*Reuss*)   149

The news and entertainment media cannot be the sole
    judges of the boundary between appropriate and exces-
    sive coverage, even for public figures (*Gordon*)   152

Commentary (*Merrill*)   160

CHAPTER 9   **Data Privacy**   **164**

The mass media—in their news, marketing, and similar
    activities—must respect informational privacy concern-
    ing personal information contained in private or govern-
    ment databases (*Gordon*)   165

There is no need for the mass media to be concerned about
    using personal information from private or government

databases, but we all should be concerned about its collection and abuse by others (*Kittross*)   171

Commentary (*Merrill*)   179

CHAPTER 10   Violence and Sexual Pornography   **182**

Violence and sexual pornography in the media, however regrettable, are merely reflections of the world, and government or group measures to control them would create a "cure" that is worse than the disease (*Kittross*)   183

There is far more violence in today's mass media than is good for society, and that violent content must somehow be controlled (*Gordon*)   189

Commentary (*Merrill*)   198

CHAPTER 11   Media Ethics and the Economic Marketplace   **202**

The economic marketplace is at best superfluous, and at worst counterproductive, with regard to media ethics (*Kittross*)   202

The "dead hand" of the economic marketplace, and more knowledgeable media consumers, are sufficient to hold the media fully accountable for their actions and are ethically beneficial to the media (*Gordon*)   213

Commentary (*Merrill*)   220

CHAPTER 12   Infotainment Programming   **223**

Tabloid news programs, talk shows, scandal sheets, and other forms of infotainment provide needed information in formats that get through to citizens and help make democracy work (*Gordon*)   223

Tabloid news publications and programs, talk shows, and other forms of infotainment confuse the public by offering entertainment at the expense of information (*Reuss*)   231

Commentary (*Merrill*)   236

CHAPTER 13   Ethics and Advertising   **239**

Everyone understands that the function of advertising is to create images that sell products and services, and there is therefore no need for it to adhere to truth as an ethical standard (*Gordon*)   240

Advertising, no less than news or public relations, should be held to standards of honesty and other ethical principles (*Reuss*)   247

Commentary (*Merrill*)   253

CHAPTER 14   Conflicts of Interest   **256**

The credibility of the mass media will not be lost if honest practitioners are left unrestricted in their roles as citizens and humans (*Kittross*)   257

Journalists and public relations practitioners must abstain from any "private" activities that might be seen as creating conflicts of interest in their professional endeavors (*Gordon*)   261

Commentary (*Merrill*)   265

CHAPTER 15   More Topics in the Ethical Debate   **268**

Bibliography   295

Index   303

PREFACE

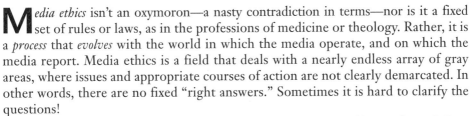

M*edia ethics* isn't an oxymoron—a nasty contradiction in terms—nor is it a fixed set of rules or laws, as in the professions of medicine or theology. Rather, it is a *process* that *evolves* with the world in which the media operate, and on which the media report. Media ethics is a field that deals with a nearly endless array of gray areas, where issues and appropriate courses of action are not clearly demarcated. In other words, there are no fixed "right answers." Sometimes it is hard to clarify the questions!

There are, however, principles that media ethicists hope will provide guidelines to assist practitioners (and their audiences) to come to grips with the ethical dilemmas that confront them every day. As John Merrill writes in his commentary for Chapter 13, "there is simply no clear and satisfying answer. But there is no reason for us to discontinue the search" (p. 254).

Even in this free form environment, and even without its inhabitants knowing, media ethics tend to follow—or can be explained by—a number of philosophical concepts: Aristotle's Golden Mean, Bentham's and Mill's utilitarian principle of the greatest good for the greatest number, Kant's categorical imperative of treating every moral rule as if it were a universal law, Rawls' veil of ignorance, and others that you will encounter in the pages that follow.

At the same time, the news, entertainment, and advertising media operate under time pressures that are matched only by those of a surgeon in an operating room. As a direct consequence of dealing continually with new events, concepts, conditions, and opinions, the mass media are continually faced with decisions that must be made with limited and imperfect data, competing goals and purposes, and a societal tendency toward *ad hoc* situational ethics. It is no wonder that there are many controversies above media ethics!

In this book, we try to provide students and practitioners with a carefully constructed set of opposing arguments focusing on more than a dozen major controversies facing mass media practitioners today. The table of contents shows that we deal with *real* and *current* problems and controversies in media ethics. In fact, every part—virtually every page—of the second edition of *Controversies in Media Ethics* has undergone major updating or clarification.

Because there are no "right" answers, we have set up this book as a series of arguments, each on a particular topic. Many of the specific cases or situations in media ethics that you will face in the future, whether as a communicator or as a member of the public, will be informed by one of these arguments. Since *you* will supply the cases in the future, we saw no reason to systematically pull examples from the past or invent hypothetical ones, although we certainly refer frequently to current ethical problems of the media. We also do not recommend that past ethical cases be used as an inflexible blueprint for determining current or future resolution to ethical dilemmas.

Each of this book's fourteen chapters deals with specific controversies and has two contrasting points of view on a major problem, written by two different authors, as do some of the less thoroughly treated topics in Chapter 15. These arguments are accompanied by brief commentaries that highlight some of the key points in each controversy. These commentaries were prepared by John Merrill, whose long experience writing and teaching in this field is evidenced by almost any bibliography on media ethics. We hope these commentaries will invite additional discussion with your peers, co-workers, and teachers. They are not intended to provide definitive summary statements on each issue.

Because our purpose is to stimulate thought and discussion, the authors have often taken fairly extreme positions in their arguments on each controversy. This is a common pedagogical approach: start at extremes in order to define alternatives clearly, and then work toward a viable middle ground. Furthermore, we stopped in each chapter before coming to the "viable middle ground," in order to leave to you the experience of defining that ground. We hope that you will consider, adopt, modify, and merge our different points of view, and apply them to the media ethics problems that face each of us literally every day. Remember that there is rarely a clear or easy solution.

We recommend reading each section completely through before going back to the individual positions for analysis. You will notice that, contrary to the linear nature of most books, the author of the first segment of each chapter will occasionally refer to points made in the second section. This also occurs because in writing the book, we had the opportunity to exchange our work more than once, allowing us to refine our positions. The selection of which author's argument is presented first is arbitrary. This give-and-take approach, while potentially confusing, allows readers the opportunity to read each argument with equal weight.

You'll find that a particular author, at times, may embrace an argument that seems to run counter to something she or he wrote in a different chapter. That doesn't indicate inconsistency or hypocrisy! It simply illustrates that these complex media questions may have many gray areas and usually can be argued cogently from different perspectives rather than lending themselves to simple and easy answers. Also, we were never required to take positions that we strongly opposed, nor did we feel compelled to defend to the death our personal favorites among the traditional ethical theories we discussed.

Although different writing and reasoning styles may have been used, and there are different levels of "heat" in our arguments, each of us supports his or her position with evidence and reason. At the same time, we each recognize, with very few exceptions, that the opposing views for each issue also have some validity. In preparing our arguments, we had the luxury of time, unlike practitioners who are suddenly faced with ethical problems, to flesh out fully the various arguments we've used, do some research, consider opposing points of view, and respond to them. Indeed, one of the major benefits of dealing with these topics in a classroom, rather than in a newsroom or studio or the offices of a public relations or advertising firm, or even sitting at home reading the paper or watching television, is the opportunity to ponder them, discuss them with fellow students or instructors, and to begin to draw some conclusions about how to "do" media ethics.

However, *Controversies in Media Ethics* also is aimed at arming today's practitioners among its readers—as well as future media practitioners—with different points of view. It is our hope that this will enable practitioners to optimize the very limited time available for discussing ethical problems with professional colleagues and making good decisions, at the same time that a deadline is looming.

We hope that the issues presented, and the various ways we analyzed them and individually resolved them, will provoke spirited discussion, even arguments, among our readers. Like defensive driving practice, it is important to become familiar with these issues now, without deadlines forcing you to make snap judgments, so that you can more easily make ethically appropriate judgments later. And, as we say throughout, media ethics is a necessity in order for the media to serve the society, culture, and body politic of which they are an essential part.

Although each of us has his or her favorite ethical theories, none of us takes a particular philosophical position and runs its logic out to the end in any given chapter. Instead, after the problem or controversy has been spelled out, each of us, independently, tries out a number of ethical principles and theories. So, while we are not case study oriented, we do treat each major ethical controversy that we deal with as something new, rather than the opportunity to demonstrate blind adherence to a particular ethical theory.

It is impossible in a book of this length to cover every media ethics issue. We have tried to focus on larger issues that most people who are interested in the mass media consider important. To further broaden this book's scope and value, some other questions are touched upon as we discuss the fourteen major controversies as well as the ten additional issues raised more briefly in Chapter 15. Our arguments aren't presented as case studies, nor are they presented as absolutes, traditions, or isolated concepts. We have, rather, tried to provide some theoretical framework that can be used to analyze one's own positions.

We have deliberately avoided the reason why we selected a particular ethical theory in a given case or controversy—and hope that you enjoy selecting your own theory and making your own decisions. It is quite possible to do "good" things for "bad" reasons and "bad" things for "good" reasons, and we want to give our readers ample opportunity to think this through for themselves.

We hope that you will remember that there are no "correct" answers to many of the questions or problems presented here. But we do believe that there are correct ways of making ethical decisions, using the facts of the case and knowledge of past philosophical thinking. Why and how you reach a particular conclusion is probably more important to your ethical development than exactly what that conclusion is. After all, reaching ethical decisions is *your* job, now and in the future.

A. David Gordon
John Michael Kittross
Carol Reuss
John C. Merrill

NOTE TO INSTRUCTORS

C ontroversies in Media Ethics is a unique series of debates that offers students and instructors multiple perspectives on a wide range of media ethics issues presenting vast "gray areas" and few, if any, easy answers. The goal of this book is to point a new generation of media practitioners, students, and interested consumers toward coherent methods of dealing with ethical problems, and toward "proper" ethical decisions. We are concerned with both philosophical ethical theory and generally accepted professional practice for *all* well-rounded media students and practitioners. But, since determining just what's "proper" and reaching those decisions is the reader's job, now and in the future, *Controversies* focuses on principles, not specific cases.

To help achieve this goal, as was true with the first edition, this book presents an innovative way to introduce students to mass media ethics. *Controversies* contains four perspectives: those of the three authors, David Gordon, John Michael Kittross, and Carol Reuss, and the commentaries and introductory Overview of John Merrill. (For the second edition, David Gordon and John Michael Kittross take responsibility for updated revisions and additions to the material originally prepared by Carol Reuss.) The different approaches taken by the authors offer more diverse views of current media ethics problems than are available in most other books on this topic.

Controversies first provides an introductory Overview by John Merrill that surveys the relevance of numerous philosophers and their ethical theories to the subject of today's mass media ethics. This Overview gives students a wealth of information on which to draw when considering the various factors and situations dealt with in the rest of the book. The Overview also will be useful to many instructors as a framework for the discussions that will evolve from the book's current issue-oriented controversies. It is intended to serve as a foundation and a reference.

Each of the next fourteen chapters and many of the ten sections of Chapter 15 present a different specific controversial issue with two sharply contrasting points of view written by two different authors. These arguments are followed by brief commentaries by Merrill that highlight some of the key points in the arguments. Because these essays express the results of our wrestling over the topics in order to sharpen the argument over each, we did not wish to bog down the narrative with a source citation for every thought or comment, although we did supply citations for quotations or other direct references. This structure is designed to promote discussion and debate in the classroom and within the media on each of these important issues.

■ NEW TO THIS EDITION

- **A new chapter on conflicts of interest,** added in response to suggestions from users and reviewers of the first edition, argues this burgeoning area of concern.
- **A new mini-chapter on deception in reporting** (sparked by the 1997 decision in the *Food Lion* case) reflects the need for new techniques of newsgathering.
- **Fully updated examples and issues** include discussions of the Clinton–Lewinsky situation in Washington, as well as the role of paparazzi in the death of Princess Diana.
- **Thoroughly updated debates** make the issues more engaging as well as easier to understand for students by making use of recent events.
- **Reference sections** at the end of each chapter provide students with additional resources on each issue.
- **A general bibliography,** greatly expanded and updated in the second edition, contains sources for cases and additional ethical decision-making tools published in more traditional texts for those who wish to delve more deeply into these topics.
- **An extensively expanded index** includes a comprehensive list of topics and names for easy reference.

Controversies in Media Ethics is intended as a primary text in upper division under-graduate ethics courses, as well as in graduate-level courses. It also is designed to be a useful supplement in a variety of courses—from advanced reporting and editing to com-munication law, and from contemporary media issues to mass media and society, not only in journalism and mass communication curricula but throughout higher education.

Although Kurt Lewin once said, "there is nothing so practical as a good theory," we are aware that some instructors will wish to start with applications and problems, bringing in ethical theory only to explain how a particular dilemma has been resolved. Obviously, such a course should start with the numbered chapters, and then return to Merrill's introductory Overview when the need and desire for more background arises. Others may wish to start with a problem or case study drawn from the daily paper or newscast (or from a good ethics casebook), and then look at the general arguments in the text to see how they apply to the new and specific situation. Finally, some will pre-fer to start from a theoretical position, using ethical theories to analyze and, ideally, to resolve ethical dilemmas. Those readers may wish to start out with the introductory Overview to this book, which is intended to provide a useful introduction to or review of some of the best and most influential thinking about ethics throughout history.

No matter how one digs into *Controversies in Media Ethics*, the focus should re-main on dealing with *real* problems faced by *real* people in the mass media, and with the impact of these problems on all of us in the media audience.

■ ACKNOWLEDGMENTS

We all have our own heroes, and the authors of this book have their own lists: the people—living and dead—who taught us ethical principles and standards, who were our colleagues and exemplars; those who are still working to ensure that the mass communication industries are also ethical professions; those who create, write, edit, and preach. Such lists are unique to each of us, although the fruits of the labors of those on our lists are to be found in the book you hold in your hands. We hope that you will be building your *own* list of mentors and role models as you face the ethical problems of your career and life.

However, there are people who deserve special thanks from us as we finish this book. One is Ed Lambeth, whose annual seminars on the teaching of ethics in journalism and mass communication have greatly expanded the rigor and the expertise of this field and have directly assisted two of this book's authors. Scholars such as Cliff Christians, Don Gillmor, Ted Glasser, Gene Goodwin, and a growing number of others, and scholar-editors such as Ralph Barney and Jay Black of the *Journal of Mass Media Ethics*, have contributed to the ethical context that enriches this volume. Of course, our families, friends, pets, and colleagues who had to make many adjustments while we worked on this book were also instrumental in its completion.

We have all learned various things from our students in media ethics courses over the years, and many of those insights are reflected in the text. Two graduate students deserve special mention for their assistance with the first edition, however. Christopher Jones at Emerson College and Robert B. Stepno at the University of North Carolina at Chapel Hill provided research help and computer expertise, respectively. Without their efforts, we might still be trying to finish this project.

Hillary Henderson, Margaret Loftus, and Kathy Schurawich, all formerly at Longman, and Donna Erickson and Priscilla McGeehon who are currently there, were also among those who helped improve this work. We are indebted to Lori Ann Smith of York Production Services for her ability to retain her cool and implement changes amid the final production crunches. Sue Gordon provided major assistance in greatly expanding the index for the second edition.

We are particularly indebted to those reviewers—Charlyne Berens, *University of Nebraska–Lincoln*; Frederick Blevens, *Southwest Texas State University*; Peter Jacobi, *Indiana University*; Val E. Limburg, *Washington State University*; Robert Picard, *California State University-Fullerton*; Herb Strentz, *Drake University*; and Tim Wulfemeyer, *San Diego State University*—whose willingness to comment on the entire manuscript were immensely helpful both early and late in the review process.

We also are grateful to all our other reviewers, whose suggestions on selected chapters were also very useful: David Arant, *University of Memphis*; William Buccalo, *Northern Michigan University*; Tim Gleason, *University of Oregon*; Richard Goedkoop, *La Salle University*; August K. Gribben, *Marquette University*; Milton Hollstein, *University of Utah*; Dominic L. Lasorsa, *University of Texas–Austin*; Sharon Murphy, *Bradley University*; Richard Alan Nelson, *Louisiana State University*; Sherry Ricchiardi, *Indiana University–Purdue University at Indianapolis*; Harold C. Shaver, *Marshall University*; Karen L. Slattery, *Marquette University*; Mindy Trossman, *Northwestern University*; and Patrick Washburn, *Ohio University*.

Any misinterpretations, lapses of logic, or other shortcomings of this book are, of course, the responsibility of the authors.

A. David Gordon
John Michael Kittross
Carol Reuss
John C. Merrill

■ ABOUT THE AUTHORS

Collectively, the four authors of this book have well over a century of teaching experience in mass communication, much of it dealing with mass media ethics. Among them, they also have several decades of professional media experience. All have earned the doctoral degree and bring to this book widely differing perspectives on social, political, economic, and philosophical issues. All of them enjoy a good debate.

A. David Gordon has taught mass media ethics and law, and a wide range of other journalism and media–society courses, at Northwestern University, the University of Miami, Emerson College, Northeastern University, and the University of Wisconsin–Eau Claire. He has been a department chair and acting dean at Miami and a department chair at Emerson and UW–EC, as well as a newspaper reporter and a mayor's administrative assistant. He is the author of *Problems in Law of Mass Communication* and of articles on ethical and legal issues, and is on the editorial board of *Mass Comm Review*. He sees himself as taking a utilitarian approach to media ethics.

John Michael Kittross is editor of *Media Ethics* and edited the *Journal of Broadcasting* for a dozen years. He is coauthor of *Stay Tuned: A Concise History of American Broadcasting*, and has written, coauthored, or edited several other books and a variety of articles. He has taught at the University of Southern California, Temple University, and Emerson College, where he also served as provost and vice president for academic affairs. He has had professional experience at several radio and television stations, in both on-air and non-air capacities. He is managing director of K\E\G Associates, an academic consulting group. As a media ethicist, he says he is a "conservative anarchist"—toward the left side of the libertarian spectrum.

John C. Merrill is a prolific writer on media ethics and journalism, with nearly two dozen books to his credit, including *The Imperative of Freedom*, *Existential Journalism*, *Legacy of Wisdom*, *Journalism Ethics*, and *The Princely Press: Machiavelli on American Journalism*. He is coauthor of the award winning *Media, Messages and Men*. His distinguished teaching career spans more than 40 years at such schools as the Universities of Missouri and Maryland and Louisiana State University, where he also served as director of the School of Journalism. He has lectured throughout the world and has considerable professional experience in both print journalism and public relations. He is an unabashed libertarian in regard to media ethics.

Carol Reuss has retired from the faculty of the University of North Carolina School of Journalism and Mass Communication, where she taught in the magazine, public relations, and mass communication and society areas. She coedited *Impact of Mass Media: Current Issues* and *Inside Organizational Communication* and is on the editorial boards for several journals, including *Public Relations Review* and *Journalism History*. As a media ethicist, she says she is a "communitarian libertarian," concerned that individual and organizational freedoms benefit society.

CONTROVERSIES
in
MEDIA ETHICS

INTRODUCTION

OVERVIEW
Foundations for Media Ethics

John C. Merrill

M edia ethics concerns right and wrong, good and bad, better and worse actions taken by people working for media. Media themselves, of course, cannot be ethical or unethical—only their staff members can. When we deal with *media ethics*, we are really concerned with ethical standards of media *workers* and what kinds of actions they take. Because this book is designed largely as a textbook for students considering the complexities of media ethics as well as for those who want an introductory view of the moral problems and dilemmas of mass communication, it is well that we use this rather long introduction to build a framework on which to attach the specific ethical controversies related to mass communication we discuss later on.

Ethics is a nebulous subject. All a person has to do is to pick up almost any book or article on ethics to see that disagreements and contradictions arise almost at once. The great moral philosophers of history have not agreed on many aspects of ethics or on the main theories and subtheories of ethics.

One thing we do know: Ethics is the study of what we ought to do. In a real sense, ethics has to do with duty—duty to self and duty to others. It is private and personal, although it relates to obligations and duties to others. The quality of human life has to do with both solitude and sociability. We do right or wrong by ourselves in the private or inward part of our lives where we are acting and reacting in a context of others. This duality of individual and social morality is implicit in the very concept of ethics, and the reader of this book will notice how these two aspects affect core arguments on each side of various issues.

For example, a journalist (or for that matter, a person who writes a television drama) is not simply writing for the consumption of others. He or she is writing as *self*-expression and *self*-gratification, and the self is developed by the very act of expression. The processes of deciding to do a story, selecting what will be used, and expressing this material all impinge on ethics and affect the moral character of the media person. What all media people communicate is, in a very real sense, what they are. They please or displease themselves, not just those for whom they are writing. What they do to live up to their personal standards affects not only the beliefs and activities of others but, in a very real sense, the very essence of their own lives. Through their actions, they existentially make their ethical selves.

■ ETHICAL CONCERN: STARTING POINT

A concern for being ethical is the starting point. If media people do not care whether what they do is good or bad, then they will have little or no interest in, or consideration of, ethics. For the average person working in the communications media, however, ethics is an important concern that permeates the entire professional activity. A sense of right conduct does not come naturally; it must be developed, thought about, reasoned through, cared deeply about. In short, it must be nurtured. Unless journalists, for example, see themselves as blotters, soaking up news-reality, how they collect this news and what they do with it is the essence of their professional life.

In recent years, an interest in making ethics relevant to the professions has become firmly entrenched. Books, articles, seminars, conferences, and workshops have stressed the need for practical ethics. Professional ethics courses have developed in many areas, especially in business, law, medicine, and journalism. Books for such courses have followed; a good example of an ethics book encompassing several professions is Serafini's *Ethics and Social Concern* (1989). Journalism and mass communications academics and practitioners have written a great number of ethics books in the last several decades. Media organizations, subject to increasing criticism from the public, have encouraged their staff members to become more concerned with moral issues.

Mass communicators are right in the middle of all sorts of ethical problems in the daily work environment. Such people must decide what is the right (or at least the best) thing to do at every turn. At the core of media ethics are certain key questions: What should I consider worth publishing, broadcasting, or disseminating in the first place? How much should I publish? Which parts should I omit? These and other questions spin out of a decision to bring a story, program, or advertisement to the public's attention. The media person works in the realm of ethics, whether or not he or she gives any thought to it *as ethics*.

Ethical concern is important, for it forces the media person to make commitments and thoughtful decisions among alternatives. Ethical concern leads the media person to seek the *summum bonum*, the highest good in professional practice, thereby heightening self-respect and public credibility and respect. The reader who expects this book to answer every question about what to do (prescriptive ethics) or not to do (proscriptive ethics) will be disappointed. In fact, as the very nature of the book attests, ethical determinations are *debatable*. What we hope to do is to serve as ethical thought-provokers and moral consciousness-raisers, and to raise significant ethical controversies in various media contexts with which readers can grapple. The purpose of this book is not to answer once and for all the basic questions of media morality, but to raise significant questions worthy of continuing concern.

Although concern with media ethics may be growing, it is still underdeveloped. Marvin Kalb, former NBC reporter now at Harvard's Kennedy School of Government, maintains that American journalism is "mean-spirited," having a "desire to tear down rather than build up" (Budiansky, 1995, p. 46). In the same article by Budiansky in *U.S. News & World Report*, Kathleen Hall Jamieson of the University of Pennsylvania says of today's journalists that "everyone operates out of cynical self-interest" (p. 46). Newton N. Minow, who called television "a vast wasteland" in 1961, reappraised the medium in 1995 and found it still lacking in quality. He writes that TV has had a "distorting influence" (1995, p. 6) and has failed to serve four main needs: properly supporting education, meeting the needs of children, adequately providing serious public programming, and supporting the political system during campaigns. Minow maintains that television has not "fulfilled our needs and will not do so in the next 30 years" (1995, p. 6). There seems to be no doubt that ethical awareness among media people is not what it ought to be.

Ethical concern is important, for it forces the media person to make commitments and thoughtful decisions among alternatives.

Two Main Ethical Emphases

Ethical concern can manifest itself in two main emphases: (1) the mass communicator can be concerned mainly with taking ethical cues from the society, from colleagues, and from the community, or (2) the mass communicator can emphasize personal ethical development and put community priorities second. The first emphasis is today called *social* or *communitarian* ethics, the second is called *personal* or *individual* ethics. In both cases, the journalist is concerned with ethics and wants to do the right or best thing. It is simply a matter of emphasis—one relying on group-driven ethics, the other on personally determined ethics. One stresses other-directed ethical action, the other inner-directed ethical action.

Actually, these two emphases are not mutually exclusive, although the proponents of each often seem hostile to one another. The communitarian does not ignore individuality; the individualist does not disdain cooperative or social concerns. It is simply a matter of emphasis. A good book that gives the communitarian perspective is *Good News,* by Clifford Christians and colleagues (1993), which proposes that journalists forget the Enlightenment concepts of individualism and libertarianism touted by such liberal thinkers throughout history as Locke, Voltaire, Constant, Adam Smith, James Mill, John Stuart Mill, and Kant. Communitarians see individual or liberal ethics as dysfunctional to the community and generally based on personal quirks rather than on group-determined standards.

Today, communitarian ethicists such as Amitai Etzioni, Alasdair MacIntyre, Christopher Lasch, Joseph de Maistre, and Michael Sandel would have journalists publish things that would bring people together, not fractionalize them. Christians et al. (1993) ask for a universal ethics, saying that journalists should realize that "universal solidarity is the normative core of the social and moral order" (p. 14) and that journalists should throw out the old concepts of journalistic autonomy, individualism, and negative freedom (pp. 42–44).

The other emphasis or ethical orientation is the liberal or libertarian one, which asks for maximum personal autonomy in ethical decision making. It does indeed stress the values of the European Enlightenment thinkers and puts the individual at the center of the ethical system. One of the best books upholding the liberal or individualistic emphasis and criticizing the communitarian perspective is Stephen Holmes's 1993 book *The Anatomy of Antiliberalism.* This University of Chicago political theorist explains both communitarianism and libertarianism, but mainly provides a critique of what he calls antiliberalism (communitarianism).

Communitarians	Libertarians
Groupists	Individualists
Egalitarians	Enlightenment liberals
Altruists	Existentialists
Traits	**Traits**
Restrained freedom	Maximum freedom
Civic transformation	Self-transformation
Normative ethics codes	Personal ethical codes
Selflessness	Self-concern
Cooperation	Self-enhancement
Social influence on policy	Personal influence
Bonding/conformity	Autonomy/diversity
Group-progress	Competition/meritocracy
"Other-directed"	"Inter-directed"
Like-minded worldview	Diverse worldviews
Positive, cohesive news	Total spectrum news
Social guidance	Social information
Universal solidarity	Universal competition
Agreement on common ethics	Disagreement on ethics
Universal-legalistic ethics	Relative-situation ethics
Media professionalism	Anti-media professionalization
Exemplars	**Exemplars**
Confucius, Plato, Marx, MacIntyre, Bellah, Lasch, Hutchins, Niebuhr, Buber, Jonas, Etzioni, Sandel, Christians	Lao-tzu, Socrates, Aristotle, Locke, Jefferson, Madison, Voltaire, Constant, Tocqueville, Mill, Thoreau, Camus, Jaspers, Rand, Nozick, Hayek, Merrill

FIGURE 1   Two ethical mega-emphases

Another defender of individualism and critic of egalitarianism and other forms of communitarianism is *Time* magazine's former media critic, William A. Henry III. In his 1994 book *In Defense of Elitism*, Henry describes the growth of the "community" emphasis, which leads to a deprecation of the individual, and of "elitism" or meritocracy—the idea that some people are smarter than others, that some ideas are better than others. Explaining the kind of elitism he supports, Henry writes:

> The kind of elitists I admire are those who ruthlessly seek out and encourage intelligence and who believe that competition—and, inevitably, some measure of failure—will do more for character than coddling ever can. My kind of elitist does not grade on a curve and is willing to flunk the whole class. My kind of elitist detests the policy of social promotion that has rendered a high school diploma meaningless and a college degree nearly so. . . . My kind of elitist hates tenure, seniority, and the whole union ethos that contends that workers are interchangeable and their performances essentially equivalent. (p. 19)

To Henry, the contemporary emphasis on community desires is taking precedence over individual preferences to the degree that the marketplace of ideas is being threatened. Even in education, which Henry believes should foster individualism, there is an "academic echo of Marxism [as] administrators join activists in celebrating the importance of 'community' over the importance of individual thought and exploration" (p. 108).

Another book, George Morgan's *The Human Predicament* (1968), is also anticommunitarian in its thrust; it extols the individual person and bemoans the drift toward standardization of social activities. In a chapter called "Dissolution of the Person," Morgan warns that increasingly one's everyday activity is modeled after the machine: standardized, automatic, and repeatable. "In all departments of life," he writes, "unceasing efforts are made to avoid, or render unnecessary, the judgments, decisions, and even the presence of the individual man" (p. 61). He continues:

> This situation is so taken for granted that few are aware of it or can see its true nature. Once recognized, however, its manifestations are found everywhere. Let it be epitomized here by a development that reaches into the core of the person: the everspreading assumption that a person's life need not be shaped through his own search, understanding, and decision—aided by the experience and wisdom of others. (p. 62)

We can see that these two emphases are important: the libertarian holds fast to individualistic ethical development and the communitarian seeks to enhance the community and take ethical nourishment from the group. The first would improve society by stressing self-improvement and individual decision making; the second would improve society by sublimating personal concerns to community wishes and cooperatively making decisions that are designed to eliminate friction.

■ INTRODUCING THE FIELD OF ETHICS

Before getting to the controversial issues in the succeeding chapters, it is well to provide an introduction to the field of ethics, to talk *about ethics*—the need for ethics and some of the theories and subtheories of ethics. Actually, this Overview deals with what moral philosophers call *theoretical* normative ethics—the theories philosophers have developed to explain moral behavior. The rest of the book considers what is called normative ethics (what ought to be done in specific situations and cases). This introductory part, along with the *pro* and *con* arguments (and the commentaries) throughout the rest of the book, provide a rather broad perspective on ethics as it relates to the problems of media people as they face real decision making.

Media ethics is a branch of philosophy seeking to help journalists and other media people determine how to behave in their work. In its practical application, it is very much a normative science of conduct, with conduct considered primarily self-determined, rational, and voluntary. It must be remembered that without freedom and sanity, ethics is meaningless to a person and impossible to take seriously as a subject of discourse. To have the option of being ethical, I must know what I am doing and I must have the freedom to decide among alternatives of action.

Many workers in the media might say that they have very little freedom because they are employees—that they must follow orders, not make their own ethical decisions. They point to the fact that jobs are scarce and that they must make a living.

Indeed, there is much pressure on media employees to conform, to give up their freedom and their integrity; to be sure, there are authoritarian bosses who give little or no leeway to the individual worker. But media people cannot adopt the defense used by the Nazis at the Nuremberg war crimes trials, and disclaim their responsibility for the actions they take. Although journalists and other media people in the United States may not have all the freedom they might want, they have a great deal—enough at least to have the force of ethical sanctions fall on them.

A media person concerned with ethics, like anyone else, goes through a process of moral development. It is generally thought there are three main levels in such a moral progress, each one more sophisticated than the last. The first level is based on *instinct*, in which right conduct is determined by the person's fundamental needs and instincts. On this primitive level, ethics comes from innate tendencies. The second level is based on *custom*—what seems right to the person is conduct that is in accordance with the customs of the various groups to which he or she belongs. The third and highest general level of morality is based on *conscience*. Here, conduct that appears right is that which is approved by the agent's own personally developed judgment of what is right or wrong. The conscience is developed by the person's own reasoning, building on custom and instinct.

Regardless of the particular theory or subtheory of ethics used, the third level of moral development is the media person's goal. Here, moral standards are actively chosen by the individual after deliberation; they are no longer accepted passively as a natural part of group-assigned conduct, although they may rely to some extent on social expectations. The person at this level senses a new personal interest in morality, recognizing that *at the level of conscience* to be good is essentially an individual matter. At this third level of moral development, which William Lillie (1961, p. 51 ff.) calls "pure morality," the agent leaves a level of ethics based on institutional or group-approved actions and enters a level where right and wrong become a matter of individual determination. James Q. Wilson, in *The Moral Sense* (1993), deals at length with this more personal kind of ethics, and his approach will be discussed later.

It is probably true that most media morality today is largely stuck at the level of custom. But there are those in the media who reflect on moral matters and, guided by conscience, refuse to follow the customs of their particular media institution or professional society. It is undoubtedly beneficial to the group or society that most people accept the group standards without question; if all journalists constantly asked questions about the rightness and wrongness of the rules of their newspaper, there would be a breakdown of stability and traditional principles would not be passed on.

It should be noted that many of the ethical principles found at the custom level actually *began* with the thoughts of some person in the past. How else could a custom get its start? So it is not true that all custom-based ethical principles are wrong. Generally, however, the level of custom in ethics is more nonrational and inflexible than the level of conscience. It is more ritualistic and conformist, making morality less likely to progress, develop, and adapt to the special needs of the individual or the particular situation. Being a group-determined morality, it is more absolutist and often insensitive to the thoughtful individual who finds a need for exceptions to rules. Such a thinking individual is often considered, on the level of customary ethics, to be a danger to social stability and harmony. (Lillie discusses this in Chapter 3, "Development of Morality," of *Introduction to Ethics*.)

Later we shall consider various theories of ethics that fall in all three of these levels of moral development—instinct, custom, and conscience. We shall see that the custom level (including various versions of social or communitarian ethics) and the conscience level (including the more individualistic, egocentric, and existential ethical inclinations) seem to manifest themselves as moral adversaries. It might be said that the two strands of moral emphasis have their genesis in the moral thinking of Plato (more aligned to communitarian, social ethics) and Aristotle (more aligned to individualistic ethics), although the ideas of both philosophers were quite complex and there are bits of both strands in each of them. At any rate, it will be interesting to keep these *levels of ethical development* in mind as we consider broad and narrow theories of ethics.

■ THREE CLASSES OF ETHICAL THEORIES

Theories of ethics abound, but we shall try to keep our explanations here as simple as possible and focus primarily on two main or mega-theories of ethics: (1) *deontological*—those that base ethical actions on a *priori* principles or maxims that are accepted as guides for such actions—and (2) *teleological*—those that base ethical actions on a consideration of their consequences. Here we shall expand this binary typology, placing several subconcepts under a third heading, which we shall call *personalist* or *subjective theories*, which provide more instinctive guidance theories.

The following sections offer brief descriptions of these three main classes or types of ethical theory: *absolutist/legalistic theories*, which are deontological (including Aristotelianism, Confucianism, Kantianism, and the divine command theory); *consequence theories*, which are teleological (including utilitarianism, altruism, egoism, the social contract theory, and the pragmatic or Machiavellian); and *personalist theories*, which are predominantly subjective and individualistic (including the instinctual, emotive, antinomian, and existential).

Deontological Ethical Theory

The first of the mega-theories, the *deontological*, has to do with duty, with following formalistic rules, principles, or maxims. If you follow them (e.g., *always* give sources of quotes in a news story), you are ethical; if you don't, you are unethical. In this sense, it is clear-cut and simple. And it has a great appeal for many people in the media. Just tell the truth. Be consistent. Have no double standards. Be forthright and full in your reporting. Let the chips fall where they will. Don't worry about consequences; just do what a mass communicator is supposed to do.

Probably history's leading *deontologist* in ethics was Immanuel Kant (1724–1804), a German philosopher who provided the fullest arguments for a duty-bound system of ethical behavior. He believed that *only* an action taken out of self-imposed duty could be ethical, and he formulated what he called the *categorical imperative*, which said that what was ethical for a person to do was what that person would will that everyone should do. Another version of the famous imperative (a kind of supermaxim from which ethical principles can be formulated) was that no person should be treated as a means to an end, but only as an end. Together, these two formulations make up the core of Kant's duty-to-principle ethics—guidelines a person can have ahead of time to guide ethical decisions.

Teleological Ethical Theory

The *teleological or consequence-related* mega-theory says that the person trying to decide what to do attempts to predict what the consequences will be if *A* is done instead of *B*. The object is to choose the action that will bring the most good to the party the actor deems most important. The altruist thinks of good to others; the egoist considers good to the self, with perhaps some benefits spinning off to others.

At any rate, the *teleological* approach to ethics is a popular one and will recur in most of the arguments found in the controversy discussions in later chapters of this book. The theorist most commonly associated with this thinking is John Stuart Mill, the nineteenth-century British philosopher who formulated the theory of *utilitarianism*—whose aim it was to bring the greatest happiness (or pleasure) to the greatest number (see Merrill's *Legacy of Wisdom*, 1994, profile 16). Many versions of teleological ethics, other than the altruistic one just mentioned, were propounded by such thinkers as Mill, Bentham, and Hume. For example, there are *egoistic* teleologists who consider consequences mainly to one's self, rather than to others. Twentieth-century writer Ayn Rand (see Merrill, 1994, profile 22) is a good example of an egoistic teleologist.

Personalist or Subjective Theory

The *personalist* or *subjective* mega-theory subsumes many subtheories lending themselves to intuitive, emotive, spiritual, and other highly personal moral factors. Unlike the deontological and teleological theories, this personal-subjective theory is nonrational. It is more spontaneous, motivated by instinct or a spiritually motivated will. The person has a kind of moral sense that nudges him or her toward right action—call it conscience, instinct, or spiritual guidance. For the Christian moralist, this ethical sense may be directed by a deep-rooted concern often called *agape* (God-centered love). Such spiritual-religious overtones are exemplified by the *religious* or *faith* level—the highest level of Kierkegaard's moral progression. It is also related to Joseph Fletcher's *situation ethics* (Fletcher, 1966), where one's actions in any situation are directed by a love (deep concern) that flows constantly through the agent and is projected to others. *Agape ethics* serves as a kind of underpinning for such a social ethical stance, in one of the domains of communitarian ethics. Personalist or subjective ethics does not have to be God-centered, however; ethical direction can also be found through various forms of meditation, mystical experiences, and existentialism.

One type of the *personalist* or *subjective* mega-theory we should mention is what C. S. Lewis (*Mere Christianity*, esp. Book III, ch. 3) and others call *conscience* and James Q. Wilson (1993) calls the *moral sense*—something genetic or biological, something, as Wilson says, that is "intuitive or directly felt . . . about how one ought to act when one is free to act voluntarily" (p. xii). Wilson says that it is impossible to define such a subjective concept any more clearly than that, and he mentions British philosopher Henry Sidgwick's struggle with the concept of "ought" through six editions of his great ethics treatise (1956); Wilson concludes that the concept "is too elementary to admit of any formal definition" (p. 30).

It seems that gender may have something to do with the moral sense Wilson talks about. Harvard's Carol Gilligan (1982) has concluded that childhood experiences coupled with innate or genetic differences may lead to the existence and development of a moral sense. She also believes that much of it is gender-based. For example, her

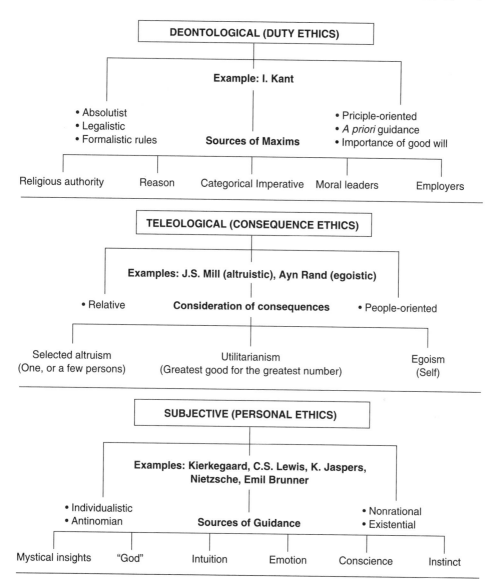

FIGURE 2　Three classes of ethical theory

research indicates that men are more prone to stress such concepts as fairness, justice, and duty, whereas women stress such moral attributes as assistance, care, and sympathy. It should be noted that these gender-based inclinations are based on what people *say* they are concerned about, not what they *do* in a real situation.

Because this third cluster of theories is personal and subjective, it is hard to make generalizations beyond the kind made by Gilligan which are applicable to the mass communicator.

At this point we shall leave this subjective macro-theory and briefly consider two perspectives that can be considered professional indicators of a journalist's basic allegiance: to norms or rules, on the one hand, and to consequences on the other. For the journalist, these legalistic and consequence theories often collide.

For example, does the journalist who claims to have some predetermined *deonto-logical* principle (for example, to be truthful and full in the report) on occasion break with these beliefs when consequences seem to warrant it? The answer usually is yes. For instance, many rule-based journalists would omit the name of a rape victim from a story, even though it would be required for a full account. Thus, deontology and teleology intermingle in the decisions and actions of most media practitioners.

■ THE PROFESSIONAL AND HUMANISTIC STANCES

We are faced with a real conundrum in ethics—two perspectives that might be called the *professional* stance and the *humanistic* stance. The professional stance, for example, is that of reporters who are dedicated to "the people's right to know," who feel an ethical obligation to let them know. They might do so without worrying about consequences and, perhaps, without considering as important the *means* of getting the story. The driving principle would be providing a truthful and full account. Neither the means of achieving this end nor the consequences would be important. For example, a reporter who prints the name of a rape victim, believing this to be good, full, accurate, and truthful reporting, could be described as taking the "professional" stance (Merrill, 1985). The corresponding *Machiavellian* principle would be that the information needed to make a full and accurate story may be obtained by any means necessary (Merrill, 1992).

The *humanistic* stance, on the other hand, is more relativistic and more teleological or consequence-motivated. It is not tied to any one professional objective, however important it might be. Of course, a person taking this stance would make exceptions to general principles, consider consequences to people involved in the situation, use ethical means to achieve desired ends, and put human sensitivities and humanistic concerns above the job of simply providing a full and truthful account or meeting some other goal.

■ A BRIEF LOOK AT SUBTHEORIES

There are many ways to look at ethics and its many theories and subtheories. The main three have been presented as teleological, deontological, and personalist. We now proceed to some of the more restricted or specific ways philosophers have classified conceptions of ethics. This is not an exhaustive list, and some concepts do not fit neatly into only one of the three basic theoretical types. We can certainly see in each of the following the genesis of many interesting controversies, some of which manifest themselves throughout the rest of this book.

Acquired-Virtue Ethics

Many ethicists actually consider *virtue ethics* one of the macro-theories, not a subtheory. At any rate, Aristotle (384–322 B.C.) can probably be called the father (or at least one of the fathers, along with Confucius) of this kind of ethical theory, which is elaborated on in his *Nicomachean Ethics*. Such an ethics is built mainly on the concept of virtue and on the habitual practice of actions that foster harmonious relations among people. Aristotle saw ethics tied to character, principles, and good will (see Merrill, 1994, profile 5.) Self-esteem was important to Aristotle and the practice of virtue was the key to self-development. He would have people concentrate on character building and the formation of intellectually sound habits, for he believed that moral virtues arise within us as a result of habits. We are not born with them. In fact, the Greek word *ethos* (habit) is similar to *ethike*, from which we get our word *ethics*.

For Aristotle, virtue is a state of character concerned with choices of a moderate nature, a kind of balance determined by a rational person of practical wisdom. This *Golden Mean* is the midpoint between two vices, one excessive (too much) and the other defective (too little). Avoid extremes in action, he seems to say; seek a moderate and rational position in ethical decision making.

In journalism, Merrill (1989) has related Aristotle's golden mean to Hegel's synthesis of the dialectic and has proposed this middle-way ethical stance as a worthy one for media people. Personal needs clash with societal needs; the resulting synthesis is moderated action. James Wilson (1993, p. 93) says that, according to Aristotle, most people become temperate as they begin to value "deferred pleasures" such as friendship, respect, and lasting happiness that come as they "subordinate their immoderate passions to moderate habits."

Many journalists feel that seeking some kind of Aristotelian mean is not very useful in journalism. Some issues, such as freedom of expression, do not lend themselves to a Golden Mean position; a journalist, they say, cannot be a "little free." However, compromise in ethics is indeed possible, and the fact that one does not have complete freedom does not keep that person from having a great degree of freedom. It seems that one can indeed be a "little free." Some media people—and entire media systems—can be freer than others.

As Anthony Serafini (1989) points out, Aristotle's approach to ethics is empirical, similar to the approach taken later on by the utilitarians and by their 20th-century followers who have modified and adapted their ideas. A person, in acquiring virtues and making them habitual in practice, brings happiness to others—and to oneself at the same time. Through reason, and through following the practices of respected people deemed virtuous in their society, one develops good habits and a moral character. That person's morality can be observed by others in everyday activities; ethics, for the person who enthrones the development of character, is not a matter of simple belief, but a matter of empirical reality where the virtuous person habituates actions on the basis of thinking, has good motives, and does nothing in excess.

Another ancient sage who proposed a variant of *acquired-virtue ethics* is Confucius (551–470 B.C.). This Chinese thinker was, in many ways, similar in his ethical outlook to Aristotle. When we think of Confucian ethics (see his *Analects*, many editions), we are mainly considering ceremonial activities, manners, and the like. In short, in Confucius we see a stress on Aristotelian habitual virtuous actions (see Merrill, 1994, profile 1).

In the ethics of Confucius, manners are extremely important; in fact, they play a key role. Life would be brutish and graceless, Confucius believed, without human ceremony. Ceremony, he said, can transform a person's life (Dawson, 1932). It can check depravity before it develops, and cause the individual to move toward what is good, keeping him or her from wrongdoing without consciously realizing it. This kind of ceremonial ethics is largely culture-bound. Moral habits come, in large degree, from community expectations and are "habits of the heart" (a term coined by Alexis de Tocqueville and discussed at length by Robert Bellah and colleagues, 1985).

Virtues can be learned and developed. They then become part of the person, and come into play automatically when they are needed to keep the person on the moral road. The virtues of work and courage and the graces of courtesy, civility, consideration, and empathy are all central to Confucian ethics. Henry Hazlitt (1972, pp. 76–77) has called this kind of ethics "major ethics," in the sense that it is an ethics of everyday life. Codes of manners, according to Hazlitt, set up an unwritten order of priorities such as the young yielding to the old, the able-bodied to the ill or crippled, the gentleman to the lady, the host to the guest. How we act toward one another was very important to Confucius. He even proposed (four centuries before Christ) what is called the Negative Golden Rule: Do not do unto others what you would not wish others to do unto you. Confucius believed that an internalized code of ethics is the foundation of morality and tends to reduce or eliminate life's irritations and traumas.

. . . Confucian ethicists believe that the person who is considerate and thoughtful in little things will also be so in big things.

Confucius recognized the importance of such an everyday morality and gave less attention to what might be called "crisis" morality and its focus on big issues. For this Chinese thinker, what was important was having good manners, being polite, being considerate of others in all the details of everyday life. The big crisis issues would tend to disappear in the presence of the continuous practice of the "little virtues."

By and large, Confucian ethicists believe that the person who is considerate and thoughtful in little things will also be so in big things. Of course, rational morality (with the possible exception of Kant's) concedes that there are exceptions to any ethical path. For example, a person can evidence perfect manners and outward manifestations of concern for others while also being cunning, devious, and scornful of others. But generally, according to Confucian thought, this is not the case; the habit of good manners and consideration casts the person in an ethical mode from which he or she seldom deviates. In a sense, we have here a kind of morality where actions (manners and ceremonial actions) destine a person to be ethical. It is the ethics of acquired virtues, habitually put into action. It is the ethics of habitual virtue, the concept of "do and you will be"—a trait of cultural morality often found in Eastern cultures.

For Confucius, the whole social order is preserved by customs (*li*, which can be defined as imperatives of conduct). Karl Jaspers (1957, p. 45) summarizes the importance that Confucius gave to *li*: "Confucius drew no distinction between custom, morality, and justice. . . . His vision embraced the whole world of Chinese customs: the right way of walking, greeting, behaving in company, always in accordance with the particular situation; the rites of marriage, birth, death, and burial; the rules of administration; the customs governing work, war, the family, the priesthood, the court; the order of the days and seasons, the stages of life."

Cultural Relativism

Many thinkers believe that different cultures have different moral codes, thus generating a system of cultural relativism. A good example of such theories can be found in anthropologist Ruth Benedict's popular book *Patterns of Culture* (1934). What one believes and does depends simply on where you are, according to Benedict. For example, in Mexico a journalist may well moonlight for a politician in the evenings, and there is nothing unethical about it, whereas in the United States such a practice would be considered unethical. The believer in ethical *cultural relativism* would claim that there is no objective standard by which we can call one societal code better than another, that different societies or cultures have differing ethical codes, that one's own moral code has no advantage over others, that there is no universal truth in ethics, and that it is nothing more than arrogance for us to judge the conduct of other peoples. Cultural relativism is closely related to contextual (sometimes called situation) ethics.

Ethical Subjectivism

This is the view of ethics that says that our moral opinions are based simply on our feelings. No objective right or wrong exists. When we say that a reporter should keep personal opinions out of a story, we are not stating a fact that putting personal opinions in the story is bad or wrong; we are only saying that we have negative feelings about doing so. If I am an ethical subjectivist, I am only recognizing that my opinions represent my own personal feelings and have nothing to do with "the truth" of the matter.

Subjectivism is by far the most common form of relative ethics. Fundamentally, the subjective ethicist who is saying that a certain action is right is simply expressing personal approval or disapproval of an action. Serious moral philosophers through the ages have not found subjectivism very convincing as an ethical theory, seeing it more as a psychological manifestation than a rational view of morality. This theory is also known as *emotivism*. It is closely related to ethical intuitionism, antinomianism, and even existentialism.

Religious Morality

Theologian Emil Brunner offered the well-known statement that doing good means always doing what God wills at any particular moment. This expresses the core idea of the ethics of religion. The problem for the media person and for anyone else, however, is knowing what "God wills" at any one moment in the decision-making workday. Holy books such as the Bible, the Talmud, and the Koran can give only general guidance not specifics about the will of some higher being or spirit. For many, a solution is found in the *divine command theory*, where "ethically correct" or "morally right" means "commanded by God" and "morally wrong" means "forbidden by God." But many problems are connected to this theory. For instance, such a theory would be of no help to the many people who are atheists. Also, as Plato asked four centuries before Christ: Is conduct right because the gods command it, or do the gods command it because it is right? Of course, there is also the basic problem of receiving specific guidelines for professional decision making via a transcendental channel.

This is nevertheless a real and important theory for many religious media people. They believe that they can take divine guidance in general things and adapt it to specific decisions; it is a matter of belief, faith, and interpretation. For them, this is sufficient ethical guidance. Related to this theory is what is often called the *theory of natural law*, which states that moral judgments are "dictates of reason," and that the best thing to do in any case is what seems most reasonable.

Natural law, which is not really in conflict with religious ethical theory, also includes the person who is not religious. There are natural laws that prescribe our behavior just as there are "laws of nature" by which nature operates. Reason, it may be said, is congenial with the idea of a rational divinity who created the world as a rational order peopled by rational creatures.

Ethical Egoism

The core of ethical egoism was well expressed by Ayn Rand (1964, p. 37) when she stated that the "achievement of his own happiness is man's highest moral purpose." Rand's version is a kind of egoistical utilitarianism that many see negatively as a form of ethical hedonism. Thomas Hobbes (1950) defended ethical egoism by connecting it with the Golden Rule: One considers the self first by thinking that if he or she does good things for others, they will do good things in return. In one way, the theory is a common-sense view of ethics, saying that we should look out for our own interests and that at least we should balance our interests against the interests of others. Whereas psychological egoism says that we do pursue our own interests, *ethical egoism* goes further and says that we *should* pursue our own self-interests.

Certainly it is a theory that challenges some of our deepest moral beliefs. Ethical egoism is a radical theory that says that one's *sole* duty is to promote one's personal interests. The theory does not forbid one from aiding others; in fact, it often sees such aid as an effective way of helping oneself. The ethical egoist believes that what makes an act ethical is the fact that it is beneficial to oneself. It should also be noted that ethical egoists do not always do what they want to do, or what might give them short-term pleasure. What a person should do is what will be the best for that person *in the long run*. It does indeed recommend selfishness, but it doesn't advocate foolishness.

Writing of the rational self-interest of Ayn Rand, Leonard Peikoff (1983) stresses that moral selfishness does not mean a license to act as one pleases or to engage in "whim" ethics. What it does mean is a disciplined defining and pursuing of one's *rational* self-interest and a rejection of all forms of sacrifice, whether of self to others or others to self. The theory upholds the virtues of reason, independence, justice, honesty, productiveness, self-pride, and integrity (pp. 308–309).

Despite a stress on such virtues, ethical egoism seems rather cold and uncaring. Maybe it is the word *egoism* that makes it hard to accept as an ethical theory. Can there be any real arguments for such a theory? There are some. For example, if we are always concerned for others, we may intrude into their privacy; it may be better for us to mind our own business. Besides, giving charity may well be degrading to others, robbing them of individual dignity and self-respect. Altruistic ethics regards the individual as sacrificial for the good of others, whereas ethical egoism permits a person to view his or her life as being of ultimate value. It seems, however, that these two contrasting ethical stances are really not "pure," for there is considerable overlap. A person living in a social situation *must* have some consideration for the welfare and progress of others—although, it may be said, this consideration stems from a selfish motivation.

Egoism is more ethically substantive than people usually think. For example, if we think of the moral end as self-perfection, then it is likely that we can do very little for the perfection of others. Egoism holds that the only contribution a person can make to a good world is to maximize his or her own goodness. One of the significant arguments against ethical egoism, however, is that it does not conform with moral intuitions. The moral sense or conscience (the highest of the development stages of morality) tells us to seek the good of others rather than our own, and it is impossible to have a meaningful ethics that goes against basic instincts.

Somewhere between egoistic ethics and the ethics of altruism is what some have called *mutualistic ethics*. Most of us are not really against the pursuit of self-interest; what we feel uncomfortable with is the pursuit of self-interest at the expense of others. Are we like the egoist (even a rational one) of Ayn Rand who would act only out of self-interest? Or, on the other hand, do we act solely out of the interest of others? For most of us, or perhaps all of us, the answer to both questions is *no*.

A society in which all people worked only for the good of others would be hard to conceive. A society in which everyone acted purely egoistically would certainly not be workable. What is important to recognize is that egoism and altruism are not mutually exclusive. What we really have as ethical motivations might be called mutualism—a kind of synthesis of symbiosis. This ethical stance shows that what promotes the well-being of the individual also promotes the well-being of society generally, and what is good for society is good for the individual. As a theory, this mutualistic ethics may seem reasonable, but in all probability each person will remain intrinsically—or mainly—an egoist or an altruist, motivated largely by concern for self or concern for others.

Machiavellian Ethics

A variant of egoistic ethics is one that might be called *pragmatic egoism*, or *Machiavellian ethics*, and its leading exemplar was Niccolò Machiavelli (1469–1527), a Florentine historian and political consultant who championed the achieving of predetermined ends. Success was his guiding principle. Use conventional ethical standards, he said, when they will work for you, but don't refrain from using *any* means if they are needed to achieve your ends. His was certainly a very pragmatic, flexible, relativistic, ego-centered *teleological* system of ethics (Merrill, 1998), predicated on personal achievement of desired ends.

Machiavelli might well be considered the father of modern propaganda and, many might say, of modern advertising and public relations. Certainly he would represent the competitive, get-the-story-at-all-costs philosophy of many modern hard-nosed investigative reporters. Machiavelli's ethics is success-driven and egoistic.

It is not hard for the viewer of today's television (and to a lesser degree the reader of today's press) to see media-Machiavellians at work. One is hardly surprised to hear even prominent journalists invoking the old saw that "the end justifies the means." Let's look at some specifics (reported in the *Washington Post National Weekly Edition*, 1992, pp. 31–32). Hidden cameras were used by ABC's *PrimeTime Live* and CBS's *60 Minutes*—is that unethical? CBS's Don Hewitt says it bothers him somewhat, but he sees it as "a minor crime versus the greater good." Richard Kaplan, executive producer of *PrimeTime Live*, also sees ends justifying the deceptive means in journalism.

Journalists have been at this undercover reporting sting business for a long time. One of the most widely discussed cases was in the late 1970s, when the Chicago *Sun-Times* and the Better Government Association set up a Chicago bar called the Mirage, secretly photographing local inspectors seeking bribes. Was this entrapment? It has been argued both ways. However, since then U.S. newspapers have avoided such operations, although similar stings have appeared on television.

Mike Wallace of CBS admits he does not like to lie or to mislead, but says it depends on your motive; each case, for Wallace, "must be weighed separately as to the cost-benefit ratio" (*Washington Post National Weekly Edition*, 1992, p. 32). Machiavelli would have been happy with that statement. There is no doubt that many leading journalists in the country subscribe to such Machiavellian or pragmatic ethics. Some ethics scholars even question whether such deceptive journalistic tactics as hiding one's identity as a journalist or surreptitiously taping are wrong, or whether some ends can indeed justify the means.

Others are more certain of the unethical nature of such activities. Tom Goldstein, long-time journalist, media critic, and now dean of the Graduate School of Journalism at Columbia University, says bluntly: "I think it is wrong. Journalists should announce who they are. I'm uncomfortable living in a world where you don't know who you're talking to" (*Washington Post National Weekly Edition*, 1992, p. 32). Despite voices such as Goldstein's that rise emphatically from time to time, the spirit of Machiavelli pervades the ranks of serious investigative reporters, who often seem to put professional expediency before traditional ethical concerns.

One thing is certain: The public does not like the media, thinking the national press is elitist, arrogant, and insensitive. Stephen Budiansky, in *U.S. News & World Report* (1995), writes that a "full 71 percent believe the media get 'in the way of society solving its problems'" (p. 45). He quotes Everette Dennis, former executive director of the Freedom Forum Media Studies Center in New York, as saying today's journalists have a sense of superiority. Dennis says, "I think a lot of journalists think they could do a better job of running the country than anyone in office" (p. 46). Much of the hatred and mistrust of the press stems from its Machiavellian penchant to succeed, to have power, to get the story by any means necessary.

Utilitarian Ethics

Now we come to *utilitarianism*, a theory that is quite different, being happiness-oriented and altruistic. This is probably the most influential of ethical theories. It belongs to the consequence, or teleological, class of theories. Utilitarianism in some form has profoundly altered the thinking about morality and pushed ethics into a new direction that emphasizes the importance of means and ends. Utilitarians (such as David Hume, Jeremy Bentham, and John Stuart Mill of 18th- and 19th-century Britain) began thinking differently about ethics. For example, Bentham (1823) said that morality was more than loyalty to abstract rules and even more than pleasing God; it was nothing less than an attempt to maximize the happiness in the world. This is one variant of *teleological ethics*, or consequence-oriented ethics, one of the great moral systems we discussed earlier.

What this means for the media person making an ethical decision is that he or she would determine which of several possible courses of action would bring about the most happiness or the greatest good to the greatest number of people. Then the ethical course could be taken. John Stuart Mill, in his *Utilitarianism*, states that the primary ethical rule is following this happiness-producing theory that he called the Greatest Happiness Principle. The end would justify the means if the end were the greatest happiness for the greatest number.

Often, the words *pleasure*, *value*, or *good* are substituted for *happiness* in the utilitarian model. Mill believed that pleasure is the only desirable end, and the only proof that something is desirable is the fact that people actually desire it, and every person's pleasure (or happiness) is a good to that person, so the general happiness is the largest good of all. The name of this theory, *utilitarianism*, is somewhat misleading, for it emphasizes utility or usefulness rather than happiness or pleasure. But the term has stuck and has taken on a meaning consistent with the slogan "the greatest happiness to the greatest number."

In the field of mass communication, such a theory is often professed by media people. The journalist, for example, may consider consequences when the story is written, and certain liberties then may be taken with the facts in the name of happiness-production or justice-production. This is the teleological approach, as we have said earlier; the journalist who would reject the utilitarian approach would be the *professional* type who would see happiness of others as irrelevant, and even damaging, to the truth of the story. Even for the utilitarian journalist, one of the main problems of using such a theory would be the difficulty (many would say the impossibility) of predicting which action would bring greater future happiness.

Ethical Absolutism

Next we come to the formalistic theory of ethics, whose foremost spokesman was Immanuel Kant (1724–1804). It is a species of what is called *deontological ethics*, and it is the opposite of such theories as utilitarianism. Consequences are not to be considered. The essential ingredient of this ethical theory is *duty* to principle. Have some *a priori* maxims, principles, rules and feel a profound duty to follow them. These are absolute principles that one imposes rationally on oneself and will serve as a guide to ethical behavior. The person who follows them, is ethical; the one who does not follow them is unethical, according to Kant (see Merrill, 1994, profile 12).

An ethical maxim, for Kant, implied obligation. You should do such-and-such, period. These duties are called categorical, as contrasted with hypothetical, which hold that if you want to achieve some desire, then do such-and-such. A categorical duty is one that, *regardless of your particular desire*, you would do. These categorical "oughts" bind rational people simply *because they are rational*. These "oughts" stem from what Kant called his *categorical imperative*, a principle that he believed every rational person would accept. This supermaxim, or imperative, went like this: "Act only according to that maxim by which you can at the same time will that it should become a universal law" (Kant, 1959).

Being an ethical person, in Kant's view, entails being guided by absolute rules, universal laws, and moral principles that hold, without exception, everywhere. Kant also enthroned people as people, and his second formulation of the categorical imperative insisted that every person should be treated as a person and not as a means to some end. A basic respect for people and a deep valuation of their human dignity were the foundation of Kant's ethics. He was saying, in effect, "Don't *use* people." Pragmatists or Machiavellians could never be Kantians. Perhaps we can summarize the essence of Kant's ethical theory in this way: Have a deep respect for human dignity and act toward others only in ways you would want everyone to act. Not a bad formula for the media person trying to make ethical decisions.

Many media people try to be Kantians, having strongly held beliefs about what to do and what not to do. Tell the truth, for example. Always give the source for quotes. Don't ever change direct quotes. On the other hand, many media people who believe in human dignity, or say they do, find nothing wrong with "using" people to garner information or to furnish tips or leads to other stories. This Kantian ethical road of ethics is a difficult one to travel, and most journalists seem to wander from it from time to time, thereby exposing many double-standards, exceptions, and contradictions in their overall moral demeanor. But Kantian ethics is a good starting point for media people, and many of the maxims found in codes of ethics seem to reflect a proclivity for this formalistic absolutism.

Antinomian Ethics

The ethics of law, of duty, of absolute obligation such as Kant recommends is a little strong for most media workers. This legalistic stance is often confronted by its opposite—what has been called *antinomianism*. The rebel against Kantian legalism has accepted what might be considered an extremely reactionary stance called by many a nonethics—a completely open kind of morality that is against any *a priori* rules, laws, or guidelines.

The antinomian has, by and large, tossed out all basic principles, precepts, codes, standards, and laws that might guide conduct. Just as the legalist tends toward absolutist or universal ethics, the antinomian tends toward anarchy or nihilism in morality. In many ways, antinomian ethics is a modern variety of what might be called Freudian ethics. Some people consider this ethic really an anti-ethical, or at least a nonethical, system. Freud at various times evidenced a hostility to self-restraint and self-discipline and showed a tolerance for self-indulgence and irresponsibility. Richard LePiere (1959) has gone deeply into this antinomian aspect of Freudian ethics.

In brief, such an ethic says that people must be socially supported and maintained and they cannot be expected to be provident and self-reliant. Support for this type of moral philosophy has been spread in America through a steady growth of permissiveness and avoidance of personal responsibility. There is a tendency to blame others or social institutions or conditions for any kind of immoral actions one may take. The person who might be said to act unethically is simply a victim of "society," limited by its rigorous moral code.

This "hostility to moral laws" ethical system places nonrational freedom above self-restraint and assumes that what comes naturally is the ethical thing to do. Such a view is based on psychology rather than moral philosophy. The antinomian clashes with the legalist. And such a clash, as Joseph Fletcher has asserted (1966), has resulted in a synthesis that is often called "situation ethics."

Another version of this kind of "nonethical" system might be that which has been suggested by analytical philosophers who have truly abandoned morality. In essence, they say that moral judgments are no more than personal preferences and not much different from a taste or distaste for apple pie. A. J. Ayer (1946), for example, maintained that because moral arguments cannot be verified scientifically, they are no more than commands or pure expressions of feeling that have absolutely no objective validity.

Situation Ethics

The basic tenet of *situation ethics* is that we must consider the particular situation before we can determine what is ethical or not ethical. Situation ethics has been around in some form for a long time, but it was Fletcher, in his popular book *Situation Ethics* (1966), who planted this term firmly in the public mind. He was talking about a special Christian concept of situationism that applied a kind of God-induced love (agape) to any moral dilemma. Love would be the guide to ethical action *in any situation*. Much of the philosophical (or theological) basis for this theory—in its Christian sense—comes largely from the writings of German theologians Dietrich Bonhoeffer, Rudolf Bultmann, and Paul Tillich.

In this Christian sense, situationism is just another variant of religious ethics, but one that eschews specific moral principles to be applied on every occasion. It certainly is different from the divine command theory of ethics. The only guide for the Christian situationist is to act out of love. *Simply apply love in every situation and you will be ethical.* Of course, this poses some problems because love can be defined differently and lead to a wide variety of destinations in ethical thinking and behavior.

These religious versions of situation ethics were, however, somewhat different from an earlier and more prominent idea of situationism in morality. More common was the idea that the situation determines the ethics—no more than a form of moral relativism that said there are no universal ethical principles that can be applied in every situation. These situation ethicists believed that only nonrational moral robots would try to adhere to an absolutist ethics.

Thus, situationism is really a type of relativistic ethics focusing on the particular situation. For Fletcher and other Christian ethicists, love determines action in each situation; for general relativists, each situation requires a special and different kind of ethical decision making, using whatever standards they think best.

An extreme variety of relativism is what Leonard Peikoff (1983) called the new relativism—a theory based on the belief that truth is unknowable, that there is no objectivity, that reason is not as reliable as passion. It dismisses values and sees society as diminishing the individual. It denies that virtue is possible, it hates standards, it despises quality and excellence, and it attacks achievement, success, and beauty. And it believes that one person's sense of morality is as good as another's.

Intuitive Ethics

Intuitive ethics is perhaps the oldest moral doctrine. It is the theory that we know what is right and what is wrong without having any *a priori* rules or without doing a lot of thinking before we act. Intuitionists give many answers when asked how they know what to do. Theorists like James Wilson (1993) say that God plants in each person a certain *moral sense*. Others call the immediate guide to ethical action *conscience*, a kind of inner voice that directs each person. At any rate, most intuitionists believe that rightness and wrongness are self-evident—simply a matter of intuition. *Conscience*, of course, means many different things, from the repressive superego of Freud (1930), to the God-given moral implantation of C. S. Lewis (1952), to the "disinterested spectator" theory of Adam Smith (1759).

Although there are philosophers who believe in ethical intuition, the doctrine does not have a wide following. Usually one who points to intuition is someone whose intuition is based on past experiences and who has thought about consequences of varying kinds of action. Or, and this perhaps is even more plausible, such an intuitionist is a person who has habituated certain actions and does certain things spontaneously. Therefore, the actions *seem* to flow from mere instinct or intuition.

Intuitionism is closely related to what has been called common-sense ethics, which draws on wisdom gleaned from large numbers of particular cases. We use traditional moral rules that have seemed to satisfy moral conditions throughout the ages.

Taken together, these traditions and rules tend to crystallize into a body of practical wisdom (as found in the philosophies of Aristotle and Confucius). This is nothing more than common sense that respects precedent. Common-sense morality, and also perhaps so-called intuitionism, recognizes the need to abide by general rules that have proved to be useful.

Having such general rules in ethics is very close to what Immanuel Kant proposed as duty ethics. Each person develops rules, maxims, or principles to which she or he is dedicated and obligated. Unlike Kant, however, modern common-sense ethicists are flexible, being willing to follow moral rules except when there are clear reasons for not doing so. It is important that exceptions be made carefully and infrequently—with the burden of proof being on the exception or on the alternative ethical innovation.

Although there may not be any ethical intuitions per se, there may be certain ethical principles or maxims that are self-evident. For example, a rule that journalists should not fabricate news stories is self-evident in that the whole concept of news and the media's credibility would disappear if it were not so; besides, no reasonable journalist would ever feel the need to ask the justification for such an ethical rule.

Social Contract Theory

Another theory or subtheory of ethics we should mention is one that links morality to the state or to society. It is a kind of citizen-volunteerism to accept socially enforced rules of conduct; because this social enforcement is by the state, it is a kind of people-state agreement or contract for a common morality. The state exists to make possible social living through external enforcement, whereas ethics deals with overarching voluntary rules that enhance social living.

This theory says that only in the context of the social contract can people be moral agents. Why? Because the contract creates the conditions necessary for us to care about other people. As the state organizes society generally, it organizes social and moral expectations of society specifically. In short, a state makes it possible for us to have civilized relations with others, giving rise to the very concept of ethics.

Harvard philosophy professor John Rawls (*A Theory of Justice*, 1971) has built on the social contract in the development of his theory of justice. In this theory, Rawls stresses that free and rational people must assume a position of equality in determining the terms of their association. These people agree on, or contract, the basis of their social cooperation. Rawls proposes what he calls *the veil of ignorance* in order to ensure that the principles agreed on will be just. Participants in such a contract, according to Rawls, are situated behind this veil of ignorance, not knowing how the decisions they make will affect their own lives. In short, they must put aside their own identities and make decisions by adopting the identities, in turn, of the other people affected by their decisions. Nobody behind this veil of ignorance knows for sure what their identities will be when the veil is lifted. This, according to Rawls, will ensure fairness and justice in the contractual situation (Rawls, 1971, pp. 136–142).

Thomas Hobbes (1588–1679), also an espouser of ethical egoism, and Jean-Jacques Rousseau (1712–1778) are most closely identified with the social contract theory. Somewhat related to this theory is one that is sometimes called the *socialist* or *Marxist* theory stressing a kind of classless utopianism in which people are bound together by a sense of community veering in the direction of egalitarianism. In the various versions, the objective is to eliminate discrepancies among people, level out material benefits and opportunities, and permit the state to play a more important part in making a fair and equitable system, after which presumably it would wither away. Probably the earliest proponent of such a theory was Plato, who saw a person's ethical duty as supporting the authority of the state and working for the public good.

The social contract theory requires people to set aside private, self-centered desires and inclinations in favor of principles that impartially promote the welfare of everyone. Of course, a person can do this only if others have agreed to do the same thing—in effect, by entering into a kind of unwritten contract. For the advocate of this theory, ethics consists of rules dealing with the way people will treat one another—rules reasonable people will accept for their mutual benefit. This is the basis of the theory in a nutshell.

One advantage of the social contract theory is that morality is simply a set of rules that reasonable people agree to accept for their mutual benefit.

Actually, a media organization—not necessarily a state or total society—can subscribe to a social contract theory. The members of the staff of a broadcast station, a public relations agency, or a newspaper can agree to follow certain institutional moral rules because it is to the advantage of each person to do so. It would not be to anyone's advantage if people violated the rules at any time. The main point of such a theory of ethics is that people must be able to *predict* what others will do; we must be able to count on one another to follow certain rules, at least most of the time.

One advantage of the social contract theory is that morality is simply a set of rules that reasonable people agree to accept for their mutual benefit. We don't need to worry about the objectivity or subjectivity of moral principles, about relativism or absolutism around the world. What we have is a socially based theory; we have socially established rules, and if we deviate from them we are being unethical. Period. It seems, in many ways, a theory akin to that of Kant—certainly a deontological one—but, unlike Kant's theory, it is socially rather than individually determined and enforced.

It is not difficult to see this social contract approach as spawning what today is often called the social responsibility media theory. The media and the people, in a sense, contract with one another to bring about certain mutual expectations, such as adequate and pluralistic information, truthfulness, reliable and credible social exposition and a meaningful context, with social good as a guiding ethical principle.

Existentialist Ethical Theory

In one sense, there is no real ethical theory of existentialism; existentialist ethics is so individualistic that many feel the term is oxymoronic. Jean-Paul Sartre (1905–1980), perhaps the best-known existentialist, said he would write on this subject of ethics specifically, but never got around to it. However, he did deal with ethical problems to some extent. For example, Sartre (1957, pp. 42–43) stresses that we cannot decide *a priori* on an ethics that will guide us in a specific action; he is certainly not a Kantian in this respect. Ethical considerations, of course, permeate the writings of all existentialists from Kierkegaard onward. At the heart of any existentialist ethics appear to lie personal authenticity, integrity, honesty, deep concern with freedom, and the acceptance of personal responsibility. One may be free to be unethical, but according to American philosopher Hazel Barnes, an authority on existentialism, the person who chooses to be unethical rejects the positive benefits of freedom. Barnes's *An Existentialist Ethics* (1978) makes the overall point that ethics and freedom are both needed for a rich, fulfilling, productive life that benefits both the individual and society.

Ethics, for the existentialist, must be personal if it is to contribute to the authenticity of the person. As I pointed out in *Existential Journalism* (1995), for a media person to follow some group-designed code or traditional manner of action, either out of blind submission or thoughtless habit, is inauthentic and depersonalizing. The basic point is that there is no blueprint for what an individual media person can become or what he or she should do. The individual must decide, for the essence of each person is self-determined.

Many see existentialist ethics as a form of egoistic ethics, and to some degree they are right. But no major existentialist philosopher has ever suggested extreme individualism and the fulfillment of all one's desires. Always there is some control. A kind of reasonableness, for instance, that keeps personal freedom in bounds, is quite common in existentialist literature. Or, as Kierkegaard believed, Christian love and a concern for others keep personal freedom under control. Or, as Sartre held, control is exercised by a person's notion of responsibility. He also said the anguish of personal choice arises from the fact that, in making the choice, a person is committing not only him- or herself but, in a certain manner, all humankind. This existentialist statement is almost Kantian: We choose only the things we would be willing to see universalized.

Also, for the existentialist, an ethical demeanor is necessary because of the necessity of accepting personal responsibility for actions. This imposes a kind of ethical restraint on a person; for example, existentialist media people would never try to escape the consequences of their freely determined actions. Media workers have superiors—and colleagues, sources, and audience members—who are affected by the workers' actions. Media people know this, understand this, and must decide whether to take certain actions. It is the ethical restraint of individual integrity.

For the existentialist, there is also the restraint of human dignity. Such dignity places just limits on action for the simple reason that a person does not live isolated in society, and all members of society have this same human dignity. Moral people have such dignity. And who are moral people? Those who do not succumb to instincts or passions, who do not change opinions without justification, who are not flatterers or falsifiers, who constantly attempt to transcend self and traditional morality.

This concept of transcendence was important to Friedrich Nietzsche, an important existentialist voice. He would have us say "yes" to life, therefore becoming more noble and heroic, always rising to our highest potential. Nietzsche sounded a common note of the existentialist concept of ethics: that the individual person is extremely valuable and worthy, more so as that person determines his or her own destiny and does not submit to any authority that restricts personal freedom or makes the person inauthentic.

One variant of existentialist ethics might be a kind of "superior person" ethics, where through existential progress an individual "transcends" normal morality and, in a sense, becomes a superior ethical person. Nietzsche, who espoused in *Beyond Good and Evil* (1866) what he called the *Overman* (usually translated as the *Superman*) and talked of a "master-morality," is probably the best example of such an ethicist.

Nietzsche drew heavily on Greek philosopher Thrasymachus, who believed that justice is no more than the interest of the stronger. Nietzsche would interpret stronger not only in terms of physical or military strength but also in terms of a full spectrum of intellectual and moral strength that transcends physical power. Nietzsche is rather vague as to how these superior people will manifest themselves. His ethical theory is a close relative of the egoistic ethical theory, but is different in that Nietzsche's Superman draws on subjective and mystical insights for transforming moral progress. Egoistic theory is based more on rationality.

■ CONCLUDING REMARKS

Now that we have taken a quick trip through many of the paths of ethics and ethical theory, we are ready to consider some specific examples of troublesome ethical problems facing people who work in mass communication. We will do so in the following chapters in the form of informal debates (or better, opposing contentions) on a variety of today's controversial ethical issues.

As we stated earlier, there are no hard and fast answers to such ethical questions, and the varying ethical positions on the issues that follow attempt to provide only some of the most salient arguments on either side. Of course, there are always *more than two sides* to these complex ethical questions, but the basic format of the chapters deals mainly with the most common two sides of the issues. Other ethical positions are mainly left to each student to grapple with. Some are suggested by questions posed by the opposing positions, or in the commentary that follows each debate; others will probably come up in class or other discussion. The important point is that this is a book of basic *positions and commentary* on some important ethical issues in the field of media studies; it is not a textbook of normative ethics intended to provide concrete answers to these many difficult moral problems.

We hope that you will weigh the evidence presented by each debater carefully, consider the commentaries, and resolve the controversies as rationally as possible. But what is truly important is that the reader realize that, in a real sense, nobody *wins* or *loses* in such controversial ethical discourse. The smart reader takes what is most meaningful, useful, and helpful from *all of the positions* presented here, integrates it into an already developing personal morality, and makes it useful in present and future relationships and activities.

Media people can progress ethically—becoming ever more consistent and sensitive to the moral environment that encompasses them. Many moral development theories are available to the serious person desiring to mature ethically. Except for the three main theories discussed early in this Overview, we have not dealt with them, but they are important and indicate that there are many levels or stages through which a person may proceed on an ethical journey. Books such as Ronald Duska and Mariellen Whelan's *Moral Development: A Guide to Piaget and Kohlberg* (1975) will acquaint the student with development models. And, of course, books by Jean Piaget (1932) and Lawrence Kohlberg (1981), both important developmental theorists, will get the reader into the intricacies of moral development theories.

The important point here is that a person does not one day just become "ethical" and that is the end of the moral story. Individuals grow ethically just as they grow physically and intellectually. Whatever ethical theory—or combination of theories— drives them through the brambles of moral choices, there is always the possibility of maturing further and making even better ethical decisions.

We hope that the controversial discussions that follow will give you the opportunity to think about ethical quandaries facing a person working in the media. By accepting or rejecting the arguments put forth by the debaters, and by considering the remarks made in the commentaries, we believe you can improve your moral reasoning and reach a higher level of ethical consciousness. But remember: There are always higher levels to strive for. The ethical journey is never over.

REFERENCES AND RELATED READINGS

Aristotle. (Many editions). *Nicomachean Ethics.*
Ayer, Alfred J. (1946). *Language, Truth and Logic.* New York: Dover.
Barnes, Hazel. (1978). *An Existentialist Ethics.* Chicago: University of Chicago Press.
Bellah, Robert N., Richard Madsen, W. M. Sullivan, Ann Swidler, and Stephen M. Tipton. (1985). *Habits of the Heart: Individualism and Commitment in American Life.* New
    York: Harper & Row.
Benedict, Ruth. (1934). *Patterns of Culture.* Boston: Houghton Mifflin.
Bentham, Jeremy. (1823). *An Introduction to the Principles of Morals and Legislation.* Oxford:
    Clarendon Press.
Budiansky, Stephen. (1995). "The Media's Message: The Public Thinks the National Press
    is Elitist, Insensitive and Arrogant." *U.S. News & World Report,* January 9, pp. 45–47.
Christians, Clifford G., John P. Ferre, and P. Mark Fackler. (1993). *Good News: Social Ethics
    and the Press.* New York: Oxford University Press.
Cooper, J. M. (1975). *Reason and the Human Good in Aristotle.* Cambridge, MA: Harvard
    University Press.
Cooper, Thomas W., Clifford G. Christians, Francis Forde Plude, and Robert A. White.
    (1989). *Communication Ethics and Global Change.* White Plains, NY: Longman.
Dawson, Miles M., ed. (1932). *The Wisdom of Confucius.* Boston: International Pocket Library.
Duska, Ronald, and Mariellen Whelan. (1975). *Moral Development: A Guide to Piaget and
    Kohlberg.* New York: Paulist Press.
Etzioni, Amitai. (1993). *The Spirit of Community: Rights, Responsibilities, and the Communitarian Agenda.* New York: Crown Publishers.
Fletcher, Joseph. (1966). *Situation Ethics: The New Morality.* Philadelphia: Westminster Press.
Freud, Sigmund. (1930). *Civilization and Its Discontents.* New York: Norton.
Gilligan, Carol. (1982). *In a Different Voice.* Cambridge, MA: Harvard University Press.
Gordon, George W. (1968). *The Human Predicament: Dissolution and Wholeness.* New
    York: Dell.
Haselden, Kyle. (1968). *Morality and the Mass Media.* Nashville, TN: Broadman Press.
Hazlitt, Henry. (1972). *The Foundations of Morality.* Los Angeles: Nash Publishing.
Henry, William A. III. (1994). *In Defense of Elitism.* New York: Doubleday.
Hobbes, Thomas. (1950). *Leviathan.* New York: E. P. Dutton.
Holmes, Stephen. (1993). *The Anatomy of Antiliberalism.* Cambridge, MA: Harvard University Press.

Jaspers, Karl. (1957). *Socrates, Buddha, Confucius, Jesus: The Paradigmatic Individuals.* Edited by Hannah Arendt. San Diego: Harcourt Brace Jovanovich.

Kant, Immanuel. (1959). *Foundations of the Metaphysics of Morals.* Indianapolis: Bobbs-Merrill.

Kohlberg, Lawrence. (1981). *The Philosophy of Moral Development: Moral Stages and the Idea of Justice.* New York: Harper & Row.

LePiere, Richard. (1959). *The Freudian Ethic.* New York: Duell, Sloan & Pearce.

Lewis, C. S. (1952). *Mere Christianity.* New York: Macmillan.

Lillie, William. (1961). *An Introduction to Ethics.* New York: Barnes & Noble.

Machiavelli, Niccolo. (Many editions). *The Prince.*

MacIntyre, Alasdair. (1966). *A Short History of Ethics.* New York: Random House.

Merrill, John C. (Summer 1985). "Is Ethical Journalism Simply Objective Reporting?" *Journalism Quarterly* 62(2), pp. 391–393.

———. (1989, 1993). *The Dialectic in Journalism: Toward a Responsible Use of Press Freedom.* Baton Rouge: Louisiana State University Press.

———. (1994). *Legacy of Wisdom: Great Thinkers and Journalism.* Ames: Iowa State University Press.

———. (1995). *Existential Journalism,* rev. ed. Ames: Iowa State University Press.

———. (1998). *The Princely Press: Machiavelli on American Journalism.* Lanham, MD: University Press of America.

Mill, John Stuart (Many editions). *On Liberty.*

———. (Many editions). *Utilitarianism.*

Minow, Newton N. (Winter 1995). "How Vast the Wasteland Now?" *Media Studies Journal* 9 (1), pp. 3–8.

Morgan, George W. (1968). *The Human Predicament: Dissolution and Wholeness.* Providence, RI: Brown University Press.

Newman, Jay. (1989). *The Journalist in Plato's Cave.* Cranbury, NJ: Associated University Presses.

Nietzsche, Friederich. (Many editions). *Beyond Good and Evil.*

Patka, Frederick, ed. (1962). *Existentialist Thinkers and Thought.* New York: Citadel Press.

Peikoff, Leonard. (1983). *Ominous Parallels.* Briarcliff Manor, NY: Stein & Day.

Piaget, Jean. (1932). *The Moral Judgment of the Child.* Glencoe, IL: Free Press.

Postman, Neil. (1985). *Amusing Ourselves to Death.* New York: Viking.

Rachels, James. (1986). *The Elements of Moral Philosophy.* New York: Random House.

Rand, Ayn. (1964). *The Virtue of Selfishness.* New York: New American Library.

Rawls, John. (1971). *A Theory of Justice.* Cambridge, MA: Belknap.

Sartre, Jean-Paul (1957). *Existentialism and Human Emotions.* New York: Philosophical Library.

Serafini, Anthony. (1989). *Ethics and Social Concern.* New York: Paragon Press.

Sidgwick, Henry. (1956). *The Methods of Ethics,* 7th ed. Indianapolis: Hackett.

Siebert, Fred S., Theodore Peterson, and Wilbur Schramm. (1956). *Four Theories of the Press.* Urbana: University of Illinois Press.

Smith, Adam. (1759). *The Theory of Moral Sentiments.* Oxford: Clarendon Press.

Washington Post National Weekly Edition. (1992). December 14–20, pp. 31–32.

Wilson, James Q. (1993). *The Moral Sense.* New York: Free Press.

C H A P T E R   1

ETHICS AND FREEDOM
Mass Media Accountability

Responsibility and freedom are two sides of the same coin when one looks at the American mass media system. But there can be major differences of opinion as to which side society most needs to have facing up.

To some degree, it's a chicken-and-egg situation. Freedom of expression, as guaranteed by the First Amendment to everyone, gives the mass media "breathing room" to make their own ethical decisions to be responsible or irresponsible. But if their decisions are seen as continually irresponsible, the result has often been public (or government) pressures to curtail the media's freedom in order to *require* increased responsibility.

That's the crux of the arguments that follow. Each author agrees that *both* freedom *and* responsibility are important if the mass media are to function properly in society. Carol Reuss stresses that the media can't be allowed to hide behind the First Amendment in order to justify irresponsible behavior. David Gordon argues that freedom of expression must be protected at almost any cost, regardless of whether the media are ethical or responsible.

One other aspect of this dilemma also merits some consideration, although it is not discussed directly in the following material. That's the question of to *whom* or *what* the media should be responsible or accountable, assuming that some level of responsibility is expected. Is it to society as a whole—i.e., to the general public? To specific audiences or subaudiences? To their owners and stockholders? To their peers, or perhaps to some general notion of "ethics" appropriate for the mass media? To more than one of these groups, or perhaps to some others as well? These questions are well worth further thought, as you ponder the different perspectives on the freedom/responsibility relationship presented here.

■ GORDON: Freedom of expression must be zealously guarded regardless of whether that freedom is exercised ethically by the mass media.

Writing for a unanimous Supreme Court in 1974, Chief Justice Warren Burger noted that the First Amendment to the U.S. Constitution guarantees a free press but does not require a responsible press. That comment, in *Miami Herald Publishing Co. v.*

Tornillo (418 U.S. 241, 1974), was part of the Court's rejection of a Florida law that *required* newspapers to provide specific reply space to political candidates whom they had attacked editorially. The decision epitomizes the position taken by those who believe that we dare not even begin to limit freedom of expression in the name of requiring the responsible use of that freedom.

The ideal situation, of course, would be to have *both* freedom of expression and responsible exercise of that freedom. However, human nature being what it is, there will always be people who abuse protected freedoms of expression. That, I believe, is simply a cost of doing business in a society that values the right to express oneself freely—a right that must be zealously protected against all incursions, even those attempted in the name of ethics. Any efforts to legislate or otherwise require ethics at the expense of the First Amendment will aim for a cure that is worse than the disease—and, as will be noted later, run the risk of preventing change in society's moral values.

To attempt to require *ethical conduct . . . would be to allow the regulatory camel to get its nose into the tent of free expression.*

To attempt to *require* ethical conduct in connection with the First Amendment would be to allow the regulatory camel to get its nose into the tent of free expression. And once that nose is in, the issue becomes not *whether* some curtailment of free expression is permissible, but rather *where* to draw the line, *how far* to extend the regulations, and *who* gets to make those decisions. I suspect that is why Chief Justice Burger—no zealot in supporting many aspects of the First Amendment—drew a sharp line in the face of Pat Tornillo's attempt to force his way onto the *Miami Herald's* front pages in response to a pair of editorials attacking his political candidacy.

Although elementary fairness might have dictated that the *Herald* give Tornillo such an opportunity to respond, Burger made it clear that this was not something the state government could mandate, as the Florida legislature had tried to do six decades earlier. Burger was willing to let the *Herald*—which had, in fact, offered reply space inside the paper under its standard procedures—determine the conditions under which Tornillo could respond. Government interference with this process, he wrote, would impinge on the paper's freedom to determine its contents.

And that's essentially as it should be for all of the mass media, with government prohibited from imposing requirements for responsible use of free speech, because any such requirements would limit that freedom. Responsibility in communication should, by definition, be an ethical rather than a legal concern. And, because meaningful ethics involves choice, people are free (and likely) to make some "wrong" decisions about what is or is not responsible communication. Additionally, there most likely will always be some segments of the audience that are interested in various types of "less ethical" media content or practices. In our society, mass media ethics must be based on a "first principle" that ensures zealous protection for freedom of expression while leaving us fallible mortals free to chart our own ethical (or unethical) courses, guided by our own principles regarding responsibility.

I won't quarrel here with the notion that private individuals ought to retain some rights to sue the media for irresponsible communication that damages their reputation or invades their privacy in an unwarranted manner. I will note, with approval, Justice Hugo Black's contention that the best response to libelous material is not a lawsuit but rather the opportunity to respond and set the record straight. The value of an approach that sets the record straight, as the remedy for defamatory publication or broadcasts, is borne out by an Iowa study reporting that libel plaintiffs—especially those allegedly damaged in connection with public rather than private matters—were far more concerned with correcting false statements about themselves than they were in recovering monetary damages (Bezanson et al., 1987, pp. 4–5 and 79–81).

Such an approach, involving "more speech" rather than monetary damages, would also help avoid the very real problems of self-censorship that have cropped up in the media in response to large libel verdicts. This "chilling effect" of large verdicts, not to mention the cost of defending a libel suit even if you win (particularly for smaller, less affluent media outlets) is a very real consequence of the law's desire to provide remedies for the more irresponsible instances of defamation. It illustrates well one type of problem that can follow the camel's regulatory nose into the free expression tent.

■ LEGAL LIMITS ON FREE EXPRESSION

Of course, some governmental limits and regulations on the exercise of free expression have received Supreme Court sanction. Such potential limitations as restraining publications that are obscene or directly incite to violence (see *Near v. Minnesota*, 283 U.S. 697, 1931) or that clearly threaten "national security" (see *New York Times Co. v. United States*, 403 U.S. 713, 1971—the *Pentagon Papers* case) come immediately to mind. In both cases, however, the Supreme Court ruled that the conditions that would permit prior restraint were *not* met. Another area where expression is regulated is seen in the federal requirements imposed on broadcasters (see especially *Red Lion Broadcasting Co. v. FCC*, 395 U.S. 367, 1969, which held that enforcement of the FCC's now-terminated Fairness Doctrine did *not* violate broadcasters' First Amendment rights). Potential restrictions on expression that safeguard a criminal defendant's right to receive a fair trial, and the remaining restrictions that place some aspects of "commercial speech" outside the protection of the First Amendment, are other examples.

None of these, with the possible exception of the "commercial speech" restrictions, are likely to be undone by the courts, although the Fairness Doctrine was repealed in the 1980s by the Federal Communications Commission and broadcasting has been greatly deregulated over the past 15 years. However, such law-based ethical notions as broadcasters serving the "public interest, convenience and necessity"— required by the federal Communications Act of 1934 (47 U.S. Code)—are unlikely to be scrapped entirely, and the repeal of the Fairness Doctrine has certainly not meant the end of broadcasters' allegiance to that general principle, nor has it ended the possibility that the doctrine might be restored if broadcasters stray too far from this principle.

My focus, therefore, is twofold: First, on the need to make sure that the government goes no further in trying to *mandate* responsibility—or even accountability—in mass media by imposing further limitations on freedom of expression; second, on the ethics-based arguments for this strong presumption in favor of protecting a full range of freedom of expression for everyone regardless of whether it is used responsibly.

There is no doubt that giving the media this kind of freedom inevitably leads to considerable discomfort in some segments of society, and sometimes to some potentially difficult or even dangerous situations. But that's really no different from the risks we accept by embracing democracy as our chosen form of government. In a democratic society, the people are given the ultimate power to decide and they retain that power even when a large minority of the people think the decisions are wrong. The antidote for wrong or even dangerous political decisions is to rejoin the political battles and convince enough people to make the right decision next time. It is *not* to impose restrictions on the political dialogue or the political process in order to prevent wrong decisions.

The approach should be no different in regard to free expression in a democratic society. The antidote for wrong, dangerous, or offensive speech should be *more* speech by those who disagree with the original statements, rather than restrictions on the original speech. The key here is that we must be willing to provide protection even for speech that offends us, and even if that speech offends us greatly. To quote Justice Oliver Wendell Holmes's dissent in *United States v. Schwimmer*, we must safeguard "freedom for the thought that we hate" (279 U.S. 644, at 655, 1929) every bit as much as freedom for words we find agreeable. Or, as Massachusetts Congressman Barney Frank said much more recently, "the First Amendment protects hateful people's right to be hateful."

A classic example of how attempts to control hateful speech can backfire is the 1978–1979 controversy surrounding the efforts of the American Nazi Party to stage a march in the Chicago suburb of Skokie. The village enacted three parade permit ordinances aimed at setting up conditions under which the Nazi Party's request could be denied. One of those required a $350,000 surety bond to be posted by the parading organization, to cover possible costs to the village if the parade resulted in any kind of disorder. And the first group to be denied a parade permit because it couldn't post that bond? The local Jewish War Veterans chapter!

The antidote for wrong, dangerous, or offensive speech should be more speech . . .

Protecting even offensive speech clearly runs counter to various contemporary efforts to deal with so-called hate speech, and in particular to campus speech codes that aim to punish such speech. The problems with such codes, as with all attempts to regulate "irresponsible" communication, are the questions of who gets to decide what "irresponsible" really means and what criteria can be used to provide consistency from one situation to another. The fact that linguistic fashions change from one generation to another further complicates this issue, because what is seen as hate speech today may become much more acceptable a decade or two from now, much as calling one a socialist in the 1920s would have been seen as highly damaging to reputation, while today it is at most a very mild epithet.

■ HATE SPEECH ON CABLE TELEVISION ACCESS CHANNELS AND THE INTERNET

More central to this discussion is the issue of whether "hate speakers" should be given free rein on cable television's public access channels or on public channels of the information superhighway. The cable access issue has arisen in a number of cities, including Kansas City, Missouri, Austin, Texas, and Cincinnati, Ohio. In all three, the eventual response was counter-programming rather than censorship of the original "hateful" programming (although in Kansas City, the counter-programs were never implemented because of developments that ended the original Ku Klux Klan telecasts). There were varying degrees of controversy and soul-searching in these three cities before the "more speech" approach was reached. In a similar controversy in Fullerton, California, however, the results were less firmly supportive of freedom for hate speech to appear on the access channel.

An analysis of these four cities demonstrated "that the most prudent, responsible, and ethical course is to permit outrageous speech and counter it with positive messages" (Harmon, 1991, p. 146). That analysis of ethical theory concluded that approaches suggested by John Milton's *Aereopagitica*, John Stuart Mill's espousal of the societal benefits of doctrinal competition, "the 'free expression as utilitarian' view espoused by David Hume" (Harmon, 1991 p. 152), John Locke's social contract approach, and John Rawls's distributive justice theory all supported the "more speech" remedy to this problem. So, we can add, does the "free marketplace of ideas" concept inherent in the social responsibility model for the mass media. In any event, Harmon offers this conclusion:

> . . . regardless of whether one views free expression as a natural right, a utilitarian tool, or a component of the social contract, one comes to exactly the same conclusion about the KKK's use of cable access. (p. 153)

In other words, hateful speech should not be restricted because it too is entitled to the freedom guaranteed by the First Amendment. But it should most certainly be countered by opposing viewpoints in an open marketplace of ideas—open even for hateful ideas.

If this is the best solution to hate speech on cable access channels, it seems logical that it is also the best approach to combatting irresponsible use of freedom of expression wherever it occurs in the mass media (or more generally throughout society, although that's a broader discussion than is appropriate here). If freedom of expression is zealously guarded for everyone, it is available for the speech we agree with as well as for speech we find offensive. And it will safeguard society—and us—if we happen *not* to be 100% correct in our view of what is and isn't hateful or offensive, or if those who find our ideas offensive are in power.

It's well worth recalling that such political and social movements as abolition, women's suffrage, civil rights, and opposition to the Vietnam War all started out as unpopular positions within the body politic. Had those in power been able to suppress the upstart opposition, American history would be vastly different.

When political positions, ideas, or social philosophies clash, as Mill would point out, the only way to modify "erroneous" ideas without resorting to force or violence is to subject them to the test of competing opinions. Mill would also note that even the most wrongheaded ideas may have a grain of truth in them, and that grain will be lost if they are silenced. In other words, we must rely on the guarantees of the First Amendment, forbidding government interference, so that we can come, sooner or later, to an appropriate societal consensus forged from unfettered, robust, and wide-open discussion and debate.

All of this is not to say that the threat—real or implied—of government action hasn't helped produce some responsible approaches to free expression. It is likely that the 1996 Communications Decency Act will have some impact on Internet users, in spite of the fact that the Supreme Court struck it down the following year. And the threat that Congress might restore the Fairness Doctrine through direct legislation, if the airwaves were to become blatantly "unfair," probably hasn't been lost on some broadcasters who otherwise might have disregarded this tenet. (But note that there certainly are broadcasters who have supported the fairness approach regardless of potential government sanctions—perhaps most notably the former Group W, where the fairness ideal took form in early Westinghouse requirements for its stations.)

In the last analysis, this is one situation where Kant's categorical imperative seems to have considerable application if we believe in the benefits of freedom of expression. Even stopping short of espousing an absolutist position, we could frame a general proposition that freedom of expression should be protected regardless of whether it is used responsibly or irresponsibly. Assuming a rule utilitarian approach, we can argue that giving the widest possible latitude to freedom of expression will, on balance and in the long run, produce the greatest amount of good and perhaps even "happiness" for the greatest number of people in the society. I believe this is true whether one focuses on the news media, as Carol Reuss has done, whether one is concerned with the legal and ethical dimensions of the contents of entertainment media, or whether one is concerned with broader issues of hate speech.

British ethicist H. L. A. Hart may have put it best when he argued that it is not morally desirable to legislate ethical behavior. He was referring primarily to the specific area of sexual morality, but his argument applies logically to the focus here on media freedom and responsibility:

> . . . the preservation of morality . . . is not identical with and does not require the preservation from change of a society's moral code as it is at any given moment of that society's existence; and *a fortiori* it does not require the legal enforcement of its rules. . . . The use of legal punishment to freeze into immobility the morality dominant at a particular time in a society's existence may possibly succeed, but even where it does it contributes nothing to the survival of the animating spirit and formal values of social morality and may do much to harm them. (Hart, 1963, p. 72)

In other words, enforcing responsible communication behavior ("morality," in Hart's terms) may well not succeed. Even if it does, such enforcement may damage both the underlying value of free expression and the societal change it can help bring about. Mill would support the latter argument, in his concern that any moment's "truth" should continually be tested rather than allowed to become unchallenged dogma.

American ethicist Deni Elliott (1987) argued more recently that First Amendment freedom is an inadequate basis for defining media responsibility. The law, she wrote, is "problematic as a basis for moral responsibilities because one cannot derive duties from rights" (p. 7). In other words—Theodore Glasser's arguments to the contrary (Glasser, 1986)—we cannot use protected rights of expression to impose duties and responsibilities on a speaker without risking serious damage to those protected rights. Thus, it may have been unfair, unethical and irresponsible for the *Dallas Morning News* to publish (on-line and then in its regular edition) confidential documents from the Timothy McVeigh defense team that reportedly said that McVeigh had admitted his guilt in the Oklahoma City bombing to his lawyers. But the paper must be left free to make that choice—even if it is "wrong." ("The McVeigh Dilemma," 1997, pp. 17 and ff.; Rosensteil, 1997.)

Thus the important thing for our purposes is to protect free expression as fully as possible. An Aristotelian balance between freedom and responsibility will not work here. If freedom is used irresponsibly (immorally, in Hart's terms), we can certainly use our own freedom of expression to argue for more responsibility, in either the news or the entertainment sectors of the media. But we may well fatally threaten our own freedom of speech, as in the Skokie march example noted earlier, if we try to legislate or otherwise impose ethical, responsible communication standards as part of our traditional freedom of expression.

■ REUSS: Freedom of expression should not be allowed to become an excuse for irresponsible media conduct.

There is an imaginary road between *shall* and *should* that is littered with obstacles, and nowhere is this more evident than during discussions about freedom of expression—especially freedom of expression enjoyed by U.S. mass media.

When civil libertarians rally for total freedom, they mean that every individual, every group and organization, and especially the mass media can say anything they wish to say. The whole potful of information, ideas, and opinions, they say, ultimately boils down to "truth"—information and ideas that benefit both individuals and society. The mass media, the libertarians insist, must be a free marketplace of ideas, guided and protected by the literal interpretation of the First Amendment: "Congress shall make no law . . . abridging the freedom of speech, or of the press . . . ." That's what Congress shall do, but no mention is made as to what the mass media should do for the public.

All but the most rigid libertarians recognize that limits are occasionally needed and useful. They accept, even as they challenge, interpretations of the First Amendment that curb the free flow of ideas and information, particularly media contents that might be considered defamatory, obscene, or seditious. These recognized limits to absolute freedom of expression open the door to what the media *should* do, and there are many interpretations of the word *should*.

David Gordon summarizes various relationships the mass media have with the First Amendment as he summarizes libertarian arguments that favor its literal interpretation. He wisely cites the need to guard—indeed, to "zealously guard"—freedom of expression. I agree. I cannot agree, however, that the media can disregard consideration of whether they exercise that freedom ethically. The news media, for example, should be concerned about the contents and the effects of what they publish or broadcast. They should be concerned about how they gather and interpret information. Entertainment media should be concerned about how audiences will be affected by their creative efforts.

Racists and other extremists have the right, under the First Amendment, to broadcast hateful statements. But should they have unlimited right to do so? Should radio and television stations allow them air time to shout falsely the social equivalent of "Fire!" in a crowded theater? Should publishers run their syndicated columns? Should advertising space or time be sold to them? Should any of the mass media assist racists in promulgating potentially incendiary messages to audiences that may or may not be able to discern the social and ethical consequences of these messages?

The publisher or broadcaster who disagrees with any message can refuse to run it, or may bury it in an unfavorable location or time slot, or may surround it with reports or editorials that offer different viewpoints. Admittedly, although such alternatives are attempts to moderate potentially damaging antisocial messages, there is no guarantee that they will. Should the government, therefore, step in at some point to prevent such potential incendiary messages from setting fire to the social fabric?

The mass media are valuable public platforms for any cause. They can promote or destroy reputations and ideologies, and the men and women who produce the media need to be wary of their own biases as well as the biases and intentions of individuals and organizations that seek their attention or respond to their inquiries.

Every day, media men and women face a Pandora's Box of choices as to what they, individually and collectively, *should* do. What information or interpretation should they include in articles or programs? How should they ask questions? Whom should they ask? How much attention should they pay to any subject, or to any advertiser, sponsor—or friend? Should they publish or broadcast now, with the information available, or should they wait and seek more information? Should they even publish or broadcast an article or program at all? These and other similar questions move beyond laws and legal precedents. They are among the obstacles that litter the road between *shall* and *should*, but they are not unsurmountable obstacles.

The great variety of mass media in the United States offers an additional challenge to this discussion. To keep it within reasonable limits, I have chosen to concentrate on the news media, which are important enough to a democratic society to be called the "Fourth Estate," the unofficial fourth branch of government.

News media work under severe time constraints. Daily newspapers and broadcast programs are crafted to appeal to large, rather homogeneous audiences who may or may not pay attention to the contents on any given day. Among all news media there are some common ethical concerns that merit consideration. Although many of the examples are situational, the intention is not to advocate situation ethics per se, but rather to suggest that even seemingly uncomplicated news decisions can be just the opposite. Accountability demands that media men and women attempt to predict the effects of their work before it is published or broadcast.

■ ETHICAL DECISIONS

Theoretically, in ordinary times there are no proscriptive or prescriptive lists of what media can and cannot investigate and cover. However, there are people and organizations who insist that their information and their interests be protected from disclosure in the news media. The challenge that journalists face, therefore, is whether to cover any subject and how to cover it. They are concerned about facts and sources as much as they are concerned about how they gather those facts and how to link them together. They are concerned about the ethics—the "oughtness"—of their decisions and their work.

Sometimes media people make good decisions—"right" decisions—and sometimes they don't. Even the best, most respected and experienced journalists may trust bad sources and incomplete information. They may conceal their intentions from potential sources, or move a story prematurely. There are dozens of ways for even the best to make errors, wittingly as well as unwittingly. When errors are made, however, good newspeople don't hide arrogantly behind the First Amendment. They don't use freedom of expression as an excuse for inappropriate actions, or "the people's right to know" to coerce potential sources to reveal potentially embarrassing information about inconsequential matters.

When errors are made . . . good newspeople don't hide arrogantly behind the First Amendment.

Philip Meyer (1983) coined the term *ethically efficient* in a report on newspaper ethics for the American Society of Newspaper Editors. An ethically efficient person, he wrote, is "persistent enough to carry his evaluations beyond snap judgments and easy conventions" (p. 53). An ethically efficient news operation, Meyer wrote, "provides an environment where decision makers have the time, the support, and the emotional capital to discover what they really value, to 'straighten out the relationship between what is valued for its own sake and what is not'" (p. 54).

Keys to both, Meyer said, are freedom from knee-jerk responses, mutual respect between editor and publisher, and high staff morale. "News people are in this business for psychic income as much as any other kind. Nothing can destroy morale as much as a perception that the place is being run without regard for moral values" (p. 54).

Meyer's concept of ethical efficiency, like so much of his work, is practical as well as philosophical. The bottom line for ethically efficient people and organizations is profitable, high-quality work. It is based on respect for the news organization and its people *and* their sources and customers.

Neither Meyer's "ethically efficient" journalists nor Edmund B. Lambeth's "virtuous" journalists (Lambeth, 1992) are immune to misjudging news significance and sources or their own reportorial techniques. So, although it doesn't fit the book and movie image of the hard-hitting newshounds, responsible journalists should regularly assess what they are doing, and why. Some do.

Today, few media people work in isolation. They need and deserve time to collaborate with others on the staff and with outsiders so their work is as accurate, complete, and fair as it can be. With few exceptions, as Meyer indicated, their rewards are often intangible.

■ PITFALLS AND OBSTACLES

What are some of the potential pitfalls that haunt even the best news staffs—roadblocks that litter the imaginary path between *shall* and *should*? Consider these:

- The tendency to place freedom and responsibility in apposition. They aren't. Both support the democratic process; they allow democracy to work. Personal or organizational freedom flows from personal and organizational responsibility.
- The tendency to emphasize press (or mass media) freedom over individual freedom. News gatherers do not have the right to invade an individual's privacy or to coerce an individual by insisting that the First Amendment supersedes individual

rights. They do not have the right to storm a home or a private business with a phalanx of sound and camera equipment or to invade a neighbor's space in the same way.

The First Amendment does not require ordinary people to respond to reporters' questions. It does not justify their being subjected to rude treatment by impertinent reporters and photographers.

Too often the media cry "freedom of the press," when in reality they mean "tell *me*." They intrude unnecessarily on unwary people. They lapse into thinking that the watchdog Press (capital P) supersedes individual rights to privacy, reputation, and information. Even the most careful reporters sometimes get so immersed in their work that, like bloodhounds hot on a scent, they inappropriately intrude on sources and fail to verify what they hear. Some coerce sources into thinking that they *have* to respond to questions or give reporters personal photos or documents.

The list of news media excesses in recent years would include many more than the following examples:

- The tendency to cover "live action" without consideration for what *might* happen and how it will affect audiences. It is immaterial whether professionals or amateurs hold the cameras that record panicked fire victims on rooftops or in windows, shootouts, or O.J. Simpson's Bronco escorted by a covey of police cruisers, or even the 1998 suicide-by-shotgun on another Los Angeles freeway. The viewing public is becoming so hardened to death and violence that life is devalued. Violent scenes are becoming frightening stereotypes that falsely categorize people who are not involved in violence and crime.
- The growing tendency to seek unedited amateur videotape and the temptation to air especially sensational footage repeatedly, even with stories that are not directly connected with the original tape.
- The tendency to let sensational stories, often from afar, crowd out stories that are more important to the public. The coverage of the death and funeral of Princess Diana in 1997—which in the United Kingdom exceeded even the World War II newspaper coverage of Dunkirk and V-E Day, and which in the United States overshadowed the death later that week of Mother Theresa—might be thought excessive. The world's news media came forth with compelling Diana stories— but at what sacrifice of attention to other local, national, and international situations and events, or even to the question of why Americans reacted so strongly to the death of a British ex-Royal?
- The widespread sensationalism in the 1998 Clinton–Lewinsky coverage—including hasty stories that later were withdrawn or corrected—that reached the point of overshadowing any truly serious questions of President Clinton's public behavior.

Too often, sensational stories with little or no local significance fill the mass media. Do such articles inform, or do they titillate or encourage others to "compete" or to copy? From newspapers and news programs, sensational situations often move to movies and especially to television programs that are emotionally charged and often explicit in showing how victims were assaulted. Should explicit coverage of assaults and other perversions—in news or entertainment format—be freely available? It has been interesting to observe a new wrinkle in the media's obsession with sensational stories. Sensationalized coverage of an event reaches the saturation point and one by one, the media decry that sensationalism but nevertheless continue to produce it.

To some degree, this is what happened in mid-1997, when several supermarket tabloid editors expressed outrage over the sale of pictures from Princess Diana's death scene, and urged their competitors to refuse to buy and run them—but continued their own heavy coverage of the princess' death and funeral using other illustrations. (Morgan, 1997) Rupert Murdoch, on the other hand, criticized the photographers supplying those photos only for charging too much! Neither of these reactions comes anywhere near the Golden Mean approach that might be most appropriate here, since sensational stories are never going to be ignored.

Another question that should be asked is whether media attention is fair to victims of crimes or to the accused. If the trial stage is reached, does saturation coverage assist or destroy public confidence in the legal system? Does it generate unwarranted fears for individual safety? Does it teach crime?

Other media practices engendering potential problems are:

- The tendency to let the VIPs, or the most colorful or persistent people or organizations, or the biggest sponsors or advertisers set the news agenda, and not to attend to the insights and the needs of the rest of society.
- The tendency to participate in "pack journalism," and not only in coverage of political candidates, which is how the term gained popularity. Pack journalism is rarely neutral, and the pack doesn't have to be big. Reporters caught in the pack tend either to overplay or underplay an event and, having done so, often regret it. For example, years ago, *Chicago Tribune* columnist Bob Greene covered the execution of Gary Gilmore in a Utah prison and wrote a gruesome, detailed story about it that was printed in newspapers across the country. Greene followed with an eloquent article lamenting the first. Was his lament necessary? In 1989 television reporter Ginger Casey covered the aftermath of a gunman's attack on a California schoolyard. Her article about her remorse for having been part of the media pack at the schoolyard was eventually reprinted in *Reader's Digest* (Casey, 1992). Was it needed? (See Chapter 15-G.)
- The tendency to follow a leader, particularly a media leader. It might be *The New York Times* or *The Washington Post*, ABC or CNN—or even The Drudge Report. Regardless, when a major player takes on a topic, others soon follow. When the "big" press covers an issue, it often sets the agenda for everyone else. When the "big" press is arrogant or insensitive, others too often follow suit. When Katherine Fanning was publisher of the *Anchorage Daily News*, she voiced her concerns at a Modern Media Institute (now Poynter Institute) session, saying that "those organizations trickle down to us way out in the boondocks and on the frontier." She added, "It's a real concern to me that we like to peek so much into peoples' private feelings that often it goes way past any news value to savor others' tragedies. . . . I think we could have an impact without in any way inhibiting public responsibility, the public's right to know. I question whether the public really has the right to know how deeply someone is hurt on the occasion of losing a family or whatever" (*The Adversary Press*, 1983, p. 109).

- The tendency to concentrate attention on only part of society and to ignore many people and groups who deserve media coverage. Banks "redline" areas they believe are high-risk (to them). Editorial redlining can work two ways: Omit coverage of selected areas and populations or concentrate only on bad news about selected areas. The "unseen" poor in many big cities have erupted without media warning far too many times—at high cost to everyone.

What will happen to cities, and to the nation, when what we now call general circulation dailies offer "customized" editions? When people will order only the sections, only the subjects they want? What will happen to the democratic process when it is easy to select? This option deserves ethical consideration because the temptation to hide behind freedom—and freedom of selection—will be great, and we should not be surprised if new media options place new strains on society.

The news media face many other ethical choices every day—not only choices of who is covered and how they are covered, but how much they are covered. More information is currently available about media effects than ever before and many men and women in the media are vitally concerned about how their work affects their communities. The professionals want to be ethical. They cannot carry the whole burden, however. Readers, listeners, and viewers should be active participants in the media ethics arena. For the most part, organized news councils have not worked in this country, but individual and organizational interaction—criticism in the fullest sense of the word—can help media men and women make good ethical decisions.

What will happen . . . when what we now call general circulation dailies offer "customized" editions?

Although this section has concentrated on news media, continuing public and professional scrutiny of the entertainment and persuasive media also is important. The men and women who staff the media are often likened to gatekeepers because they monitor what their publics will see and hear. They know that the First Amendment protects individuals and the media alike. Their hardest job is often deciding what *should* be said—what should be included in news accounts and in entertainment programs that are published and broadcast to mass audiences. Indeed, freedom of expression is guaranteed and should be guarded, but it should not be allowed to become an excuse for irresponsible media conduct, particularly conduct that does not consider the potential social effects of what is included or excluded from the media.

This entire chapter reflects one of the major arguments about the mass media of the 20th century: will the public be better served with *access* or with *fairness?* Mass media access requires merely the technological support for members of the public to reach a large number of their fellows, but in no way guarantees that anyone will pay attention. Fairness, however, implies using a professional cadre that selects, edits and otherwise ensures that the public receives the information, entertainment and persuasive messages that it wants or needs. It is to be expected that most professional communicators will take the latter position.

■ MERRILL: Commentary

David Gordon is taking the radical libertarian position on this controversial issue. It happens to be the one I prefer, although I recognize the problems it brings to a discussion of ethics. The more moderate—and perhaps, intelligent—position discussed by Carol Reuss is the one that most media practitioners would probably agree with today. It is actually the position that is more *ethically based* and, after all, this book is about ethics.

Reuss's position is somewhat puzzling, however, in that she hedges her position by simply saying that freedom of expression should not be allowed to become an excuse for irresponsible media conduct. Who is it that will not allow it? And who is it that will define *irresponsible?* She solves the quandary, finally, by denying that freedom and responsibility are mutually opposed. In other words, she maintains that one can be both free and responsible. True. But does this eliminate the controversy discussed in this chapter? Does not freedom also include the right to be irresponsible? Certainly, most "big" stories are irresponsible *in somebody's opinion.*

The libertarian position is that the ethical journalist will want to be responsible, but that his or her freedom includes the right *not to be.* Gordon comes close to saying this, but it's hard to say because most people want to limit freedom to suit their own beliefs. On the other hand, *responsibility* is extremely relative and devoid of substantive meaning.

The libertarian position espoused by Gordon also expresses hope that such free expression would not be limited in any way whatsoever. This is, as Gordon recognizes, a difficult position to defend in this day of communitarian concerns that have grown out of the social responsibility theory of the (Hutchins) Commission on Freedom of the Press of the 1940s and the communitarians of the 1990s. However, many media people take Gordon's position; they are strict constructionists of the First Amendment and pure libertarians caught somewhere in the eighteenth-century Enlightenment. Freedom to them means "freedom," pure and simple. It should not be abridged in any way; a foot-in-the-door by some "ethically correct" authority is the height of arrogance, and it is dangerous to an open and contentious society.

Does not freedom also include the right to be irresponsible?

People who side with Reuss and who would limit free expression contend that morality dictates such a stance. Unlimited freedom, they say, is socially harmful, counterproductive to the development of a moral sense, unintelligent, and potentially disruptive to social harmony, and perhaps even to national security. Any reasonable person, they say, knows that there are limits to freedom, that anyone concerned with ethical behavior is automatically enjoined to place ethics ahead of freedom, the community good ahead of individualistic proclivities.

People siding with Gordon—and I am one of them—see any limitation of freedom of expression (by outside forces) as dangerous. It is dangerous for several reasons: It opens the door to any would-be determiner of "right" or "correct" expression, it assumes that media people cannot make their own decisions, it propagates a monistic concept of responsible communication, and it is nothing more than incipient authoritarianism in the guise of ethical communications behavior.

Don't misunderstand me. I am concerned about responsible communication. I want to be ethical—and I will be, according to *my own* concepts of morality. It is not that I am *against* ethics; it is just that I wish to be ethical in my way and let you be ethical in yours. This means—in the context of communication and journalism— that program directors, news directors, and editors will operate their ethical decision making in a context of pluralism, of diversity. They will limit *their own* expression, and therefore there will be a diversity of what is published and what is not published.

Now, if Reuss means that free expression may be limited in some ways (meaning *self*-control or *self*-limitation), then I agree with her. But if she implies that an outside person or entity will do the limiting, even in the name of morality, then I cannot agree with her. And if she does mean what I suggest above, then I would ask how her position differs from that of Gordon. Voluntary self-restraint or self-limitation of free expression is not at all inconsistent with libertarianism, even *radical* libertarianism. Every libertarian has always accepted the fact that a person imposes limits on one's own freedom. This is part of freedom: the freedom to restrict one's own freedom.

REFERENCES

The Adversary Press. (1983). St. Petersburg, FL: Modern Media Institute.

Bezanson, Randall P., Gilbert Cranberg, and John Soloski (1987). *Libel Law and the Press: Myth and Reality.* New York: Free Press.

Casey, Ginger. (July 1992). "Have They No Shame?" *Reader's Digest,* pp. 185–188, condensed from *Image,* the magazine of the San Francisco *Examiner,* January 19, 1992.

Commission on Freedom of the Press. (1947). *A Free and Responsible Press.* Chicago: University of Chicago Press.

Elliott, Deni, ed. (1986). *Responsible Journalism.* Newbury Park, CA: Sage.

Elliott, Deni. (Fall 1987). "Creating Conditions for Ethical Journalism." *Mass Comm Review* 14 (3), pp. 6–10.

Glasser, Theodore L. (1986). "Press Responsibility and First Amendment Values." In Deni Elliott, ed., *Responsible Journalism.* Beverly Hills, CA: Sage, pp. 81–98.

Harmon, Mark. (1991). "Hate Groups and Cable Public Access." *Journal of Mass Media Ethics* 6(3), pp. 146–155.

Hart, H. L. A. (1963). *Law, Liberty, and Morality.* New York: Vintage Books.

Lambeth, Edmund B. (1992). *Committed Journalism: An Ethic for the Profession,* 2nd ed. Bloomington: Indiana University Press.

"The McVeigh Dilemma." (April 1997). *Quill,* p. 17.

Meyer, Philip. (1983). *Editors, Publishers, and Newspaper Ethics.* Washington: American Society of Newspaper Editors.

Morgan, David. (September 3, 1997). "U.S. supermarkets join anti-tabloid backlash." Reuters story at http://www.infoseek.com/Content?col=NX&.

Rosenstiel, Tom. (March 21, 1997). "The Promise, and Perils, of On-Line Journalism." *Chronicle of Higher Education,* p. B6.

CHAPTER 2

INDIVIDUAL AUTONOMY AND ETHICAL DECISIONS

Those who study the principles that ought to shape human behavior—those whom we call ethicists—generally have agreed that unless an individual is free to choose what courses of action to take, there is little point in discussing ethical decision making. However, that does not allow individuals to ponder ethics decisions in a vacuum. Inevitably, various real-world factors enter into the decision-making process.

This doesn't invalidate the idea of individuals as moral agents, able to determine their own ethical criteria, directions, and behavior. It also does not mean that individuals are controlled by any or all of those real-world factors. But it does mean that some of those factors may well have an influence on some people's ethical decisions. *Applied*, as contrasted with *theoretical*, ethics often revolves around the tensions created by the clash of individual moral autonomy and organizational, cultural, or societal pressures.

This chapter focuses on how much influence is exerted on the individual moral agent, under what circumstances outside factors may become important, and whether—and how far—those factors may constrain the individual. Carol Reuss argues that the individual values of media people are by far the most potent forces in shaping ethical decisions and, thereby, the contents of the mass media. David Gordon responds that economic and other forces in society impact severely on the ethical decisions made by media practitioners, who may well believe that they are acting independently.

■ REUSS: The values of individual mass media practitioners shape their ethical decision making and the contents of the mass media.

The media cannot be ethical or unethical, John Merrill wrote in the Overview to this book, because media contents stem from decisions made by *workers* in the media. That's a good starting point for this discussion of media people and the media.

The mass media are synergistic. They are the result of the combined decisions and actions of many people—reporters, editors, producers, designers, managers—and the results are more potent than the sum of the individual decisions and actions those people make. The combined values of media people and all the other individuals and groups who are involved—suppliers and audiences, potential audiences, and even critics of the mass media—are more potent still. The basis of it all, though, is individual values. The collective decisions made by men and women who work for news and entertainment media flow from their individual values. Sometimes individuals' values, or their perceptions of their values, align with those of colleagues and sometimes they compete with them. This can be frustrating for the individuals who produce mass media and for those who evaluate mass media content, especially those who want to be comfortable in relying on particular media for information and interpretation of events.

Very often, neither the public nor the mass media community pays much attention to professional values until a situation arises that prompts questions about the rightness or wrongness of a person's or an organization's actions. Then a firestorm erupts, with questions about that person or organization and eventually about other persons or organizations, some of which might not be even remotely connected with the first. A case in point: a reporter, followed by a pack of other reporters, asked a presidential nominee for a cabinet position whether she had paid Social Security taxes for the services of a domestic worker. It made no difference if the question originated in the reporter's mind or if it was suggested to him or her or if the reporter were guilty of similar transgressions. The result was the same. There was a chain reaction of information, questions, and interpretations, not only about this candidate but about many others who were nominated for office. The media coverage concentrated on Social Security payments (nonpayment is against the law) to the exclusion of other information about the nominee's abilities, views and characteristics. The ethical standard for acceptable public service became, temporarily, payment or nonpayment of Social Security taxes for domestic help.

As often happens when a topic hits the news and then begins to play out, the deluge of news coverage about cabinet nominees sparked reporters' interests in other arenas. They shifted the angle away from politics and public service and toward ordinary citizens' everyday decision making. Chicago Tribune Syndicate writer Barbara Brotman, for example, challenged her readers to examine their own moral values as well as those of the nominees. "We obey the laws of the land," she wrote. "We uphold the highest moral values. We do not lie. We do not cheat. We do not steal. If we can help it" (Brotman, 1993, p. 1E).

In a sidebar article, Brotman listed questions based on material from the Josephson Institute of Ethics. She asked her readers to explore their own ethics as well as those of the nominees. Had they ever inflated claims on expense accounts; lied about age to get a discount; copied someone else's computer software; taken office supplies home; employed a housekeeper or baby-sitter without paying Social Security taxes; misrepresented a material fact on a resume; parked illegally; or taken credit for something they didn't do? Her questions about relatively common activities are as appropriate to media men and women as they are to her readers. They demonstrate basic values, and they suggest that ethical perfection is an elusive goal—but one that should be striven for.

■ SOURCES OF ETHICS

The values and the kinds of ethical decisions media people and the public make are based on life experiences, education, and interactions with others in various social groups. There are no studies of ethical decision making across all of the mass media or across all the different job categories in any one medium, but Fred F. Endres's (1985) study of newspaper journalists offers insight into the socialization processes that influence personal values.

Endres asked a representative sample of journalists to list the influences on their professional values and attitudes. When the study was completed, parents and early home life were at the top of the list. Next came journalistic experience, colleagues' behavior, religious upbringing, current family life, education, and the behavior of others. Journalists don't live or work in isolation, nor do other men and women who produce mass media. The values on which they base their professional ethical choices are rooted in experience, including social experience.

David Weaver and G. Cleveland Wilhoit (1991, 1993) completed two extensive studies of journalists in the 1980s and 1990s that offer additional perspective on the backgrounds, values, and interests of men and women who staff U.S. newspapers, wire services, newsmagazines, radio and television stations, and networks. Anyone interested in changes over the decade should read both studies.

The "typical" journalist in the early 1990s, Weaver and Wilhoit reported, was a married white Protestant male in his mid-30s who earned a bachelor's degree from a public college and had about 12 years of media experience. He worked for a medium-size group-owned daily newspaper with 42 journalists on staff, and did not belong to a journalism association. (Weaver and Wilhoit, 1993). Far more numerous and varied than "Mr. Typical," are the more than 100,000 other women and men who work at newspapers, newsmagazines, and broadcasting companies. Their individual similarities and differences affect the content of the news media.

What are some of their similarities? Hard-nosed journalists may prefer to be seen as cynical critics of almost everything, but Weaver and Wilhoit found that basically they are altruistic. They like the public service aspects of the work they do, and they believe it is important to get information to the public quickly and to provide analysis of complex problems. They are concerned about the impact of government on the people and thus believe it is essential to investigate the claims and actions of government at every level; journalists who are not on the government beat support the efforts of those who are.

The Weaver–Wilhoit studies indicate that journalists value autonomy, which is more difficult to find in large media organizations, especially organizations that use complex and sophisticated technology. Television journalists, for instance, work closely with video and sound crews and have less opportunity for autonomy than do print reporters. One might surmise that the men and women who create entertainment programs, which require even more specialists and elaborate equipment, have even less opportunity for autonomy, so they are probably most likely either to be extremely strong advocates for their own values or willing team players—or unhappy, unsatisfied professionals.

Weaver and Wilhoit found that although salaries are usually larger in the "big" media, many journalists willingly leave chain- and group-owned media and seek other kinds of employment when they feel their freedom and autonomy are in danger of being curtailed. A result of such personal independence is the loss of highly skilled people, who are often replaced by newcomers with much less experience.

From a positive perspective, such independence exemplifies the power of personal decision making—the ethical factor in occupation choice—and faith in the new talent available for jobs in journalism.

Men and women now entering professional journalism, Weaver and Wilhoit report, are likely to be college-educated. Although years in school cannot guarantee that anyone is a mature ethical decision maker, college-level work both teaches and requires critical thinking, which is very important in journalism. College-level work involves the ability to analyze, to seek and document facts, to synthesize, evaluate, and communicate—all activities that are important to journalism and the journalist's work.

The autonomy that journalists value is two-pronged, and they know it. On one side are the opportunities that journalists have to work independently, with minimal supervision. On the other side is the obligation journalists have to be independent of activities, associations, and ideologies that might be or appear to be conflicts of interest that would affect their credibility (see Chapter 14).

The traditions or conventions of journalism put high value on freedom, truth, and justice. Freedom includes freedom of the press, as guaranteed by the First Amendment. It also means that journalists and the media have the freedom to consider all viewpoints as well as the freedom to publish and broadcast opposing viewpoints. It implies that journalists should be independent and not do anything that might compromise or seem to compromise their integrity. Truth telling implies that journalists make every effort to make sure their work is accurate, thorough, and bias-free. Justice implies that journalists be fair, that they be thorough in their investigations, and that they offer honest information and relevant interpretation of their findings.

Competent journalists base their actions on those traditions, knowing, however, that they sometimes fall short. "All" information and viewpoints might not be available on deadline, for example, but ethical journalists should seek the full story even as they work against strict deadlines.

■ COMPETENCE AND COMMITMENT

While I use the word *competent* to describe ethical journalists, Edmund B. Lambeth uses the word *committed* in his excellent book *Committed Journalism: An Ethic for the Profession* (1992). Lambeth maintains that five principles distinguish ethical journalists and journalism: truth telling, justice, freedom, humaneness, and stewardship. These, he says, encompass both the techniques that ethical journalists use and the motivations for their work.

Ethical, competent, committed journalists work both for themselves and for the common good, but not without problems of interpretation of the information they seek and provide for their audiences. Weaver and Wilhoit asked for opinions about the ethics of various reporting practices in two surveys conducted a decade apart. In each study, there were disagreements about the ethics of news gathering and reporting practices. Some of the journalists they interviewed said that undercover reporting can be justified, some did not. Some said that it is acceptable to use unauthorized business and government documents, while others disagreed. Some said it is acceptable to use personal documents, such as letters and photographs, without authorization, some said it is not. Some said that journalists don't have to identify themselves as journalists when they seek information for a story, that it is all right to use hidden cameras, to disclose confidential sources, to badger sources for information. Some said it is acceptable to pay for confidential information.

For better or worse, the operative word was *some* because there was no consensus on any of the topics. Instead, individual differences, backgrounds, values, and perceptions strongly influenced responses to the Weaver-Wilhoit questions, just as they influence the decisions journalists make as they cover the news.

When Weaver and Wilhoit analyzed their data they found only slight differences between broadcast and print journalists, between people who worked for large and small media, and between old and young journalists. But, they said, there were some differences. Older and more experienced journalists are more apt to hold to the tradition that journalists should work in the open, be up front in identifying themselves, and respect confidences. Journalists in the larger media organizations are more likely to say that cutting corners may be justified.

Unfortunately, Weaver and Wilhoit did not ask questions about the use of composite characters, or about the ethics of not identifying sources, especially those who are directly quoted. They did not ask whether or when it is acceptable to omit personal characteristics about important subjects. For years White House reporters kept from their stories any indication that President Franklin D. Roosevelt was crippled from polio. They omitted knowledge of other personal traits, too, just as their predecessors had done for earlier presidents. Public and journalistic tolerance for keeping personal information private has now changed, as exemplified by the Clinton-Lewinsky coverage of 1998. However, disclosure of such information in the mass media still rests on decisions that often start with journalists on the beat and with the values these men and women hold. Sometimes they rigidly embrace values they have learned to trust over the years; sometimes they and their values are malleable, just as the values of their audiences also change.

... individual differences, backgrounds, values, and perceptions strongly ... influence the decisions journalists make as they cover the news.

The broadly stated traditions of journalism—honesty, accuracy, thoroughness, objectivity, fairness, freedom from compromising entanglements—appear to be relatively simple and clear-cut, but they are not. The pressures of covering news include the pressures of time and competition as well as the availability of adequate sources and information. Events often erupt simultaneously, and with little warning. Journalists try to make decisions equitably, but sometimes even the best make poor decisions. The worst—the weakest—set the pace for biased, sensational, inaccurate reports generated within a system that takes pride in First Amendment freedoms.

Some ethical questions or problems can be resolved quickly and without discussion. A subject is or is not newsworthy, a source is or is not trustworthy. Other questions, including many about fairness, balance, objectivity, and appropriateness, merit newsroom discussion before articles are written and published and before broadcasts are produced and aired. During the discussions, individual values and professional and social values may be, or may appear to be, in conflict. To get a sense of how competing values complicate news decisions, ask yourself and others the following questions, based loosely on the questions Barbara Brotman (1993) asked her readers:

- Is it ever acceptable for media people deliberately to deceive a potential source of information about their professional identity or intentions?

- Is it ever acceptable to steal documents, photographs, or other material from a source or to copy them without first asking permission?
- Is it ever acceptable to stage or re-create an event without telling the audience?
- Is it ever acceptable for media people to accept gifts, tickets, or other freebies?
- Is it ever acceptable for media people to seek or give special treatment for themselves, their families, or causes they favor?
- Finally, is it ever acceptable for media people to violate laws, including speeding and parking laws? Are they "above" them?

Longtime newsman Michael Gartner was forced to resign the presidency of NBC News after its *Dateline* program aired a segment about GM truck safety. The segment's producers planned a crash to prove their point that the truck's gas tanks were poorly placed. To make sure the truck they filmed caught fire, they attached detonators to it! Gartner's words after the faulted crash summarize well the risk attached to decision making: "[Y]ou can write all the rules you want, you can make all the pronouncements you want, you can set all the examples you want, you can hold all the seminars you want—and indeed you must do all those things—but there's no way you can totally keep folks from doing dumb things," he said soon after the episode. "And even if you have a tradition of dealing fairly—of listening to the outraged, of correcting the mistakes, of fixing the system—you may still find that you suddenly have a lot more time to spend at home with your family" (Gartner, 1993, pp. 8–9).

The individual values of mass media people are indeed important in shaping their ethical decision making, but these individuals work with others in relatively complex media organizations and the final decisions that are made every day may not align exactly with each person's values. If this happens too often, ethical men and women look for other jobs.

So far, this chapter has concentrated on the people who manage and staff the news media—how their ethical values shape their decisions and, ultimately, the news media contents. The equation is incomplete, however, if we rely solely on media practitioners' values and omit consideration of the individual and social values of media audiences—actual and potential.

There are different kinds of audience participation in media decision making. Public opinion about a topic or about the media is a strong collective influence on mass media contents and formats, and on public acceptance and interpretation of media offerings. It is generated by people who are active members of media audiences and by those who, for any number of reasons, have opinions about media that they publicly express even if they pay little or no attention to mass media.

People who make up actual and potential mass media audiences, as well as media men and women, need to recognize the importance of audience values to media contents. As David Gordon recommends in Chapter 11, media audiences need to be media literate—to know the nuances of different media and media techniques and to know how to react to media because they *are* participants in decision making about mass media contents. The values, principles, knowledge, and even the biases and prejudices of mass media audiences show up in broadcast ratings and in circulation statistics. They influence the work of the men and women who staff the mass media; they help determine the quality and the quantity of media contents. The opinions of any media audience will of course be more valid if they are knowledgeable about the media.

■ GORDON: Social, economic, and political forces severely constrain the ethical decisions of individual media practitioners.

Media content—both in entertainment and news media—is determined by a vast series of individual decisions made by those working in the media, but it is far from accurate to say that the individual decision makers are free to act based only on their own ethical values (or lack of them). They may think this is the case, but experience argues to the contrary. There appears to be considerable evidence that decisions at key points are influenced heavily—and, in some cases, are dictated—by various political, social, and especially economic forces that operate in society.

■ POLITICAL PRESSURES

Although American mass media are basically free to operate without political interference, the specter of government regulation or influence certainly cannot be ignored. The beginnings of federal regulation of broadcasting go back to the early days of radio. More specifically, the Federal Communications Commission's late (and occasionally lamented) Fairness Doctrine exemplified how government and the political system can get involved with mass media ethics and values.

The Fairness Doctrine—adopted by the FCC in 1949 (13 *FCC Reports* 1246) and codified in FCC Public Notice 63-734 of July 23, 1963—can be traced back at least to the 1941 Mayflower case (8 FCC Reports 333). (Ford, 1963–1964) With respect to controversial issues, in particular, it can also be traced back to operating procedures established by Westinghouse (Group W) for its stations in the late 1940s. Many broadcasters still have not gone so far as to specify in writing the need to treat controversial issues—and people—fairly. But most of them would certainly agree at least in the abstract with the need for "fairness" as an ethical principle.

However, broadcasters' varying interpretations of what "fairness" means and how it should be implemented were constrained when the FCC adopted and applied—enforced would certainly overstate what actually took place—the fairness principle to all broadcasters. In the last analysis, whenever the issue was joined, *fairness* came to mean whatever the FCC and the courts said it did or did not mean. Even after the Fairness Doctrine was repealed as part of the broadcasting deregulation of the 1980s, station owners and managers were not totally free to establish or change their own definitions of fairness because there have been sporadic rumbles from Congress that it might adopt legislation reinstating the Fairness Doctrine if broadcasters stray too far from this principle in the new, deregulated atmosphere.

Among the most frightening examples of government constraints on media practitioners were the results of the investigations by the House Un-American Activities Committee (the infamous HUAC) of alleged Communist influence in Hollywood, in 1947 and again in 1951–1952. The climate of fear these investigations engendered sent a clear message to the film industry and, to some extent, to radio and television, that certain subjects were not fit topics for loyal Americans to feature in their productions.

HUAC also sent the message that anti-Communist films were appropriate to the political climate, and the film industry responded with more than 50 such movies between 1947 and 1954, even though most of them were box office failures (Sayre,

1978, pp. 79–80). Movies such as *I Married a Communist*, *The Red Menace*, and *My Son John* were among the commercially unsuccessful examples of this "interplay between American film and politics" that resulted from "a ferocious campaign to draft Hollywood into the Cold War" (Doherty, 1988, pp. 15–16).

There are also more recent and much more specific examples of how government and political pressures can become more important than individual decision makers and their values. One need look no further than the 1992 cable television re-regulation law, which gained major impetus from perceptions that cable rates were skyrocketing beyond reasonable levels. True or not, this concern fueled what was essentially a congressional backlash against the cable industry, resulting in legislation intended to provide at least limited rate protection to cable consumers and imposing constraints on decision making in the cable industry.

Because of pressure from over-the-air TV broadcasters, the legislation also allowed local stations to charge cable systems a fee, and gave cable operators the option not to carry local broadcasts and thereby avoid paying the fee. In a handful of markets where some local stations were taken off the cable systems, subscribers were caught squarely in the middle as the cable and broadcast industries fought over an economic issue that wouldn't have existed had the government not stepped in. (Ironically, this legislation became the first and only veto by President Bush that Congress was able to override. Its content was relatively minor in comparison to such issues as gun control or family leave, where presidential vetoes were upheld, but the cable bill was widely perceived as a consumer protection measure and the veto went to Congress just before the 1992 elections. Score one for political impact on the media and their consumers!)

A second example of political forces influencing the mass media is the pressure to label if not actually reduce violence in TV programming. Organized groups (such as the Reverend Donald Wildmon's American Family Association) and congressional hearings fueled the concern from 1993 on, culminating in a "voluntary" TV rating system that was begun in 1997. In this instance, threats of organized social and political action, economic boycotts, and potential government regulation put major pressures on the gatekeepers both within the television industry—particularly made-for-TV movie producers, who supply sizable portions of TV programming—and elsewhere. Decision makers in advertising agencies and television advertisers, who had to decide whether to sponsor programs with high violence quotients, were also directly constrained by these developments.

A third example was the attempt to regulate Internet content through the 1996 Communications Decency Act, which certainly will not disappear from the political or cultural arenas despite being held unconstitutional by the Supreme Court in 1997.

■ SOCIETAL AND OTHER PRESSURES

Organized pressure groups are only one aspect of the social constraints affecting the mass media. No matter how altruistic journalists—or anyone else in the media— may be, they must pay attention to the size and reactions of the audience. Ratings, subscriptions, single-copy or single-play sales, and movie attendance all have a direct impact on how the final media product turns out, as does direct feedback such as complaints to the editor, general manager, or advertiser. If an altruistic approach to the media product engenders serious resistance from the intended audience, either the altruism or the individual displaying it is likely to be gone quite soon. What often happens is that the ethical framework of media workers takes second place to the likes and dislikes—and on some issues, the ethical concerns—of the media audience and the advertisers trying to reach them.

Altruism isn't the only quality in media people that may be severely constrained by outside forces. Independence is another . . . .

Altruism isn't the only quality in media people that may be severely constrained by outside forces. Independence is another, particularly as economic factors become more and more important in all aspects of the media business. As Carol Reuss noted in referring to the Weaver and Wilhoit studies, autonomy is reduced in large media organizations. And economic factors are increasingly producing such large media organizations. As Weaver and Wilhoit (1993) note, many journalists have left chain-owned or group media organizations because they didn't want to see their independence and autonomy threatened. But what of the media people who don't or can't make such a career change? It is reasonable to conclude that by opting to stay rather than to leave such situations, they are giving up some of their moral independence in trade for the benefits derived from that job.

Internal organizational norms and customs may also exert negative as well as positive influences on individual moral autonomy. An early study by Warren Breed (1955) found that the newsroom culture was usually sufficiently strong to socialize new reporters into the established way of doing things, at least on the medium-sized papers included in his study. A more recent in-depth study of the overall operation of a major newspaper—widely believed to be *The New York Times*—indicated that the internal dynamics of the organization might be at least as important as economic pressures in terms of the impact on individuals and their ethical independence (Argyris, 1974).

Another type of internal pressure can come from technological changes. Although new technologies can relax deadline pressures in some media, they can increase them in others. Look, for example, at the electronic newsgathering (ENG) equipment in broadcast journalism, which allows faster turnaround of taped stories and encourages more live reports. The faster deadlines occasioned by ENG reporting mean less time for ethical concerns to surface and more need to "go by the book"—or by "how it's always been done here"—in putting stories together, rather than making ethical awareness part of the story preparation process.

■ CONGLOMERATES AND INDIVIDUAL AUTONOMY

Economic pressures on individual autonomy are increasingly common in media conglomerates, where top management may have little familiarity with traditions that historically have been important to their media subsidiaries. For publicly owned parent companies, the bottom line is usually more important (and sometimes *far* more important) than maintaining traditional standards, because the shareholders can't bank traditional standards.

James Squires, former editor of the *Chicago Tribune*, discusses this issue in considerable detail in his 1993 book, *Read All About It!* His analysis provides examples of the economic forces that take content decisions out of the hands of the media people who have made them in the past.

Newspapers, Squires notes, traditionally have sought, and fought, to obtain the greatest market penetration possible by providing news, information, and entertainment that interests wide cross-sections of people in their circulation areas. With the increase of publicly held companies as newspaper owners, though, the focus has shifted sharply to the affluent readers in the top 35 or 40% of the economic scale. This more affluent audience, if it can be captured, enhances the desirability of the paper for advertisers who are aiming at upscale customers. At the same time, it eliminates from the newspaper's consideration the needs and interests of the other 60 or 65% of the population, a fact that Squires says runs counter to the traditional role of the newspaper as the vehicle through which a self-governing society becomes more informed. In his words:

> Nowhere does the Constitution define "the people" as the predominantly white upper 35 percent of the population between twenty-five and fifty years of age who make $50,000 a year. Yet newspapers routinely control costs and enhance profits by cutting off circulation that is unprofitable because it lacks value as a quality audience. (Squires, 1993, p. 90)

Wall Street, Squires alleges, has made prisoners of the editors and publishers in America's most powerful newspaper companies. Although the editors and publishers still nominally make the decisions, "they are now compelled to find the most profitable way to deliver information, even if it means abandoning their traditional form, their traditional function, and their traditional definition of excellence" (145–146).

Thus, bottom-line pressures to maintain and increase profit margins can take away the autonomy and independence that Weaver and Wilhoit found to be an important value to American journalists. It is important to note that Weaver and Wilhoit's "typical" 1990s journalist works for a group-owned paper, most likely a local monopoly paper that can survive quite well without diverting potential profits to improve quality. Furthermore, this group-owned paper is increasingly likely to be part of a conglomerate where the parent firm may have interests that differ greatly from traditional journalistic values, such as Rupert Murdoch's News Corp.

Corporate pressures to produce profits in such situations remove much of journalists' past freedom to make decisions based on their own ethical frameworks. Thus it is no longer correct, if it ever was, to say that news media content is determined mainly through the decisions made by various individual journalists. Of course, those decisions are still made and do influence media content, but increasingly, those decisions are being made within a profit-driven context that removes important choices from the realistic options available to individual practitioners.

If this is happening in American newspapers, especially as conglomerate ownership increases, it is certainly happening in other segments of the mass media where ownership is also solidifying. Is it possible that the management of Time-Warner, to take one huge example, is going to be more influenced by ethics and values issues than by the need to return the greatest possible profit to its shareholders and creditors? One need not look far for part of the answer: Time-Warner representatives praising "the 'artistic integrity' of the racist and sadistic outpourings of the rappers Ice-T and 2 Live Crew" (Harwood, 1992)—recordings produced and distributed by a Time-Warner company.

Or, in another segment of the mass communication field, will conglomerate owners of advertising agencies give free rein to employees' creativity if the economic results are decidedly less certain than profits previously produced by less imaginative, "tried and true" ad campaigns? I wouldn't bet on ethics overcoming economics in this case, either.

Pragmatism—particularly as it relates to economic survival and growth, as reflected in the bottom line and in the stockholders' expectations—has become far more important than the individual values of media people in determining content. Even top media decision makers cannot ignore this perspective because they are increasingly being held responsible and accountable to the officers of a parent company and to stockholders. Media critic Ben Bagdikian (1989) noted this with regard to Time-Warner:

> Thousands of shareholders now have to be satisfied, the largest being a number of banks, institutions not widely known for their interest in magazines, movies or television programming that push beyond the safe perimeters of conventional wisdom and popular entertainment. (p. 808)

■ ETHICAL FRAMEWORKS

If bottom-line considerations are replacing some long-standing customs in the mass media, are there any useful ethical frameworks other than the pragmatic ends-justify-the-means approach of Machiavelli? Edmund Lambeth warns against using utilitarianism as a guide because it may be "ever so easy and often tempting to choose as a 'maximizer of the good' the path that suits the individual [practitioner's] or media organization's interest rather than the course [an individual], as a moral agent, would decide" (Lambeth, 1992, p. 57). Ethical egoism might be a viable alternative in a context where rational pursuit of self-interest is the accepted approach. However, it might not be useful if one looks at *long-run* self-interest while the corporate bean counters are trying to maximize short-term profits.

Unless you are going to rely on "gut feeling" (or on John Merrill's notion of a "moral epiphany"), the only useful ethical guideline in these situations comes from Aristotle's Golden Mean. That approach might suggest staying in a job as long as you can live with the ethical constraints imposed by outside forces. When things get too bad, then it's time to leave, a move that may be possible if you have built up what might be called a go-to-hell fund so you can tell that to your boss when you're asked to step across a line that takes you too far from your basic ethical principles.

James Squires used the pragmatic, Machiavellian approach in dealing with the head of the business side of the operation at the *Chicago Tribune* and at *The Sentinel* in Orlando, Florida. He struck what he later came to view as a Faustian bargain. He would control what went into the paper, its editorial opinions, when it went to press, and the face it presented to its community; in return, he would "run the tightest ship in the business. It was a deal designed to deliver both prizes and profits" (Squires, 1993, pp. 57–58).

This agreement did deliver considerable success, in terms of both journalistic recognition and steadily rising profit margins. It is an approach that, increasingly, seems necessary if editors are to have any hope of obtaining the resources they need to do their jobs and improve their product. But attaining one's goal at any cost is not comforting to people concerned with ethics. This approach also runs the risk of having the focus on profits override the use of resources for the editorial product, which illustrates once again the way in which corporate economics are increasingly more important than individual value systems.

Similarly, executives who are responsible for making television programming decisions are increasingly likely to be constrained by economic factors. For example, if a potential program isn't likely to appeal to viewers in a desired niche of the overall audience, it is unlikely to be seen on a national network no matter how good it is or how much "good" it might bring to a large number of viewers.

Perhaps even more frightening is the picture painted by Bagdikian, who commented that the relationships between various parts of mass media conglomerates could—with only a little imagination—override most if not all traditional values in the gatekeeping process. For instance, consider the possibility of a magazine editor commissioning an article that can then be expanded into a book published by another subsidiary of the same parent firm. The book could then be plugged on talk shows on the radio and TV stations owned by the publisher's conglomerate parent, featured and perhaps serialized in the parent company's newspapers or magazines, and made into a movie produced by the conglomerate's Hollywood studio. The film would then be booked through the company's distribution arm and have its soundtrack released on the company's record label. The vocalist could be turned into an instant celebrity by being featured in the company's magazines and interviewed on its radio and TV stations, the soundtrack album could be played on the conglomerate's radio stations, and the movie could eventually be issued on videocassette by still another arm of the parent firm (Bagdikian, 1989, p. 812).

[T]he very structure of American media industries is increasingly creating conditions in which both individual ethical values and media traditions are less important than economics.

Note that this scenario has not even considered how the work, and various tie-in commercial products, might be merchandised through cable networks or local cable systems owned by the conglomerate, with the assistance of affiliated ad agencies or marketing specialists—all with little consideration of the quality of the original article and its offspring, or of the impact these various commercial activities may have on individuals or society as a whole.

Conglomerate ownership has produced relationships—and the potential for decisions about the media—that extend well beyond the gatekeepers of mass media. For example, the tie-ins between the Disney Corporation's various media activities, including ABC, and its ownership of theme parks and the Anaheim Mighty Ducks and Angels pro sports franchises, could easily produce some media content decisions based on considerations about the marketing of these nonmedia activities.

Thus, the very structure of American media industries is increasingly creating conditions in which both individual ethical values and media traditions are less important than economics. When the actual and potential influence of government, politics, and the social system are added to the equation, the constraints on individual ethics, values, and autonomy should be obvious.

■ MERRILL: Commentary

David Gordon is right when he maintains that ethical decisions in the media are greatly influenced by forces operating in the larger society. Certainly it would be simplistic to believe that individual media people make their decisions based solely on their own ethical values. Media policy, peer expectations, and social pressures of many kinds inevitably have an impact on individual ethical determinations. Journalists, for example, often can avoid ethical decision making if they are willing to follow the traditional media or social expectations. Sociologists would not quarrel with Gordon on this score; it is well known that people tend to conform to the policies of the institutions they work for.

Although such a position is not too bothersome in most areas of social activity, when it comes to *ethics*, the concept of social conformity is rather worrisome, at least to those who feel that the individual should have the courage to carry the moral burden independently of external expectations. Even the immoral person can conform to the group, as we know. Like Kant, some believe that the "principled" media worker would be guided by a reasoned duty to do the right or the better thing—*regardless of the social sentiment of the day.*

Certainly we do not want to go too far in such thinking, however. We know that a meaningful ethics is not isolated from society, that in reality there is no ethics that is not *social ethics*. At least this is what a large segment of ethicists—especially communitarians—tell us. Religious, political, economic, and other forces, as Gordon argues, have their impact on media ethics. Organized social and political action, boycotts, and government regulation do indeed make independent ethical determinations difficult, if not impossible—or so it seems. But a question persists: *Should they?*

Gordon gets very close to saying that the free-market capitalist economy, with its normal pressures, keeps journalists from making their own ethical decisions. It is incorrect, he maintains, to attribute significant media content to *editorial* decisions; he argues that such decisions are made in a profit-driven context that largely omits moral considerations from the model. If this is true, then it is indeed a sad day for media morality. Journalists become no more than slaves to forces outside themselves, mere functionaries operating in an institutional environment without morals. Like Machiavelli (and American journalist James Squires, quoted often above), Gordon seems to see pragmatism replacing the individual values of media people.

Taking issue with Gordon, Carol Reuss puts considerable stress on the importance of individual moral values and decisions. Question your own ethical premises, think out your own ethical problems, act out your own moral strategies, take responsibility for your own ethical action: These are individualistic mandates, according to Reuss, that fall on every media functionary. This is only right; according to Reuss's position, ethics largely comes down to one's own value system, one's own moral reasoning.

However, Reuss is not naïve in her individualistic proclivities. She realizes that journalists are both individuals and group members. They have institutional expectations in addition to having a desire to fulfill personal moral commitments. These collective and individual expectations may or may not be in conflict, but it would seem that if they are, the journalist would have to come down on the side of *individual* expectations. Why? Because morality is not determined by a majority vote or even a desire to do what the crowd desires or demands. Reuss's argument seems to be that moral reasoning is distinctly different from some kind of decision making based on a democratic calculus.

Why should I individually *feel any ethical mandate placed on me?*

Of course, out of such discussions as this comes the inevitable question: Why should I *individually* feel any ethical mandate placed on me? If I do, does it perhaps come from the expectations of my colleagues in the media or from those in the audience I serve? These are good questions, and ones that are usually avoided in media ethics books. I'm not sure that I can answer them—or that I really want to at this point. But I will say that a *concern* with being ethical must always precede any wrestling with moral dilemmas and any systematic concern for doing the right or best thing.

Many would say that a moral consciousness, with its determination to be ethical, derives from a deep-seated selfishness, a kind of doing unto others *as you would have them do unto you.* Be honest with others because you want them to be honest with you. Don't lie, said Kant, unless you would be willing to say that everyone should be allowed to lie. This is ethical reasoning, all right, but it is built on a foundation of selfishness. It makes sense, no doubt, but does it make *moral* as well as *logical* sense? Perhaps *I* should not lie *even though everyone else, indeed, does lie.*

Is it possible that I should have a desire to be ethical simply for the sake of being ethical—and for no other reason? Just because I sense that it is good to be ethical? No consideration of Millian consequences here. No dedication to a Kantian universalizing principle here. Just a deep-seated, *personal* commitment to doing right, regardless of what others might do or think, or what the social repercussions might be. This would free me from the formalistic ethical strictures of Immanuel Kant and also from the altruistic consequentialism of John Stuart Mill. It would throw me, existentially, into the moral maelstrom and force me momentarily to make ethical decisions and accept responsibility for them.

This might be called a kind of motivation ethics. It is somewhere between the social determinism of Gordon's argument and the personal autonomy of Reuss's position. My *motive* is simply to do what *I* think is right, or what I feel or intuit is right. The simple motive of doing good, of following the righteous path as I see it in the existential context of the moment and situation—this is the *reasonless* stimulant to ethical concern that may well lie at the foundation of much moral motivation.

This will not appeal to everyone; in fact it will probably not appeal to very many. It has Kierkegaardian overtones that rise to a kind of religious apex of faith, intuition, and personal spontaneity. Not to be found here is an overriding concern with moral reasoning, or with "doing ethics." It is not exactly the philosopher's way—it is perhaps more the theological or the mystical way. It is coming at ethics from the subjective side, not the objective side. It is unfolding ethics from the inside out, not from the outside in. It is more *feeling* ethics than *thinking* ethics. Of course, when we talk like this we are getting into the religious sphere, but it is a sphere that many philosophers (such as Kierkegaard, Nietzsche, Schopenhauer, and Jaspers) and many religious figures (such as Buddha and Jesus) have endorsed wholeheartedly.

I have departed considerably from Gordon's and Reuss's main arguments, perhaps. But perhaps not. Such an inward-motivational stance is certainly an *individualistic* one, based not on social conformity and peer expectations but rather on a personal, almost transcendental moral consciousness that rises from spiritual awareness of what is better or worse, right or wrong, not from worldly reasoning. It derives from a kind of subjective inflation of the *humanity-sense*, a form of flooding the spiritual aspects of personhood with mystical positive overtones, and it results in a moral epiphany quite different from the purely philosophical *reasons* for being ethical.

The arguments of Gordon and Reuss deal with much more mundane matters. Certainly, they stay far away from the mystical moral epiphany that I have just suggested. But they are facing the same sort of question, an old question with which many thinkers have grappled: Is ethics mainly individualistic or social? Many agree with Hegel, who saw each of us as insignificant, no more than an expression of the grand forces of society and history, believing that an ethical sense must flow from the needs and wishes of society. The modern *communitarians*, under the leadership of sociologist Amitai Etzioni, are busy reinforcing the appeal of a socially endowed and concerned ethics.

Others, like Kierkegaard and Nietzsche, see the individual as of more importance than society, and make the case for personal moral accountability. Supporters of Carol Reuss would be psychiatrist Carl Jung and philosopher Karl Jaspers, who believed that the individual matters more than the system, thus reversing the idea of Hegel, Marx, and other "groupist" thinkers. Contemporary Harvard philosopher Robert Nozick would support Reuss, and his colleague John Rawls would support Gordon.

What I think is clear is that the *individual* is essential to ethics, but at the same time others are also needed. The individual cannot be ethical in a vacuum. Without a doubt, media people must consider the human environment in which they function. Of course, this will lead to a certain moderation of action and to a certain conformity. At the same time, it is necessary to recognize that the media person must often be willing to make ethical decisions in a courageous and independent manner regardless of social expectations.

REFERENCES

Argyris, Chris. (1974). *Behind the Front Page*. San Francisco: Jossey-Bass.

Bagdikian, Ben. (June 12, 1989). "The Lords of the Global Village." *The Nation*, pp. 805–820.

Breed, Warren. (1955). "Social Control in the Newsroom." *Social Forces* 33(4), pp. 326–335.

Brotman, Barbara. (March 7, 1993). "When Conscience Fails to Guide." *The News & Observer*, Raleigh, NC, pp. 1E, 5E.

Doherty, Thomas. (Fall 1988). "Hollywood Agit-Prop: The Anti-Communist Cycle, 1948–1954." *Journal of Film and Video* 40(4), pp. 15–27.

Endres, Fred F. (Spring 1985). "Influences on the Ethical Socialization of U.S. Newspaper Journalists." *Newspaper Research Journal* 6(3), pp. 47–56.

Ford, Frederick W. (Winter 1963–1964). "The Fairness Doctrine." *Journal of Broadcasting* 8(1), pp. 3–16.

"Gartner Shares Lessons He Learned from NBC Years." (June 1, 1993). *SNPA Bulletin,* pp. 8–9.

Harwood, Richard. (December 5, 1992). "Knights of the Fourth Estate." *The Washington Post,* p. A23.

Lambeth, Edmund. (1992). *Committed Journalism: An Ethic for the Profession,* 2nd ed. Bloomington: Indiana University Press.

Sayre, Nora. (1978). *Running Time: Films of the Cold War.* New York: Dial Press.

Squires, James D. (1993). *Read All About It!: The Corporate Takeover of America's Newspapers.* New York: Times Books.

Weaver, David H., and G. Cleveland Wilhoit. (1991). *The American Journalist: A Portrait of U.S. News People and Their Work,* 2nd ed. Bloomington: Indiana University Press.

Weaver, David H., and G. Cleveland Wilhoit. (1993). *The American Journalist in the 1990s. Preliminary Report.* Arlington, VA: The Freedom Forum.

C H A P T E R   3

CODES OF
ETHICS

O ne of the hallmarks of a profession (as distinct from an occupation or a trade)—or a field with pretensions to professionalism—is that it has a code of ethics, often with teeth to enforce it.

Some of these codes are primarily for the benefit of practitioners in the profession. A good example is the original Hippocratic Oath, which focuses on such things as economics and control over entrance to the field of medicine and its practice. Codes may also be public relations exercises, intended to make customers or the general public look more favorably on the profession. The injunction against administering poisons in the Hippocratic Oath can be read this way because its concern is for the reputation of all doctors. Finally, codes can also form a useful set of guidelines for practitioners, with the best interests of the public—the profession's customers—at heart.

There are many codes of ethics in the mass media fields. Various organizations in print and broadcast journalism, such as the Society of Professional Journalists (SPJ), the National Press Photographers Association (NPPA), and the Radio-Television News Directors Association (RTNDA), have developed, and argued over, their own codes. So have individual newspapers and, since the demise of the National Association of Broadcasters' code of practice, various broadcast stations, networks, and groups.

Ethics codes also exist in public relations, business communication, and advertising, not to mention technical writing and political campaigns. But there is considerable debate about their value, or the lack of it. "For some people, formal codes are a necessary mark of a true profession. For others, codes are worthless exercises in vagueness, irrelevance, and slick public relations" (Johannesen, 1996, p. 197).

Codes of ethics in the mass media can be traced back at least to 1910, when the state press association in Kansas adopted one. By 1929 some newspapers and at least a dozen state press associations had adopted ethics codes, fueled in part by concerns over the re-emergence of newspaper sensationalism and an increasing erosion of newspapers' credibility (Cronin and McPherson, 1995). A code with national dimensions emerged in 1923, when the Canons of Journalism were adopted by the American Society of Newspaper Editors (ASNE).

The early codes and those that have followed tend to be worded quite generally. Almost all are voluntary, without enforcement provisions. One exception is in public relations, where complaints can be filed against practitioners who have allegedly violated provisions of the Code of Professional Standards of the Public Relations Society of America (PRSA). Such complaints are heard either by a PRSA national grievance board or by regional panels. In several cases, complaints have led to the expulsion, suspension, or censure of public relations personnel by the PRSA, but that does not bar them from continuing to practice public relations.

Arguments for and against media codes of ethics have been made in many forums over the years. Usually, these have focused on the philosophical implications of codes (Johannesen, 1996, pp. 198–199, provides a concise summary of arguments against formal codes). Sometimes, they have reflected fears that a voluntary code will be taken over and enforced by government. Occasionally, the arguments have focused on fears that those who adhere to a code may find themselves at a competitive disadvantage to those who ignore it, on specific revisions in a code, or on whether any enforcement provisions should be added. Some of those disputes have reached vitriolic levels.

In the calmer and more reasoned discussion that follows, Carol Reuss argues that codes have no power and are not important to either the media or the society. David Gordon maintains that ethics codes are valuable both to the mass media themselves and to society.

■ REUSS: Media codes of ethics are impotent, and too often they are facades that imply ethical behavior.

Will Irwin implied that newspaper reporters had a code of ethics when he wrote his 15-part critique of the American newspaper for *Collier's* in 1911. "[M]en at the bottom of the profession—if we measure standing by salary and public esteem," he said, "have come closest of all American journalists to forming a professional spirit and formulating an ethical code" (Irwin, 1911, p. 19). Irwin summarized the four standards of the unwritten code:

> Never, without special permission, print information that you learned at your friend's house, or in your club. In short, draw a strict line between your social and professional life. . . .
>
> Except in the case of criminals, publish nothing without full permission of your informant. . . .
>
> Never sail under false colors. State who you are, what newspaper you represent, and whether or not your informant is talking for publication. . . .
>
> Keep this side of the home boundary. Remember that when the suicide lies dead in the chamber there are wretched hearts in the hall, that when the son is newly in jail intrusion is torment to the mother. . . . (pp. 19, 30)

"Not all reporters hold that code, of course," Irwin wrote, "but the best, the directing journalists of tomorrow do" (p. 17).

The implied code Irwin described, dramatically phrased, is repeated in contemporary codes, which are as self-serving as they are protective of the rights and feelings of others.

. . . contemporary codes . . . are as self-serving as they are protective of the rights and feelings of others.

Today, handsomely framed copies of codes of ethics decorate the walls in many mass media offices, and copies of codes are often included in textbooks about mass media. They are impressive, even inspirational—but, like Irwin's implied code, they're of limited value.

Written codes of ethics suggest that mass media, and the men and women who produce them, are virtuous servants of society. They imply unified allegiance to professional standards of performance in a business where the media and the assignments undertaken by those who produce them are so varied that codes cannot describe, prescribe or proscribe their activities. The contents of the excellent news media are accurate, balanced, and fair because the individuals responsible for them work tirelessly and under pressure to be accurate, balanced, and fair. Excellent entertainment media are the product of creative, capable men and women. At the other end of the spectrum, media of poor quality are also produced by people, not codes.

The mass media codes may suggest nirvana—uniformly applicable practices, universally accepted and applied—but that is not possible. Codes do have some influence on media practitioners and practices, but because they are neither universally applicable nor enforceable they are, at best, of limited importance. They are at worst impotent facades or at best "they leave a lot to be desired in terms of implementation and efficiency" (Nordenstreng, 1995, p. 2).

Moreover, most existing codes of ethics are aimed entirely wrong, in focusing on journalists rather than on owners, who are the ones with real autonomy and decision-making power. As John McManus points out, because "journalists are more decision takers than decision makers . . . their authority to produce high-quality ethical news reports is circumscribed, tightly for some, loosely for others. . . . Journalism's ethical codes have it backwards." (McManus, 1997, p. 13)

Codes of ethics might even be unethical if they are so stringently applied and monitored as to restrict or constrain autonomous decision making, placing government in the position of enforcing what originally may have been a "voluntary" code. That is unlikely unless there is a total disintegration of the First Amendment, whose protectors—like John Merrill—abhor any restrictions on the free flow of information, any regulation or licensing. But such dire consequences of tightly administered codes of ethics are also unlikely because, although sponsoring organizations occasionally review and revise their codes and regularly emphasize and renew organizational support for them, the codes of ethics in general are ambiguous and unenforceable.

■ THE CODE MAKERS

There are two major kinds of codes of ethics: professional organization codes and company codes, which often are similar.

Professional organization codes are by and for the members of professional organizations—ASNE, NPPA, RTNDA, SPJ, and PRSA, as well as the National Conference of Editorial Writers, the Associated Press Managing Editors, the Associated Press Sports Editors Association, the Society of American Travel Writers, the International Association of Business Communicators, the American Advertising Federation, the American Association of Advertising Agencies, and various other voluntary associations that individuals can join if they wish and if their work is within the scope of the organization.

Will Irwin implied that newspapers had a code of ethics in 1911, and some state press associations did have written codes of ethics before the first national mass media code, the Canons of Journalism, was announced in 1923 at the first meeting of the

American Society of Newspaper Editors. The Canons heralded the rights and freedom of the press, fidelity to the public interest, and the power of journalists but said little about specific responsibilities of journalists. The ASNE code was revised in 1975 and the APME code in the mid-1990s. In 1995, the ASNE launched the Journalism Values Institute, a program whose goal is to deepen newsroom understanding and discussion of core journalism values in an evolving media environment rather than codify them.

Broadcasters' codes (radio in 1930 and television in 1952) and the movie industry's code (1930) were written on the heels of criticism that some feared would bring government intervention. In those days, these were primarily entertainment media and their critics expressed fear that they might corrupt public morals, especially in their depiction of marriage and family life, religion, law, and justice. There's a ring of repetition in contemporary criticism of these media.

Other codes of ethics were prompted by sincere efforts of media people to be "professional." Unlike the professions of law and medicine, the mass media on the whole do not require job applicants to have specific educational or other credentials or evidence of passing media-specific examinations. Instead, media organizations hire men and women whom they believe can do the work involved. Although the acknowledgment of a code of ethics is often interpreted as a sign of professionalism, it is just that—a sign.

Company codes are imposed on the employees of specific media organizations. There are hundreds of individual company codes of ethics. A 1985 survey by Ohio University researchers (Davenport and Izard, 1985–1986) indicated that nearly two-thirds of the nation's news organizations have their own written codes or policy statements, many of which apparently were written in response to the surge of media criticism in the 1970s and 1980s. Some media attorneys, however, consider company codes to be dangerous with respect to libel suits because they establish a standard to which the company might be held.

There are similarities and differences between professional organization codes and company codes. First the similarities: Although some are more eloquent than others, codes support the importance of mass media in a democratic society and they articulate standards and practices that members or employees should strive to attain. They support the news, interpretation, entertainment, and advertising functions of the mass media, even as they delineate the differences among these functions. Print and broadcast journalists' codes of ethics, for instance, center on accurate, unbiased reporting, separation of news and commentary, and concern for the public interest. Journalists are to respect confidences, to rectify quickly any harmful and inaccurate information they disseminate, and to offer opportunity for reply if they publish or broadcast charges against reputation or character. They are to avoid any activities that are or might seem to be conflicts of interest. It's hard to argue against any of those goals or attributes for the news media and their staffs.

The major difference between the professional organization codes and the company codes is enforcement. Company codes have enforcement power, if management wishes to use it—and, in the case of companies that deal with unions, if the unions accept the code and the enforcement procedures as part of their collective bargaining agreements. The company sets and disseminates the policies it expects its employees to maintain, including the procedures for assessing adherence to them and potential sanctions for deviations from them. If a company code forbids reporters from accepting gifts, for instance, they should know that and should know also the potential penalty for accepting a gift. The code in this case is a policy document that governs employment. This is significantly different from what can happen with voluntary professional codes of ethics.

Many company-specific codes state what employees may and may not do, both on the job and off. Changing times, changing opinions about workplace regulations, and even media competition can soften interpretations of the codes. Prestigious awards have been presented to individuals and media that, in retrospect, have admitted that they bent their own rules against using anonymous sources or stolen documents.

Media organizations have also been reviewing the policies that forbid employees from participating in community, social, or political activities. If publishers and broadcasters can be on community boards, many ask, why can't reporters do likewise? If entertainers can participate openly in public service activities in their communities, why shouldn't others do likewise? Needless to say, there is not total agreement about specific prohibitions, or about promoting participation in social, political or other public service activities. There has to be concern as to how the public will perceive such participation as well as whether it will become a real conflict of interest for the individuals involved (see Chapter 14).

At one time, company codes were adamantly against staff members moonlighting for non-news organizations, including being paid to keep score at athletic events, writing copy for political candidates or marketing organizations, and appearing as commentators on radio or television programs. Big companies probably can continue to restrict employees' activities but smaller ones, which pay far smaller salaries, may lose valuable employees if they do. The distinguishing point should be "if the activity is or appears to be a significant conflict of interest."

Because company codes are, in effect, company regulations, individuals can be fired or suspended for violating them. Some codes sponsored by voluntary professional organizations, on the other hand, may contain strong statements about members' roles and responsibilities and sanctions for violation of the codes, but because membership is voluntary there is no strong power of enforcement.

There have been attempts to strengthen professional organization codes by requiring members to pledge allegiance to them and by establishing review boards to examine alleged infractions. For the most part they remain attempts, largely because voluntary organizations rarely put burdensome restrictions on members and depend on voluntary allegiance to their codes of ethics.

Weaver and Wilhoit noted in 1991 that the typical journalist still did not belong to a national association, despite a membership surge from the 1970s into the 1980s. Without a groundswell of support, the voluntary organizations are probably wise not to impose unnecessary regulations on members or potential members.

The Society of Professional Journalists recently published a 271-page handbook to accompany its three-page Code of Ethics. The coauthors of the handbook wisely warn that it is not a directory of correct answers and quick fixes. "Such a book does not exist; you should distrust one that promises an ethics panacea" (Black, Barney, and Steele, 1995, p. 1).

Other organizations also have written interpretations of their codes. There is as yet no evidence that having two documents, a code and an interpretation, improves decision making, especially when decisions have to be made quickly and in competitive media situations.

■ THE ENFORCEMENT ISSUE

One organization, the Public Relations Society of America, does have enforcement sanctions built into its code. The procedure for adjudicating alleged violations of the PRSA code includes review of all evidence by a committee sworn to confidentiality. The code is powerless, however, if the accused simply quits the organization, which is what happened when its president-elect was accused of a code violation. Soon after the review committee began its confidential assessment of the situation, this prominent member resigned. Neither PRSA membership nor allegiance to the PRSA Code is required of public relations practitioners, so he was free to continue to practice his craft.

Some members of PRSA have suggested that members sign a pledge to indicate allegiance to the PRSA code, and that their employers monitor the member's performance. Such an arrangement, though an admirable attempt to put teeth in an otherwise voluntary code, can be only as strong as the people who participate allow it to be. The test would come when the arrangement is publicly questioned by someone who refuses to pledge allegiance to the PRSA code as a condition of employment, or when someone sues after being fired because the boss says he or she violated a tenet of the otherwise voluntary professional code.

Lack of enforcement is not the only weakness of codes of ethics. There is no agreement whether codes of ethics prescribe the highest or the lowest acceptable standards of practice, describe attainable or ideal performance, or can ensure the media quality society needs and deserves. There is no agreement about how fully codes are understood and embraced by those for whom they are written. There is concern that codes are laden with ambiguities—fuzzy, imprecise words and statements that are subject to interpretation. There is also concern that the codes are more show than substance, that their major role is to give the public the impression that the media and the people who work for them have high standards of professionalism. There is concern that the codes are aspirations that are unattainable in a world where situations change rapidly, where competition forces communications people to make quick decisions about complex subjects, where instant criticism is as prevalent as instant replay and can skew media attention and content.

Even experienced professionals cannot agree on the value of codes. Charles B. Seib, long-time managing editor of *The Washington Star* and one-time ombudsman for *The Washington Post*, said that he had never seen an editor turn to a code or set of rules for guidance when faced with a real ethical call. "Codes do not touch the broader ethical issues confronting today's journalists" (1981, p. 6). Not everyone agrees with him. Newsman-turned-professor Philip Meyer maintains that codes cannot be written to cover all situations but "they can surely at least be used to denote a sensitivity to certain values and desires" (1983, p. 60).

That's probably as much as we can expect of mass media codes of ethics—to inspire those who are willing to accept them to be sensitive to professional values and practices.

■ GORDON: Media codes of ethics are useful and necessary to the mass media and to society.

Even if codes of ethics cannot be enforced, they serve an important purpose by setting standards against which conduct can be measured and evaluated. This is important both for the media themselves and for society.

Within the media, codes serve several purposes. Perhaps the least important, overall, is to ensure that standards are set internally, rather than having either the courts or the legislatures take on this responsibility. More important, codes of ethics can provide an ideal standard by which the industry can evaluate its own performance and—on a more personal level—against which individual practitioners can measure their own values and performance. Codes can "act as the conscience of the professional, of the organization, of the enterprise" (Black, Barney, and Steele, 1995, p. 13).

For both the media industry as a whole and for individuals within it, codes can also help keep attention directed toward principles that are particularly important as guidelines for appropriate behavior. Codes can also serve as a starting point—a threshold, if you will—for considering which principles deserve to be honored by ethical practitioners in the mass media. Indeed, because ethics deals with normative behavior as well as philosophy, codes of ethics can be a major factor in helping to establish those norms, especially if they provoke discussion as to what they should cover and how that coverage should be worded.

As Richard Johannesen has argued, ethics codes "should not require heroic virtue, extreme sacrifice, or doing right no matter what the obstacles," but rather should aim at people of ordinary conscientiousness (1996, p. 199, citing Kultgen, 1983). Johannesen provides 10 other guidelines to overcome what might otherwise be valid objections to ethics codes. Among them are the need to specify which parts of the codes represent *ideal* goals and which are *minimum* conditions that must be met in order to be considered ethical or to avoid punishment. Other guidelines include clear, specific language, logical coherence, protection of *both* the general public interest and the practitioners covered by the code, and stimulation by the code of "continued discussion and reflection leading to possible modification or revision" (p. 199).

. . . codes may provide reasonable standards and guidelines that help the public discuss, debate, and measure the media's performance.

In society as a whole, codes may provide reasonable standards and guidelines that help the public discuss, debate, and measure the media's performance. In that respect, if the codes are realistic, they can also help to *protect* the mass media and media practitioners from unrealistic expectations, demands, and criticism. On the other side of that coin, they can help the public express reasonable demands and criticism of the media when that is warranted. In all three situations, codes can help make the mass media more accountable to their various publics.

As an aside, many of the same arguments noted in the preceding paragraph can also be used in favor of news councils, which have always faced strong opposition from many news organizations and have now largely disappeared from the American journalistic scene. Much opposition to news councils seemed to be rooted in a fear that they would provide too easy an opportunity for the public to attack the news media. But as the Minnesota News Council has proven since its founding in 1971, the availability of an institutionalized procedure to consider and evaluate complaints against the media has benefited the media as much as it has the public. The disposition of complaints brought to that press council has resulted in reasonable guidelines that have protected and supported Minnesota news media when complaints went beyond what might reasonably be expected of the media.

■ FURTHER BENEFITS OF ETHICS CODES

Codes of ethics do more than help to protect the public from unethical performance and the media from unreasonable public demands. They also provide a reference point that can be invoked to protect workers in the media from internal pressures that could force them to violate their own consciences. Written codes also help acquaint media neophytes with some of the key ethical issues and principles they will face as practitioners, and can increase their understanding of professional values. More generally, codes can sharpen the focus on ethical issues that people in all branches of the media must face regularly. As noted above, codes can also provide a context for media practitioners to discuss and reflect on their responsibilities and obligations—as this discussion may do in a general way for you as you read it.

Eric W. Allen, an early dean of the journalism school at the University of Oregon, writing in 1922 about early state codes of ethics, noted that they could serve as a sound basis "for much further study and discussion" (1922, p. 173) and added, "The publication of a written code brings [important questions] to the forefront of discussion. They become more likely to receive thoughtful consideration" (p. 175; see also Cronin and McPherson, 1995, pp. 896–897).

I will concede without hesitation that written codes of ethics generally reflect compromises that fall below what some individuals see as an appropriate standard for ethical conduct. Some codes use terminology that is too vague to have much meaning (such as the reference to "good taste" in the code of ethics of the Public Relations Society of America) or omit some standards that many observers and practitioners consider important (such as the failure of some journalism codes of ethics to mention truth—which most people would consider an essential element of the business as well as of its ethics).

It is also true that codes of ethics *cannot* be universal in their application, given human ingenuity in creating unique dilemmas. But even though codes can't possibly be tailored to every situation where media ethics issues arise, they certainly can be quite useful in dealing with general concerns that face most practitioners in a given medium. Some 30 years ago, a distinguished clergyman responded to one aspect of this problem by arguing that ethics codes governing any aspect of public life must be *both* absolute and relative, drawing on the Judeo-Christian tradition that places on humankind the responsibility to avoid both the morass of excessive relativism and the pretension of rigid absolutism (Blake, 1966).

Beyond such concerns, and as noted above, a written code may provide ideal standards of excellence to strive for, although few people are able to live up to an ideal level of morality under all circumstances. Even codes that fall short of such an idealized level can usually provide some worthwhile ethical goals toward which individuals in that field can aim. As the honorary president of the International Organization of Journalists noted in 1977, an ethics code can proclaim "the elementary rules of the morality of our profession" (Jones, 1980, p. 12, quoting Jean-Maurice Hermann).

Codes can also establish an ethical threshold as a starting point from which individual (or corporate) ethics standards can be developed. Various additional ethical standards (perhaps exceeding the code's provisions) may be formulated by individual practitioners or organizations to deal with specific situations or problems, or matters of personal concern.

Jeffrey Marks, former news director of a Portland, Maine, television station and primary author of the most recent revision of the ethics code of the Radio-Television News Directors Association, dealt with these points in defending that code from charges that it was incomplete and not credible:

> The RTNDA Code of Ethics represents an attempt to cover the spectrum of journalism in the electronic media. In doing so, it must be fairly broad. Many newsrooms have specific policies which go much further. (1989, p. 6)

Codes of ethics have often been criticized because they have no teeth; they are seen as lofty rhetoric that has no real meaning because the ideals cannot be enforced in any way. This is a somewhat specious argument, however. Ethics, by its nature, deals with what "should" happen rather than what can be legalistically enforced. An enforceable code could raise the specter of government control and enforcement and, moreover, would lose some of the necessary flexibility such relativity requires, because ethics often must be relative rather than absolute.

A notable example of the problems potential enforcement can create involved the Society of Professional Journalists in the 1980s. The organization become embroiled in an extremely bitter debate over whether the group's code should specify that violators would be censured or even expelled from SPJ. The idea of a useful but voluntary ethics code almost got lost in the vitriol. That's a textbook case of how *not* to go about formulating and implementing a useful code of ethics, but it does not prove that other groups (or SPJ in the mid-1990s—see Hodges, 1995) cannot successfully codify ethical standards.

■ PITFALLS TO AVOID

It does seem fair to say that if codes of ethics get too watered down, or perhaps even too vague and general, they can dilute the ethical standards within the medium to which they apply. Codes that are too general can also produce ethics so closely bound to the existing (majority) culture that they provide little or no guidance to individuals who tend to think for themselves. Specifics can help make written ethics codes more useful, especially because general language makes it much less likely that there will be widespread agreement on what the code means.

Similarly, if codes are so strict and rigid that no one can realistically live up to them, they can become objects of derision and thus become counterproductive. As with so many other aspects of ethics, the Aristotelian Golden Mean has much to recommend it in approaching the matter of codes. Striking a balance between specificity and universality, between absolutism and pure situational ethics, between the ideal and the pragmatic can help produce a code of ethics that is highly useful. One would certainly get into trouble with a Kantian approach, insisting that code provisions must be absolute, formal, or universal in order to be worthwhile.

Handled properly, ethics codes can be of considerable value, to stimulate thought and discussion at a minimum. For example, Professor Alan Dershowitz of the Harvard Law School argued in 1993 that American journalism needs some type of national ethical standards, and that they would help safeguard the First Amendment by helping to maintain the public's confidence in the news media. In a talk to the newspaper publishers' association, he suggested what he called an "internal court of corrections," in which three respected journalists would hear complaints and try to determine whether the record needed to be corrected.

Such an approach would require some agreement on the basic ethical standards at issue, not to mention agreement on the three respected journalists. The idea is an interesting one, and certainly focuses concern on the need for defined ethical standards—a code of ethics—although its practical possibilities seem limited at best.

Similarly, the public relations field—which has had an ethics code since the Public Relations Society of America adopted one in 1950—still debates the viability of an ethics code for practitioners. Edward Bernays, the centenarian public relations pioneer widely regarded as the father of the field, argued repeatedly before his death in 1995 for some form of certification or licensing to denote PR practitioners who have mastered a specified body of knowledge *and* who promise adherence to a recognized code of ethics.

Ethics codes could also be helpful on another score. As new technologies take the various media into previously uncharted areas, there is arguably an increased need for codes of ethics to help provide some useful guidelines. For example, how do privacy concerns relate to the various electronic databases available to marketers, journalists, and others (a topic discussed in detail in Chapter 9)? Some guidance on such emerging concerns would be useful, as would some systematic thought about the issue in preparation for putting ethical guidelines down on paper or into an electronic database.

Karen Lebacqz (1985), writing on codes of ethics in the professions, suggested that they must go beyond prescriptive rules for behavior. Rather, they should describe the "moral character" expected of—and needed by—practitioners in a particular field. They should illuminate "where stresses and tensions have been felt within the profession and what image of the good professional is held up to assist professionals through those stresses and tensions" (p. 68).

Johannesen's guidelines for developing useful ethics codes, noted earlier, also suggest that such codes "should go beyond general admonitions against lying and cheating to focus on those facets of the group's functions 'that pose particular and specialized temptations to its members'" (1996, p. 199, quoting DeGeorge, 1986, p. 342). "Problems" and "concerns" are perhaps of more relevance than "temptations" today. For example, references to journalists' potential conflicts of interest were missing from many of the early codes in that field, but the phrase is now standard in most journalism codes. The codes are also quite—perhaps overly—explicit in defining the term, reflecting increased attention paid to this topic by both society as a whole and the journalism field (see Chapter 14).

Similarly, a 1952 draft of a proposed international code of ethics stressed the need for immediate and spontaneous correction of errors, as part of the need to keep faith with the public. The introduction to a more recent study of ethics codes in some 50 countries noted that voluntary codes can serve "as a life-line tracing the way back to responsibility and to credibility" (Jones, 1980, p. 7), both areas of increasing concern to journalists and their critics.

It seems likely that the early journalism codes of ethics, written in the 1920s, were intended at least in part to be public relations tools aimed at enhancing media credibility with the public. Many state press associations formulated codes that focused on such concerns as propaganda in the media, the influence of press agents, and a resurgence of sensationalism. There is also some evidence that the early codes were seen as buttresses for many journalists' desire that their occupation be regarded as a profession (Cronin and McPherson, 1995, pp. 892–893). But even if these were the only reasons that the pioneering codes were written—and even if there are still overtones of some of those goals inherent in today's codes—their purpose and value have evolved on a much broader scale in the 1990s, especially in light of current interest in, and concern for, mass media ethics.

■ INTERNAL ETHICS CODES

So far, this side of the argument has not dealt with company codes of ethics. Obviously, a company that believes strongly in its code of ethics or conduct is in a position to enforce it, so such codes are clearly *not* impotent. Nor are they unimportant, at the very least to the people who could lose their jobs by violating them. The real question here might better be whether company codes really come to grips with ethical issues in a meaningful way.

No blanket assessment of this is possible because media companies deal with ethics in many different ways (or not at all) on a corporate level. One example, however, can drive home the fact that company codes *can* deal head-on with important ethical issues, and do so meaningfully. In 1991, the U.S. Supreme Court ruled that several Minnesota news organizations were liable for damages (under the theory of a breached contract) because their editors had overridden pledges of confidentiality given to a source by reporters and published the source's identity. (See *Cohen v. Cowles Media Co.*, 1991.) Beyond the highly relevant ethical question of whether confidentiality should have been promised at all in this instance, the case focused on the issue of whether a reporter could bind a news organization to respect a pledge of confidentiality regardless of what editors thought about the situation.

The upshot of this case, in many newsrooms, was a revision of company codes, or clarification of what had been hazy guidelines, to require that reporters henceforth must obtain an editor's agreement before promising confidentiality to a source. News organizations taking this approach came directly to grips with an important ethical (and legal) issue in a way that set standards that their employees had little choice but to observe, however adversely it might affect getting sources to talk.

In regard to newsrooms more generally, a 1987 survey of radio and TV news directors indicated that about 40% of broadcast news operations have some type of ethics code. The responses indicated a considerable degree of agreement by the news directors on such issues as not naming rape victims and granting confidentiality to sources. On other issues, such as the use of ambush interviews, opinions were more evenly divided (Wulfemeyer, 1990).

A survey by the Ethics Committee of the American Society of Newspaper Editors a few years earlier indicated that ethics requirements were being enforced in many print newsrooms. The committee reported that at least 78 newspaper journalists had been dismissed or suspended in the three prior years for ethics violations ranging from sports editors using the paper's telephones to take bets, to plagiarism, to outright fabrication of stories (American Society of Newspaper Editors, 1986–87, p. 7). That survey also found considerable disagreement on a variety of ethics issues, a problem that might be clarified if codes of ethics could be developed to specify acceptable standards of behavior:

> [The editors often] couldn't even agree on what is ethical or unethical. For example, 34 percent of the editors who responded see no violation if a staffer makes a campaign contribution to a candidate that he or she doesn't cover while 31 percent say it would violate ethics.

There was, however, general agreement on such serious violations of ethics as plagiarism, profiting from insider information, and accepting discounts from businesses about which stories are being written or edited (p. 9). The study also tended to support the value of written company ethics codes. It indicated that editors of both large and small papers with written codes "were more likely to take a stricter view of what constitutes an ethics violation than newspapers without codes" (p. 11). This tends to support the argument that written codes can—at least in the case of company ethics codes—help produce a meaningful ethical context.

■ SOME FINAL THOUGHTS

The bottom line on this topic is that ethics codes will never be a total cure for the problems of the news and entertainment media. Even if they're not perfect, however, ethics codes can be useful in pointing the way to self-improvement in the media and greater accountability to the public. When codes work well, they can focus attention on key issues and help make those concerns part of the media's general decision-making process. As Lebacqz has suggested (1985, p. 83), they can also be very useful to individuals concerned about their own character because "each choice about what to do is also a choice about whom to be—or, more accurately, whom to become."

To dismiss ethics codes out of hand as worthless and counterproductive seems to be throwing out the baby with the bath water merely because perfection is beyond our grasp.

A set of three general goals for any code of ethics, developed as part of the transnational study noted earlier, illustrates some basic values of such a code and might form a broad philosophical context for ethics codes:

1. Protecting the audience toward whom mass communication is directed "from any irresponsible, antisocial or propaganda use of the media."
2. Protecting people working in the media "from being forced to act in ways which are irresponsible, humiliating or in any manner contrary to the dictates of their consciences."
3. Keeping "open all channels of communication, both from above and from below," to make sure that the public gets the information needed in a self-governing society, and to ensure that ordinary people can always register their opinions through the media (Jones, 1980, p. 14.).

Of course, those goals would require some agreement on the meaning of key terms such as *irresponsible* before they can be implemented. There are inherent short-comings in any code of ethics, but that does not mean that this approach should be completely avoided. To dismiss ethics codes out of hand as worthless and counterpro-ductive seems to be throwing out the baby with the bath water merely because perfec-tion is beyond our grasp.

■ MERRILL: Commentary

Probably what the reader comes away with, after reading the positions presented above, is that ethical codes in journalism are sometimes meaningful and helpful and sometimes not. Most of us, I believe, would be somewhere in the middle, seeing codes as an indication of good faith or good will on the part of the media organiza-tions that frame them, but recognizing that they are largely window-dressing and do not mean much to many media functionaries unless—and this is important—their provisions agree with the basic concerns and values these media people carry around in their heads.

Carol Reuss quotes Philip Meyer (1983) as saying that codes at least can be used to "denote a sensitivity to certain values and desires." If this is true, it tends to lessen Reuss's argument that they are impotent—for they would be an overt indica-tion of moral caring and motivation to right actions. But I doubt very much that it is indeed true. Codes may *denote* some sensitivity to the *idea of values* on the part of the person (or small committee) writing the codes, but denote little or nothing about their real concerns or those of the journalists or communicators represented by the code.

This certainly has been the case with many members of the Society of Profes-sional Journalists in respect to their code. First, not many have even read the code, and second, those who have read it have done so quickly and without careful analysis and questioning. There is no evidence that those "professional" journalists are any more ethical than any other journalists.

Beyond this, Reuss notes that various media organizations "have written interpre-tations of their codes." This is rather strange. If their members cannot read the codes and make *their own* interpretations, then such codes are not very useful. Now, say the organizations, let us tell you what we really *meant* in our codes. Reuss is right when she asks: Does the availability of *two* documents instead of one improve the journal-ist's decision making when faced with ethical problems? I doubt it very much.

Although Reuss makes some valid points about codes of ethics, she does not ad-minister the killing blow. In fact, as I read her argument, she sees them as exerting some good influence on media people, but says they are "of limited importance." So should we do away with them? If they are unimportant and impotent, perhaps we should. If they have even "limited importance," perhaps we should not.

David Gordon, on the other hand, seems to feel the validity of his side of the ar-gument somewhat more strongly. He sees codes as providing a standard against which organizations and practitioners in the media can evaluate their own perfor-mance. This is a tangible and perhaps worthy rationale for codes. They may not help much in ensuring ethical practices by the media, but they may well *identify* those that ought to prevail. Or, perhaps we should say—they may identify the practices that the *writers of the code say ought to prevail.* If this is the case, then a code is a rather authoritarian document, intending to impose on a body of workers the belief system of the code writers.

Codes of ethics are obviously here to stay in journalism and mass communication. They at least serve a public relations purpose for the media organizations that publish them. They say in effect that such-and-such a group is public-minded, conscious of its actions, desirous to do the right—or at least the best—thing, and is not just a money-making, cold business enterprise. They attest to the social consciousness of the media organization. They imply a concern and a desire to act responsibly. And they do provide a document—a kind of foil, however vague and ill-written—against which people can react.

Just as the Bible in a person's home does not indicate that the person is really religious, a code of ethics hanging on the wall of a newspaper office does not mean that the journalists there are ethical. What really counts in both instances is what goes on inside the people attaching themselves to these written words. A meaningful ethics, like a meaningful religion, lies within the person, and what really counts for a journalist trying to be ethical are the internalized convictions personally accepted, not someone else's words codified in some document. So I would say that the only meaningful code of ethics is one that is journalistically *self-determined.* We can have institutionalized laws (which can be enforced), but a journalistic ethics must be personal, and it cannot be enforced.

A meaningful ethics, like a meaningful religion, lies within the person . . .

As I see it, a main problem with most codes of ethics is that they try to do too many things at once. Their writers are never quite sure whether to make them *inspirational* (credal) or *normative* (legalistic), to make them personal or impersonal, formal or informal, relative or absolute, directive or suggestive. A good example of such a quandary in code writing is offered by the Society of Professional Journalists.

That group's code deals with freedom of the press, calling on journalists to guard it, but failing to note that it is just this freedom that calls into play many *unethical* practices that the SPJ code writers would condemn. The code brings up such concepts as the "public's right to know" without considering that such a right may contradict the press's freedom. Of course, many credal, inspirational, general statements are slipped into the code—for example, that "we believe in public enlightenment as the forerunner of justice" and such outright misstatements as "We believe . . . in our *Constitutional* [emphasis added] role to seek the truth." (Journalists may feel that it is their *ethical* role to seek the truth, but such a role is not found in the Constitution.)

The SPJ Code of Ethics is rather typical of codes of ethics in the communication fields. It is hard to see how such codes can be of much real guidance to media practitioners; the language is too vague, general, and subject to individual interpretation. Their ethical admonitions are devoid of contextual exceptions, and their normative parts are notable for their many gaps and omissions. For example, prior to its 1995 revision, the SPJ code mentioned (in Part IV, 4) that photographs and telecasts "should give an accurate picture of an event and not highlight an incident out of context." This was obviously an effort to try to cover as many aspects of journalism as possible with *something* of an ethical nature, but it might be noted that the code failed to say the same thing about newspaper or newsmagazine stories.

What do journalistic codes of ethics imply? That there are standardized good or right actions to be taken in the field? Perhaps. Gordon says that Alan Dershowitz has argued that national ethical standards are needed in American journalism to safeguard the First Amendment. I would say that the First Amendment, providing for freedom of the press, is not in need of safeguarding (at least by something that might restrict it). If so, then the First Amendment is rather meaningless. The free press provision doesn't say that Congress shall make no law abridging freedom of the press *except when so-called unethical practices occur.* This would certainly open the door to all kinds of authoritarian interpretations and visions of ethics used to direct the press.

Codes of ethics, it seems to me, are *controlling* mechanisms, not freeing ones. Certainly journalists should discuss ethics among themselves; they should be concerned with being ethical, but they should recognize that their particular beliefs about ethical practice might not be those of others. Attempts to impose one's ethics on another (through codes or in other ways) are intrinsically *authoritarian* and even arrogant. Certainly, such attempts are not consistent with the spirit of the First Amendment or, it might be added, with the whole spirit of message pluralism, which we claim to value so much.

The recent emphasis in American journalistic circles (mainly in communications schools and other academic venues) on *communitarian* ethics goes against the more individualistic and libertarian comments made in the previous paragraph. A growing concern is evident in the increased talk about "public" ethics, not "private" ethics. A belief in some kind of community-sanctioned and community-directed ethics is in ascendancy in our ethics courses and texts. Such collective or social emphasis, rather than individual, in the area of morality adds weight to the advocacy of ethical codes.

As I have written elsewhere, the *existential* concern of the journalist should, in a free society, take precedence over the communitarian dimension. The precept of the authentic free person inhibits the existentialist from embracing a code of ethics. But the existentialist, propelled by humanitarian concern, does venture a guiding principle for the ethical decision-making process: *One should choose what one would wish all other people to choose under the same circumstances.* But this universalizing choice does not mean altruism in every case. One thinks of existentialist Martin Heidegger, who found that his existentialist philosophy did not deter his acceptance of the Nazi ideology. Likewise, the free journalist may well *not* agree to follow some organizational code, instead using freedom to make an independent decision.

Regardless of the weaknesses of codes of ethics, they are doubtless here to stay. In this day of "image," they play their part and, admittedly, they may actually be of some value to some journalists in some situations. If they are, then perhaps they can be justified. Readers will surely have other arguments to present on both sides. Most readers will probably endorse codes, or at least they will see no harm in them. But regardless of how we feel about ethical codes, I have one suggestion to make: If we must have them, then let's try harder to write better ones than we currently have, and make them more credal than normative. The very least the code writers can do is to write well and provide inspiration.

REFERENCES

Allen, Eric W. (May 1922). "The Social Value of a Code of Ethics for Journalists." *The Annals of the American Academy of Political and Social Sciences*, pp. 170–179.

American Society of Newspaper Editors, Ethics Committee. (Fall/Winter 1986–1987). "Newsroom Ethics: How Tough Is Enforcement?" *Journal of Mass Media Ethics* 2(1), pp. 7–16.

Black, Jay, and Ralph Barney. (Fall/Winter 1985–1986). "The Case Against Mass Media Codes of Ethics," *Journal of Mass Media Ethics* 1(1), pp. 27–36.

Black, Jay, Bob Steele, and Ralph Barney. (1995). *Doing Ethics in Journalism: A Handbook with Case Studies*, 2nd ed. Boston: Allyn & Bacon.

Blake, Eugene Carson. (January 1966). "Should the Code of Ethics in Public Life Be Absolute or Relative?" *The Annals of the American Academy of Political and Social Science*, pp. 4–11.

Cohen v. *Cowles Media Co.*, 501 U.S. 663 (1991).

Cronin, Mary M., and James B. McPherson. (Winter 1995). "Pronouncements and Denunciations: An Analysis of State Press Association Ethics Codes from the 1920s." *Journalism & Mass Communication Quarterly* 72 (4), pp. 890–901.

Davenport, Lucinda D., and Ralph S. Izard. (Fall/Winter 1985–1986). "Restrictive Policies of the Mass Media." *Journal of Mass Media Ethics* 1(1), pp. 4–9.

DeGeorge, Richard T. (1986). *Business Ethics*, 2nd ed, New York: Macmillan.

Hodges, Lou. (July–August 1995). "Code Changes: The Why and How." *Quill*, p. 51.

Irwin, Will. (1911). *The American Newspaper* (reprinted with commentaries by Clifford F. Weigle and David G. Clark, 1969). Ames: Iowa State University Press.

Johannesen, Richard L. (1996). *Ethics in Human Communication*, 4th ed. Prospect Heights, IL: Waveland Press.

Jones, J. Clement. (1980). *Mass Media Codes of Ethics and Councils*. Paris: Unesco Press.

Journalism Values Handbook. (1996). Reston, VA: (ASNE) Journalism Values Institute.

Kittross, John M. (Spring 1988). "New, Improved RTNDA Ethics Code?" *Media Ethics Update* 1(1), pp. 7, 16.

Kultgen, John. (1983). "Evaluating Codes of Professional Ethics." In Wade Robison, L., Michael S. Pritchard, and Joseph Ellin, eds., *Profits and Professions: Essays in Business and Professional Ethics*. Clifton, NJ: Humana Press, pp. 225–264.

Lebacqz, Karen. (1985). *Professional Ethics: Power and Paradox*. Nashville, TN: Abingdon Press.

Marks, Jeffrey. (Spring 1989). "New Improved RTNDA Ethics Code!" *Media Ethics Update* 2(1), p. 6.

McManus, John H. (1997). "Who's Responsible for Journalism?" *Journal of Mass Media Ethics* 12 (1), pp. 5–17.

Meyer, Philip. (1983). *Editors, Publishers and Newspaper Ethics*. Washington DC: American Society of Newspaper Editors.

Nordenstreng, Kaarle, ed. (1995). *Reports on Media Ethics in Europe*. Tampere, Finland: University of Tampere, Department of Journalism and Mass Communication, Series B 41/1995.

Seib, Charles B. (February 1981). "Ethics: Many Questions, Few Right or Wrong Answers." *Presstime*, pp. 4–10.

Weaver, David H., and G. Cleveland Wilhoit. (1991). *The American Journalist: A Portrait of U.S. News People and Their Work*, 2nd ed., Bloomington: Indiana University Press.

Wulfemeyer, K. Tim. (Winter 1990). "Defining Ethics in Electronic Journalism: Perceptions of News Directors," *Journalism Quarterly* 67(4), pp. 984–991.

CHAPTER 4

MANIPULATION BY THE MEDIA
Truth, Fairness, and Objectivity

O ver the years, news media practitioners, as well as their critics, have expressed considerable concern about what is meant by *objectivity*, whether it is possible to achieve it, and whether the focus ought to be on "accuracy," "reality," "truth," "fairness," or some similar referent to the world portrayed by the media. And, if the focus should be on other terms, how should they be defined?

The controversy in this chapter focuses on the news media, but it has overtones in the wider media world as well. The arguments in Chapter 7, which focus on the portrayal of race and gender in both news and entertainment media, are one offshoot of these concerns. So are the questions raised here about how truthful docudramas or historically based films must be in order to stay within appropriate ethical boundaries.

Although concerns over such concepts as truth and objectivity must focus first on the news media, they also resonate more widely. They affect everyone in society who is a news media consumer and who (ideally) should know something about how the various news products are put together. They certainly should be of concern to public relations practitioners, who must work symbiotically with news media personnel and who must therefore understand thoroughly how these concepts should play out in journalistic practice, not to mention the ethical boundaries of truthfulness that relate directly to their own public relations work.

Although entertainment media normally need not be as concerned as news media with the line between fiction and fact, this isn't always the case. It can be argued coherently that the public has a legitimate interest in knowing the amount of truth in historical films, docudramas, and similar productions.

In this chapter, both authors agree that mass communicators—from entertainers to journalists to public relations practitioners—must be concerned about the elusive concept of truth. But they suggest that there are different ways of defining and operationalizing that term, and they differ on whether other ethical concepts may be of equal or greater importance. David Gordon does not quarrel with such additional ethical standards, but focuses on truth as both a necessary and sufficient condition for ethical performance in the mass media. John Michael Kittross suggests a further operationalization, and concentrates on two related concepts that he considers more attainable than truth: accuracy and fairness.

■ GORDON: Truth precludes any need for further ethical concerns in journalism and public relations.

I'm not about to argue that ethical concerns beyond truth are inappropriate, just that they are not needed. If practitioners in the journalism and public relations fields choose to concern themselves with additional matters of ethics, that's all to the good. Edmund Lambeth (1992), in his excellent treatise *Committed Journalism*, provides an extremely useful discussion of some of these other principles in a chapter that begins to develop "a framework of principles for journalism ethics" (p. 23). In that chapter, he suggests the principles of truth telling, justice, freedom, humaneness, and steward-ship. I have no quarrel with the value of the last four of these principles, nor do I ob-ject to others that people have stressed over the years, including John Michael Kit-tross's upcoming emphasis on fairness, accuracy, and the definitionally elusive concept of objectivity.

What I am arguing is that truth telling is a first principle in journalism, to the point where if choices must be made, truth must be given primacy over any other ethical concerns. Ideally, as Kittross will argue, those truths should be told within a context of fairness and balance. Certainly, as Jim Willis (1991) and others have pointed out, truth is an ideal that is hard to attain and doesn't always reflect all of "reality."

There may well be circumstances where non–news media people's allegiance can be to something other than the "whole truth." Those in the entertainment industry obviously have some license to deviate from, or embellish, the literal truth of settings drawn from history and, in fact, the constraints of the narrative form may require this in most cases. But when this is done, I believe that the audience should be made aware of the changes and whether they are major or minor ones. Similarly, some public rela-tions people may believe that lies—or something other than 100% of the truth—are perfectly acceptable under some conditions. Sissela Bok (1978), while advocating strongly the need to respect veracity and tell the truth, rejects Kant's absolutist posi-tion against *any* lie. She acknowledges that there are some situations where a lie would be warranted, especially "those where innocent lives are at stake, and where only a lie can deflect the danger" (p. 45).

But the question of whether one may ever lie and still be ethical is a topic for a different discussion, for which Bok provides some excellent insights. Rather, our focus here is on whether truth telling is the *key* ethical concern in situations where lying is not acceptable, or whether other ethical standards must also be of concern. I believe that truth is a sufficient condition for the practitioner to claim to be acting ethically and, furthermore, that being truthful is almost always necessary for ethical practice in the mass media. I also suggest that in the few cases where lies may be acceptable, other ethical considerations must then assume much greater importance than when truth is the most important ethical principle.

For journalists in particular, Walter Lippmann's approach nearly 80 years ago still has an immense amount to recommend it as an ideal. In his ground-breaking book *Public Opinion*, Lippmann wrote that the "function of news is to signalize an event, the function of truth is to bring to light the hidden facts, to set them into relation with each other, and make a picture of reality . . ." (1922, p. 271). The telling of truth—es-pecially in Lippmann's suggested framework—should be the crux of the ethical focus, despite Kittross's concerns about how fragile truth really is or how many different truths can be brought to bear on a particular set of events.

The criticism leveled at *Time* magazine in June 1994 for altering its cover photo of O. J. Simpson illustrates the importance of telling the truth without embellishment. Both *Time* and *Newsweek* used the police mug shot of Simpson on their covers the week after he was arrested and charged with the murder of his ex-wife and her male acquaintance. *Newsweek* ran the photo unaltered but *Time* darkened Simpson's face digitally and gave him a darker, more brooding and sinister appearance, in the opinion of a number of critics. The result, in their view, was an unethical bending of the truth-telling principle and one that—intentionally or not—had racial overtones.

Telling the truth as fully as possible should be a "first principle" for journalists and public relations practitioners, in the spirit of Kant's categorical imperative, even if one agrees with Bok that a few exceptions are needed to that absolutist stance. Objectivity, even if it could be defined succinctly, doesn't come close to reaching that level of primal importance, even for journalists. As Everette Dennis has pointed out, objectivity is an approach "that almost always valued official sources over ordinary people" and that has contributed to "the straitjacket of unelaborated fact" (1990, p. 8).

At first glance, those last comments might seem to put me in agreement with Kittross's argument that fairness is as essential as truth. Indeed, we may be closer to agreement on that point than on any other. But it seems to me that everything starts with an emphasis on truth—which certainly should include some *context* as well as "unelaborated fact." If proper attention is paid to truth telling as the key ethical principle, the other ethical concerns will resolve themselves.

■ TRUTH IN PREPARING AND PRESENTING NEWS AND ENTERTAINMENT

To take just one example, the goal of reporting the truth is so important that it also overcomes any concerns about what some people call deception in the gathering of news. So, using hidden cameras or undercover reporting, as illustrated by the 1997 Food Lion case, should not be at issue as long as they produce truthful reports on topics that are (or should be) of concern to the public.

Bob Steele of the Poynter Institute has expressed concern about any kind of deception in reporting, noting that "anything that hides the truth contradicts journalism's basic mission: to seek the truth." Whether this takes the form of "outright lying, misleading, misrepresenting, or merely being less than forthright," he argues that it can damage the necessary level of trust in the truthfulness of shared information, which he regards as vital to a democratic society (1993, p. 3).

Black, Steele, and Barney (1995, p. 120) suggest criteria that can be used to weigh whether any type of deceptive information gathering is ethical. For them, *all* of these guidelines must be met to justify lying or any other deceptive means of obtaining information that may be necessary to unearth and report the full truth:

- The information must be vitally important to the public or it must prevent profound harm to individuals.
- Every alternative to obtain the information must have been exhausted.
- The journalists involved must be willing to disclose publicly the type of deception used and the reason for using it.

- The harm prevented by obtaining the information must outweigh whatever harm is caused by deception.
- The individuals and their news organization must be willing to commit time and money to pursue the story fully and to use a high degree of "craftsmanship" in presenting it.
- There must be a full examination, by the journalists involved, of their motivations, the consistency of their decision, the consequences on those being deceived, the deception's impact on credibility, and the legal implications of the action.

Perhaps ironically, deception in order to get at the truth is something on which Kant and Machiavelli might agree, perhaps even without the list of qualifying criteria. Kant—if he could get past his absolutist opposition to lying—might well argue that reporting of "the truth," or perhaps even a full account of different "truths," is the kind of universal law he had in mind in formulating his first categorical imperative. Machiavelli would agree that the end—here, providing accurate information on matters of public importance—certainly justifies even deceptive means of acquiring that information. As Don Hewitt, the long-time producer of *60 Minutes* put it, "If you can catch a thief with lies and deception, . . . 'that's a pretty good trade-off'" (Harwood, 1992, p. A23).

Machiavelli might also argue that dramatic re-creations of news events could be justifiable means of attracting television viewers' attention to various worthwhile news stories. I would disagree strongly on the grounds that such re-creations do not adhere to the concept of truthful presentation of material, whether they occur on regular news programs or on the so-called tabloid news programs, where they are more common.

Machiavelli would also see no problem with docudramas or films that take considerable and unnoted liberty with historical fact; he would argue that those liberties are justified because they enhance the entertainment value of the presentation. Indeed, to the degree that the audience realizes that the film or docudrama is a fictionalized account of real events, the question of truth is much less important than it is in the nonentertainment portions of the mass media sphere. But are the audiences that sophisticated?

Perhaps ironically, deception in order to get at the truth is something on which Kant and Machiavelli might agree. . . .

To take an extreme example, did the docudrama that portrayed a completely fictional court-martial of General George Armstrong Custer leave viewers with the belief that this is what really happened, ignoring the fact that Custer was killed at the Little Big Horn and couldn't have been court-martialed in its aftermath? A somewhat less extreme example, from the film world, involves the changes made to civil rights history for dramatic purposes in the 1989 film *Mississippi Burning*. Many of those changes made the *white* FBI agents seem more heroic, and downplayed the real 1964 roles and actions of blacks in Mississippi.

How many people in these audiences wound up accepting the revised versions as being the literal truth of what really happened? And, even if most people were generally aware that liberties had been taken with historical fact, would it not have been more ethical for the audiences to know how "true" such accounts were? If entertainment media are to be accepted as accurate sources for history—and there is some evidence that they are—shouldn't this impose some kind of ethical requirement on them not to rewrite that history in ways that deceive their audiences? I believe that these questions raise some major ethical concerns for writers and producers of docudramas, although entertainment media normally need not be anywhere near as concerned with truth as are the news media.

One possible cure for the specific dilemma posed by changes made for entertainment purposes would be to apply the third Black-Steele-Barney guideline to the presentation of such docudramas or films. Under this approach, audiences would be given full disclosure regarding whatever changes have been made in the historical record for the sake of increased entertainment values, and the burden would be placed on them to use or to ignore that information.

On the news and information side of mass communication, Dennis (1990, p. 10) has proposed fuller disclosure by media organizations about how they operate, which fits in nicely with an emphasis on truth as the key ethical concern. He suggests that the news media tell their audiences how many people cover major stories and, more important, provide information about their backgrounds, interests and ideological preferences, if any.

A similar type of disclosure was used by *The Miami Herald* in 1984 when it told readers about a major disagreement between its publisher and editorial board over the paper's endorsement in that year's presidential election. The publisher, Richard Capen Jr., disregarded the editorial board's recommendation and directed the paper to endorse Ronald Reagan rather than Walter Mondale. But Capen also wrote a column telling readers why he made this decision, noting that the editorial board disagreed, and adding that the paper's editor would argue his position in a column that ran simultaneously. He said that the "ethics of credibility" entitled the readers to know of the split and of the reasoning that underlay both his position and that of the editor (Fink, 1988, p. 142).

■ DIFFERING PERCEPTIONS OF THE TRUTH

One important question that arises regarding the news and information media is *whose* truth or whose version of the truth are we referring to? Or, to approach this another way, does telling the truth require us to reveal every single fact we have learned?

The answers to those questions are perhaps easier to deal with in public relations than in journalism. The public relations practitioner is concerned with presenting as positive an image of his or her client as is possible. For a practitioner concerned with ethics, that requires telling the truth in the sense of presenting no material that is *untrue*, as well as answering questions truthfully or avoiding uncomfortable questions without lying.

. . . credibility in public relations depends first and foremost on telling the truth.

I believe that it also requires one to avoid presenting truthful information—either selectively or in a slanted manner—so as to paint an overall picture that is untrue. Any departures from this general approach, which would involve lying on behalf of a client, should come only after applying an adaptation of the six Black-Steele-Barney criteria noted earlier. If these overall general principles are adhered to, there is—with one key exception—no need for the public relations practitioner to *volunteer* additional facts that might detract in some way from the client's overall image or lead reporters or the public to raise questions about the client. It is perfectly appropriate for public relations practitioners to emphasize the good points of their clients, as long as the truth is acknowledged about any warts that also exist. This approach is also important to emphasize as part of the counseling and guidance that public relations practitioners provide to clients.

The exception here has to do with credibility, which might sometimes be enhanced (as Kittross says) by providing information that casts the client in a less favorable light. In this case, the end—enhanced credibility—justifies the means, and Machiavelli would be happy.

But I suggest that credibility in public relations depends first and foremost on telling the truth. Neither the public nor journalists should be so naïve as to expect public relations practitioners to be objective or even fair all of the time. That's not what the business is about. However, they should be expected to tell the truth if they see themselves as ethical and effective practitioners. Kittross's notion that the essence of public relations is simply to get people to like the client vastly oversimplifies that field of endeavor, as any good PR text makes quite clear.

For journalists, the issue is a bit more complex. Let's begin this part of the discussion by focusing on privacy law, where the courts have held that under some circumstances, truthful publication of embarrassing facts that an individual has a right to keep private can be punished by the award of monetary damages. This legal guideline is one that the news media may want to take into account in their considerations of how much of the truth to tell, to reduce their risk of exposure to legal liability if not for ethical reasons.

But it must be noted that the courts have also generally held that where information is legitimately newsworthy, it can be published even if it is embarrassing. This brings us back to the key ethical concern—namely, the need to publish truthful reports on newsworthy topics (i.e., those of concern and interest to the public). If you do that, the rest of the potential ethical issues will take care of themselves, as will most of the legal ones.

Although the legal guideline may provide an ethical threshold if there is some question about an item's newsworthiness, it fails to provide sufficient guidance in situations where invasion of privacy is not a potential legal danger. For example, in political campaign coverage, is there a need to think twice about reporting material that is true, potentially embarrassing to a candidate, but only marginally relevant to the story at hand?

If the material is clearly irrelevant, it shouldn't be included whether it's embarrassing to the candidate or not. That seems not so much an ethical guideline as simply a principle of competent news judgment and reporting. If the material falls into the gray area of possible relevance—as so many items seem to do—then I believe that once a reporter has verified its accuracy, the material should be reported and the audience members should be given the privilege of making up their own minds about its relevance. To handle the situation any other way smacks of an elitist approach, with the reporter determining what her or his audience should be allowed to know. Reporters have long been cautioned against trying to play God by including or withholding various types of information, and that admonition seems highly appropriate in this situation.

Journalists who provide as much truthful information as is relevant, and report the material in context, serve the public well and need not worry about additional ethical concerns. Conversely, reporters are *not* serving the public well if they tailor a story to avoid a possible negative impact on some of the people mentioned in it, provided the material at issue is relevant and of concern to the public. If the subject is important for the public to know about, then even the possibility that it might cause a suicide, though not to be taken lightly, is an insufficient ethical concern to overcome the principle that one reports accurate information and lets the other ethical concerns fall where they may.

This puts a considerable burden on journalists and their editors to determine when any particular item of information is so important to the public that it justifies the risk of personal harm resulting from its publication. This becomes very much a situational ethics issue, because one must weigh the importance against the likelihood of harm. In addition, one must consider whether the information is so crucial to the topic that the story can't be told fully without this particular item.

To me, if the material is highly relevant to the story, and if the story is one that the public needs to know about, it would require an almost inevitable likelihood of a human life being lost to justify even considering the withholding of truthful information. Even then, the best approach might well be to withhold the information only temporarily. Kittross's upcoming query about running a kidnapping story that could endanger the victim's life raises this question, and I'd respond—in advance—that if releasing the story would truly endanger the victim, there are strong ethical reasons for telling something other than the whole truth, at least for the moment.

However, I can't justify an outright lie, in print or on the air, even to avoid endangering the victim, but this is based more on the credibility issue than on Kant's categorical imperative mentioned earlier. Withholding information would fall short of an absolutist Kantian position to tell the whole truth under all circumstances. Thereby, it would recognize preventing harm to a fellow human being as another ethical concern that may on occasion merit consideration along with truth telling.

But, one might ask, is telling all of the truth a viable position if the material under consideration is merely titillation rather than important information for the public? Because I have little use for mere titillation as a valid part of journalism, I find the answer to that question quite simple. Leave the titillation to mass communicators who deal with entertainment rather than news (even if they purport to call themselves journalists), and the issue never arises. (This perspective does raise some other important questions, but this is not the place to discuss them. Some of them are dealt with in Chapters 10 and 12.)

■ A RULE UTILITARIAN PERSPECTIVE

This whole argument is essentially framed in utilitarian terms. This shouldn't be surprising because—as John Merrill notes in his introductory Overview to this book—utilitarianism is probably the most influential ethical framework in general, and the ethical approach most often professed by mass media practitioners. But the utilitarian perspective used here is somewhat different from the one Merrill outlined. He emphasized the aspect of utilitarianism that focuses on the greatest happiness for the largest number of people, thus requiring an attempt to predict the consequences of a specific act or decision.

In contrast to that *act utilitarianism* approach, my focus requires agreement that truthful and complete reporting—and truthful public relations—as a general *rule* will produce the greatest good (or "happiness," in at least a loosely defined sense) for the greatest number of people—i.e., that it will provide the greatest service to the public. This approach to utilitarianism holds that predictions of specific consequences are not important because the general results are assumed when one follows the relevant guideline—in this case, truth telling. In a sense, this approach lets one use the strengths of both the Kantian and utilitarian approaches while avoiding some of their pitfalls.

Such a *rule utilitarian* perspective requires one to reject alternative ethical principles if they interfere in any way with this greatest good of providing the greatest amount of (relevant) truthful information to the audience. If there is no such interference, then complying with additional ethical principles would be perfectly appropriate, even though they are not necessary to meet the threshold definition of ethical behavior.

Kittross begins his discussion of this topic by referring to the need—in court and, assumedly, in the media—to tell "the whole truth." He goes on to note the difficulty of including every important detail. In fact, the requirements of the news media make such a goal both impossible and undesirable. There isn't print space or air time sufficient to do that, and reporters can't be everywhere. Even without those impediments, the audience wouldn't be interested in that much detail on the vast majority of topics.

However, there is a need to provide context for the information provided to the public. One part of this is to provide historical perspective along with reports on breaking news, thereby viewing "news stories not as single, isolated events but rather as links in a longer chain" (Willis, 1991, p. 11). Such an approach demands that the media devote enough time and resources to gathering information to reflect the historical context, and enough space or air time to present it to the public. It certainly will raise costs for the news media, but the result will be a more complete truth in the information presented to the public. Ethical news reporting seems to require this kind of investment.

In addition, the relatively recent development of computer-assisted reporting, with its access to huge amounts of information that can be retrieved from a wide variety of databases, provides new opportunities for telling "the whole truth" and doing so more easily than was possible for earlier generations of reporters. But these opportunities also raise concerns regarding information overload, going beyond what the audience can or will absorb. Kittross's reference to the horde of topics and details that might provide appropriate context for the report of an earthquake seems excessive, for the same reason. With too much context and too many details, audience members can too easily become distracted from the essence of the news, or be led to misinterpret what happened.

However, I don't want to denigrate the need to give the audience a complete picture—within reasonable limits—of what took place. That's been implicit in my stress on truth telling as the prime principle for the news, information, and persuasive media. When the reporting is markedly incomplete, the results can be very serious both for the community in general and for the media's credibility.

■ SOME EXAMPLES

Two unfortunate examples of such incomplete reporting and its results can close this discussion. One was the news media's failure to provide timely coverage of the AIDS epidemic during its early years, a gap Everette Dennis (1990) called a "sad chapter in American journalism." Dennis said that the news media largely ignored the story

> because editors believed it affected unattractive and unimportant constituencies. Only after the Rock Hudson revelations and some other instances when individual journalists' families were involved did the press begin with any seriousness to cover this critical public health problem. There are angry critics who say the press should shoulder some of the blame for the spread of the disease because of a kind of de facto censorship that deprived the American people of important information. (pp. 9–10, citing Kinsella, 1989)

The second example was the incomplete and distorted coverage of the 1989 murder of Carol DiMaiti Stuart in Boston. News media—as well as police and other government officials—were taken in by Charles Stuart's bogus claim that a "raspy-voiced black man" shot and killed his pregnant wife while wounding him. For much of the 10 weeks before Stuart committed suicide after becoming the prime suspect in the case, the media accepted Stuart's account. They asked far too few questions about the willingness of a city with a history of strong racist overtones to accept a story that had an inner-city black man attacking a supposedly "all-American" suburban white couple (Christians et al., 1998, pp. 95–98). Although the media were not totally to blame, their failure to report (or even to begin to report) the truth in this situation did immense damage to race relations, law enforcement, and various other aspects of the urban fabric in Boston. In retrospect, much of that media coverage *was* "objective" and accurate, at least to the degree that official sources were used and quoted quite accurately. Skepticism about Stuart's story was not reported because no official sources would go on the record with those doubts, which turned out to be quite valid in the end.

In neither of these cases did the news media do an adequate job of reporting the truth of the situation. In the AIDS context, it was simply a lack of coverage until the disease had spread widely. Regarding the Stuart murder, it was incomplete reporting, based on stereotyped thinking and a lack of skepticism, that omitted far too much of the truth. To be sure, greater accuracy would have helped, as would fairness (and perhaps even objectivity, if we could ever define the term usefully). But first and foremost in these situations, for very different reasons, the news was not reported fully enough or truthfully enough, and the resulting shortages of "truth" were bad for both society and the media's credibility. The slogan used by *The Capital Times*, the afternoon paper in Madison, Wisconsin, would be a good reminder here: "Let the people have the truth and the freedom to discuss it, and all will go well."

■ KITTROSS: The social value of journalism and public relations requires high-quality practices reflecting ethical considerations that go beyond truth and objectivity to accuracy and fairness.

When one takes an oath in a court of law, it is to tell "the truth, the whole truth, and nothing but the truth." Not an easy task, when constrained to answer only "yes" or "no" to the specific questions asked by attorneys who have specific clients to serve. But it is much easier than being asked to be objective and fair at the same time, as journalists always are, and even as some in the entertainment media are expected to be.

For many journalists, the concept of truth has become a deontological standard—requiring specific rules of or obligations for ethical conduct: Thou shall speak or write the truth. But it isn't so simple, as the prevalence of lying and fictionalizing in mass media content illustrates.

Are truth and objectivity adequate standards for the news media? Indeed, are they attainable? Would a teleological or "consequence" (dealing with results rather than causes) approach be better?

Or, expanding this argument, is it too easy to use traditional journalistic standards of truth and objectivity as a smokescreen to hide what really may be falsehood and inaccuracy—maybe even dishonesty? Don't we need to be *fair* as well as truthful, *accurate* as well as objective?

If the media are, as is traditionally held, surrogates for the citizens in a democracy, providing information that is necessary in order for the citizenry to make valid and reliable decisions, then even standards of truth higher than those of the courtroom may be inadequate. Hence, I believe that truth alone is not—despite David Gordon's opinion—"sufficient . . . for the practitioner to claim to be acting ethically."

Don't we need to be* fair *as well as truthful,* accurate *as well as objective?

Neither is balance an adequate substitute for truth—a position Gordon tries to put in my mouth. I hold that balance is *not* a substitute for either fairness, accuracy, or truth, although Aristotle might find it in accord with his Golden Mean.

Although this chapter deals largely with the journalistic function of the mass media, and not the entertainment function, almost all of what is said also applies to persuasive communication such as propaganda, advertising, and public relations. Propaganda might be defined as getting an idea from the brain of communicator A to the brain of receiver B, with the best interests of A at heart. Advertising uses similar techniques to sell goods and services rather than ideas. Much education also is persuasive but supposedly also has the interests of "B" at heart. Public relations, when relating to the general public, operates at a more visceral level. It is intended, in its most simple form, to get people to like clients both through what PR says *and* what it doesn't say, whether creating an image or engaging in damage control. Often, public relations has to perform many of the same tasks and functions as journalism, and even more commonly must help journalists fulfill their own duties. To be effective, the PR practitioner must be credible—and truth is usually, but unfortunately not always, more credible than fiction produced either by commission or omission. Hence, public relations practitioners also continually need to consider truth, objectivity, accuracy and fairness.

■ TRUTH

At the very best, truth is "truth as we know it." Griffiths (1996, p. 85) maintains that "journalists seek the truth and public relations professionals never lie." Some reporters have another definition: as long as we got someone to say it on the record, it must be true, or at least reportable without cautionary notices. The definition of *truth* is not self-evident, despite Gordon's attempts to wiggle out of this basic problem. Fairy tales, legends, and even psychological studies show us how fragile the concept of truth may be. The film *Rashomon* portrays an event as perceived very differently by different characters in the drama, and there is no single correct view of the event. Prosecutors in criminal trials are well aware that witnesses' memories of events are often faulty. When we tell a story among friends, we tend to polish off its rough edges and reduce its complexities. When talking with children, we simplify as much as we can. We often forget—or try to forget—unpleasant memories.

These are normal human traits. Good reporters are aware of them and are constantly looking for additional objective evidence to back up the accounts of those they interview. But often, reporters are unaware of their own perceptual biases or motivations. A reporter, like a pollster, may unconsciously seek to interview only those who are well-dressed, seem rational, appear to be articulate—or who are conveniently located. It is easier to get a story from such a person than from someone who is dressed in rags, who may appear irrational or inarticulate, or who must be sought out.

A 1940s study on rumor dissemination and stereotyping—what Walter Lippmann in 1922 called "the world inside our heads"—found that, when an oral description of a picture of a white man holding a straight razor during an apparent confrontation with a black was relayed through two or three people who hadn't seen the picture, then the razor—a "stereotypical symbol of Negro violence"—migrated in the final telling to the hand of the black man, even though the original picture clearly showed it in the white man's hand (Allport and Postman, 1945, p. 75). Similar stereotypes or expectancies are part of what each of us learned unconsciously as we grew up.

There is an old joke about a weather forecast: "snow, followed by small boys on sleds." It is stereotypical to think of "snow, sleds, small children" as belonging together. But suppose we saw the snow and the sled—but there was a dog riding the sled. Would we notice? If it didn't make sense according to our stereotypes, would we report it?

This happens over and over again in all sorts of newsmaking situations. During the Cold War, the Soviet Union was the enemy of the United States, and it was always a shock when a report of cooperation or agreement or laudable behavior came along. During the civil rights marches of the 1960s in the South, Northerners rarely heard about the many police officers in Dixie who did *not* attack the black marchers. Could the film *Schindler's List*, which portrayed a Nazi Party member who saved hundreds of Jews from the Holocaust, have been understood—or even made—immediately after World War II?

Hollywood understood early on that people were complex and that many of its most popular and potent characters were the "good bad girl" or the "bad good man." But such complexity is almost never shown in television news or on the pages of American newspapers. We stereotype and simplify the news without even thinking about it.

Another assault on the absolutist conception of truth is the "little white lie," where an untruth is told because we believe that it will benefit the listener or reader more than the truth will—the "Yes, Virginia, there *is* a Santa Claus" syndrome, where the media have the arrogance to assume that they have the right to prevent harm to the audience. Additionally, and with less concern for the recipient of a message than for its sender, we have the relatively harmless spin put on a political or other utterance by a public relations practitioner, or the puffery created by an advertising agency.

Worse yet, it isn't unknown for a reporter or an advertiser to deliberately lie, by omission or commission. A reporter who lies deliberately isn't a reporter, of course, but a whore. Lying is unacceptable and unprofessional behavior because, among other things, it misleads the publics whom the reporter serves and challenges every justification for the news media's existence.

Then there is what may be the biggest *unconscious* bias of all: the reporter has a mental picture of a specific audience—those attending to a particular newspaper or broadcast station—and wants to satisfy them and secure the largest possible audience for the story. Reporters and advertising copywriters use simplification as a useful tool. This is like the parents who simplify bedtime stories, so there is no possibility of the children misunderstanding the main points, by taking out most of the potentially confusing detail, contradictions, and complexity that are part of any "real" story. Reporters and editors, for the same reason, usually simplify the stories they cover and present to their readers, listeners, and viewers.

Telling the "whole truth" is rarely an option, although reporters often use this idea as an excuse for covering too much. For example, sometimes "the truth" *shouldn't* be told (at least not for a while)—as, for example, when the life of a kidnap victim is at stake and the police need some room to maneuver. Frankly, there aren't enough rolls of newsprint or feet of videotape ever to present "the *whole* truth."

■ OBJECTIVITY

Many journalists and teachers of journalism become uneasy at the very mention of objectivity, for the same reasons that they find truth to be such an elusive concept: It may be impossible to be 100% objective about anything. The reason is simple: We are human beings. But Rawls's veil of ignorance allows us to achieve objectivity—reporting without bias—more easily than achieving more complex ethical goals, such as truth.

Most of what was said earlier in the section on truth dealt with what might be called honest untruths. But reporters, like everyone else, have their own axes to grind. A reporter, after all, lives a life outside of the newsroom. He or she may be a liberal, a conservative, a feminist, an environmentalist, or a racist. Background—urban/suburban, white/black, old/young, fundamentalist/agnostic, male/female, poor/rich—may control the reporter's value system. On any day a reporter may get up on the wrong side of the bed, may allow personal impressions of events or subjects to color what and who is reported.

Reporters are trained to stand outside of controversies, although this is hard to do and still report fully. How can someone sitting in an auditorium know what is happening backstage? How can someone reporting from the police station under siege during a riot, or from one election headquarters during a campaign, be fully objective? Can a foreign correspondent, reporting on a country where the language, the customs, and the politics are strange, *ever* get beneath the surface? If only superficial reports are prepared, is this really an objective or a truthful view of that country?

Even more important is the relationship of the concept of objectivity to the journalistic function and purpose. Is journalism's role to produce "a truthful, comprehensive, and intelligent account of the day's events in a context which gives them meaning" (Commission on Freedom of the Press, 1947, p. 21), or is journalism merely a conduit, carrying whatever happens to get inside, without context, comprehensiveness, or intelligence? Is the provision of context, or using the writer's intelligence to accept or discard data, ever truly objective?

It is this need for context that makes it so necessary for reporters and editors to be widely read and curious about many things. Otherwise, it is truly impossible to interpret what is going on—and the news media become, at best, a conduit for the words of those who want to say something (and who are selected by the media to say it). Photographs then are selected mostly for immediate reward—titillation—rather than information.

Of course, there is nothing intrinsically wrong with titillation, or trying to gain the audience's attention. In fact, for any of the other mass media effects (such as attitude change, opinion formation, or overt behavior such as shopping, voting, or demonstrating) to take place one must first gain public attention.

But news must go beyond titillation and gossip. It is history in the making; it enables the public to make its decisions. The choice of stories is important: Watergate dealt with misconduct by President Nixon while in office, but the Whitewater scandal originally dealt with a time before President Clinton took office and with events in which he was passive, not active—events that had nothing to do with the U.S. Constitution. Are they equally significant with respect to the public's ability to make rational decisions? Why do mobs of reporters try to photograph or interview the victims of disasters—as when the emotional children in Christa McAuliffe's classroom were cornered by photographers after the spacecraft *Challenger* exploded with her aboard in 1986? (See Chapter 15-G and 15-I.)

To prevent one's own feelings from affecting the story in some way probably is impossible, but to prevent them from affecting the story grossly is not difficult. If eternal vigilance is the price of liberty, as John Philpot Curran said in 1790, then it also is the price of the journalist's objectivity.

Reporters covering the 1994 Los Angeles earthquake needed more than the ability to paraphrase lines from a steamy movie ("the earth shook at 4:31 A.M."). They needed a background in Southern California geography, politics, transportation, economics, history, sociology, demography, and many other matters, in addition to a general knowledge of government, technology, and geology. With adequate context, reportage may be quite "objective." But it still has to assume a point of view: that of the temporarily (or permanently) homeless, the politicians, the technocrats, the victims, the predators, the good, the bad, the altruistic, the unaware, or the uncaring. The reporter's location and view of the scene often determine what the audience sees and hears and, as a result, thinks. Television journalism, in particular, tends to select stories with dramatic pictures rather than those that give a comprehensive and intelligent context for the day's events. Although a picture may be "truthful" in the sense of not having been staged or digitally manipulated (unfortunately, a growing practice; see Chapter 15-F), this is not sufficient for the citizen who must make decisions on the basis of the available news.

This point is illustrated by the folk story about the blind men and the elephant: The first feels the tusks and describes them, the second feels the ears and describes them, and so on. But none of them is able to describe the elephant until, or unless, all of the smaller pictures are put together and given context. It might be argued that in many instances the connections are far more important than what is being connected.

But if, as posited above, neither truth nor objectivity are fully realizable, on what shall we base our professional journalistic standards?

First, I do not propose that we just surrender, whining that because entertainment communication isn't expected to be truthful (although often documentary, cinema verité, or other "truthful" production techniques are used), we should classify media by their entertainment function and ignore the entire concept of truth. (As John Stossel, an ABC investigative reporter, once arrogantly said to his colleagues at an Investigative Reporters and Editors convention, "once *we* decide who the 'bad guy' is, it's show biz.")

Instead, I suggest that journalists must meet two other standards or factors, interwoven with but distinct from truth and objectivity: accuracy and fairness, with fairness being more important.

■ ACCURACY

One of the most entertaining and useful books on research methods is Darryl Huff's *How to Lie with Statistics* (1954). Among the many fallacies illustrated in this book is that of "false accuracy." To say that "33.333% of the female students at Such-and-so University in 1890 married members of the faculty" may be true—but it may mean that there were only three women in the student body that year, and one can't generalize from that year to another.

Other fallacies or errors that are technically accurate but actually false abound in journalism, as they do in scholarly or commercial research. The researcher distinguishes between validity (something measures what we say it does), reliability (repeated measurements of the same phenomenon have the same result), and precision. The journalist often tends to ignore these distinctions and is concerned only with a somewhat fuzzy concept of accuracy.

This can be serious. Without carefully defined standards, it is unlikely that high quality will be achieved. Traditionally, embryonic reporters—whether they went into journalism or public relations—were taught that "it doesn't matter what you call someone as long as you get the name right." But we all know that there is a declining standard, even of spelling proper names. The use of tape recorders hasn't helped much, and if a newspaper reporter hears one thing being said at a presidential news conference and millions of viewers and listeners hear something else, what happens to the paper's credibility? If one has selected the wrong words, no spell-check computer program will help. These computer programs may be reliable (they spell the word the same way each time), but may not be valid (they are checking the wrong word).

Furthermore, if a reporter is "accurate," but doesn't give the whole story, the overall effect is one of inaccuracy. The old advertising slogan that "four out of five doctors prefer" a particular product may be accurate and truthful as far as it goes, but suppose that only five doctors were asked and all of them worked for the firm producing the product?

To achieve accuracy is one reason that we have editors—and the shortsighted money-pinching of some publishers with respect to copyediting and fact-checking is a major factor leading to loss of credibility and damaging libel suits. I was an expert witness in one libel case where a magazine's top management bragged about its almost universal fact-checking, an editor said that there was some fact-checking, but the reporter testified to complete ignorance of this stage in the process. The judgment against the magazine was for $6 million. The then-president of the national Society of Professional Journalists, Paul McMasters, four-fifths of the way through a 50-state tour (Boston, May 24, 1994), told of his surprise and dismay over the number of times his name had been spelled wrong and his views distorted in "quotes" published and aired by many of his own members.

■ FAIRNESS

Fairness is the act of keeping an open mind, of suspending individual judgment until enough information is available so that judgments or decisions can validly be made. It is impartiality, but not ignorance. The media are not merely a conduit; they have the responsibility to assess the validity or truth of the information they disseminate. Of particular importance is the need to provide sufficient valid and reliable information that will allow readers, listeners, and viewers to reach their own conclusions.

The media are not merely a conduit; they have the responsibility to assess the validity or truth of the information they disseminate.

One must continually assess whether something is fair. Is "one man, one vote" inherently fair if it excludes women? Or is it fair if the effect is to give *all* power to 51% of the electorate and *none* to the other 49% (and those too young or otherwise disqualified from voting)? Is two people ganging up on one fair? But suppose the one was a professional prizefighter and the two were small children? Is it fair to select an obvious "kook" as a spokesperson for a position frowned on by the reporter? Should the names of rape victims be published? How about the names of accused rapists?

The now-defunct FCC Fairness Doctrine, which dealt only with personal attacks and controversial issues, often got confused with the statutory requirement (47 USC 315) that bona fide candidates for political office are entitled to equal opportunity to be seen or heard on the air during a campaign. The public has picked up this idea, and tends to believe that opposing views on all sorts of matters should have "equal time," regardless of the medium. Allied with this is a belief that all views are equally valid. (Another acquired belief appears to be that all quotations are sacrosanct, and that there is no need to provide valid and reliable proof of what someone says; see Chapter 15-I.)

To a certain extent, we can think of fairness in terms of what *not* to air or publish.

Should a mass murderer have as much attention as the victims? During the Gulf War, should the ruler of Iraq automatically have rated "equal time" or "equal space" with the combined leadership of the coalition arrayed against him? Was the situation different in 1998? Should a spokesperson for an unpopular view or other controversial position—perhaps one favoring pornography or on either side of the abortion, gun control, or smoking issues—automatically have exactly the same attention from the media as those on the other side? Should a station run a story about a kidnapping when it has been warned that it may put the victim's life in danger? Should a newspaper bring up old, unpleasant memories when dealing with a subject such as incest or rape?

Fairness can be complex, as are other ethical questions. If ethics involves what we ought to do, then fairness asks, "For whom?" It isn't a game: Identifying oneself as a reporter may be morally correct and truthful, but doing so may mean that the public doesn't get the information it needs. On a pragmatic level, libel and privacy law cases often involve questions of fairness, and most juries with which I'm familiar see it that way; in contrast the traditional plea of "provable truth" has undergone many changes in recent libel litigation (e.g., *Milkovich v. Lorain Journal Co.*, 497 U.S. 1, 1990) and no longer protects the media absolutely.

Although reporters may start to feel as if they are playing God, they must concern themselves with individuals as well as with a mass or general audience. "Playing fair" may not yet have achieved the status in law that injuries to reputation (libel) and the right to be let alone (privacy) have. Indeed, because our legal system tends to be proscriptive ("thou shalt not") rather than prescriptive ("thou shall"), it may never reach that status. But invasion of privacy became a tort only after it was described just over a century ago (Warren and Brandeis, 1890), and fairness may well become a similar requirement in the next century, as the population burgeons and competition for resources and amenities becomes ever fiercer.

■ CONCLUSIONS

Now that I've set up truth, objectivity, accuracy, and fairness as straw figures to be knocked down, what do I believe journalists should do? And why?

The second question is the easier, and may be answered in two ways: Journalists and public relations specialists should do what is "right" or what will help them to sleep well nights; *and* they should do what will create the greatest credibility for the media. The public good fits in on both levels: That which is "right" will benefit the greatest number of people, in a utilitarian sense, but without credibility the media will not be believed even when acting strictly for the public good. With respect to affecting public opinion, credibility is much more important than truth, which may not be believed. For example, most of the people in the world would find incredible and unbelievable the fact that almost every home in the United States has a television set, a flush toilet, a working telephone, and bathing facilities. Public relations and business communication practitioners are particularly aware of the need for credibility, and today public relations groups (such as the Public Relations Society of America, the International Association of Business Communicators, and the Southern Public Relations Federation) are among the few professional communications associations to provide certification intended to provide additional credibility for practitioners whose education and standards measure up.

So, one should *try* to meet the highest standards for truth, objectivity, accuracy, and fairness that one can and, beyond that moral approach, exercise any other techniques that will at least mitigate any unfairness, untruth, inaccuracy, or lack of objectivity because (despite the example given in the previous paragraph) truth usually is more credible than fiction.

One technique, used rarely, for improving the media's credibility is to state in advance any connections or conditions that might lead the reader or the viewer to suspect bias (particularly if unsuccessfully concealed). An example of this approach was Peter Arnett's reminders, in his broadcasts from Teheran over CNN during the Gulf War, that his material was subject to censorship by the Iranian government. Another example is that of Jeffrey Schmalz, an editor and reporter on *The New York Times*, afflicted with AIDS, who nevertheless was assigned/allowed to report on AIDS and similar health matters, but with full disclosure to his readers in every column ("The Changing Times," 1992).

Another method that encourages reader trust is the prominent use of corrections whenever a publication has been in error. There are at least 19 other "media accountability systems" used in various countries (Bertrand, 1993, p. 9), including opinion surveys, accuracy and fairness questionnaires mailed to people mentioned in the news, ombudsmen, and press councils.

A technique often reflected in journalistic and public relations codes of ethics might be thought of as the Caesar's wife approach. In other words, be above reproach. To achieve this status, however, often requires that one become a political and social eunuch. Reporters are often required to forgo political activity, although most publishers consider that it is permissible for themselves (see Chapter 14).

Finally, there is the "I must be doing a good job" logic of the beleaguered journalist when *both* sides to a controversy accuse the same media outlet (or individual) of bias and dishonesty! After all, we must convince ourselves that we are the "good guys" because we tell the truth—which is more than just conveying "facts"—and that we are fair, accurate, and objective. This, of course, is a teleological (and perhaps theological) argument: Our strength is the strength of 10 because our hearts are pure.

In all of this, I am definitely *not* advocating that the reporter should be ignorant as well as unbiased, as trial jurors, in contravention of any rational principle, are expected to be today. Rawls's veil of ignorance concept merely points out that we should make an ethical decision as though we are unaware of which side we are on; such "ignorance" allows us better to evaluate whether the outcome of that decision was fair. (Note that Rawls does not advocate the common meaning of the word *ignorance*—that is, not knowing the facts.)

In the long run, if we go beyond rules or codes that are unreliable and impossible to follow, into the realm of morality—and try to do the best job we can—our reputations will be so high that we will gain credibility even as we provide our readers, viewers, and listeners with the information they need. To some extent, this is "doing well by doing good" because the only way the media can be successful—financially, journalistically, personally—is to maintain a reputation for *honesty*, which goes far beyond the copout of saying that we are attempting merely to be "truthful" and "objective." (See also Chapter 15-J for another aspect of honesty.)

■ MERRILL: Commentary

For me, this is perhaps the most important controversy dealt with in this book—a subject especially important to anyone concerned about the ethics of *journalistic reporting*. But it is likewise important to those who are in the field of public relations. It gets us to a central dilemma of ethics: the importance of truth as contrasted with something-less-than-the-truth. It gets the journalistic reporter to the nub of his or her basic responsibility *qua* reporter.

Many hard-nosed reporters, in both the print and electronic media, come at ethics from a mainly *deontological* (principle-bound) perspective. A dominant principle for them is the presentation of a truthful, unbiased, and thorough account of an event. They believe that it is not only their *professional* duty but also their *ethical* duty to do this. These are the reporters who report; they do not distort, hide certain things, tamper with quotes, and in other ways provide a "report" that is flawed intentionally to fulfill some personal agenda. Connie Chung of CBS probably would not fall into this category with her promising (in January 1995) that information from Newt Gingrich's mother (that son Newt considered Hillary Clinton a bitch) would be "just between you and me" and then proceeding to telecast it. This is *Machiavellian* and puts reportorial ends ahead of ethical means.

And then there are the overt *ethicists*, who agree with John Michael Kittross and take the more *teleological* ethical stance (consideration of consequences) in making decisions that might well go beyond a concern for the truth or objectivity. In journalism, these practitioners probably outnumber the truth-oriented ones, and in public relations almost everyone is such a practitioner. The very nature of public relations is consequence-oriented, whereas presumably the *reporter* in journalism is largely directed by duty to the simple principle of truth telling.

I can imagine that the dedicated *deontological reporter* would say something like the following concerning the reporter who would shape the story in the name of proper consequences: *Such a consequence-oriented reporter is not really a reporter. He or she is perhaps a good person, a person concerned with ethical action, but a flawed reporter. In one sense the more a journalist becomes concerned about treating people fairly, the poorer he or she becomes as a reporter.*

Perhaps I am being unfair to consequentialist reporters, but I think not. Such reporters are, indeed, being ethical, but hardly reportorial. A significant object for them is fairness to somebody, not providing an accurate reflection of the real event. The disclosure-bound reporter, on the other hand, is dedicated to the truth of the event, not to fairness to somebody. If this reporter thinks of fairness, it is only fairness to the *integrity of the story.*

What I think is important to remember here is that *both* types of practitioner can be thought of as being ethical. The hard-nosed, full-disclosure types feel ethical when they provide a full and virtually truthful account with the verifiable facts included. Their reportorial ethics are based on a belief that the people have a right to know the truth. In revealing the truth, such reporters consider themselves as also being fair. The other type of media practitioners—the consequence ethicists—would feel ethical when they, through purposely tampering with the facts in some way, bring about fairness to some principal in the story, or some other desirable consequence. This type of reporter, for example, would withhold the name of the rape victim while knowing that the integrity of the story is being compromised. The possible consequences, for this reporter, outweigh the full disclosure of relevant facts in the story.

Let us look briefly, in conclusion, at the public relations enterprise. Truth, though important, is not the main concern of the public relations practitioner—at least not *all* the truth. The main objective of PR is to provide the most positive image of the client or the institution possible. This may necessitate manipulating the facts, stressing some and omitting others, revealing some and omitting others. This is the name of the game. One hardly expects a public relations person (or an advertiser) to have the same dedication to truthful (complete, unbiased, balanced) information expected of a news reporter.

So what would an ethical public relations person be like? That's difficult to say, because of the implicit loyalty issue. The PR person's loyalty is to the client or employer who wants good relations with various publics. Theoretically, at least, the media reporter's loyalty is to the report—or to truth or objectivity, and therefore ultimately to each audience member. This is a big difference in basic loyalties, and it tells you much about the eagerness with which each type of practitioner is dedicated to truth and fairness.

REFERENCES

Allport, Gordon W., and Leo J. Postman. (1945). "The Basic Psychology of Rumor." *Transactions of the New York Academy of Sciences Series* 2(8), pp. 61–81. (Reprinted in numerous collections.)

Bertrand, Claude-Jean. (Fall 1993). "Media Ethics in Europe: Media Accountability Systems." *Media Ethics* 6(1), pp. 7–9.

Black, Jay, Bob Steele, and Ralph Barney. (1995). *Doing Ethics in Journalism: A Handbook with Case Studies*, 2nd ed. Boston: Allyn & Bacon.

Bok, Sissela. (1978). *Lying: Moral Choice in Public and Private Life*. New York: Pantheon.

Christians, Clifford G., Mark Fackler, Kim B. Rotzoll, and Kathy Brittain McKee. (1998). *Media Ethics: Cases and Moral Reasoning*, 5th ed. New York: Longman.

Commission on Freedom of the Press. (1947). *A Free and Responsible Press*. Chicago: University of Chicago Press.

Curran, John Philpot. (1790). *Speech upon the Right of Election*.

Dennis, Everette E. (1990). "In Allegiance to Truth: News, Ethics and Split-Personality Journalism." Gannett Center for Media Studies, speech delivered March 6, Honolulu.

Fink, Conrad. (1988). *Media Ethics: In the Newsroom and Beyond*. New York: McGraw-Hill.

Griffiths, David. (Spring 1996). "Teaching Journalism Skills Courses to New Public Relations Majors." *Journalism & Mass Communication Educator* 51(1), pp. 82–86.

Harwood, Richard. (1992). "Knights of the Fourth Estate." *The Washington Post*, December 5, p. A23.

Huff, Darryl. (1954). *How to Lie with Statistics*. New York: Norton.

Kinsella, James. (1989). *Covering the Plague: AIDS and the American Media*. New Brunswick, NJ: Rutgers University Press.

Lambeth, Edmund B. (1992). *Committed Journalism: An Ethic for the Profession*, 2nd ed. Bloomington: Indiana University Press.

Lippmann, Walter. (1922). *Public Opinion*. New York: Macmillan.

Rawls, John. (1971). *A Theory of Justice*. Cambridge, MA: Belknap.

Steele, Bob. (Winter 1993). "Lying to Tell the Truth: Is it Ever OK?" *Poynter Report*, p. 3.

"The Changing Times." (October 5, 1992). *The New Yorker*, p. 63.

Warren, Samuel D., and Louis D. Brandeis. (December 15, 1890). "The Right to Privacy." *Harvard Law Review* 4(5), pp. 193–220.

Willis, W. J. (Jim). (1991). *The Shadow World: Life Between the News Media and Reality*. New York: Praeger.

CHAPTER 5

INFLUENCES ON MEDIA CONTENT
The Public Relations Factor

Should the news media act merely as conduits for what others want to bring to the audience's attention? How much should media gatekeepers screen and modify that material before it is transmitted to the public? The answers to these questions affect not only the news media and their consumers, but also public relations practitioners, whose job is to deal with the news media on behalf of their clients.

The news media certainly cannot function without using a variety of sources. But the question remains as to how much responsibility rests on them to avoid taking the easy route and relying heavily on material that is furnished by sources with axes to grind. Entertainment media can also be manipulated by people who want them to bring certain topics to the public's attention or by companies that arrange to have their products featured prominently in a film or television program.

In the discussion that follows, Carol Reuss argues that the media—particularly the news media—have a symbiotic relationship with their sources and there is nothing inherently wrong with using press releases and other materials furnished by those sources. David Gordon takes the somewhat extreme position that the media must ignore material from people whose motives are to manipulate media content.

■ REUSS: The mass media cannot ignore individuals and groups seeking to manipulate media content, nor should they ignore such sources of news and information.

If I'm in a building that's on fire, I don't care if an arsonist pulls the alarm. The source of the information and the cause of the fire are far less important to me and my welfare than the warning. Hearing it, though, I must decide whether to heed the alarm.

News and information media hear alarms many times every day. Some are newsworthy tips and some are false alarms. But because the media are not omniscient and cannot afford to be omnipresent, they have to depend on others for information about situations that may be important to their audiences and their communities, even on people and organizations that are intent on getting *their* stories or their viewpoints told in the public arena.

This approach doesn't sit well with David Gordon and those who argue that media staffs don't need—indeed, shouldn't use—material from sources they don't seek and select. News reporters and editors often boast that they alone are capable of covering the news—every aspect of it. The most boastful say, "News is what I say it is, period," which is true to a point because as media gatekeepers they control the flow of what is in the mass media.

These men and women control what the public sees and hears. But, try as they might, they cannot know or see everything, so they need more help than any single mass medium can supply. Sometimes news reporters have a double standard about accepting help. They all use their lists of sources, which they guard like gold, but many of them curse news releases from public relations departments or firms. They scoff at what public information officers do. They cannot admit that many public relations practitioners learned media relations from the news side and many of them are highly skilled about news practices. Reporters frequently complain shortsightedly that public relations and public information officers are spin doctors instead of seeing their opportunity to be "de-spinners" who serve the public by offering full, fair, and accurate news and information that counteract undue PR influences.

The news media routinely augment the work of their own staffs by subscribing to news services and syndicates, by retaining freelancers, and by soliciting news tips, letters, essays, photographs, and videotape from the public. Sometimes a news medium wants outside contributions to broaden the interpretation of topics or events; other times it is to boost circulation or ratings. Regardless, people often respond to the media because they want their side aired or their cause promoted, or because they enjoy the opportunity for public recognition the mass media offer. Whatever the reason, the media often receive ideas, articles, illustrations, and audio- and videotapes they would not otherwise have.

The bulk of outside contributions probably comes from news releases and other materials prepared by individuals or organizations. Untold thousands of print, audio, and video news releases (VNRs) are delivered to news organizations every day. Many offer information that the media might not otherwise be aware of; most promote special interests or causes. The list of potential topics is long—from information about people, products, and facilities, to school cafeteria menus and bus schedules, cultural calendars, and even complex discussions of social, technological, cultural, and political ideas. The list of sources is equally long—from attorneys to zoos, government offices to local clubs.

The media practitioners who evaluate news releases look for the usual standards of newsworthiness: proximity, timeliness, and significance. The subject, the source, and even the physical appearance of the release can affect potential use. A reporter's or editor's prejudices may open or close a gate on a release and so can the amount of space or time available on a given day.

News release writers know that the releases they prepare may be revised or even discarded, but they are willing to take the chance because they want the media coverage for themselves or their clients.

Both the preparation and the use of news releases are awash in ethical considerations. At both ends—the sender's and the receiver's—questions about accuracy and honesty must be asked. News releases cannot be accepted blindly. They must be evaluated for newsworthiness, unwarranted bias, plausibility, and appropriateness. They must be judged by the same standards of newsworthiness and significance to audiences that are applied to staff work. News releases from friends and from organizations that offer special considerations or gifts should be scrutinized as fully as those from unknown sources. Staff reporters, writers, and producers should never take credit for or put their bylines on articles or features that are run verbatim or paraphrased from news releases.

The development of video news releases has raised related ethical issues, such as making sure that their technical quality doesn't mask the newsworthiness of the information itself. In other words, technical proficiency should not bias news judgment, and the individual or organization by or for whom the release was prepared should be identified clearly to the audience.

Years ago *The Wall Street Journal* was criticized for publishing news releases verbatim but without bylines. The paper responded to the criticism by saying that releases were well-written and, as far as the editors could ascertain they were accurate, and readers were well-served by the paper's publishing them. Not all concerned media people were satisfied by the *Journal's* response; they seemed to believe in a mythical ethical standard that news releases are tainted because they are supplied by vested interests, that no news release, no matter how accurate and well-developed, should be published or broadcast as is. But news releases are often prepared by writers who have solid news experience so it seems foolish—and potentially expensive—to mandate changes of copy merely for the sake of change.

■ MUTUAL ADVANTAGES

Many media professionals know how publicists and special interest groups operate, and they know how to use them to their advantage and the advantage of their audiences. They may call them when they want to verify or expand the facts and opinions they have gathered from other sources. They may want help understanding a complicated subject. They may want to be able to present more than one side in their reports and programs.

Reporters and editors who deny the value of news releases . . . from "outside" deny their audiences the full range of information and ideas . . . .

Reporters and editors who deny the value of news releases and other materials that are delivered from "outside" deny their audiences the full range of information and ideas that may be important or of interest to them.

For years, radio and television stations have promoted audience participation by asking people to call in news tips and write responses to editorials. More recently, with the wide availability of inexpensive audio and video taping equipment, they are asking listeners and viewers to submit audio- and videotapes for possible use on-air. The amateur movie footage of the assassination of President John F. Kennedy that was purchased by *Life* magazine is probably the best known precursor to the current use of amateur video in news broadcasts. The news media gatekeepers must evaluate all such submissions for validity, worthiness, taste, and potential legal implications. Amateur video has entered yet another dimension, sometimes moving from broadcast use to courtroom use that has affected legal decisions and generated even more coverage. The 1992 tape of Rodney King being beaten by police in Los Angeles is a notable example.

There are other ways to involve the public in broadcasts and producers' standards and needs vary. Some want many "other sides" represented on-air and others refuse anything that does not follow their particular ideology; some want contributions that are logical and well-written and others want bombast and innuendo; some don't care about technical quality and some do.

The motivations and the ethical values of sources vary, as do those of media organizations and practitioners. Some are experts on important topics and some may only think they are. Some represent special interests and say so, some do not. Some are skillful communicators, some are not. The bottom-line ethical consideration is whether the finished products match the ethical standards and expectations of the media to which they are submitted and of their potential audiences.

Producers of media entertainment often accept fees to include brand-name products in their films or television productions. Marketing and sales people like this practice because it offers opportunities to show off their products. Many others condemn it, saying that it gives undue promotion to certain products, such as expensive brand-name or age-restricted products such as alcoholic beverages, which many viewers cannot afford or should not be tempted to crave. This is serious business: Reebok recently sued the producers of the film *Jerry McGuire* for failing to insert the promised scenes after accepting a considerable contribution. (See a further discussion of this point in Chapter 15-D.)

Increasingly, entertainment television has involved public participation in programs. Like movie producers, television now often buys rights to individuals' life stories. In addition, television producers in recent years have capitalized on programs that are based on individuals freely sharing their personal experiences—talk shows, lengthy docudramas, and vignettes for such series as *Rescue 911* and *Cops*. They also compete for amateur footage for programs such as *America's Funniest Home Videos*. Amateur video footage also is sought for various information and news programs. People send in their stories and cassettes because they seek mass media notoriety as much as any financial rewards that might be offered.

Entertainment media executives make many ethical decisions as they evaluate and approve or reject films and programs, and even as they evaluate public input. They balance available material with their organizations' standards of taste and ethics, their estimates of what audiences will accept, and potential profits. The most highly publicized decisions usually involve violence and sexuality in a film or a program, and the treatment of religious beliefs. Often, criticism of entertainment television is developed by organized groups such as the Catholic religious organizations that pressured sponsors to drop *Nothing Sacred* even before it aired in the fall of 1997. Like others desiring to be seen and heard, such groups frequently attempt to intensify their voices by staging "events" that are intended to generate coverage by the news media.

■ THE PUBLIC ROLE

Talk shows, which have proliferated in recent years, invite a wide range of questions pertaining to ethics and ethical decision making. Some shows tend toward news and information, some are strictly entertainment, and some contain sensationalism, misinformation, opinion-mongering, and low-level, tasteless "performance." They all invite public participation, however, and the ethics of the public participation as well as the subjects covered can be complicated. Are the invitations to participate open or selective? Does the audience know which? Does the participation inform or encourage public debate, or doesn't that matter? Does it entertain, and at what level of entertainment quality? Do the programs build up or tear down accepted social standards? Who benefits, and how? Questions like these must be asked by the media gatekeepers, by audiences and potential audiences, and by critics of the media.

When there is strong criticism of the entertainment media from groups and from individuals, media decision makers may make content changes, because they fear turning off their audiences. The age-related labels affixed to a movie or television program (e.g., PG-13 or TV-14) presumably indicate that not every person should view it or try to insulate it against criticism. Similarly, television programmers move potentially offensive programs to a different time slot or venue. Rarely is there widespread agreement as to whether such decisions are more ethics- or marketing-motivated.

Thomas Griffith wrote in *Time* in 1984, "The need for a diverse press makes for strange and incompatible bedfellows" (p. 103). He was referring to the difference between a raunchy "skin" magazine and main-line journalism, both of which have a right to exist under the First Amendment. His quote could be used to describe the relationship of the news media and groups that are critical of the media. Some of these groups are highly organized and highly visible. They are based on every possible topic, from abortion (both for and against) to zoos. Pressure groups are as varied as the nation's population. Mothers Against Drunk Driving is as free to seek media attention as are the Tobacco Institute, the National Dairy Council, the National Rifle Association, ACT-UP, and the Moral Majority. Some of these groups or coalitions were formed to promote specific causes, some to defend against what they perceive as unfair coverage of their causes or criticism of them.

The single attribute that marks each is the need to find ways to get the mass media to pay attention to them and their causes. They need mass media coverage to legitimize their causes and to draw recruits. They vie for media coverage in many ways—by sending news releases, by talking with and writing to media people at every level, and by staging media events and demonstrations that they hope will generate media coverage. The creativity of special interest groups that vie for media and public attention is limitless. Media men and women know this and they also know that the public should have information about changing ideologies and contemporary causes. They must ask the same kinds of questions about newsworthiness and public interests of special interest groups that they ask of other news and information sources.

Some special interest groups take the mass media as their raison d'être. They regularly face off with the media and media contents. There are scores of media watchdog groups that enlist members and financial support from individuals and organizations that are displeased with media contents or activities. Five that have become prominent nationally were analyzed by Chip Rowe for the *American Journalism Review* (1993). They are (1) Accuracy in Media, founded in 1969 by Reed Irvine; (2) Media Research Center, founded in 1987 by L. Brent Bozell; (3) Center for Media and Public Affairs, founded in 1986 by S. Robert Lichter and Linda Lichter; (4) Fairness & Accuracy in Reporting, founded in 1986 by Jeff Cohen; and (5) the Institute for Media Analysis, founded in 1986 by William Schaap and Ellen Ray. These organizations conduct studies of media fairness and accuracy, but each has its own special mission and concept of what constitutes these attributes.

Media people know that the sting of criticism can come soon after an issue is published or a program is broadcast. Phone calls, letters, even the way a publisher, reporter, or anchor is greeted on Main Street, can indicate agreement or disagreement with what had been published or aired. So can subscription orders and cancellations and broadcast ratings.

The Commission on Freedom of the Press in 1947 recommended public participation in media criticism. It suggested that press councils be established to evaluate and help improve news media performance. Supporters envisioned press councils as being egalitarian in terms of membership and mission. The call was unheeded until the late 1960s, when several local press councils were organized. Minnesota's statewide press council followed in 1971 and the National News Council in 1973.

The National News Council lasted a decade and its files are probably larger than its impact on the nation's media. The Minnesota News Council is the sole survivor of about a dozen state and local news councils. All of the news councils invited both media and nonmedia people to examine complaints about media contents and assess media effectiveness. They were well-intended but they didn't succeed, in part because they were voluntary organizations that didn't have clearly defined roles and responsibilities. In addition, they got little support, attention, or cooperation from the mass media, which they were supposed to criticize or defend from unwarranted complaints, or from the general public.

The National News Council was practically unknown nationally when it ceased operations. It had been established to assess the nation's news media. Its deliberations were limited, however, to the wire services, the national news magazines, and network television news. Unlike its counterpart, the British Press Council, it could not afford to publish or broadcast information about its deliberations and, with few exceptions, the media were not interested in spending time and money to do this.

Special interest groups, however, many of which could afford to be represented by highly paid counselors, tried to make the National News Council a platform to argue their special causes by initiating complaints that they and their interests were inaccurately or inadequately covered in the media. Ironically, the council that had been established in 1973 to improve news media content and impact was in danger of becoming a platform for special interests when it died. It was increasingly approached by organizations that wanted public redress for perceived or claimed media wrongs.

■ TWO SIDES TO MANIPULATION

The potential for media manipulation is immense. Innumerable individuals and organizations want the mass media to support their causes, to give them legitimacy in their communities and beyond. The ethical dimensions include how thoroughly the media evaluate what they are offered and what they choose to do with it. If media people sanctimoniously insist that they alone have good judgment and professional skills, they risk subverting the mission of the media organizations that pay their wages. They need to evaluate carefully the news and information supplied to them, and to identify contributions that might confuse or enlighten their audiences just as they identify news and analysis supplied by their own staffs. They need not rewrite news releases that are of high quality, but they should not add staff bylines to them.

Media staff can be as manipulative as outside organizations. They can just as easily open the gates to causes they espouse as they can close them to others. An obvious example is a publisher who supports local businesses, especially advertisers, and who commands space for stories about them. Less obvious but increasing are the influx of new activists—reporters, for example, who promote social causes but maintain that they are simply but effectively reporting the news. As mentioned briefly in Chapter 4, the late Jeffrey Schmalz was an exceptionally talented reporter for *The New York Times*. His articles about HIV, AIDS, and the gay community, and especially about his experiences with all three (which were identified in the articles), were painfully insightful. But were they manipulations of the media? Did he use his experience and his status as a *Times* reporter to manipulate the coverage of HIV, AIDS, and the gay community? Did the readership benefit? These are difficult ethical questions that must be examined.

The entertainment media are not immune from pressures—from insiders and outsiders alike—to support special causes. Talk shows, soap operas, comedies, and prime time blockbuster dramas all need current, stimulating, even controversial content, in great quantity, to get and sustain audiences. Entertainment media gatekeepers are no less immune from the "pressure game" than journalists are. They too must evaluate their own motives as well as the motives of the people and organizations that seek their attention. They must evaluate the contents of the information and ideas being promoted—for truthfulness, for appropriateness to the media audiences, and for value to the medium itself.

■ GORDON: The mass media should ignore material submitted by sources who want to manipulate their content.

Although it is part of the conventional wisdom that reporters need both news releases and public relations practitioners to help them do their job, this idea is increasingly a dangerous oversimplification. In practice, it has become extremely difficult for journalists and special interest groups to maintain a healthy symbiotic relationship.

Technology and human ingenuity have combined to produce a situation where it is far more beneficial for society if journalists can find ways to do their own work rather than relying on people with their own axes to grind regarding the information that reaches the public. I believe that this approach will also benefit public relations practitioners, who will have to succeed on the basis of their overall professional skills rather than merely on how well they can manipulate various news personnel.

The advent of video news releases, on top of audio news releases, has made it too easy for broadcast journalists to air material furnished by sources who want to use the media to tell their own story their own way. The news media have been subject to this same problem for the decades that written news releases have existed but there, too, the ground rules are changing. Such developments as public relations wire services, which blend a traditional news source with a PR tool, increase the possibilities that lazy, careless, or penny-pinching news media can be easily manipulated. Internet technologies only increase these possibilities.

The would-be manipulators of the media are not necessarily bad people. They include business firms, attorneys, politicians, special interest and pressure groups of various kinds, and of course public relations practitioners representing many of these sources. Also in this category are cultural and civic groups (such as PTAs, garden clubs, the League of Women Voters, and the local choral society) plus educational institutions and other nonprofit organizations that need media attention to accomplish their worthy goals. In addition, the various levels of government have also developed huge publicity arms to get their own messages through the media to the public.

All of these groups are simply trying to use the American media system to get the attention of the public or to make sure their particular point of view on an issue or a story receives at least equal prominence with any others. As Christopher Lasch (1990) has noted, they are succeeding and that success blurs the line between information and publicity:

> Increasingly information is generated by those who wish to promote something or someone—a product, a cause, a political candidate or officeholder—without arguing their case on its merits or explicitly advertising it as self-interested material either. Much of the press, in its eagerness to inform the public, has become a conduit for the equivalent of junk mail. (p. 10)

When the news media become overly reliant on such sources, two unfortunate results may occur. First, news accounts can become weighted too heavily toward the positions of sources with their own agendas and thus become slanted. A second result, which isn't always obvious, is that the information and points of view provided by the various would-be media manipulators can crowd out information and points of view from people and groups who lack the money, skill, or status to make their voices heard.

Nearly three decades ago, Tom Wicker of *The New York Times* noted the tendency of reporters to rely too heavily on sources representing established institutions (Wicker, 1971). Such institutional news sources usually have well-developed public relations arms and make full use of a wide range of techniques to influence what eventually appears in the news media.

This tendency puts people without access to institutionalized public relations efforts at a huge disadvantage when it comes to getting their ideas or concerns into the media. This is particularly true if such individuals are criticizing established institutions, whose PR people can command much greater media attention in response. Wicker suggested that some counterbalancing approach would improve the quality of American journalism by providing a wider range of sources. One way to move toward Wicker's goal would be for news media workers to ignore the output of the PR efforts, even those in the service of groups or causes that we all might agree are worthy.

It can be argued, as Carol Reuss has done, that journalists should use news releases and other materials furnished by interested sources, but that in doing so they must apply their own standards and ground rules. However, at the very least this appears to require that written news releases should be used only as a starting point for a story rather than presented as a finished product, with little or no change. It would also seem to mandate going beyond Reuss's admonition that journalists should never take credit for material run verbatim from news releases. Rather, if material from an audio or video press release is used at all, it should be clearly labeled as such, as should printed material that draws heavily on news releases.

This approach, even with the clear labeling beyond Reuss's suggestions, might be fine in the abstract, but it simply isn't working. Even if news releases are carefully evaluated for newsworthiness, bias, and the other criteria Reuss noted, there is great danger that people or groups with the resources to put out well-crafted releases will succeed in buying an improved opportunity to get their point of view past the media gatekeepers.

Beyond this concern is the fact that, in too many small news operations, there is little independent evaluation of what comes in from the would-be media manipulators. If there is space or air time to be filled, and if the news release is smoothly done, it all too often is put into the paper or onto the airwaves unedited. With the advent of audio and video news releases, this has become even more of a danger. This approach reduces the significant costs of producing on-air news stories or writing them for the paper and may well enhance media bottom-line profits. But although this practice may serve the media's economic needs, it can run roughshod over ethical concerns.

Some studies have indicated that, even in major metropolitan markets, the availability of video footage and how well it's packaged have a definite impact on news directors' and producers' decisions to air them. One study examined nearly 400 items, such as news releases and meeting notices, and concluded in part that the ease and efficiency with which information could be gathered, along with a station's resource constraints, were among the strongest influences on whether a particular story would be considered for broadcast. Other important factors included a balancing of the story's visual impact with its importance (Berkowitz, 1990).

All this can lead to a violation of virtually every major perspective on ethical issues involving the news media. Both of Kant's categorical imperatives (acting on a maxim that you would like to see as a universal law, and not "using" people in order to achieve your ends) are ignored when media manipulators succeed in getting their self-serving messages to the public without appropriate scrutiny from the usual gatekeepers. The utilitarian ideal of the greatest good for the greatest number of people is in serious danger when the good of the manipulators is served at the expense of the public as a whole.

John Rawls's concern for protecting a situation's most vulnerable participants fares no better in such circumstances. Even Aristotle's Golden Mean approach is in danger if the manipulators become better at presenting their messages than media people are at screening and evaluating them, as—arguably—happens regularly in smaller (and some larger) news operations. This trend makes a travesty of the social responsibility ideal.

One observer has argued that the use of video news releases without clearly identifying their source breaches the unwritten "covenant between news producers and news audiences that the news will be independently gathered and produced" (Linn, 1992, p. 15). Indeed, one could make a similar argument against the widespread use of news releases in general, labeled or not. About the only ethical system that can be applied to the successes achieved by the media manipulators is Machiavelli's contention that any means are justified if they are needed to reach one's goal. That brand of ethics holds up only from the standpoint of the media manipulators. A recent example was the manipulation of information for publicity purposes by the family of six-year-old beauty pageant contestant JonBenet Ramsey—both before her murder, and to protect the family afterward.

■ FINDING A MIDDLE GROUND

All of this is not to argue that the news media should shun *all* contact with people and groups who are trying to get their point of view into print or on the air. Such an extreme approach would greatly handicap the media in trying to be fair to those actual or potential newsmakers, because their side of the story would not be available to the media or to their audiences. This, in itself, would run counter to the utilitarian perspective of providing the greatest good for the society as a whole.

I do not disagree with the desirable practice of news media inviting audience participation through news tips, editorial responses, letters to the editor, home videotapes, or whatever. That's a far different situation than granting almost automatic access to people or groups with specific causes or agendas to advance.

What I am arguing is more the avoidance of extremes, in favor of Aristotle's Golden Mean—that contacts with people or groups with their own issues to promote should be initiated only by the media. (Granted, this is a different use of the Aristotelian balance than the one hinted at by Carol Reuss in this chapter.) Journalists should solicit information or help or guidance only if *they* see this as necessary. This was the approach generally followed by I. F. Stone in his long and distinguished career as "a self-proclaimed 'radical reporter'" whose goal was to search out uncovered stories, and who often "berated the establishment press for its laziness and acquiescence" (Lule, 1993, p. 88).

> . . . Stone was wary of traditional conventions, such as press conferences, news releases, leaks, and interviews, that allowed sources to control information and forced reporters to rely on those in power. Such practices, for Stone, were ethically flawed as well as professionally unsound.
>
> . . . And, he said [even] interviews should be the culmination of research and analysis. Only after information was collected and research documented should reporters confront those in power. (pp. 90–91)

This kind of approach might help level the playing field, so that less affluent and less powerful sources have a more equal chance of having their points of view represented. Radical as it may seem, these reporting techniques offer one of the few chances to improve if not cure the present situation in which many well-written or slickly produced news releases receive prominent play without having to face the screen of news judgments or skeptical questions from reporters covering a story. Indeed, the gatekeeping study of TV news mentioned earlier found that the people making the news-gathering decisions "assumed that television news stories *should* be gathered by sifting through information provided by sources" (Berkowitz, 1991, p. 249). Such expectations destroy a great deal of the autonomy that observers such as Edmund Lambeth and John Merrill see as a crucial ingredient in news media ethics.

Manipulation problems are not limited to the news portions of the media. The growing specialty of getting brand-name products placed in highly visible parts of films or TV programs is something that deserves increased scrutiny—as part of truth-in-labeling, if nothing else—because the practice will probably be nearly impossible to stop (see Chapter 15-C)—although the tobacco companies did agree to stop paying to place their products in films or on television as part of the 1998 settlement of Minnesota's lawsuit against them ("Terms of the Settlement").

The Disney studio is one of the leading players in this game, featuring specific brands of products in its productions in return for fees paid for this exposure, and it has a great deal of company. By one count, more than 50 products were displayed in the movie *Total Recall*.

Although including a can of Coke or Pepsi as a prop may be perfectly natural to lend authenticity to a scene, it takes on less benign overtones when the display is conditioned on the payment of a fee or some bartered tradeoff. It raises even more ethical concerns if the display is enhanced beyond what's called for by the script because of that consideration. At the very least, a disclaimer should tell the movie and TV audiences when fees have been paid to ensure that certain products are displayed.

The practice of trying to manipulate the media also raises ethical issues for the people who practice this crafty art. Among those practitioners are lawyers who try to use the media to create more favorable contexts for their clients, or to advance their own reputations, or both. In 1993, the attorney for Amy Fisher (the so-called Long Island Lolita) said he would have no qualms about misleading the news media if it benefited his client. His comment, on a panel at a journalism and mass communication educators' convention, drew a sharp response from an Associated Press reporter who questioned whether the use of public relations in such high-profile cases might be just "a marketing tool for attorneys."

Public relations practitioners hired to put their clients in the best possible light also have to answer questions regarding how truthful, or even how forthcoming with the truth, they choose to be. They might also do well to have some guidelines in place as to whom they will accept as clients. During the 1991 Gulf War, for instance, the Hill & Knowlton public relations firm drew heavy criticism for taking on as a client a Kuwaiti group that some critics saw as just a front for the government of Kuwait, a charge denied strongly by Hill & Knowlton. Although there is no rule that American public relations practitioners cannot represent foreign governments or that they must agree with the positions of their clients, the industry—and society as a whole—might benefit if decisions about taking on clients were made in contexts with ethical as well as financial overtones.

Public relations practitioners also need to consider how far they will go on behalf of a client whose demands raise ethical concerns. A 1992 study reported that practitioners rated responsibility to themselves as a third priority, behind responsibilities to their clients or to the publics relevant to those clients—but ahead of responsibility to the public at large. This approach, the authors warned, could "result in personal and organizational mind sets that 'anything goes' . . . [which is] hardly the mark of a true professional" (Newsom et al., 1992, p. 7).

Let's return to what might be the appropriate relationship between the news media and political/government processes. Traditionally, the news media have been seen as having an adversarial relationship with politicians and the government. In theory, this is a healthy situation, with the media serving the public as watchdogs of the political and government processes. However, this can be carried to unhealthy extremes, as was the case in the early 1970s when the news media repeatedly and heatedly responded to criticism from then–Vice President Spiro Agnew. Neither side displayed much respect for the other.

In recent decades, the growth of the government's public relations apparatus (generally called, a bit euphemistically, its public information function) has led to new sets of problems and concerns. The government information apparatus now has the enhanced technological tools to get its messages to the news media more efficiently and effectively. In some instances it bypasses the traditional news media entirely in getting those messages to the public—for example, by using the Internet to make the text of proposed bills, or of speeches, available to anyone who is plugged in.

The U.S. House and Senate have steadily increased facilities for their members to transmit material to news media in their home areas, undoubtedly motivated heavily by incumbents' concern for their electoral strength. This trend includes the growing tendency to send video news releases by satellite, a technique used especially by incumbents from districts considered "marginal" rather than "safe." As networks and local stations reduced their bureaus and freelance coverage in Washington at the end of the 1980s, the increased availability of video news releases helped provide broadcast-quality material for local newscasts at greatly reduced costs, an option that was particularly attractive to stations in smaller markets (McKay, 1992). The ability to download video clips from Internet websites provides an even easier way of delivering such materials.

These developments tend to bypass traditional journalistic news values and move Washington news coverage "toward the politics of image and away from the politics of policy" (McKay, 1992, p. 15). Although this may benefit both congressional incumbents and news directors with tight budgets, I doubt that this sharing of the gatekeeping function benefits the public.

The entire political public relations industry has undergone dramatic transformations in recent years, using not only the various new technologies but also the new phenomenon of spin doctors. These people meet with the media after political campaign events such as the presidential debates and do their best to explain or even reinterpret their candidates' performances so they are perceived in the most favorable light by the media people reporting the event. It is easy to see how this practice can benefit the candidates; it is a lot harder to understand how it benefits the news media, much less the electorate. This is another example of media manipulation efforts that ought to be ignored by the news media—though, were that to happen, the spin doctors would make even greater use of talk shows, computer networks, and other channels that provide direct access to voters.

It is easy to see how [spin doctors] can benefit the candidates; it is a lot harder to understand how [they benefit] the news media, much less the electorate.

None of these developments lend themselves to easy answers. But it would be useful if media practitioners took the time to think a bit more about the ethical dimensions of these concerns before confronting them and being forced to retreat into a situational ethic for lack of any more structured approach.

■ SOME ETHICAL GUIDELINES

Which ethics, then, *should* guide news media practitioners in dealing with sources who would use the media primarily for their own ends? On the other side of the coin, what ethical standards are most appropriate for the people or groups who are trying to use the media to spread their messages and points of view?

Let's take the second question first; most public relations practitioners would profess a higher set of standards than the Machiavellian code of conduct. They would probably agree that outright lying and deception exceed the limits of acceptable conduct, and that certain amounts of respect for both the news media and the public are both pragmatic and ethically sound. Although they are almost certain to reject Kant's stricture against using people (both those in the media and the public more generally) to accomplish their ends, many PR people would argue that their craft is one that, when practiced properly, helps to provide needed information for the good of the overall society—almost a utilitarian approach, if by the back door.

On the other hand, a media practitioner looking for philosophical guidance might seek a middle path between outright acceptance of public relations materials and total rejection of them. This Aristotelian approach might be argued as the rationale for using selected PR offerings and handling them according to strict journalistic criteria (such as relevance, importance, and accuracy). However, as noted earlier, it can also be used as the foundation for another middle ground approach—namely, *not* accepting any material from would-be media manipulators of any stripe *unless* this material is something the journalist finds so useful or necessary as to justify requesting it.

The latter approach might also be grounded in the utilitarian concern for the greatest good. It could be based even more strongly on Rawls's ideal of safeguarding the weakest participants, applied here so as to protect members of the public from material that could easily manipulate their attitudes unduly or unfairly simply because it appears in the news media. Whichever of these three ethical theories is used, one can justify guidelines that call for disregarding material furnished by potential news sources who want to manipulate mass media content for their own purposes.

This whole argument gets more complex when we move beyond the realm of news releases and similar publicity activities, to confront the question of "media events"—activities planned and designed to attract media attention and get exposure for the sponsoring individual or group. Daniel Boorstin (1961) referred to them nearly four decades ago as pseudo-events and argued that such developments create a kind of artificial reality that is often reported to the public as reality.

Such pseudo-events or media events range from news conferences and press previews to demonstrations and civil disobedience to political party conventions. Even such events as the taking of prison hostages or the hijacking of airplanes have on some occasions been aimed at securing media exposure in order to air demands that the perpetrators thought were not reaching the general public. On a different level, most events during the week preceding the Super Bowl are designed in large part to attract media coverage and thereby focus the country's attention on the upcoming football game, which itself has become a kind of pseudo-event. This game, and its half-time show, have become a marvelous vehicle both for broadcasters to sell the most expensive advertising spots and for advertisers to buy those spots because they provide access to an extremely large and desirable market.

Even an event such as the president's annual State of the Union address, whose constitutional origins far predate the concept of media events, has fallen into that category. It has become an occasion on which the president can almost automatically command media attention and through that attention get a message out to the voters.

The dilemma this poses for the news media is a difficult one indeed. Many of these staged events do have some legitimate news value; as Reuss pointed out, the public does need information about contemporary causes and changing ideologies, and there is certainly legitimate interest among sports fans as to which team prevails in the Super Bowl. Thus it is far more difficult for the news media to ignore these events than it is to disregard news releases or phone calls. But at the same time, the media must guard against being used or manipulated by individuals or groups that are particularly clever and creative in staging their events, and must exercise news judgment carefully in deciding whether coverage is warranted and, if so, how much.

The major television networks, for example, have cut back considerably in their coverage of the quadrennial conventions of the Democratic and Republican parties. They did so on the grounds that much of what takes place does, indeed, constitute pseudo-events that are not important enough to warrant the kind of gavel-to-gavel coverage that once was the norm.

A classic instance of using a pseudo-event to capture media attention took place more than two decades ago when the Illinois attorney general called an afternoon press conference to announce a new consumer protection initiative. As it happened, it was a heavy news day, and virtually none of the Chicago radio or TV stations covered the press conference. Undaunted, the attorney general scheduled another news conference for the following morning and (with the electronic media present this time) reread word-for-word the news release that had been ignored the previous afternoon.

If you had been the news director of one of the local stations, would you have covered the second press conference at all? Is this pseudo-event repetition of an earlier pseudo-event even worth reporting, when it added nothing to what had been available (and not covered) a day earlier? If you believe the second news conference is worth covering, is the best approach to report it straight? Should the previous day's news hole have been enlarged? Would it be appropriate to explain why the first conference wasn't covered? Or might it be better to report that the attorney general called a press conference to repeat a press release that had been largely ignored the previous day, thus providing a fuller context for your audience? Attractive as that last approach might seem in the abstract, most media people at the time apparently felt either that it ridiculed the attorney general too much or that it departed far too radically from the journalistic objectivity/fairness norm. The result was that most coverage of the second press conference never even mentioned that there had been an identical event the previous day.

I don't believe that the public was well-served by that kind of coverage, which seems to encourage increased efforts to manipulate the media. Audiences are better served if media gatekeepers take effective steps to ensure that they, rather than the would-be manipulators, are really in control of what goes through the media's gates.

■ MERRILL: Commentary

In a way, the whole subject of mass media ignoring or not ignoring material designed by outsiders to manipulate the media's content seems peripheral to media ethics. Is it not parallel to a more general professional question: Should the mass media ignore certain events and personalities that they deem to be not newsworthy? Perhaps this is a *professional* question rather than an ethical one. After all, manipulation of content is the name of the journalistic game, whether it is practiced by those within the media or by those outside the media. Selection and rejection of stories and information is at the very heart of journalism.

Perhaps this is a* professional *question rather than an ethical one.

Naturally, a conscientious medium will question the accuracy and honesty of news releases sent it. This is the natural or professional thing to do, just as the medium would question its own reportorial accuracy and honesty. One might say that this is an ethical question. In fact, that is what both Carol Reuss and David Gordon are saying. On the other hand, it might be considered merely a routine, professional question, hinging as it does on the basic journalistic tenet of accurate, unbiased reporting. At any rate, it is an important consideration for journalists and other media functionaries because the world is filled with people and institutions intent on using the media for their own ends.

Reuss notes that news releases cannot be accepted blindly. They can, of course, but the ethical operative verb might well be *should not* instead of *cannot.* However, if an editor decides to accept a news release blindly, without verifying its accuracy in all details, does this mean that the editor is *unethical?* Or might it not simply mean that he or she is careless, or lazy, or simply trusting? Are there *ethical* problems here, or merely *professional* ones?

The reader will note that we are getting into the areas of content selection, news judgment, and communication skills, and probably most media workers think of such factors as *extra*-ethical and related more to effective work habits than to morality. Nevertheless, even the most prosaic media practices do, indeed, have ethical overtones. A good case can be made that sloppy quoting of a source is both poor reporting and bad ethics—*poor reporting* because it distorts reality and *bad* ethics because it misleads the audience.

Reuss is correct in saying that editors who deny the value of a news release simply because it comes from outside are in a sense *censors* (she doesn't use that term) in that they keep from their audiences a full range of information and ideas. This *is* an ethical consideration, especially if the journalists claim they support full-disclosure reporting and content diversity. News management stemming from a personal bias, even when coming from a media functionary, is a form of purposeful informational control—and that would be, in the eyes of most journalists at least, unethical.

Gordon takes on a much more difficult task: He makes the case that media should ignore material submitted by outside sources. Of course, this position is modified by the important phrase "by sources who want to manipulate." What he is saying, essentially, is this: Media should not accept material from *manipulators* of the content. The problem here is that an editor does not know at the time he or she receives such material *whether the source wants to manipulate the content or not.*

The news release, to use an example, may be proffered in perfectly good faith, designed to impart balanced and truthful information about the institution or candidate and *not to manipulate.* How does the editor who receives such a release know the motivation of the sender? For example, if the editor assumes that all news releases are manipulative, then he or she will ignore the release. This may be the *safe* position for the editor to take, but as Reuss points out, it may keep important information away from the audience.

Gordon points out that today it is better for journalists to find ways "to do their own work rather than relying on people with their own axes to grind." It might be noted here that when a reporter, for example, interviews a public official or any other source (i.e., does his or her "own work"), this interviewed source may well manipulate the content (and the medium) just as much as a news release sent from that source's office would. Manipulators, in my view, are everywhere out there working in their own little ways to present themselves and their positions and institutions in the best possible light. Of course, a good journalist will try to reduce such manipulation to a minimum, but the idea that it can be eliminated would be hard to defend.

A very good point made by Gordon is that *media*, not outside groups, should initiate invitations for incoming information. Journalists, he says, should solicit material or assistance in developing a story *only if they see this as necessary*. This is an interesting suggestion, one that I have not seen before. It would definitely keep the media people in control of information, and would eliminate a plethora of unsolicited material that floods in from public relations offices.

Gordon also gets into the ethical problems faced by people who try to manipulate the media's content—lawyers being a prominent example. For the sake of this commentary and chapter, let us just say that lawyers, doctors, politicians, and others—even public relations agencies—must be responsible for their own ethical standards. Here we are concerned with *media ethics*, and therefore must not worry too much about the ethical practices outside the media. But you may insist that media ethics and ethics of media-related entities cannot be separated. Perhaps this is true, but it would be difficult for an editor to *know* how ethical a public relations release-writer is when the release comes to the newspaper. The decision is the editor's: accept or reject, or accept with follow-up, verification, and perhaps rewriting.

The adversarial relationship between the press and the government, according to Gordon, is a healthy situation—at least in theory. Gordon points out that such a relationship can be carried to extremes that are unhealthy, where both institutions are harmed and little respect is shown on either side. That's one truth about *adversaries:* They are opponents, they fight, they want to win; quite often, wide moral gulfs appear because of this inclination to succeed in combat. Government, says Gordon, increasingly uses various new technologies and techniques (such as spin doctors) to fight its battles in the public opinion arena.

The implication is that government information sent directly to the public, thus bypassing the traditional media, is at least to some degree unethical. And spin doctors are unethical. The media have their own spin doctors; the government has its own. What is the difference? Gordon might well answer: The media's are legitimate and ethical; the government's are illegitimate and unethical. But why so? Why are journalists any more legitimate and ethical than our elected representatives and their minions? If they are, there is no real evidence that this is so—at least that I have seen.

Gordon ends his argument with the contention that audiences are better served if media gatekeepers take effective steps to ensure that they, rather than the would-be manipulators, are really in control. Although there is something a little strange about one institution (the media) *being in control*, rather than the more democratic idea of a pluralism of controllers sharing power with the media establishment, Gordon's statement is given in the spirit of the First Amendment and the traditional American concept of an autonomous media system making independent content determinations.

This is a difficult topic, one with which the reader could wrestle for a long time. It gets us into the areas of power, power-sharing, journalistic purpose, conflict of interest, the public's right to know, the "right" of public access to the media, and the basic meaning of press freedom in our society. It is certainly a topic in which broadcasters, print media people, advertisers, movie producers, and public relations practitioners all have a vital and vested interest. It should stimulate considerable discussion.

REFERENCES

Berkowitz, Daniel A. (Winter 1990). "Refining the Gatekeeping Metaphor for Local Television News." *Journal of Broadcasting and Electronic Media* 34(1), pp. 55–68.

———. (Spring 1991). "Assessing Forces in Selection of Local Television News." *Journal of Broadcasting and Electronic Media* 35(2), pp. 245–251.

Boorstin, Daniel. (1961). *The Image: A Guide to Pseudo-Events in America*. New York: Harper and Row.

Commission on Freedom of the Press. (1947). *A Free and Responsible Press*. Chicago: University of Chicago Press.

Griffith, Thomas. (April 9, 1984). "Watchdog Without a Bite." *Time*, p. 103.

Lasch, Christopher. (Spring 1990). "Journalism, Publicity and the Lost Art of Argument." *Gannett Center Journal* 4(2), pp. 1–11.

Linn, Travis. (1992). "Video News Releases: Breaching the Covenant with Viewers." Paper presented at the annual convention of the Association for Education in Journalism and Mass Communication, Montreal, August 5–8.

Lule, Jack. (1993). "Radical Rules: I. F. Stone's Ethical Perspective." *Journal of Mass Media Ethics* 8(2), pp. 88–102.

McKay, Floyd J. (1992). "Filling the Gap: Congress Increases Its Video as TV News Cuts Budgets." Paper presented at the annual convention of the Association for Education in Journalism and Mass Communication, Montreal, August 5–8.

Newsom, Doug A., Shirley A. Ramsey, and Bob J. Carrell. (1992). "Chameleon Chasing II: A Replication." Paper presented at the annual convention of the Association for Education in Journalism and Mass Communication, Montreal, August 5–8.

Rowe, Chip. (April 1993). "Watchdog Watch." *American Journalism Review*, pp. 32–34.

"Terms of the Settlement." (May 9, 1998). Eau Claire (WI) *Leader-Telegram*, p. 1A.

Wicker, Tom. (May/June 1971). "The Greening of the Press." *Columbia Journalism Review*, pp. 7–12.

CHAPTER 6

ACCESSING
THE MEDIA
Information Equity Versus Apartheid

S ince information is power in our increasingly information-based society, some equality of access to it is crucial unless we are willing to settle for a society where some people or groups are disadvantaged because they can't obtain access. The risk is that society could become stratified on the basis of information available for people to use, as well as along economic, educational, racial, or other lines.

A number of observers of the media-society relationship have raised this issue recently. Concerns have ranged from general warnings about a possible "informational underclass" (McQuail, 1993) or "informational apartheid" (Representative Edward Markey, in a 1992 commencement address) to newspaper subscription drives that deliberately ignore poor rural areas and low-income city neighborhoods where the delivery risks and costs outweigh the possible subscriber and advertiser cash flow (Ghiglione, 1992).

Much of the recent discussion has focused on new information technologies—such as fiber-optic or satellite transmission systems that simultaneously carry TV signals, voice, and printed data, or digital networks that use other technologies—and whether such communication networks will be accessible to people who are disadvantaged physically, economically, linguistically, socially, or even educationally. Conceived most broadly, a huge proportion of the population does not have full access to the mass media, for a variety of reasons, and this group may grow as the information superhighway develops further.

The first question here might well be whether this is really a media *ethics* issue. After all, why should the purveyors of media products have any greater responsibility than the producers of other goods and services to ensure access to those products? The answer, of course, is that the media industries have First Amendment protection precisely because they fulfill a societal role that is different from that of other businesses. The media's role is taking on some added dimensions as new transmission and distribution systems emerge, but the inherent questions of ethics and responsibility are similar regardless of whether new or traditional channels are used for access to mass-mediated content. Our discussion here therefore focuses on both older and emerging forms of mass communication.

Everette Dennis put the issue succinctly when he noted the "reasons to be concerned about information-rich people versus information-poor people. Information is power and some information will no doubt be priced so high that it will be out of the reach of many people" (Dennis and Merrill, 1991, p. 75).

Eric Elbot, former director of communications for the National Center for Accessible Media in Boston, has noted that America has always stood for access—to education, politics, libraries, and (perhaps with the most roadblocks) the economy. With the advent of the information age, he suggested, the focus must shift to include access to information and entertainment available through the various new media channels.

The key issue seems to be not what must be accomplished but whose responsibility it is and how far this responsibility extends. David Gordon maintains that the mass media must make some special efforts to ensure that they continue to reach a truly mass audience and, in the process, bring the information age to all strata of the society. Carol Reuss responds that market forces and competition are sufficient safeguards to provide the access that's needed, and questions just how much access is really required.

■ GORDON: The mass media must guard against practices that isolate some groups in society from access to information they need.

The mass media not only have an ethical obligation to help ensure "information equity" throughout society, but also have some very practical reasons for doing so.

Some of those practical reasons are grounded in economics: If groups in society are deprived of access to information, the media lose potential customers and, therefore, potential targets for advertisers. Another reason is that as society becomes more aware of the importance of access to diverse sources of information, pressure is likely to build for government action to ensure this if the media themselves don't take steps to see that it happens.

But the most important reason for the media to be concerned about information equity is the utilitarian viewpoint that it is right for the society as well as for the media. The ethical consequences of information "apartheid" are simply too serious to be tolerated by the media or by the society they serve.

My concern is equity of access to information that the various gatekeepers have already put into the media conduits. News media access to the information needed to report fully on society is a related but separate concern, and Carol Reuss is correct in noting that it's also important. For me, however, the key issue is providing opportunities for access to information that has passed the scrutiny of various gatekeepers and has been made available to the public. This goal, in an age of increasing dependence on information, impresses me as a truly ethical concern, and one that demands attention.

American mass media have First Amendment protection so they can help create an informed citizenry that is capable of governing itself. But we can't expect a fully participatory democracy unless we aim for the ideal of allowing *all* citizens the opportunity to acquire information on a relatively equal footing. As information becomes more and more important in society, it becomes ever more crucial to ensure access to broad strata of that information.

Perhaps oversimplifying, an essential question emerges: Will our mass media remain *mass?* Or will we see a combination of economics, new media technologies, and even new niche marketing techniques reduce greatly—or even eliminate—the media's ability to serve society as a whole? Might those same factors curtail seriously the ability of many different people and groups at all levels of society—such as the 33 million or so Americans with visual or hearing impairments—to use media of their choice in obtaining information? At stake are the ability of citizens to participate fully in the American democracy and their ability to obtain information or entertainment that will increase both their satisfaction with such participation and their general quality of life.

What's really at issue here is the 20th- (and 21st-) century version of the lesser-known part of one of Thomas Jefferson's statements. This is the second sentence in his well-known comment about newspapers and government, the part that is almost never included when newspaper folk quote Jefferson on the importance of their calling:

> The basis of our government being the opinion of the people, the very first object should be to keep that right; and were it left to me to decide whether we should have a government without newspapers or newspapers without a government, I should not hesitate a moment to prefer the latter. But I should mean that every man should receive those papers & be capable of reading them. (Jefferson, [1787] 1984, p. 880)

Jefferson's second sentence is really the crux of a key issue the mass media face today in a democratic society: the need to ensure that everyone who is capable (or potentially capable) of understanding the information transmitted by the various mass media has an opportunity to connect to media distribution systems and receive that information. It is an ethical necessity to expand the marketplace of ideas into a marketplace of both ideas *and* information, with assurances that everyone—including the physically disabled and those low on the economic scale—will have the opportunity to participate in that marketplace and to share in the benefits of access to diverse kinds of information services.

■ THE PROBLEM OF LESS AFFLUENT AUDIENCES

Magazines, newspapers, radio, and television (both cable and over-the-air broadcasters) have all aimed at least some of their content at specialized audiences, often at more affluent segments of the mass audience because that's what appeals to advertisers. This is just good business sense, rooted in the American free enterprise system. With the dependence of the American media system on advertising revenues, the media have little choice but to sell the audiences that advertisers want to buy.

But this approach can also leave less affluent segments of society cut off from considerable amounts of entertainment, news, and advertising that would interest them. A 1991 situation illustrates such "media redlining," a term derived from the practice by some lending institutions of literally drawing on a map a red line around low income areas—most often occupied predominantly by members of minority groups—where they refused to make mortgage loans. *The Courier–Journal* in Louisville, Kentucky, allowed home sellers to run *and pay for* their real estate ads *only* in editions going to more affluent circulation zones, without the cost of serving the poorer and predominantly minority circulation areas (Barr, 1991).

This practice in Louisville kept lower-income, typically minority residents from knowing about homes for sale in the more affluent part of the newspaper's circulation area unless they made special efforts to obtain a copy of the paper zoned for areas other than their own. This particular situation was eventually resolved by the paper's offer to dump press overruns of two zoned inserts at convenience stores in the less affluent neighborhoods. The paper dealt with the ethical issue—by providing the inserts—in part because of its commitment to its community, although legally it may not have been required to do so.

Related problems involving the print or broadcast media include the pricing of various tiers of cable TV service beyond the means of some economic groups or the removal of newspaper sales racks from areas where they are repeatedly vandalized. Reuss deals with only half of the problem in explaining why newspapers sell fewer copies in high-crime areas—it's not just concern for safety of newspaper carriers, but also the fact that readers in less-affluent areas are far less important to most advertisers than are more upscale readers.

There has been a recent and increasing trend toward putting concerts and sports events on premium cable channels or on a pay-per-view basis. What do we lose if this trend accelerates, to the point where events of major societal import (such as the presidential debates) are available only on pay-per-view to the people who can afford them?

Local cable TV operators have also been criticized for rushing to wire more affluent neighborhoods while dragging their feet in providing service to lower-income areas, where they are less likely to sell their add-on packages. Some magazines have adopted a strategy of selectivity in soliciting subscriptions, preferring in some cases to exclude lower-income zip codes from their mailings in order to concentrate on areas with family income levels that appeal more to their advertisers. *Life* magazine, in its last throes as a weekly, publicly decided not to accept subscriptions from counties with low average income. These market-driven forces are all perfectly logical from an economic perspective, but they pose a serious ethical question about our willingness to cut off certain segments of society from access to various *supposedly mass* media channels.

[W]hose responsibility is it to see that information apartheid doesn't subvert the democratic goal of an informed citizenry?

Among the new information technology issues is one posed by the electronic forum that developed shortly before the 1992 presidential election. This Internet forum allowed citizens with computer access to obtain information on the presidential race, pose direct questions to campaign staff, and debate the issues among themselves, all free of intermediaries. The question of information equity should not have been overlooked under these circumstances.

> "There is an issue of information rights that we have got to drum home," said John Mallery, a Ph.D. candidate in international relations and machine learning who is chief engineer of the service. "The rich and powerful are going to have this stuff. The question is whether the average person is going to get it, and, if so, how?" (Radin, 1992, p. 26)

If these concerns are valid, what, if anything, might be done to provide broad access? And, most important, whose responsibility is it to see that information apartheid doesn't subvert the democratic goal of an informed citizenry? The key question may be who should pay for the added costs of producing greater social benefits (i.e., spreading those benefits to the greatest number of people) by preventing or at least reducing inequities of informational access.

Only five possible groups can take separate or combined responsibility for ensuring information equity in the emerging information society—media consumers, the nonprofit sector, the government, advertisers, and the media themselves. Because income (economic capability) varies widely among media consumers, it is useless to rely on the economic marketplace to cure inequities that stem originally from this economic disparity. The nonprofit sector has little to do today with traditional mass media, although historically foundations, universities, churches, and other groups have been active in supporting public broadcasting. Many are now promoting equitable availability of computers and the Internet through such institutions as libraries and schools, an approach reminiscent of Andrew Carnegie's funding of hundreds of public libraries.

Relying more heavily on government financing of some parts of the mass media system carries with it risks of increased government control, not to mention even more unbalanced budgets. Government support and control have been rare under the American constitutional and economic systems, with the exception of some indirect support to National Public Radio and television's Public Broadcasting System, postal and legal advertising subsidies, and the government's own publications and electronic output.

Advertisers are not likely to contribute voluntarily to any approach that forces them to help pay for getting their messages to people they don't really care about reaching. In the absence of some sort of "carrot" for the advertisers, extracting such financial support may be both politically and constitutionally difficult.

The last option is to make the media themselves responsible for achieving information equity, perhaps as part of what Theodore Glasser (1986) has called the affirmative responsibilities imposed, as a matter of ethics if not law, by the First Amendment. Here, too, constitutional issues must be dealt with, unless the mass media agree that they have a responsibility to their community—or to society—to provide more equal opportunity for information access.

■ MASS MEDIA RESPONSIBILITIES

Given both the need for equity of access and the lack of acceptable alternatives, there seems to be no viable alternative to the mass media taking on this responsibility as fully as is necessary. Such an ethical obligation clearly stems from both the utilitarian concern for providing the greatest benefit for the greatest number of people and John Rawls's emphasis on protecting the most vulnerable members of the community. It can also be argued cogently that if social responsibility means anything at all, it means finding a way to avoid creating a clearly defined group of second-class citizens in an information society.

Working out access in practice remains a difficult question, but many possibilities exist. Newspapers might, for example, *give* merchants advertising that runs in all editions, charge them only for zoned ads (if that's what they want), and write off the lost revenue to the paper's social responsibility to make information available to all readers regardless of their ability to pay. Alternatively, the Louisville approach regarding real estate ad sections might be expanded to include some or all advertising inserts.

Cable television operators might agree (or be persuaded by government) to provide at least minimal access to information sources at a rate that most people can afford. This might include a very inexpensive basic package that includes all local TV stations plus public access channels and such information staples as CNN and C-SPAN.

Emerging media and new information technologies may provide a better opportunity than do existing mass media operations to establish new practices and—more important—public policies that foster rather than discourage information equity. If economic barriers to user access can be overcome, intelligent communication networks or other new means of communication could give the public a great deal of control over information dissemination.

This, in turn, would help overcome increasing selectivity by information sources in targeting their desired audience. For example, the audience—regardless of economic status—would be given an *opportunity* for access to ads even about goods that conventional wisdom says are beyond the interest or economic reach of many people. And the mass media system would provide real *opportunities* for all strata of the mass audience to obtain information on topics that conventional wisdom says are of interest only to certain elites.

One attempt to provide such an equality of informational opportunity was suggested by an Alabama state task force concerned with the implementation and potential impact of intelligent communication networks. With some input from groups that were marginalized—because of such factors as physical disabilities, low income, or lack of education—it recommended the establishment of public access points in libraries and shopping malls that would be available to everyone (Jennings Bryant, chair of the Alabama Information Age Task Force, telephone interview, October 21, 1992).

The task force report zeroed in on some specific access problems and suggested a rationale of equity as the basis for dealing with them:

> [A] philosophy of social equity and social responsibility should guide planning for the network. Special efforts should be made to guarantee extended universal information service . . . to the poor, the disabled, and minorities. (Alabama Information Age Task Force, 1991, pp. 5–6)

The report also made some specific recommendations for implementing that philosophy, which in essence embraces the utilitarian approach. These include the possibility of rate structures that take ability to pay into account, the public access points mentioned above, and subsidized access to the network for the disabled, funded by the state and federal governments, private industry, and the disabled community. Although it is still too soon to tell whether this approach has any chance of successful implementation, the involvement of several major information industry players in the process leaves the door open for its concerns to be discussed further.

Other states have also moved ahead with similar efforts, with Maryland as one of the leaders. By 1996, a system was in place there to provide statewide citizen access to the Internet through the library system, on a walk-in basis or for the price of a local telephone call.

The Alabama task force recommendations could be adapted to more traditional mass media, in such ways as newspapers making their electronic news libraries more accessible to the general public than has traditionally been the practice. Making that access free would reduce a potential source of added income for the papers, but would add little or nothing to existing costs of operation. In light of newspapers' continuing explorations of new ways to relate to and serve their communities (such as the Gannett 2000 project and Knight Ridder's 25-43 Project)—efforts that relate fundamentally to the need to stem, if not reverse, the persistent decline in newspaper readership—the opportunity seems well worth seizing.

The alternative—a multitier information economy, with the information-rich media (print and electronic) costing considerably more than those in the lower tiers—is something that should frighten us both practically and ethically. As a society, and as media practitioners, we must be concerned that economics could deprive some citizens of the opportunity to obtain various types of information. (The question of equality of access to entertainment is a related issue, but one that falls outside the bounds of this discussion.)

The increasing potential for differential access to information in a society that is increasingly information-oriented is one that must be addressed by the media themselves with some assistance from government, particularly in regard to the formation of policies to regulate new information technologies. The government might also help by creating economic incentives for the existing, traditional mass media to address this growing problem.

But the basic responsibility must remain with the media, derived from the freedoms conferred by the First Amendment. To let government shoulder this burden would raise the possibility for further government intrusion into areas where the media should have the choice of responsible actions. Failing to deal at all with the information equity gap would be an ethical abdication, and equally unacceptable.

The information gap clearly runs counter to the ideal of an informed citizenry exercising control over its society. If the media are to serve the mass society, they bear a responsibility for trying to reduce the gap—a step that is also likely to lead to the development of more consumers for the mass media and their advertisers.

Although it will not be easy to close this gap significantly within the existing media structure, it may be less difficult in regard to new media technologies if we focus *now* on these concerns. Some new and innovative expectations may well be realistic where new media and media technologies—or use patterns—are concerned, perhaps especially for younger readers who may be attracted to the print media through easily available newspaper Websites. A little creative thought should enable us to adapt some of those innovative approaches to new developments in the existing media as well.

In its references to making intelligent communication network services available and affordable to disabled citizens in Alabama, the state task force summed up the crux of the larger issue for society as a whole. Such availability, the task force said, would allow all citizens to play more active and independent roles in both the social and commercial aspects of the information age society (Alabama Information Age Task Force, 1991, pp. 8–9). That goal is one that the mass media must work actively to implement, as one of the key players in and beneficiaries from an information age society.

■ REUSS: Market forces are sufficient safeguards against any groups in society being deprived of access to necessary information.

The mass media are important participants in society. According to Hiebert, Ungurait, and Bohn (1991, p. 565), they are "the central nervous system of the United States, the critical information chain that vibrates without pause." The media help to keep people informed and entertained, help shape opinions about all sorts of issues, survey the environment, transmit culture, and help the economy by promoting goods and services. They help educate and socialize diverse populations. But the mass media are not a direct conduit to social unity, even though many of them look or sound alike and cover the same topics and sources.

At the outset, understand that there are two definitions of media access. One is the ability of any individual or group to receive the media. The second is the ability of any individual or group to have its story told by the mass media.

Some people give more credit to the media than the media can possibly deserve, and more responsibilities than they can possibly fulfill, when they propose that both kinds of access to the media are moral rights, and that any limit on access is unethical. It may be unwise for a news or entertainment medium to disregard an individual's or a group's desire for media and for media attention, but it is not unethical. These people err when they interpret literally Thomas Jefferson's words, "were it left to me to decide whether we should have a government without newspapers or newspapers without a government, I should not hesitate . . . to prefer the latter. But I should mean that every man should receive those papers & be capable of reading them" (Jefferson [1787] 1984, p. 88).

David Gordon refers to Jefferson when he argues that the mass media have an ethical obligation to ensure information equity. The mass media are but one part of the communications equation, so they are not solely responsible for keeping the public informed, and no single mass medium can presume to have that kind of obligation.

At the end of the equation are media audiences, both actual and potential, who also bear responsibility as discerning information seekers. Putting ethical responsibility for access to media coverage on one erroneously omits the other.

Research indicates that people make decisions based on information from many sources and that the media have varied and limited effects on individuals and groups (Lowery and DeFleur, 1988). This does not mean that individuals should be passive about the mass media, nor that the mass media can be passive and not seek public acceptance.

■ ACCESS AND AUDIENCE

The mass media are not ethically responsible for public access but they need to be concerned about it—and many are. Special-interest media cater to specific audiences and audience interests, some of which are on the fringe of social acceptability. They live by giving voice to the interests of specific groups. That is the service they render, and like any other mass medium, when they cease serving their audiences they die, sometimes leaving an intellectual or informational void that the general interest media cannot fill.

The general interest media, particularly the newspapers and broadcasters that serve the masses, have both economic and social reasons to be concerned about reaching a broad spectrum of the population. Large audiences generate operating funds and profits for the media, and they also influence social action and policies about everything from the arts to zoning. These media need to cover the interests of huge audiences but they cannot possibly cover every topic or include every person or group that wants media attention. They must be concerned about the ethics of their decisions about who or what should get media attention, and they must also be pragmatic. For instance, newspapers don't sell many papers in high-crime neighborhoods, and carriers often are afraid to deliver there; consequently, newspapers can be accused of selectively denying access to news and information to residents of those neighborhoods. However, broadcast programs are available even in high-risk neighborhoods, so the people in them are not without news, information, and entertainment.

The variety of mass media available to the public helps guard against what Gordon fears: information apartheid. The marketplace has many, many sources. The challenges are to find ways to entice the public to pay attention to more than one information source and to more than sensational topics.

Access to media is desirable, but it is not as important as media access to information and their perseverance in disseminating even information that some of the public doesn't want to hear about. Routine beat reporting, for example, uncovered the tip of the Watergate iceberg. Persistent, skillful reporting unraveled the complex set of situations connected with the Watergate burglary and led eventually to the resignation of President Richard M. Nixon and the prosecution of a number of his closest aides. When doors were closed to reporters working on the story, when access was denied, reporters from *The Washington Post* did not quit, nor did their counterparts at other media.

The Watergate coverage is a good example of the trickle-down effect of media coverage of a news event. What started out as prosaic coverage of an apparent break-in at the Democratic headquarters in the Watergate complex grew to a flood of information that Congress and the American public could not ignore.

The flip side to media access is access to media—in its negative aspect, what Gordon describes as media red-lining or avoiding designated neighborhoods. Too many U.S. cities have paid the price of the media not covering low-income neighborhoods and not describing the frustrations of the poor. I agree with Gordon that the media paint an incomplete, even false, picture when they ignore less affluent neighborhoods instead of forcing civic attention on such conditions.

Access to media is desirable, but it is not as important as media access to information. . . .

For too many years, the mass media were WM—white males owned and staffed the media, and contents were based on their experiences and their perceptions of the world. This has changed in major cities and is beginning to change in other areas; the experiences and insights of the integrated staffs are opening opportunities to gain access to ideas as well as news sources that they ignored in the past.

The opposite of access is totalitarianism, whether by governments that try to control information or news reporters, editors, or producers who think that their viewpoints are *the* viewpoint, and who want to impose that viewpoint on everyone else. This is the manifestation of arrogance that blocks convenient access to information, and it is a form of deception that should not occur in mass media.

■ MARKETPLACE POLARITY

In the end, we have to guard against isolation. Media audiences have to know how to use the media of communication and how to separate the chaff from the wheat of those who communicate. The social marketplaces and the intellectual marketplaces must function as much as the communication marketplaces.

Access is polar. At one side is the concern that everyone have access to the mass media, which offer information, interpretation, and entertainment and help shape public opinions that shape society. At the other pole is concern that the mass media have access to the sources and contents they need in order to present a full array of topics and information about and to a wide range of society's strata.

The media marketplace is polar too (perhaps tripolar if sources are considered), and it is dynamic, ever changing. The two poles with which we are concerned are the media and the public, which constantly test one another. They benefit one another and society when established practices are challenged by new ideas and new problems.

Marketplace polarity is complicated by the concern, admittedly not a universal concern, that not everyone has the ability to choose media or media offerings wisely for their own best interests or the interests of society. Thus, there are those within the free marketplace who are concerned that some citizens, particularly children and those who could bring harm on themselves and others, should not have unlimited access to mass media offerings.

One marketplace response to children's access to "adult" media is Johnny telling Tommy, "Let's go over to your house to watch TV. Your Mom and Dad let you watch everything." Their marketplace is free but selective, and wrapped in deceit. Another marketplace response is people forcefully telling the media what they want and don't want their children to be exposed to (see Chapter 10).

Advertisers are sensitive about the environments in which their advertisements run. When big advertisers refuse to buy time during programs that they believe will offend important audiences, they may be limiting public access to media contents. Public pressure and government action banned tobacco advertising on television and required that manufacturers print health warnings on packages of tobacco and alcohol products. Public pressure also supports the idea of requiring disclaimers before the broadcast of "adult" programs and age-related classification labels before all non-news programs.

The general interest media need alternative sources of information, including alternative media—city and regional magazines, "minority" newspapers and newsletters, low-power community radio stations that broadcast throughout apartment complexes and neighborhoods (some of which stretch the patience of broadcast regulators because they are not licensed and they ignore technical regulations intended to avoid interference with other signals), and community access programs on cable systems—as much as the audiences of these media do. Traditional news and information media that ignore the messages disseminated by alternative media risk being uninformed about significant problems their communities face and achievements their communities should know about. They may not be able to give comparable space and time to information from alternative and mainstream sources, but the media need to be informed and to keep their audiences informed about what is happening in less well-reported neighborhoods and organizations. In short, a balanced utilitarian approach.

The message thus far is that there must be many news and entertainment channels, and there are. No one medium or channel, by itself, can gather or disseminate all the news and information that is available. Any that say they cover "everything" are naïve or just plain wrong. This becomes an ethical question only when mass media purport to be inclusive but deliberately omit or skew their contents and coverage. This rarely happens.

Members of the public, whether they regularly read news publications or listen to radio or watch television, have responsibilities, too. Media literacy is more than the ability to read and write. It also includes the ability to recognize that nonverbal communications are part of the contemporary mass media. It includes the ability to evaluate article placement and display in print media, to "read" the posture, diction, story introductions, soundbites, and visuals that are incorporated in television news and information programs. It includes the ability to distinguish facts from generalizations, information from misinformation. It includes the ability to choose wisely among causes presented, among commentators, and even among media. It includes willingness to criticize the media and to support media that serve audiences and society well, even morally and financially supporting so-called alternative media.

Discussions about media access will continue as long as individuals and groups believe that they are entitled to the media and to media coverage, and that the mass media are the preeminent channels of communication. In a free society, market forces will continue to safeguard against any individuals or groups being deprived of access to necessary information and desired entertainment—except, of course, when sponsors cancel popular programs because they don't reach the desired demographic groups. They might not have easy access to every desired mass medium but that does not indicate that individuals and groups have no means of social communication.

■ MERRILL: Commentary

In the discussions above, the contending authors have pitched into what is certainly an interesting and important topic: inequalities among various audience segments. Most of us, I'm sure, would agree—at least at first glance—with David Gordon's rather vague concept that the mass media should avoid practices that isolate certain groups in society from access to information. But once that is said, and we consider the statement more closely, the real problem arises. Just what are such practices and how do we avoid them? And should each medium embrace such a stance for inclusion of all segments of the audience, or is it assumed that the total media system, in its corporate pluralism, will provide access to a wide assortment of information?

Information equity is a fine-sounding term. Gordon says that the mass media have an ethical obligation to help ensure information equity. But in addition to being semantically fuzzy, it perhaps is an impossible goal. Media have enough trouble just trying to be thorough, accurate, and meaningful in their information; Gordon would have them also worry about making sure that this information reaches everyone. Should all people be equal in their access to information (*all* information? *some* information?)—or does it mean that various types of information shall get equal exposure to audiences (some audiences? all audiences?)?

Gordon says that we cannot have a fully participatory democracy until all citizens can acquire information on a relatively equal basis. Again the haunting questions:

What kind of information is necessary? How much information is enough? How can all citizens process this information equally? The questions go on and on. What about the ethics of all this? An ethical medium is one that does *what* in respect to reaching all citizens? And, to be ethical, *what kinds of information* must it provide these citizens?

Presumably some media will provide some individuals in some audience segments with some types of messages necessary (for a participatory democracy, whatever that might mean exactly). Carol Reuss makes a point well in her argument: There is, indeed, a wide assortment of media providing many perspectives, but do we assume that *each citizen* will have exposure to all these specialized or segmented bits of necessary information? No. Such an assumption is absurd.

What we are left with is the fact that many (actually most) of the American people are exposed to very little of what somebody would consider essential information for intelligent popular governance. Even if all Americans had access to all broadcast programming and to all newspapers and magazines, at least three-fourths of them probably would not avail themselves of even the obviously important information they contain. They either could not read the print media (because of some state of illiteracy) or could not find or appreciate high-quality programs on radio and TV. And, if they did get the "appropriate" information, would they vote or otherwise participate in government?

Could it be that the responsibility for access to media messages lies with the public, not with the media?

Could it be that the responsibility for access to media messages lies with the *public*, not with the media? Assuming there is, indeed, inequity in the way our media reach various audiences, could it possibly be that individuals and social segments slighted in the process bear at least some responsibility for their underrepresentation? The disputants in this chapter do not pay enough attention to audience responsibility. Actually, I am not trying to place any kind of obligation on the public; I am simply saying that if portions of this public desire more access, then they need to get busy trying to get it. It is not enough to sit back and expect the media, government, or somebody else to see that they are supplied with increased amounts of information.

How can there be safeguards in our society to ensure that everyone has the opportunity to participate in the marketplace of ideas and information? Would it mean that government should provide subscriptions to newspapers and magazines for all citizens? It is true that the less-affluent segments of society have less chance to access news. But there are libraries, usually well-stocked with a wide variety of reading material. Most citizens simply don't wish to be informed about critical issues. Perhaps this is some kind of ethical problem for *the citizens*, rather than the media.

Then we have the new information technology—increasingly available in public libraries—such as computer-linked forums, which on occasion allow citizens to obtain information on events such as a presidential race. The users would be able to question and debate issues among themselves. All right. But again we have the question of access, of most people not having the hardware for such participation. Again we have the problem of the affluent and the poor—the inequity of possibility.

So many nonmedia factors enter into a discussion such as this that the sense of frustration is almost overpowering. For example, if we could overcome the inequity of media availability (which we can't), we would still be confronted by the lack of interest on the part of vast segments of the population. And even if we could get everyone interested in important information "for democracy," we would still be confronted by the illiteracy problem. In the general public, we would still have the problem of the inequality of education. Some people are highly educated, others marginally educated, and others have little or no formal education. Because we know that financial status is positively related to education, it is little wonder that the typical uneducated person is at a disadvantage when it comes to affording the technology for receiving media messages.

The option most congenial to Gordon for providing information equity is that the media themselves be the providers. He mentions Theodore Glasser and his idea that the media have affirmative responsibilities imposed by the First Amendment. This seems to be a rather strange concept of equal opportunity brought into the communications area. I find no affirmative responsibilities imposed on the media by the First Amendment. In fact, the thrust of the First Amendment is that the press be left free to determine its own responsibilities. Certainly none is imposed in the Bill of Rights.

Of course, today such an idea goes against the whole thrust of the new communitarianism (discussed in the Overview). Sociologists such as Amitai Etzioni, communications scholars such as Clifford Christians and Ted Glasser, and political leaders such as President Clinton have emphasized the *nonautonomous person*, the socialized functionary loaded down with responsibilities and guilt. At risk are the "old dinosaurs" of classical liberalism—the libertarians and the individualists (the "new eccentrics")—who are reluctant to offer up their selves on the altar of community solidarity and collective values. *Information equity*—the subject of controversy for this chapter—is a term congenial with this communitarian spirit; it implies a responsibility on the government or the media, or both. At the same time, it implies a *right* of the people to have equal access to information. I certainly won't try to answer the question as to the source of such a questionable "right" here, but it might be well for media students to consider it.

Just what could the media themselves do to ensure information equity? Well, they could give away their services. Then *everybody* could have equal access to the information. Gordon gives some suggestions in his arguments; although these are quite interesting (especially the experiment in Alabama), they would still fall far short of providing all citizens with equal information. Emerging media and new technologies are mentioned as possible solutions to this problem. But it seems that here we are simply pushing the problem into another area—the availability of technology for citizens. Who will supply the technology to the poor? The media themselves? The government (taxpayers)? Wealthy philanthropists? Foundations?

It seems that perhaps we are worrying too much about the quantity of information that gets to the American citizen and about the availability of the technology that gets the information there. Perhaps we need to put more emphasis on the *quality* and the kind of information that media supply—on the social benefits of such information for those who receive it. Maybe it counts more to get the right kind of information to interested people (the opinion leaders and educated disseminators) than to try to spoon-feed *everybody* with a plethora of mainly entertainment-oriented material. Neil Postman, in his excellent *Amusing Ourselves to Death* (1985), provides insights into the increasing proclivity of the media to titillate and entertain us. Certainly the media come in for their share of blame for this situation, but audience members confound the situation by their growing and enthusiastic attention to such stories and programming.

After all, in a representative democracy *the people* are, by and large, satisfied to be passive and let their representatives make the decisions. Basically, they form a community of passivity and relative unconcern. Great masses of citizens show this by the low voter turnout in every election. A case might be made for the proposition that the uninterested masses, for the sake of an ongoing society, *should not* have information equity with interested, educated, and politically active citizens. William Henry III, formerly of *Time* magazine, develops this theme in his book *In Defense of Elitism* (1994). There is no doubt that the American public generally is not obsessed by serious news and interpretation. The mass media, except possibly for television, touch the masses of the population very peripherally—and even TV impacts mainly on the emotions, not on the mind.

It is improbable that market forces can ensure all groups in society information equity; the market was never set up to do that. But market forces are not alone in being incapable of providing total access to various kinds of information. The government is also incapable, as are the media themselves. Community consciousness and a social concern on the part of the media will not get the job done. Certainly, as Reuss mentions, the audience members themselves bear responsibility for getting information that will make them better citizens. A personal desire to be informed, an educational system that prepares citizens for the complexities of the modern world, and an insatiable hunger for diverse perspectives—these are vitally important factors in the whole discussion of information equity.

Let's face it. The bottom line is that there will never be information equity. It is an unrealistic, albeit worthy, expectation. Certain groups in society had best resign themselves to information apartheid, to being isolated from information of various kinds. Most of them probably won't care very much, although their spokespersons may moan and groan about the inequities of the world, including those related to information.

REFERENCES

Alabama Information Age Task Force. (1991). *Founding a First World Alabama: A Summary of the Information Age Task Force Report.*

Barr, Stephen. (December 1991). "Careless Zoning Can Look a Lot Like Redlining." *NewsInc.*, p. 37 ff.

Bryant, Jennings. (1993). "Will Traditional Media Research Paradigms Be Obsolete in the Era of Intelligent Communication Networks?" In Philip Gaunt, ed., *Beyond Agendas: New Directions in Communication Research.* Westport, CT: Greenwood Press, pp. 149–67.

Dennis, Everette, and John Merrill. (1991). *Media Debates.* New York: Longman.

Ghiglione, Loren. (1992). "Are Marketplace Values Overwhelming the News Media?" *Social Responsibility: Business, Journalism, Law, Medicine* 18, pp. 21–30.

Glasser, Theodore L. (1986). "Press Responsibility and First Amendment Values." In Deni Elliott, ed., *Responsible Journalism.* Beverly Hills, CA: Sage, pp. 81–98.

Henry, William A. III. (1994). *In Defense of Elitism.* New York: Doubleday.

Hiebert, Ray Eldon, Donald F. Ungurait, and Thomas W. Bohn. (1991). *Mass Media VI: An Introduction to Modern Communication.* New York: Longman.

Jefferson, Thomas ([1787] 1984). "The People Are the Only Censors," letter to Edward Carrington, Paris, January 16. In Jefferson, *Writings*, selected and with notes by Merrill D. Peterson. New York: Library of America, published by Literary Classics of the United States, p. 880.

Lowery, Shearon A., and Melvin L. DeFleur. (1988). *Milestones in Mass Communication Research*, 2nd ed. New York: Longman.

McQuail, Denis. (1993). "Informing the Information Society: The Task for Communication Science." In Philip Gaunt, ed., *Beyond Agendas: New Directions in Communication Research*. Westport, CT: Greenwood Press, pp. 185–198.

Postman, Neil. (1985). *Amusing Ourselves to Death*. New York: Viking.

Radin, Charles A. (November 2, 1992). "MIT Plugs Citizens into President Race." *The Boston Globe*, pp. 23, 26.

CHAPTER 7

THE ETHICS OF "CORRECTNESS" AND "INCLUSIVENESS"
Culture, Race, and Gender in the Mass Media

I t is inevitable that the mass media will reflect as well as define their world to an extent that isn't always realized. All media—news or information, persuasive, or entertainment—contribute to society's expectations of what is "usual" or "normal."

However, the media do not always carry out these socialization functions in ways that all groups living in the society consider inclusive. The charges against the media range from simply omitting people from nonmainstream groups to distorted representations of various groups and points of view. These omissions and distortions may refer to media content, to ownership of media companies, and to the fact that most employees in key decision-making positions currently are white men.

Arguments against media shortcomings in these areas have been recounted for decades. Although many people would agree that large segments of the media have shown improvement during this period, there is still considerable concern that its pace is slow, uneven, and uncertain. Therefore, some say, additional efforts are required if the media are to serve a diverse society well.

On the other side of the argument are those who believe that additional efforts can skew the equation too far the other way and completely politicize the media. They maintain that it is far better to aim for fairness and balance than for representation of each of many diverse groups in a "politically correct" manner.

In this chapter, David Gordon supports the need for special efforts by the media to become more inclusive of society's diversity in their news and entertainment content and in their employment practices. John Michael Kittross argues against simplistic, or "quota," approaches to such issues as race, gender, and ethnicity. He is more concerned with individuals than with groups, and holds that no special efforts are necessary—that the media belong to society at large more than to any one part of it.

■ GORDON: The mass media must make special efforts to deal with concerns about race, gender, culture, and ethnicity in both their news and entertainment functions.

If the mass media omit minorities from their portrayals of society—or if they misrepresent those groups—the result is unfair and damaging to more than just the ignored or misrepresented sectors of society. Such an inaccurate mediated picture also harms the many people in society who know little or nothing about their fellow citizens with different backgrounds—about the so called "others" in the society.

As a consequence, media that deal realistically with society's diversity are important to members of both the majority and minority groups in society. It has been argued that media portrayals and news coverage of the society influence what takes place between individuals and groups in their *un*mediated social, political, and economic interactions. If this is at all valid, ignoring minorities or regularly portraying them negatively rather than as contributors to the society will make it hard for anyone (majority or minority) to view them—or interact with them—as if they have a real share in the life of the society or a stake in it and its institutions.

There certainly has been progress toward including a diverse portrait of society in news and entertainment media. Still, a great deal of further effort—and sensitivity on the part of media people—is required. Indeed, two knowledgeable observers of the media diversity scene noted in 1994 that many minorities who are outside society's mainstream still have good reason

> . . . to think their perspectives are at best warped by the media or, worse, not heard at all. In the year that saw a black man elected president of South Africa, there is irony in the fact that apartheid still rules the information age in America. (Dates and Pease, 1994, p. 90)

Indeed, one of the mandates presented to the news media in 1947 by the Commission on Freedom of the Press—to provide a representative picture of society's various groups—is one that should be applied to all forms of American mass media in this last decade of the 20th century. To provide relevant and adequate information or entertainment to a broad cross-section of America's pluralistic society, the mass media must strive both to be inclusive and to reflect that the society is made up of diverse groups and individuals even if that isn't immediately obvious in some geographic (or economic) areas.

Given American society's increasing pluralism—and the heightened recognition of it—such portrayals require the media to go beyond a casual recognition of society as a so-called melting pot. That somewhat outdated metaphor views society from an assimilationist perspective that expects different groups to blend into the majoritarian culture. In recent years, various people have suggested that a more appropriate metaphor is the salad bowl (or a pizza), in which the various groups in our society retain a great deal of their own individuality while contributing their unique flavors to the larger culture.

I believe that it will require special efforts on the part of the media to move beyond the comfortable majoritarian perspective of the melting pot. Those efforts are required so the media can focus instead on the existing diversity in ways that reasonably reflect—and therefore help define—the legitimacy of different traditions, perspectives and values. This is true whether one is concerned with the news media, advertising and other persuasive media, or entertainment media, because all of them in various ways help to reflect and transmit the society's cultures and values.

This certainly does *not* mean—as John Michael Kittross points out—that editors of given genders, races, or political perspectives be given veto power over content. It *does* require a heightened sensitivity to diversity concerns that goes well beyond just opening the doors to equal-opportunity hiring or general ethical behavior. It is important to remember that—contrary to what Kittross seems to say—special efforts, such as trying to increase one's sensitivity to or empathy for others, are *not* necessarily special treatment. It is equally important to note that unintentional insensitivity can be just as damaging—though often easier to overcome—as intentional disrespect for those who are different.

Aside from outright racism, sexism, and other prejudice, three points can sum up succinctly, if in a somewhat oversimplified fashion, why special efforts are needed:

- Stereotypes
- The human tendency to view the world from familiar perspectives and to be insensitive—*often without even knowing it*—to those who view things from different perspectives
- Simple ignorance about cultures, groups, and traditions that are different from one's own.

Thus, men may see nothing out of line or offensive in a newspaper column that refers to a male who, "like you and me, has to look himself in the mirror every morning when he shaves." Women's reactions could range from simply tuning out an irrelevant message to anger or feeling belittled or otherwise offended. And what about blacks who read in the late 1960s, in *The New York Times*, about the several hundred "well-dressed Negro officials and their wives" who attended a White House function in Washington. Was it really news (i.e., worth noting) that people invited to White House functions dress up for the occasion? Or was it simply an old stereotype in the mind of the white reporter who wrote the story? (See Smith, 1969.)

Even an entertainment program as sensitive as the original *Star Trek*—which regularly tackled issues of "being different"—couldn't escape the insensitive use of language. At the beginning of each episode, the mission of the *Enterprise* was clearly stated: "to boldly go where no man has gone before." It was not until the show's *Next Generation*, with its considerable increase in the number of women in the ship's crew, that this all-male perspective was eliminated and the gender reference was changed from "no man" to "no one." Even such a minor bow toward greater sensitivity apparently didn't come immediately to the creators of the series.

One way in which the mass media have contributed strongly to public acceptance of society's diversity is TV's coverage of integrated sports events. In the mid-1970s, less than a decade after Governor George Wallace stood "in the schoolhouse door" in Alabama, the University of Alabama basketball team, with five black starters, was applauded enthusiastically by its (predominantly white) fans during introductions before an NCAA tournament game. Similar attitude change has been aided by increasing TV coverage of women's college (and, recently, professional) sports. In these instances, the media have portrayed realities of participation by women and African-Americans and some parts of society have learned more about these groups. Other factors (e.g., Title IX) have also played important roles. But the impact of media portrayals can't be ignored.

■ THE ENTERTAINMENT MEDIA: DIVERSITY AND STEREOTYPING

Beyond language concerns, the complexity of this issue is compounded when one looks at entertainment media. First, there is the question of what characters are chosen to be portrayed. Because many of those decisions are made by white men, it's not surprising that the TV view of our society lacks significant numbers of women over 35, disabled people, and minorities. This picture, drawn from Gerbner's (1993) academic study of 10 years of programming on over-the-air and cable TV, had some further details that drove home the concerns strongly:

- The disparity between male and female roles on TV remained nearly the same (about 2:1) between the 1982–1983 and the 1991–1992 television seasons.
- Elderly characters of both genders seem to be decreasing in number on TV, even as this group is growing faster in American society than any other age group.
- Hispanic characters comprised about 1% of prime-time roles on major network television, and Native Americans and Asian-Americans were almost invisible. African-Americans had nearly 11% of these roles, which was fairly close to their population percentage (Gerbner, 1993).

That 11% figure for prime-time black roles represents an improvement, as does the increasingly frequent appearance of African-Americans and Hispanics in television advertisements. Until recent decades, these groups were largely absent from the TV mainstream, both in programs and ads. As recently as 1996, observers noted that few programs feature blacks in major roles on the three major networks and even on Fox, while the two newer networks (WB and UPN) had more ("TV's Black Flight," 1996).

When entertainment media did include blacks in the cast, the portrayal was often unflattering. Black characters in early films were usually portrayed with negative stereotypes—in some cases, outright caricatures—if they appeared at all. Early television programming had similar problems, with blacks appearing mainly in subservient roles or in sitcoms. Heavy criticism of the *Amos 'n' Andy* television series was directed at the stereotypical caricatures of blacks presented by the program's white producers. (The African-American community had both positive and negative reactions to the original radio program, with the criticism reaching its height in 1931 as the result of a campaign led by the editor of *The Pittsburgh Courier*, a black weekly newspaper; see Dates and Barlow, 1990, pp. 180–181.)

Even a diversity of positive roles is no guarantee that society will be reflected realistically.

Similar problems have existed for other groups. A 1980s study by the Center for Media and Public Affairs concluded that although Hispanic characters appear rarely on TV, they commit many more TV crimes per person than non-Hispanic white characters do.

Even a diversity of positive roles is no guarantee that society will be reflected realistically. In movies or TV programs, time is limited and the nuances of the various characters can't be fully developed and illustrated. Therefore, writers and producers have little choice but to rely on stereotypes, defined by Walter Lippmann as the "pictures inside our heads," which necessarily have a major impact on our perceptions of "reality" (or of various social realities) (Lippmann, 1922). Such mental pictures act as a shorthand or shortcut to developing the nuances of film or TV characters, and the writers and producers must rely on the ones in their own minds, which often *don't* portray fully or accurately the groups to which the characters belong.

Stereotypes often offend members of the audience who see themselves as differing from the blanket description applied simplistically to their group. In arguing against using this kind of categorized description for men and women, Deborah Tannen explained the dilemma concisely:

> We all know we are unique individuals, but we tend to see others as representatives of groups. It's a natural tendency, since we must see the world in patterns in order to make sense of it; we wouldn't be able to deal with the daily onslaught of people and objects if we couldn't predict a lot about them and feel that we know who and what they are. (Tannen, 1990, pp. 15–16)

But this also requires the media to work seriously, and unceasingly, to transcend stereotypes, especially those relevant only to the majority groups in the audience. Otherwise, there is little hope of portraying society's real complexity and diversity.

The majority/minority distinction used here itself oversimplifies—stereotypes, if you prefer—a situation that is in considerable flux. It is estimated by Gerbner and others that today's "minority" groups—African-Americans, Hispanics, Asians, and others—will outnumber non-Hispanic whites in the United States fairly early in the 21st century, if current birth and immigration trends continue (see also Centron and Davies, 1989, p. 23). Worldwide, of course, that's always been the case, as it also is in several major American cities. And females have outnumbered males in the United States for some time now. Thus, we may be overdue in reconsidering just who is in the majority. In addition, the word *minority* contains the word *minor*, which might signify a lesser status for the group being referred to. In view of all this, some different terminology may well be warranted.

■ OTHER DIMENSIONS OF DIVERSITY

News coverage of minorities is often criticized either for its almost total absence or for its focus on violence and crime. Often, even that focus emphasized black-on-white crime, while the much more prevalent instances of black-on-black crime rated considerably less attention. With a little thought, and some sensitivity to groups that are often seen as outside the mainstream, a broad spectrum of potentially newsworthy stories might well be developed about African-American, Latino, Asian, and Native American communities, along with continued coverage for those of European descent.

News coverage also tends to portray minority groups as monolithic and to ignore or gloss over some very real differences within those groups. Consider, as just one example, that the term *Hispanic* is sometimes applied without regard for the fact that it can include people with roots in Cuba, Mexico, Puerto Rico—and even Spain.

The portrayals of women in advertisements and entertainment, and their coverage in the news media, also reflect many of these same concerns, if through a different prism. It is interesting to note some additional details from the 10-year programming study conducted by Gerbner (1993), among them that in *daytime* programming, when women are a prime target audience, women had 45% of the roles. In prime time, however, women had only one-third of the roles, and in children's programming they filled just under 25% of the roles (Gerbner, 1993).

White males have continued to dominate TV commercials on Saturday morning children's programs as well. A 1991 study of Boston's ABC, CBS, Fox, and NBC affiliates indicated that 95% of the characters shown during those commercials were white, and males outnumbered females by about two to one. In addition, female characters portrayed in the ads were more likely than not to be children. This study updated two earlier ones from the 1970s, and found that relatively little had changed in the interim (Pecora, 1993).

These commercials, aimed directly at children, were not just pitches for products, but also subtle messages about the societal importance of different genders and races. Even if such messages are unintentional, they still may indicate to young viewers that ratios such as these are normal or expected. (It's also noteworthy that girls usually appeared in toy ads playing with dolls while boys were shown with toy cars, in the 1970s and again in 1991.)

One instance of news coverage where greater sensitivity to women's perspectives might have raised public awareness on an important issue occurred in the accounts of the 1989 "Central Park jogger" case. Most coverage of that case emphasized the racial angle of a white female victim and black and Hispanic teenagers accused of the gang rape and beating. Some analyses tried to deal with the larger question of why *anyone* would commit such a vicious crime. Very little of the coverage looked at the general question of rape in the context of society's attitude toward women. Helen Benedict, a Columbia University journalism professor who studied the case, concluded that only female columnists and alternative papers and magazines (such as *The Village Voice*, *The Nation*, and *Ms.*) raised the issue of societal attitudes toward women.

Benedict interviewed many (mostly male) editors and reporters and learned that most were almost totally ignorant of the phenomenon of gang rape. Nor had it apparently occurred to them that they might fill in that ignorance by calling a rape crisis center or looking at some of the studies on the subject of gang rape (Benedict, 1992). It's hard to dispute that coverage of this story would have been more useful to the news consumers had it included diverse perspectives and a wider range of background information. And, despite Kittross's dismissal of the possibility later in this chapter, there may well be valid female perspectives on a town council meeting.

■ EMPLOYMENT STATISTICS

One reason that such special efforts are needed is the relative shortage of female and nonwhite perspectives among media employees generally, but especially in decision-making positions in the news and entertainment media. For instance, surveys of Hollywood employment in the early 1990s found that women were considerably underrepresented in many key entertainment industry positions. They held about 30% of the middle management positions in 20 major film and TV studios, but only three women—compared to 45 men—held the title of president of any of those studios' operations. Less than 25% of TV writers and only about 17% of film writers were women—and they were paid an average of 25% less than white male writers.

The figures were even lower (about 10%) for female members of the Directors Guild of America; in addition, women accounted only for 5.5% of directors' working days between 1990 and 1992, which means that they actually were able to use their talents about half as much as their membership percentage would seem to warrant. It should therefore be no surprise to learn that a 1991 Screen Actors Guild survey found men outnumbering women about two to one in lead and supporting roles on TV and in film, and that actresses earned about 25% less than their male counterparts.

The numbers are similar—but changing—regarding women and members of minority groups in authority in the news media. Although studies from the 1980s found that women held few of the top news media jobs, that they were paid considerably less than men in similar positions, and that they received proportionately fewer by-lines and photo credits than men did, new figures show a different picture—particularly in the electronic media. For example, a survey (Papper et al., 1997) for the Radio-Television News Directors Association showed that in 1996 14% of local television news directors and 23% of local radio news directors were women (down from 17% and 26% the year before), while 8% of news directors in both media were members of minority groups (down from 9%). Overall, however, the television broadcast news workforce was 21% non-Caucasian, and the radio news force 12%, and women constituted 37% of the television broadcast news workforce and 31% of radio's. Some 41% of middle management, 43% of assignment editors, and almost two-thirds (64%) of television producers were female in 1995.

The picture is different in the newspaper industry. According to data from the American Society of Newspaper Editors during the same mid-1990s time frame, only 11% of newspaper newsroom workers were members of minority groups (compared to 21% in television), 57% of daily newspapers employed minorities (compared to 87% for television stations), and 8.9% of minorities were "supervisors" in 1996, compared to 9.3% in the top four television news positions in 1995.

Three decades after the 1968 Kerner Commission strongly urged the news media to train minority group members and promote them to decision-making positions, whites (usually white males) still were the main occupants of those positions. As recently as the early 1990s, a majority of American newspapers still had *no* people of color on their professional staffs. To be sure, the numbers have changed today and more minority group members and women are employed in the news media, but it is still relatively rare to find them in policy-making and decision-making roles in some media organizations.

If the decisions about what to cover and how to cover it are made mainly by white men, and if that coverage is mainly guided and edited by white men, it's not surprising that operative news values reflect mainly white male perspectives and sensitivities. One result is that some people or groups are measured by a different scale in determining their newsworthiness. Another is the frequent reliance on white men as experts in news stories, and even as nonexperts who are quoted in stories. Such results paint an increasingly inaccurate picture of society and send both subtle and direct messages about whom society values enough to include in the news.

Similarly, if white men are deciding what entertainment programs will air on TV and what films are going to be made, the subject matter is very likely to reflect mostly a white male perspective of the subject matter and of the society. Again, this sends messages to the viewers about what really matters. Such messages create ethical concerns for the media that must be addressed much more strongly than they have been in the past.

■ ETHICAL FRAMEWORKS

Media that purport to serve a diverse, pluralistic society—and receive First Amendment protection to do so—have an ethical obligation to provide a spectrum of perspectives reflecting that pluralism. This obligation can be based on the overall balance required by the Aristotelian Golden Mean or on utilitarianism's dictum of the greatest good for the society as a whole.

Media that purport to serve a diverse, pluralistic society . . . have an ethical obligation to provide a spectrum of perspectives reflecting that pluralism.

This same obligation it can also be grounded, strongly, in the need for social and journalistic pluralism for which Ralph Barney (1986) has argued eloquently. Barney was focusing specifically on the value of a variety of information sources in a participatory society, to offset the professional persuasion that is increasingly occupying mass media channels. He was also concerned about the need to make these different information sources available within the relatively narrow and often specialized range of media outlets used by any one person, which makes the need for special efforts even more urgent.

Although Barney's concerns about pluralism were not specifically directed at ensuring diverse perspectives about race, gender, culture, and ethnicity—or, for that matter, age, lifestyle, sexual orientation, religion, or economic status—they are highly applicable to those issues. Barney discussed the need for journalists to "distribute views that may be personally repugnant" (p. 76) under an ethic of pluralism, and to avoid falling too far under the spell of whoever is in positions of power and authority at a given time (that is, to avoid blindly extending the status quo).

Extrapolating from those concerns, a more general approach to pluralism would require the news and entertainment media to distribute "pictures" of the society that may be personally unfamiliar to the media gatekeepers but nonetheless portray real and important aspects of the society. A media pluralist, to paraphrase Barney, would almost automatically have empathy for many societal perspectives, and would introduce as many of them as possible into both professional media messages and private conversations.

Clifford Christians (1986), among others, has stressed the social responsibility theory of the press put forward in 1947 by the Commission on Freedom of the Press and amplified in *Four Theories of the Press* (Siebert, Peterson, and Schramm, 1956) as a guiding ethic for the mass media. Christians has suggested a communitarian approach in which the news media have a responsibility to report thoroughly on the powerless segments of society and to give voice to their needs. To do this, he wrote, requires the media to overcome their middle-class ethnocentrism (and he might well have added *white* and *male* to his middle class reference).

That, of course, is the crux of the problem we have been discussing here. Christians relies heavily on John Rawls's veil of ignorance approach to ethics, where fairness is the cornerstone of social justice, and where the weaker, more vulnerable parties must be protected to the same degree that everyone else is. If this approach is applied to the need to counteract current deficiencies in mass media representations of society, the need for special efforts to include all portions of the social spectrum in those portrayals seems both logical and obvious.

■ ETHICS PLUS ECONOMICS

For the mass media, this matter has become much more than just an ethical issue. It is increasingly a matter of long-term economic survival as well. In Atlanta, for instance, *The Journal-Constitution* in early 1993 began a weekly broadsheet publication for insertion into papers delivered and sold in the inner city. Named "City Life," this publication was launched with the goal of providing the same kind of localized, interesting, and useful coverage that had been available in similar suburban inserts for quite some time. The approach stemmed in part from the ethical conviction that the newspapers had an obligation to cover the less affluent, primarily black inner-city communities as thoroughly as they did the more affluent suburbs.

During the planning stages, the working assumption was that this insert would not make money quickly, if at all. As it turned out, advertising for its inaugural edition sold much better than was anticipated, and made its startup a financial success. The commitment to publish, though, stemmed from sound *long*-term economic reasons as well as from a desire to meet the paper's social responsibility. It was clear to some key officials at the Atlanta papers that they needed to look ahead and to build readership among the groups that were then in the minority in their circulation area. Only by doing this, the argument went, might readership levels be maintained when these groups become the Atlanta-area majority sometime in the 21st century.

Even if we all agree that some special efforts are needed to make American mass media more pluralistic, we must face some valid questions as to what should be done. Some suggestions have already been noted. Others probably can't be specified in much more detail than stressing the need for empathy and sensitivity toward the perspectives and experiences of all groups other than the ones we grew up in or the circles we now move in.

But at least one specific approach can be noted. That is to get a greater diversity of people (and therefore, additional perspectives) involved at the decision-making levels so that previously ignored subjects can be considered for mass media content. For example, the recent increase in the number of African-American filmmakers has added some very different, if sometimes controversial, perspectives to American cinema. A capsule newspaper review of Mario Van Peebles's *Posse* in mid-1993 called it a "revisionist Western [that] makes room for the historically real but cinematically invisible African-American cowboy." The fact that movies have generally ignored black cowboys is just one illustration of how nonmainstream groups have been disenfranchised by the media over the years, and thereby kept from the consciousness of *both* majority and minority members of society. Consider that it took until 1993 for mainstream Hollywood filmmakers to release their first movies dealing with AIDS.

Another fairly basic approach would require greater efforts to eliminate the more subtle sexism and racism from the mass media's language. This might be something as simple as being sensitive to language that says women "giggle" while men "chuckle." It might mean omitting physical descriptions of women—or their clothing—when none are provided for men. It could mean being sensitive enough to realize that phrases such as "black reputation" or "yellow coward" can be very offensive to members of nonwhite groups.

Possibly the simplest way to raise our consciousness about language use is to be aware of what has been called the we/they syndrome. This is simply the human tendency to see the world as made up of two groups: people "like us" and "others." It shows up most readily, perhaps, in news reports (or in everyday conversations) about "the enemy" in wartime. To realize this, we need only think back to news coverage of the 1991 Gulf War, or go back and reread the 1960s news media references to the North (and South) Vietnamese as "gooks" or subhuman forms of life.

At the same time, there is a need to avoid going so far in the name of inclusiveness or pluralism that we stumble into the "political correctness" thicket. For example, was it appropriate, or overreacting, for the Minneapolis *Star Tribune* and *The Oregonian* in Portland to drop the use of American Indian team nicknames—such as "Redskins"—on their sports pages, as they did in 1993 (Fitzgerald, 1994; Jensen, 1994)? That question could be argued both ways, but suffice it to say that a realistic picture of a diverse society requires that details about that society be included, warts and all. The problem with some media content at the end of the 20th century is that it has focused too often on the warts at the expense of positive material that might well have been included.

You may remember the story of the group of blind men who touched different parts of an elephant and argued heatedly over what it was they were touching. Pamela Creedon, then an Ohio State journalism professor, raised the intriguing question of what would have changed had this parable been based on blind women, or blind women of color. Would that have added other perspectives to the argument? "Would they notice its smell?" she asked. "Would they feel its body heat?" She concluded by asking

> . . . how much richer, more complete would the whole be if the touching were done by many different people from many different standpoints—men and women—of different classes, races, sexual preferences or ethnicities? (1993, pp. 73–74)

This creates a striking analogy to the mass media and their attempts to portray for their audience a realistic picture of a world that media people as well as their audiences may be familiar with only via the societal equivalent of the elephant's trunk or ear. Too often, media portrayals come from middle-class white males, without the richness and the texture that could have been added "by many different people from many different standpoints." The challenge facing the mass media is to take the necessary steps to add those diverse perspectives both in their professional workforces and in their content. Let me state emphatically, though, that I advocate making media content truly reflective of society's real diversity, *not* shaping it to some artificial "content quota" formula, as Kittross tries to paint my argument.

What's really needed here is to acknowledge that if the news and entertainment media continually overlook minorities in general or portray them negatively (for example, as violent criminals) beyond what reality dictates, such snapshots of society will become part of the pictures inside the heads of the audience. Those incessantly negative stereotypes will inevitably determine how members of the media audience act toward people who are different from themselves in some way and, perhaps, how those "others" regard themselves.

Meeting this challenge won't be easy to accomplish, but it's necessary if American society is to become truly inclusive. To do anything less is to fall well short of meeting the mass media's responsibilities as major players in American society, both in reflecting it and in helping to shape its present and its future. Although this argument rests firmly on the grounds of media ethics and societal need, it also appears to make good business sense in view of the changing composition of potential media consumers in America.

However, if history means anything at all, this goal will not be accomplished unless the mass media renew their efforts and go well beyond what has been done in the past to make real diversity seem more natural both in themselves and in their society.

■ KITTROSS: No special efforts are required on the part of the mass media to deal "correctly" with race, gender, culture, religion, and ethnicity.

We each are different. No doubt about it. Human beings have not (yet) been cloned. But all of us are members of the same overall human community.

We have more similarities than differences. The very fact that we are of one species ensures this. Regardless of our racial, religious, ethnic, gender, age, sexual orientation, and other differences, I doubt that anyone disagrees with the precept that we live in a global community and that the mass media link this community.

Indeed, the very phrase *mass medium* implies a community of attention to a particular medium—a number of people united by that attention, if by nothing else. Although political correctness demands that we dismiss much of our common intellectual heritage, such as a literary canon (e.g., Shakespeare and the Bible; see Bloom, 1994) and our common sense of history (such as the American Revolution, the Civil War, the Great Depression) formerly familiar to every person with a smattering of schooling, if the United States is to be a nation we must have things in common. To try to talk with a college senior today about the battles of Lexington and Concord, or about the parable of the prodigal son, or about Lady Macbeth often is a fruitless exercise. Today, what we have in common is network television and mass circulation magazines. And yet, for a single network to reach a quarter of the population is a rare event, and even the largest circulation magazines, such as *TV Guide, Modern Maturity, National Geographic*, and *Readers Digest*, reach only one-tenth to one-fifth of American homes. And, in so doing, these "mainstream" media really are trying to appeal to a varied collection of small groups while hoping that other small groups will not turn away.

William Butler Yeats, in his poem "The Second Coming," laments: "things fall apart; the centre cannot hold." Today, we have no center, yet it is absolutely necessary that we find one if we are to survive as a political, economic, and cultural entity.

■ (OVER)SIMPLICITY

One approach to discussing these issues is to concentrate—as David Gordon does—on such simplistic facets of a larger problem as how many members of one group or another are shown on television or movie screens, how many are found in advertisements in a particular medium, and how many are employed by a media company—and whether that number is proportional to the numbers in the labor force or the entire population. Such a focus assumes that, contrary to what its backers maintain, we are all identical—cogs in the same wheel, no matter what our gender, age, race, or religious belief.

But my position is that we are all *individuals*, and that this individuality is precious—not to be submerged into a politically correct or stereotypical grouping. Why in the world would we classify Tiger Woods as anything other than a superb golfer—even with his rich racial/ethnic background? My own age, gender, etc., would call forth a number of stereotypes, few of which are valid in my case. I think too highly of individuality to allow myself the easy approach, and find some of today's shortsighted and often selfish attempts to glorify differences between groups rather than similarity between individuals very disturbing.

As a result, although Gordon and I are discussing the same controversy, we do so from very different philosophical positions and using very different logical and ethical tools.

The 1947 (Hutchins) Commission on Freedom of the Press posed the following five requirements for a free and responsible press:

- A truthful, comprehensive, and intelligent account of the day's events in a context which gives them meaning.
- A forum for the exchange of comment and criticism.
- The projection of a representative picture of the constituent groups in the society.
- The presentation and clarification of the goals and values of the society.
- Full access to the day's intelligence. (pp. 21–27)

As an example, Gordon interprets *one* of the five requirements of the Hutchins Commission in a very different way than I do. I believe that where Gordon and others make their mistake is in forgetting that the groups referred to by the Hutchins Commission are *constituent* groups in a *single* society—a common humanity. Throughout my part of this chapter, I express my fear that the societally necessary concepts of unity and cooperation are being replaced. The word *representation* today often means content and employment quotas, *diversity* tends to mean divisiveness, and *plurality* is a code word for separatism. This was not the Hutchins Commission's view. In its discussion of this requirement it was concerned about stereotypes and called for publication of "the truth about any social group, though it should not exclude its weaknesses and vices, [including] also recognition of its values, its aspirations, and its common humanity" (Commission, 1947, pp. 26–27). Throughout its publications are found the words *society* (singular) and *community* (singular)—without the modifications used today by Gordon and the politically correct.

■ COMMUNITY

The primary problem reflected in this chapter is that there is little agreement today on what community (or society or culture) means.

The expressed need of individuals for identity as members of a group—generally spelled out in terms of membership, roots, or family—may have established an artificial diversity in the larger American society that actually is divisive in its effect. Robert Heinlein (1982, p. 240) argues persuasively that it is a bad sign when the people of a country stop identifying themselves with the country and start identifying with a racial, religious, linguistic, or other group that is less than the whole population. Today's ethnic strife in Eastern Europe has little to do with the modern Western concept of nation. Virtually all psychological, sociological, and physiological research has concluded that there are greater human differences *within* groups than *between* them, as a careful reading of *The Bell Curve* (Herrnstein and Murray, 1994) will show. (The authors argue that society is becoming increasingly stratified by I.Q. This controversial—because of its discussion of race—book and the methodology of I.Q. testing have been defended by some scientists and attacked by others, most cogently by Gould, 1994 and 1995.)

A recent article by Ivan Hannaford points out that "[g]enuine public life—not to mention a genuine solution to racial problems—becomes impossible when a society allows race or ethnicity to displace citizenship as one's badge of identity" (1994, p. 8).

... it is a bad sign when the people of a country stop identifying themselves with the country and start identifying with a ... group that is less than the whole population.

Certainly, individuals and groups have the right to name themselves, although it may be difficult for outsiders to follow the evolution or the emotional content of such nomenclature. (The terms *Negroes, colored people, blacks, Afro-Americans, African-Americans,* and *people of color* have nuances that the larger community may find confusing—but all agree, I believe, that any of these terms is better than those intended to be derogatory or insulting, such as *nigger*—even though it sometimes may be used jocularly among blacks—or *coon*). Each individual member of a group, even the smallest, has the right to life, liberty, and the pursuit of happiness. As members of the larger society, they also have the right to be treated fairly, politely, and responsibly. Unfortunately, in the past—and present—the members of some more easily identified groups have been discriminated against shamelessly, in many ways.

For hundreds of years, this discrimination was sanctioned by the law as well as by custom. Extralegal, stereotypical discrimination was as bad. *Los Angeles Times* columnist Art Seidenbaum wrote in the aftermath of the riots in the mid-1960s (quoted in an editorial in the spring 1968 *Journal of Broadcasting*, p. 95). "There is nothing wrong with growing up to be a maid. There is a dreadful wrong when one child assumes another child has been born a maid."

In the past 35 years, almost all legally sanctioned discriminatory practices on the basis of race, religion, and gender have, thank goodness, been outlawed. However, many people still feel disadvantaged or discriminated against and believe that they should have redress for perceived past and present discrimination. This includes both blacks whose ancestors were slaves and whites who think that affirmative action is a hurtful form of "reverse racism."

But is the best solution or remedy for either legal or extralegal discrimination to seek monetary reparations? Or to insist that only members of legally established "protected classes" should have the right to sue for damages, regardless of who is harmed by the practice being frowned on today? Or should one group attempt to bring down other groups, in the expectation that their own group would be raised as a result (which cavalierly denies the aphorism that a rising tide raises all boats)? Or to use arbitrary definitions to describe the rapidly growing number of people whose parents have come from different ethnic groups, such as Tiger Woods? Or to dismiss the thoughts and wishes of independent individuals who, because of their gender, color, or heritage are listed as "belonging" to a group only because others believe they so belong? Or to insist on special treatment or special efforts in society's institutions—including the media?

More than in any other time during the human history of the planet, we are part of *one* community. By and large, globally speaking, those of similar ages tend to watch the same kinds of TV, listen to the same kinds of music (Seabrook, 1994), and worry about the same crimes, economic situations, and foreign threats. Coca-Cola is sold almost everywhere, at the height of his popularity Michael Jackson was a worldwide entertainment and news media phenomenon, and big business is almost synonymous with the major multinational or global corporations.

We cannot help this interaction with other cultures, brought about by unprecedented improvements in communication and transportation since the mid-nineteenth century. Roughly 85 years ago, the assassination of a little-known Grand Duke in an obscure Balkan town stimulated most of the world, like lemmings, to enter into a great war. What happened in that little city of Sarajevo—in 1914, during the 1984 Olympic games, or during the bloody consequences of the breakup of Yugoslavia in the 1990s—affected the entire world.

■ SPECIALIZATION

What does this mean with respect to mass media ethics? With respect to what is meant by *community?*

A century ago, the United States was proud of its status as a melting pot for immigrants. A strong nation was constructed from many peoples. They came from many different (mostly European) cultures, nationalities, and religions and found America bewildering. Often, they were exploited and discriminated against. Slaves and their "free" descendants were discriminated against the most, unless one counts the virtually complete exclusion of Asians before the last few decades. To help ease the transition, many newspapers aimed at particular ethnic groups were established. Even today, New Yorkers can purchase such newspapers as *The Jewish Forward* (in English and Yiddish—and Russian), *France-Amerique, America Oggi, The New Yorker Staats-Zeitung, El Diario-La Prensa, Novoye Russoye Slovo. The China Press, The Amsterdam News* (edited for New York blacks), *Korea Central Daily News, Hellenic Times,* and others. *The Forward,* at one time, had a daily circulation of a quarter of a million (Remnick, 1994).

This situation—a myriad of specialized media outlets—is analogous to what might be desired by some of the groups that today complain about the existing *mass* media: a station or a paper aimed specifically at and prepared by members of one group. This specialization often is welcomed by advertisers, and provides a localized sense of community, although it rejects the melting pot concept of an American nation that was current for most of the past two hundred years. Although such specialization is a fairly well-established idea—for example, there is the Black Entertainment Network and the Spanish Information Network, together with numerous magazines (including some segregated by gender), and a few "minority" daily papers in large cities—it has three significant drawbacks as a universal solution.

First, much of the agitation for specialized outlets comes from entrepreneurs who are anxious to focus on narrow demographic classifications desired by some advertisers so that they can get the financial rewards of a *niche* pioneer long after successful *mass* media pioneers have reaped theirs. In other instances, it represents an opportunity for promoters, politicians, and others to be the big fish in a small pond. Their audiences, many of which might benefit from gaining their information from more broadly based media, often are thought of solely as potential customers, as is true of almost any audience in a commercial environment, where the term *public interest* has devolved into "what can we get the public interested in."

Second, the economics of establishing a newspaper, magazine, or broadcasting station are very risky. Even if we accept the doubtful assumption that start-up capital is available, there still remains the need to develop a revenue stream that can be counted on. Most American mass media rely on purchases (such as subscriptions or paying at a newsstand or box office), advertising, or a combination of these. Mass media advertising can be described as the process of selling an audience to an advertiser who wishes to reach that audience with a message. If the audience is small, or if the audience has limited economic resources, few advertisers are interested. True, some communication industries relying on talent and ingenuity do not need large amounts of capital to get started—the head of the American Association of Advertising Agencies once said that his was the only industry where all the assets go down the elevator at the end of the day—but, in general, mass communication industries are capital- rather than labor-intensive.

The third drawback is less obvious. Is it a good thing only to be talking with oneself (or one's group)? No—not if we wish to participate fully in the economic and political life of this country. As Hannaford (1994, p. 12) points out:

> The Greeks taught us the importance of living as a community of citizens bound together by law. If we are to rise above our current condition—a national society of ethnic groups cleaving only to kith and kin—Americans, as well as Bosnians and innumerable others, will need to act politically, rethinking the nature of citizenship and of the civic compact.

No matter how comforting, there is little that can be communicated within a society as large and diverse as ours if we restrict ourselves to our own little (or big) groups. I use the plural because we are claimed by (even if we don't always care to be associated with) many different groups. We each are in so many minorities that logically it isn't impossible that this emphasis on belonging eventually might lead to "one-person groups" or—to use the old-fashioned word I prefer—individuals, with groups becoming unimportant, as I think they should be. The media themselves also are stereotyped: Often-heard phrases such as the *liberal media* ignore the essentially conservative leanings of most publishers, licensees, and talk show hosts.

Even the most stereotypical male WASP is in the minority with respect to gender, religion, and ethnic background. In terms of power, or potential power, white males, as a demographically defined group if not as individuals, are still in the minority because the combination of all females and male people of color far outnumber white males and because females are the beneficiaries of most of the nation's wealth (partly because they live, on average, seven to eight years longer than men). On the other hand, those who maintain, as Gordon does, that "today's 'minority' groups—

African-Americans, Hispanics, Asians, and others—will outnumber non-Hispanic whites in the United States fairly early in the 21st century" may be surprised to learn that Bureau of the Census data published in the *Statistical Abstract of the United States* do not confirm this. Non-Hispanic whites (but not white males) are projected to still constitute a majority of the U.S. population several decades into the 21st century.

To return to media aimed at specialized audiences, why today does the *Forward*, now a weekly with Yiddish, English, and Russian editions, have a circulation of less than 15,000? Is it because there are fewer Jews in New York? No. It is because the mainstream media provide all that a largely assimilated population believes necessary—and do so without singling out Jews as somehow separate from other New Yorkers or requiring them to learn Yiddish (Remnick, 1994). Remember, the very definition of *mass medium* refers to a relatively undifferentiated—"to whom it may concern"—audience united primarily by the act of paying attention to identical mediated content.

■ "POLITICAL CORRECTNESS": INDIVIDUALITY, SENSITIVITY, AND PROTECTIVITY

But do the mainstream media, now serving a less-differentiated audience, still have an obligation (since they must serve everybody) to make special efforts with respect to various "protected groups" or others who want additional coverage? Is "sensitivity," in the way Gordon uses it, the *primary* consideration the media should use for hiring, casting, writing, and illustrating? Should we believe that, in light of new and "sensitive" standards, the opening words of the original *Star Trek* series ("to boldly go where no man has gone before") were *intentionally* disrespectful to all women, and had no legitimacy, despite the hundreds of years of generic use of the noun *man* to refer to all members of the human race? We can acknowledge that in today's more aware climate, it is good that the opening words of *Star Trek: The Next Generation* are "where no one has gone before." But should we now go back and change history, change the words of the first person to land on the moon ("one giant step for mankind") presumably in the interests of giving females a feeling of participation?

I think not. I believe that the media have only the obligation to be fair and civil to all *individuals*—and that membership in a group often is a meaningless distinction. If stereotypes of religion, race, or gender overshadow one's personal attributes and accomplishments, then we may devolve into a system of government of quotas rather than government of the people. Each of us has—or should have—knowledge of and interest in the broader news of politics, social trends, and economics that help us make the decisions that rule our lives—what Schramm (1949, p. 260) calls a "delayed reward" in contrast to titillation's "immediate reward."

The media's obligations are to individuals and cannot be sloughed off merely because the individual in question is or is not a member of a group. Tony Hillerman, the southwestern mystery writer, could have identified one of his characters as a "native American," "native person," "indigenous person," "Indian," "Navajo," or "Lt. Joseph Leaphorn," but he still is referring to a single (fictional) human being who shares space on the planet and in this nation with individuals of many other races, cultures, ethnic groups, and religions. Even in our "winner takes all" political system, the key is the number of individuals, not the number of groups. The handicapped are to be found in almost any group, as are members of both genders and the elderly. Differences between individuals are, as mentioned in the first paragraph of my argument here, to be expected. But similarities also should be expected.

The handicapped are to be found in almost any group, as are members of both genders and the elderly.

Unfortunately, there has been a growing dependence on what is pejoratively called "politically correct" language as a cure-all for everything that ails us. Hannaford (1994, p. 33) says that "a new, more 'correct' derivative of the orthodoxy is imposing itself upon the literature and language of Western politics, an orthodoxy that vainly seeks to end racial discrimination by identifying pernicious language wherever it appears, in the home, the factory, the school, even the university, and eradicating it entirely from the conversation of humankind."

Some of the newer language changes makes a great deal of sense—*fire fighter* is more descriptive than *fireman* and reflects current hiring patterns—but some are merely an awkward genuflecting to the principle, such as "waitpersons" or "wait staff" rather than the gender-free "server." (However, it is unlikely that any label that implies a subservient relationship will survive, even though the relationship may. Think about, for example, the growing use of *associate* to replace *salesperson*).

The use of "politically correct" language and behavior may be intended to achieve, through constant repetition, a society free of language that may offend, intentionally or unintentionally. The editor of the *Los Angeles Times* claims that the use of such language promotes "greater clarity" (Coffey, 1994). Stuart Hall (1994) points out that to focus on language alone reflects a mistaken belief that calling things by a different name will make them disappear or, in the dialogue Edward Borgers put into the mouth of Saint Paul (formerly known as Roman tax collector Saul of Tarsus): "if you don't like something, change the name." Often, the results are absurd, as when the children's book *Thomas the Tank Engine* came under attack for "sexism, sizeism and distorted values" (Lester, 1994).

The politically correct approach places the burden of communication solely on the shoulders of the communicator, ignoring the fact that the act of communication requires a receiver as well. Consequently, the media may be out in front of this trend, and style books of many newspapers (such as the *Los Angeles Times*) have adopted cautions—which could turn into outright prohibitions—against words that have "potentially offensive connotations." Even worse is the use of computer programs not merely to flag, but to modify offending words—such as the (possibly apocryphal) reference to "African-American holes in space" in an astronomy article. These practices appear to be extensions of the earlier "let's avoid harming the sensibilities of the faint-hearted" use of euphemisms such as *departed* rather than *dead, sanitary engineer* instead of *garbage collector,* or similar examples of what Fowler (1965) calls genteelisms. A buffalo chip by any other name would smell as sweet.

■ THE PROFESSIONAL APPROACH

I look for the media to be professional, which must include the Kantian need to be ethical and altruistic, and to think of the welfare of others (which itself is utilitarian), and not merely of the financial bottom line. If the media are truly professional, many of the arguments against the media—going so far as to propose that there be an editor of specified gender, race, or politics to have veto power over what is being aired or published that involves these categories—fall from their own weight of selfishness. Gordon's reliance on employment statistics to justify what are, in effect, hiring quotas falls into this trap.

Essentially my position is a Kantian approach to the problem of defining *community*. If everyone acts according to the categorical imperative that what is ethical for a person to do is what that person would want everyone to do, then there is no need for special language or special efforts such as quotas. Everyone wanting to enter a career would be able to apply for the training involved based on ability and motivation. Equal opportunity would replace affirmative action.

But isn't there a current need for affirmative action? Perhaps, but there also is a need to remove the need for affirmative action as rapidly as possible, to reach a time when all humans are treated with equal fairness and civility. To overcome past discrimination requires special efforts to make sure that discrimination no longer is an influence—but affirmative action should not be an end in itself, without a statement of the criteria that will let us decide to put it away, sometime in the future, as no longer being needed. Great strides have been made toward equality, or at least equal opportunity, as anyone born early enough to compare the present to the early 1960s or before can testify—but in addition to needing additional strides, we must also cast a wary eye on the bureaucratic processes themselves. Equality is the goal, not bureaucracy—although the aphorism "God is in the details" may apply. Recent legislative debates, appellate court decisions, White House pronouncements, and similar policy decisions and referenda in states such as California (Proposition 209) illustrate the ongoing debate on this issue.

■ QUOTAS

Would it be good if each media outlet (station, channel, magazine, or paper), or possibly only the handful of national and international wire services or other news sources used by these media outlets, were required to provide news of specific interest to several specifically named groups, in the way that some "politically correct" college newspapers provide a page (and editor's slot) to the louder or stronger groups? This would require special care to ensure that women have roughly the same amount of news of interest to them as do men; Hispanics, Asians, blacks all should have their percentages; the young and the elderly their quotas; and so on through the list of those groups that have managed to aggregate enough political clout to be listed as an identifiable "minority." But how would one choose between them, if there aren't enough media minutes or column inches in the day? How can one know what would be of interest to a particular group? Editors are individuals, not pollsters, and owe their primary duty to serve the community or, at least, all of their readers, listeners, and viewers rather than stereotypes or meaningless averages. To say that sports are the domain of men and soap operas the territory of women is to ignore the millions of fans of the "wrong" gender. Not even an honest and objective general report on a neutral and universal topic such as the U.S. budget could be expected to be equally acceptable even to every one of the major, identified groups!

Under such a system, would content-quota obligations also accrue to the few media outlets owned or controlled by the specialized groups themselves? Would a black-owned newspaper have to ensure space for whites? Must *The Sheepherder's Gazette* be sure to provide coverage directed toward cattle ranchers, or would it be permitted to focus on those who have found a career among sheep? Must every mention of breast cancer be balanced by a mention of prostate cancer? How do we determine what is of interest (preferably of importance) to each group?

And what about the equally common misrepresentations of and ignoring the interests of some very large, even majority, groups? Although many Americans are religious, this aspect of their lives rarely is given much attention in the mass media. The growing proportion of the elderly, or those with vision or hearing problems, is given similarly short shrift. On the other hand, when possible, the media try to demonstrate their open-mindedness through tokenism and quotas: There is a far greater proportion of black judges on TV than in America's courtrooms, and even as far back as World War II, an army squad in a feature film had to have its quota of one soldier from Brooklyn, one from the Ozarks or Appalachians, and so on.

How could we provide true representation without giving every person his or her own station and newspaper? Economically and technologically this would be impossible, even without considering the question of finding viewers, listeners, and readers for each such media outlet. This might be paraphrased as "if everyone is talking, who will be there to listen?"

And, although we might try to answer the problem posed by the previous question through selection of staff, we might actually compound it by requiring that the reporters, anchors, editors, publishers, and station owners be present in the media workforce in proportion to the number of each of these groups in the total population, regardless of individual training, talent, or wealth. Even now, some call for an instant fulfillment of quotas. But is there a black view of earthquakes? An Hispanic view of the Gulf War? A male view of the town council meeting? Earlier chapters in this book suggest that the answer is *no*.

After all, we are individuals and should have the right to select our own representatives, and not be forced to accept those who put themselves forward in that role on the basis of their color, religion, gender, or other attributes. For example, the fact that there are "feminists" who believe variously in beauty contests, no makeup, lesbianism, heterosexuality, running a household, independence, abortion access, abortion bans, equal opportunity, reparations, and dozens of other beliefs explains both the internecine conflicts between one type of "feminist" and another and the difficulty in selecting a good spokesperson for feminism or women in general. A single representative chosen on the basis of a single attribute that appeals to all people classified as being in that group is unlikely to be found.

Let us not think that the content-quota approach is merely a straw figure, a *reductio ad absurdum* approach to the problem. It has been adopted by a number of advocates. Every year, letters to the editor—as well as content analyses in scholarly journals—draw conclusions about the worth of advertising, entertainment, and news, based solely on counts of the number of people of various groups who are shown on the screen, quoted in the newspaper, or featured in the advertising, and not on the quality of their ideas. In this chapter, Gordon implicitly adopts this approach.

The opposite of specialization is a general service that appeals to *all* groups. (This is, of course, subject to some practical limitations: Not all media owners have the financial strength to reach the entire public, nor would they want to; although FM station transmitter subcarriers can provide teletype service to the deaf, by definition they can't provide *the same* programming that they give their hearing audience; if newspapers are designed for the illiterate, the literate will stop reading them.)

In the heyday of the national television networks, of course, universality was their strategy. As fewer and fewer competing newspapers are published, their strategy of appealing to the widest possible audience of readers is similar, although their goal is to avoid losing readers (and consequently, being forced to lower advertising rates). But how is this done without appealing only to baser interests and instincts, by covering sex crimes rather than science, sports rather than foreign affairs, or gossip rather than news? I'm afraid that, in order to appeal to the largest number for economic reasons, the media are finding it increasingly difficult to provide anything other than "immediate reward" news (Schramm, 1949, p. 260)—the "titillate, don't educate," "whatever bleeds, leads" programming and editing mentality that shows little respect for the audience.

As a consequence, efforts by some media outlets to be attractive to everybody mean that they may well be attractive to nobody.

■ CONCLUSION

Let's go back to my original thesis: In the mass media the only real obligation we each have (with respect to the matters discussed in this chapter) is to be civil and fair to our fellow humans. Regardless of whether we think certain people are overly touchy, or that euphemisms (*handicapped* = *differently abled* = *challenged* = e.g., *blind* or *deaf*) are either silly or empowering, our recourse should be through education, not insult. This wasn't true in the past: Blacks were mostly ignored in most mainstream papers (unless they were being accused of a crime against a white person), honorifics (Mr., Mrs., Dr.) were omitted, reporters weren't assigned to stories in neighborhoods frequented by members of minority groups, and no blacks were accepted by the white media as spokespersons for the community. Women, as recently as two generations ago, weren't hired for some jobs, and rarely took (or were allowed to take) the training that would better qualify them.

There is good evidence, however, that social equality, even if not carried to the extreme of homogenization, requires economic equality. The disgraceful lack of trained journalists familiar with all areas of the geographic and economic community in which they work shows itself every time an important story shows up in a "minority neighborhood"—whether a *de facto* ghetto or merely an inconvenient rural area. Obviously, any job discrimination on the basis of anything other than quality, ability, and potential should be rooted out, including that directed against the elderly, the handicapped, or the "different."

The fact that the majority of students in communication schools now are female, but that the proportion of students who are members of minority groups has shrunk, cannot be explained on the basis of deliberate discrimination. Regardless of the fate of the affirmative action rules, it is in everyone's self-interest that communication schools recruit aggressively and educate all qualified applicants who wish to enter the field, just as the media need to hire those who meet their legitimate qualifications without regard to their gender, sexual orientation, age, religion, race, or ethnicity. We must remember, however, that short of firing all those who are now perceived to have too large a slice of the pie, it will take time for new generations to enter the executive suites. The glass ceiling really is composed of human beings who achieved their level. Neither affirmative action nor fairness can mandate outcomes that most of us would philosophically desire. Fairness should be inclusive, not exclusive.

So, if the basic obligation is to be fair and polite—e.g., using honorifics for all, rather than removing them so that whites are treated as badly as blacks—we can achieve some of that inclusiveness. If we develop ways to hire and promote that are as truly color- and gender-blind as the methods practiced by major symphony orchestras (auditions and competitions with the unidentified contestants hidden behind a screen), we may defuse some of the "I want mine, Jack" attitudes in the applicant pool. If the nitpicking of "political correctness" in language and content is abandoned in favor of the use of civil language rather than dogma, as gender-free as understanding and common sense permit (don't call my 92-year-old mother "Ms"!), reality may prevail over rhetoric in helping each person to be equal under the law and able to achieve the highest goal of which he or she is individually capable.

Defining *common sense* may not be easy, but it is usually the opposite of the doctrinaire: thinking things through rather than reacting, considering an idea on its own merits and not on the merits or demerits of its supporters. If all Americans, as Martin Luther King Jr. said, are to be judged by the content of their character rather than by the color of their skins, there may be less political satisfaction, but a better metaculture and civic polity in America—one that doesn't confound gender, race, religion, ethnicity, and politics.

■ MERRILL: Commentary

My natural inclination is to agree with David Gordon's position that media should make special efforts to deal with concerns about race, gender, culture, and ethnicity. After all, who would disagree with making "special efforts"? Well, in a way John Michael Kittross is disagreeing. He contends that no special effort is really needed—that the media *naturally* consider these things. Obviously such "natural" consideration is not good enough for many segments of the population that believe themselves discriminated against in the media. Therefore, Gordon calls for a greater media effort.

What is called "political correctness" today is invading almost every aspect of American life. And certainly it has made inroads into media consciousness, leading to considerable self-examination and even to some rather ludicrous attempts to be fair to every possible cultural cause and constituency. Multiculturalism clamors for some kind of proportional representation of the pluralism of society in the contents of the media. Feminists bemoan the "unfair" treatment afforded women in the media. Ditto for blacks (or should the media call them African-Americans?). Ditto for Indians (or should the media call them Native Americans?).

Gordon endorses the Hutchins Commission's 1947 mandate for the American press: to present a representative picture of society's various groups. If this is done, Gordon believes, the culture/race/gender problem will take care of itself. Of course, the problem is that the press does not give, nor has it ever given, a representative picture of the constituent groups in society. In fact, journalists can't even list the constituent groups, much less provide a reliable picture of them. No doubt Gordon would agree with this but would stress that the media must have a heightened sensitivity to diversity concerns. I could not disagree.

On the other hand, Kittross makes a good point when he expresses his belief that mainstream media do not have a special obligation to any particular groups; they have only the obligation, he says, to be fair and civil to *all* individuals, recognizing that membership in a group is often a meaningless distinction. For Kittross, the media's obligations are to *individuals*, not to groups. Kittross offers some fine examples of how "political correctness" has infiltrated the media and has introduced a plethora of euphemisms, even going beyond earlier terminology such as *sanitary engineer* instead of *garbage collector*. But, as Kittross says, a "buffalo chip by any other name would smell as sweet."

It is all getting very complicated for the media person who wants to understand just who everyone is, what to call social groups and races, and what should be changed to make everybody happy. What we are getting is an increasing concern for "communities" or special segments (or constituencies) in society, all clamoring to be treated equitably or fairly (as they define it) by the mass media. How can the media be fair to every one of these "communities" or cultures? This is a big and important question, but a puzzling and traumatic one for mass communicators.

Such communities as Hispanics, suburbanites, inner-city dwellers, environmentalists, blacks, gays and lesbians, Polish Americans, German Americans, religious fundamentalists, liberal Protestants, American Muslims, Catholics, American and Southern Baptists, lawyers, doctors, skinheads, drug dealers, and on and on—are all constituencies or "communities" that have their particular messages and want to be treated "fairly." Gordon talks of making special efforts to deal with them. Just what kind of efforts is he referring to?

It is all getting very complicated for the media person who wants to understand just who everyone is ...

Kittross would not have the media do anything other than what all conscientious media people already do: make content decisions as intelligently as possible, a practice that he contends is the perpetual ideal for the media. Gordon makes some suggestions that would focus more media attention on special multicultural concerns and calls for a sociocultural consciousness-raising in media decision-making. It is obvious that he feels the media can do much better than they are doing. And, of course, they can.

We can see certain changes in the direction Gordon is suggesting. Media are demasculinizing certain terms, such as routinely changing *chairman* to *chairperson* or simply to *chair*. And they are making sure to use *he* and *she* and *him* and *her*, or are simply using the plural *they* or *their*. I suppose that if the print media take this very far, they'll be avoiding "*man*-words" such as "management" "penmanship," and so on. At any rate, it is obvious that media consciousness has been raised, but perhaps, as Gordon says, it can be raised much more.

It may well be that before long various media groups will again revise their codes of ethics and deal with such multicultural labels. Perhaps they can also provide a calculus to be used by editors and news directors (and producers of TV drama) in determining the fair and equitable amount of space or time to be allotted to the various social groups.

My position is that the media can never please everyone. Some person or group will always feel ignored, slighted, misrepresented, stereotyped, or "put down" by some segment of the communication media. Such is the nature of mass communication. It cannot be objective, nor can it ever be truly fair. Its very nature determines that it will ignore some things, minimize or exaggerate others, and misrepresent still others. It's a complex, multifaceted, rather chaotic world out there with its legions of cultures, and the media can only distort it. The various constituencies may not like how they are treated in the media, but they had best get used to it.

REFERENCES

Barney, Ralph D. (1986). "The Journalist and a Pluralistic Society: An Ethical Approach." In Deni Elliott, ed., *Responsible Journalism*. Beverly Hills, CA: Sage, pp. 60–80.

Benedict, Helen. (1992). *Virgin or Vamp: How the Press Covers Sex Crimes*. New York: Oxford University Press.

Bloom, Harold. (1994). *The Western Canon—the Books and School of the Ages*. New York: Harcourt Brace.

Borgers, Edward W. (1961). "The Credentials Argument." (Unpublished dramatic reading of a dialogue between Saint Paul and Saint James.)

Centron, Marvin, and Owen Davies. (1989). *American Renaissance: Our Life at the Turn of the Twenty-first Century*. New York: St. Martin's.

Christians, Clifford G. (1986). "Reporting and the Oppressed." In Deni Elliott, *Responsible Journalism*. Beverly Hills, CA: Sage, pp. 109–130.

Coffey, Shelby. (April 8, 1994). "Why Newspapers Watch Their Language." Letter to *The New York Times*.

Commission on Freedom of the Press. (1947). *A Free and Responsible Press*. Chicago: University of Chicago Press.

Creedon, Pamela. (Winter-Spring 1993). "Framing Feminism—a Feminist Primer for the Mass Media." *Media Studies Journal* 7(2), pp. 69–80.

Dates, Jannette L., and William Barlow. (1990). *Split Image: African Americans in the Mass Media*. Washington: Howard University Press.

Dates, Jannette L., and Edward C. Pease. (Summer 1994). "Warping the World: Media's Mangled Images of Race." *Media Studies Journal* 8(3), pp. 89–95.

Fitzgerald, Mark. (June 11, 1994). "Downside of Political Correctness." *Editor & Publisher*, p. 9.

Fowler, H. W. (1965). *A Dictionary of Modern English Usage*, 2nd ed. New York: Oxford University Press.

Gerbner, George. (1993). "Women and Minorities on Television: A Study in Casting and Fate." (Unpublished report). Philadelphia: Annenberg School for Communication.

Gould, Stephen Jay. (November 28, 1994). "Review of *The Bell Curve*." *The New Yorker*, pp. 139–49.

Gould, Stephen Jay. (February 1995). "Review of *The Bell Curve*," *Natural History*, pp. 12–19.

Hall, Stuart. (1994). *In The War of the Words: The Political Correctness Debate*. London: Virago Press.

Hannaford, Ivan. (Spring 1994). "The Idiocy of Race." *The Wilson Quarterly* 18(2), pp. 8–35.

Heinlein, Robert A. (1982). *Friday*. New York: Ballantine.

Herrnstein, Richard J., and Charles Murray. (1994). *The Bell Curve*. New York: Free Press.

Jensen, Robert. (1994). "Banning 'Redskins' from the Sports Page: The Ethics and Politics of Native American Nicknames." *Journal of Mass Media Ethics* 9(1), pp. 16–25.

Lester, Gideon. (October 2, 1994). "Thomasina the Tank Engine Steams into a Sex Storm." *The Times* (London).

Lippmann, Walter. (1922). "The World Outside and the Pictures in Our Heads." In *Public Opinion*. New York: Macmillan.

Papper, Bob, and Michael Gerhard. (October 1997). "Moving Forward, Falling Back." RTNDA *Communicator*, pp. 24–30. The 1995 survey is reported in Bob Papper, Michael Gerhard, and Andrew Sharma (August 1996), "More Women and Minorities in Broadcast News." RTNDA *Communicator*, pp. 8–15.

Pease, Edward C. (Summer 1990). "Ducking the Diversity Issue." *Newspaper Research Journal* 11(2), pp. 24–37.

Pecora, Norma. (May 1993). "The Environment of Children's Advertising." Paper presented to the International Communication Association, Washington.

Rawls, John. (1971). *A Theory of Justice*. Cambridge, MA: Belknap.

Remnick, David. (January 10, 1994). "News in a Dying Language." *The New Yorker*, pp. 40–47.

Schramm, Wilbur. (September 1949). "The Nature of News." *Journalism Quarterly* 26(3), pp. 259–269.

Seabrook, John. (October 1994). "Rocking in Shangri-La." *The New Yorker*, pp. 64–78.

Siebert, Fred S., Theodore Peterson, and Wilbur Schramm. (1956). *Four Theories of the Press*. Urbana: University of Illinois Press.

Smith, Robert E. (Spring 1969). "They Still Write it White." *Columbia Journalism Review*, pp. 36–38.

Tannen, Deborah. (1990). *You Just Don't Understand*. New York: Morrow.

"TV's Black Flight." (June 3, 1996). *Time*, pp. 66–68.

CHAPTER 8

PRIVATE LIVES, PUBLIC INTERESTS

The search for blame after the death of Princess Diana of Wales in 1997 was immediately directed at the media that were following her car—mostly freelance photographers or "paparazzi"—without looking at any other contributing factors. For decades, concerns have surfaced about supposed news media excesses in reporting various aspects of the private lives of people who find themselves in the limelight. Indeed, the legal concept of invasion of privacy in the United States can be traced back to the late 19th century, when a pair of noted Boston lawyers used the *Harvard Law Review* to argue for legal recognition of a protected zone around what they called "the sacred precincts of private and domestic life" (Warren and Brandeis, 1890, p. 195). Although there are conflicting interpretations of what provoked the article, there is general agreement that the authors were upset with the attention (including photographs) given by some Boston newspapers to the personal lives of people in their social circles, including their own families.

Although the privacy issue goes back over a hundred years, new aspects of it continue to surface and threaten to make the dilemma more difficult as we move toward the 21st century. Publications such as *The National Enquirer* and, more recently, tabloid TV shows such as *Hard Copy* raise serious concerns about how far the media should pursue and transmit details of individuals' private lives, and under what circumstances this is justifiable.

In its most elemental form, *privacy* can be defined—as it was in the Warren and Brandeis article—as an individual's right to be let alone (see also p. 173). It has also been defined as the right to peace of mind, in contrast to defamation, which is an attack on one's reputation. Those definitions are only a start, however, toward the difficult task of pinning down privacy as a concept. One individual may not be bothered by the revelation of personal information that would drive the next person up the wall. There can be honest and principled disagreements about the degree to which "newsworthy" people must give up some of their right to be left alone in the interest of providing information that the public either needs or wants to have. Resolving this conflict of individual, public, and media rights and needs seems to call for the application of ethical principles at least as much as legal ones.

Confronting these issues, as they play out in everyday decisions, can often leave media people in a quandary. In the discussion that follows, Carol Reuss maintains that the media themselves should make the decisions concerning the boundary between newsworthiness and individual rights of privacy. David Gordon argues that leaving such decisions solely to the media hasn't worked in the past, and other controls may well be needed.

■ REUSS: The news and entertainment media should be the sole judges of how their activities impinge on individual rights of privacy.

The most important word in the premise for this discussion is the word *should*. The media *should* be the sole judges of how their activities impinge on individual rights of privacy. The men and women who staff the mass media *should* be capable of assessing what the public needs to know and willing to accept criticism, even rebukes, when they are wrong.

The issue of privacy is a partially charted mine field and no one is guaranteed safe passage through it. It is arguably the most sensitive, most controversial issue that the mass media face, and possibly the most common one. Journalists must scrutinize their own motives as carefully as those of their sources and the people and organizations they are reporting about. They must validate facts and contexts and they must judge the possible consequences of their work—that is, take a teleological view of ethical issues—well before they allow it to be published or broadcast. Decisions they make that even *might* impinge on others' rights to privacy cannot be made casually. The potential consequences to them and their organizations, as well as to the individuals or organizations whose privacy is jeopardized, are serious. Media reputations and financial security are as much at stake as are individual reputations, and the media know it.

The right of privacy is based on the tradition that individuals have the right to be let alone. Upholding that tradition are some state laws that regulate privacy. However, people are inquisitive—even nosey—and they want news about other people. They want details, even (or especially) sordid or scandalous details and they pay attention when the mass media focus on celebrities. When there is a possibility of an inside story, they want docudramas—even gossip—about people. They are mesmerized by unedited television feeds and impromptu street-side interviews, without much concern about the expertise of the interviewee.

It may take longer to process print stories, but public reactions are much the same. The public likes to read articles about other people, even articles that don't tell them more than they already knew or articles that merely suggest new possibilities.

There are basically three kinds of mass media decisions about privacy: those that involve people who are voluntarily in the public eye, people who are or might be involuntarily public, and people who, for any number of reasons, remain private.

Media scrutiny of public persons has been defended by the courts as a "greater good" that results when the public has as complete information as possible about a person who works or offers to work in the public arena. Political candidates and public officials are voluntarily public people. So are performers and other individuals who seek and achieve public attention. As David Gordon will explain, even aspects of their lives and activities that they prefer not to be subject to public scrutiny often are deemed appropriate for media coverage.

Years ago, the qualifications of aspiring political candidates were scrutinized in smoke-filled rooms. The fraternal assessments made there usually screened out unacceptable candidates, concentrated on electability, and often concluded with unspoken agreements to overlook or remain silent about anything that would handicap the favored candidate. This system that worked in the past has been greatly changed. Reporters have become more skillful, and perhaps bolder, and they use portable electronic equipment to record words and images verbatim and to access data about candidates that once was hidden in dusty files. And there is considerable competition among media to report details about political figures to a public that has more education and more opportunities to use the mass media than ever before.

No one knows for sure whether mass media scrutiny gives the public better government, but it is becoming evident that any person even considering running for office has to be ready to affirm or defend virtually every minute of his or her past. This is a serious matter for potential candidates and the public. Candidates now must be able to respond clearly and quickly to questions about their past activities and associations. Few subjects involving political figures are taboo, but the media can err egregiously when they blithely accept and use information supplied by candidates or by any other source without seeking verification. The media have the responsibility to weigh information carefully and present it in accurate and fair context.

■ THE SIMPSON CASE

The public arena is not limited to government and politics. The 1994–1995 media coverage of ex-football star O.J. Simpson's arrest and criminal trial is a case in point. Few people were *directly* affected by either the murders that precipitated the arrest or the trial coverage that followed. But millions of us (yes, including me) watched, listened, and read about O.J. until we got bored or distracted by some more important events in our lives. We remained uninformed about many other issues. The thrill of the "chase," then of the case, grabbed us as much as it grabbed the media. The media didn't have to worry about privacy because O.J. Simpson was a public person: an athlete, sports commentator, and actor who sought to be in the public spotlight. Until he was arrested, however, some aspects of his life were private; the media, for example, had rarely noted Simpson's reputation for domestic violence. After his arrest, Simpson's attorneys and the prosecutors sought media coverage, each apparently assuming that heavy media play would help its case.

... millions of us ... watched, listened, and read about O.J. [and] remained uninformed about many other issues.

A callous view of the widespread media coverage of O.J. Simpson shows little concern for his being public or private. Rather, the timing and the drama of "the chase" (the dozens of police cars escorting O.J. Simpson's white Bronco on Los Angeles area freeways), and the technology (such as the television-equipped helicopters) gave it made-for-prime-time immediacy. It also kicked off a return of the kind of "sob sister" reporting that was the staple of daily newspaper competition in the 1920s. Some might argue that the saturation coverage could prejudice subsequent legal actions, but the media knew Simpson was a public person, and the attorneys seemed willing to participate, so why not give the public every dramatic moment?

Many other individuals became involved in the Simpson case as potential witnesses and news sources. Some with only tenuous ties to the case convinced the media that they had little to offer, while others sought the limelight. Others rather quickly moved from being private persons to being public because of the momentum and scope of the case. Regardless of how or whether they participated publicly in the Simpson proceedings, some of them will have to guard their own privacy in the future if they wish to maintain it.

In any number of situations involving voluntarily public people, media men and women make decisions about what information to include and what sources to use, and they must take responsibility for the decisions they make and the reasons for making them.

Media people, too, are subject to the same consequences of being public as the subjects they cover, whether they like it or not. The bigger their reputations, the greater the scrutiny paid to their activities. Some grumble about it and others are diligent in trying to avoid any association or activity that brings unwanted public attention. But some become savory fare for the media's piranha-like feeding frenzy. One of the most egregious examples was the 1997 case of network sportscaster Marv Albert, who lost a sexual assault case and his job in the glare of what a punster might call a media full court press.

■ THE UNEXPECTED SPOTLIGHT

Many questions about privacy arise when people are thrust into the public spotlight by circumstances over which they have little control. These people may be living quietly, not seeking attention, when an event or situation intrudes and thrusts them into the news. The starting point may be an innocuous article based on a police report of an alleged crime. Before such a person knows it, reporters are on the phone or at the door, asking questions of neighbors, coworkers, anyone even remotely connected with him or her. Sometimes opinions and speculations expressed by these "sources" overshadow or obliterate any facts that are available and sometimes reporters begin to believe that opinions repeated often enough verify the facts, much to the disquiet of the person about whom the reporter is seeking information. Ethical questions of propriety, on the part of information seekers and tellers alike, abound in such situations.

Gordon discusses criteria to evaluate methods for obtaining private information. When media people—or organizations—apply these criteria, they can judge whether they are invading an individual's privacy. Likewise, media can control how information is gathered, especially whether hidden cameras, false identifications, and disguises are used to uncover important information that the public needs to know.

Media mailboxes, phone lines, and e-mail are often filled with offers from people who want even the most sordid details of their lives told for a variety of reasons. The mass media market is big and enticing to them. These people display their ethics selectively, and so do the media that use such material, so few steps are made without legal consultations and firm contracts. Personal fame and financial gain don't always equate well with public well-being, standards of taste, and ethics.

The media people who make decisions about who and what is public or private have serious obligations to the individuals involved and to the public—as well as to themselves and the media they represent. They must regularly ask themselves whether the invigorating highs they get when they uncover a story are in accord with the real significance of the tale.

A few "name" people are able to remove themselves from media attention even though the media and their audiences would prefer that they don't. Jacqueline Kennedy Onassis lived an extraordinary public life as First Lady. After President Kennedy's assassination in 1963, she remained on public view until shortly after his funeral. As a beautiful, young, brave widow, the media felt she still *was* news.

She determined, though, that she and her children deserved privacy and she was persistent in protecting it. She developed what one reporter called "a passion for privacy" and defended it for years, with every means at her disposal, including lawsuits. Major media players, many of whom had covered the White House, began to respect her wishes. Reporters often knew about her activities but didn't report them. They continued that reserve in their coverage of her final illness and death, even though millions of people probably wanted to know as many details as possible. Her legacy is that privacy is possible in a very public media world.

Crime and accident victims are involuntarily public people. In big cities, there are so many of them that only the most dramatic or gruesome usually make it into the media. Big city or small town, the media decide who and what will be published or broadcast and they must be able to justify their decisions both to those who want more and those who want less coverage of such violence.

Reporters and others who process crime and accident stories should also be sensitive to injured people or grieving families. The media have no special right to information from or about them, nor do their audiences. Often, however, media people assume they have the right to invade a family's privacy simply because one of its members was victimized. Helen Benedict (1992), in her excellent study of media coverage of sex crimes, suggests that reporters wait at least until after the first shock of the crime, and then tell families that they can choose to be interviewed or not and that they can ask not to be identified.

Media people should identify themselves to every person they interview, and they should remind distressed or traumatized individuals that they do not have to reply to any question. And, as Gordon explains, reporters should not include any information in their reports that could further endanger a crime victim. If all this sounds like a *Miranda* warning, it stems from the same goal: ordinary people need protection in moments of crisis.

Media sometimes pay a price for being ethical—such as reduced audiences, revenues, nitty-gritty government cooperation. Media people also may pay a personal price for being ethical. When they reveal information that the public needs but that public officials or candidates for public office would prefer not be discussed publicly, they may have doors closed to them, sources cut off. When they are compassionate, they may be criticized for not being aggressive or for being "soft." When they don't heed the public's cry for details about the private lives of people, they may lose audiences. But they can live with themselves. They can enjoy the confidence and support of people who understand and respect individual rights of privacy. And they strengthen the argument that they alone *should* be the sole decision-makers in matters of individual privacy.

■ GORDON: The news and entertainment media cannot be the sole judges of the boundary between appropriate and excessive coverage, even for public figures.

Beyond the broad right to be let alone, privacy is an important concept for anyone who respects the dignity and autonomy of fellow human beings. To avoid inflicting needless embarrassment or emotional distress, or the possibility that people could gain power over us if they "manage to obtain sensitive personal knowledge about us" (Parent, 1992, p. 97), there is general agreement that some things about almost any person should remain private. The issue arises over when those bounds of privacy can justifiably be breached, who makes those decisions, and what criteria should be used.

In a nutshell, I agree completely that in an ideal world, the mass media could and should be allowed to be the sole judges of where to draw the line between appropriate and excessive coverage of individuals' private lives. However, we operate in a less than ideal world, and too many media people have made poor and sometimes indefensible decisions on such issues. Therefore, there seems to be little alternative but to rely on more than just the good judgment of media practitioners, by backstopping those judgments where necessary with some forms of outside guidance or pressure.

This argument is usually a much easier one to make when the subject matter involves privacy for people who have *not* opted to enter the public sphere, but who have inadvertently become newsworthy through circumstances such as becoming an accident or crime victim. Even a Good Samaritan, like security guard Richard Jewell, was widely reported as a suspect in the Atlanta Olympic Park bombing of 1996 and his private life became "fair game." But even for people who have voluntarily entered some aspect of public life, the mass media have proven time and again that they—and society—would benefit from some external checks on their sense of what is fair game and what should be allowed to remain private.

Perhaps, for someone as powerful as the president of the United States, it can be argued that there are few if any areas where privacy concerns outweigh the public's right and need to know. Even Paula Jones's allegations about President Clinton's genital markings and detailed allegations about the president with Monica Lewinsky have been considered appropriate by the mainstream media as a matter for discussion. (See, among many useful sources, Witcover, 1998.) The power of the president is so wide-ranging that *almost* any aspect of the incumbent's life has some relationship to the way official duties are carried out—or not carried out. This wasn't always the case, and presidents before World War II enjoyed a great deal of privacy. For example, Franklin D. Roosevelt—arguably the most important president of this century—benefited from this reticence with respect to stories or photos showing the effects of his bout with polio or his relationship with Lucy Mercer.

Similar reasoning was expressed in 1979 by the then-editor of *People* magazine regarding its detailed coverage of speculation that former Vice President Nelson Rockefeller died while engaged in sex with his mistress. Richard Stolley argued that members of the Rockefeller family simply have *no* right to privacy:

"They've had such a profound effect on this country, its society, its politics, and its image of itself, that any inquiry into the circumstances of a Rockefeller's life or death, particularly one who lived in the public arena as Nelson did, is important." (Anderson, 1979, p. 2)

Men and women who enter the public arena at lower levels, in efforts to exercise leadership or make money or achieve fame, must also realize that they cannot fully shield areas of their lives that the media may deem appropriate for coverage. Even people thrust into the public arena only by the force of circumstances, who have far less power or importance than more willing participants, cannot entirely avoid media attention to the aspects of their lives that are deemed relevant or newsworthy. But using a newsworthiness standard opens the door to abuses. Unfortunately, the media haven't always lived up to their ethical obligation to use some discretion in deciding how far to go in covering the private portions of individuals' lives.

Edmund Lambeth (1992, pp. 57–58) criticized utilitarianism as one reason for that failure. He argued that the utilitarian approach can lead media people to define the maximization of *good* in terms that enhance the media organization's interest rather than seeking to define that greatest good from an independent ethical perspective. Too often, he wrote, the organizational good translates as sensational material designed to increase audience size, sometimes justified on the basis of the public's "right" to know anything that the media learn about.

. . . the knee-jerk invocation of that **right** *to know doesn't always justify printing or broadcasting intimate personal details.*

It would be well for media people—and the public—to keep firmly in mind that the knee-jerk invocation of that *right* to know doesn't always justify printing or broadcasting intimate personal details. This so-called right is not always the same as the public's *need* to know. Both of those certainly differ from the public's *desire* to know. If the latter is used as the only standard for invading individual privacy, the media stand guilty of simple pandering to the audience, and that has happened more often than is comfortable, sometimes spurred by an excess of media competition. It is not enough for us as a society just to hope that the media will exercise both good news judgment and good taste in deciding how far to go in revealing personal information. Some outside catalyst clearly seems to be needed in order to help the media maintain appropriate standards here. At a minimum, the privacy pendulum may need to swing back a bit so as not to discourage the best candidates from competing for high governmental posts.

The privacy issue affects not just what news the media print or broadcast, but also how that information is gathered. For example, should news reporters (print or broadcast) go undercover and use that fairly mild form of deception to further their newsgathering? Should they lie to gain access? Or use hidden cameras or recorders? A North Carolina jury emphatically said "no!" early in 1997, when it awarded $5.5 million (later reduced) to the Food Lion supermarket chain on the grounds that ABC producers had used fraud to obtain jobs where they could use hidden cameras to document a story about tainted meat.

Ethicist Deni Elliott argues even more broadly that

> . . . trickery, sleight of hand, and misrepresentation are tools for the magician, not for the journalist. From the passive practice of a journalist allowing a source to erroneously believe that the intended story will be a flattering one to the elaborate illusion of the journalistic mole in corporations and convalescent homes, deceptive gathering techniques cause more harm than good to the profession of journalism and to society as a whole (1997, p. 3).

Similar questions related to new technologies, such as e-mail, electronic bulletin boards, and databases, pose privacy concerns related to both the content and the method of gathering information. These are discussed further in Chapter 9.

■ PRIVACY ISSUES IN OBTAINING INFORMATION

One very useful set of criteria for weighing whether methods to *obtain* private information are ethically sound is paraphrased from W. A. Parent (1992), who listed six questions:

1. What is the purpose for which the information will be used?
2. Is the purpose legitimate and important?
3. Is the desired information relevant to this purpose? [And I would also ask whether it is *necessary* to the purpose.]
4. Is invading an individual's privacy the only—or the least offensive—way to obtain the information?
5. Does the technique to be used to obtain the information have some sort of restrictive safeguards built into it, or will it likely result in indiscriminate invasions of the individual's privacy?
6. What safeguards will exist to insure that the information will be used only for appropriate purposes once it is obtained? (p. 100)

Some critics insist that any misrepresentation, such as undercover reporting, is a form of lying and is not appropriate. Sissela Bok, while not ruling it out in cases of extreme importance, called such deception "morally questionable" (Bok, 1982, p. 263) and noted that it may well lead to reduced media credibility. She found some irony in the news media's often unquestioning acceptance of the need for undercover reporting, which she called "a stance that challenges every collective rationale for secrecy save the media's own" (p. 264).

Bob Steele of the Poynter Institute has compared the use of hidden cameras to lying, and has argued that they should be used only if other concerns—such as a need to protect vulnerable members of society, for example, by reporting consumer fraud as it happens—clearly outweigh reservations about such deception. That situational ethics approach meshes well with the criteria suggested by Parent. In essence, such approaches weigh the importance and benefits of the story—and the relevance of the information—against the degree of deception or invasion required. Many journalists argued that the Food Lion story failed on all counts, especially since ABC delayed airing it until sweeps month. (*Media Ethics*, 1997)

Whereas the ethical issues involved in straight undercover reporting usually focus on deception by the reporter and touch only tangentially on privacy concerns, the use of hidden cameras in TV newsgathering focuses much more centrally on this topic. As Supreme Court reporter Lyle Denniston (1994) pointed out, the use of hidden cameras "is, by definition, an intrusion that raises ethical questions" (p. 54). This practice can easily lead to such specific invasions of privacy as displaying hospital patients on screen as part of an investigative report of the hospital. Although some such reports may well be worthwhile, others may present footage taken by hidden cameras when other means could have been used to tell the story just as effectively.

At such times, the use of hidden cameras seems to be more a technique to boost ratings than one required to obtain important information that would otherwise be unavailable. For this reason, among others, the media cannot be allowed to be the sole judges of when to use hidden cameras. The same rationale holds in other areas where invasion of privacy is a serious risk (see also Chapter 9).

A related issue of concern here is the place—if any—of so-called ambush journalism in the gathering of information for television. Although this isn't as deceptive as the use of hidden cameras, it still raises questions as to how fair it is to the subjects of the interview, perhaps especially if they have not been avoiding attempts to interview them. Considerable criticism was leveled at *60 Minutes* at the end of the 1980s because of its heavy reliance on interviews in which the camera crew burst upon the interviewee with tape rolling and a reporter ready to pounce with questions. A number of observers questioned whether this technique was necessary in all instances where it was used, and such concerns might well have been reduced or eliminated if CBS had not been the sole judge of when to employ ambush journalism.

The whole area of visual communication often threatens to invade privacy and raises questions of taste. This is true whether one is talking about still photos, motion pictures, or video cameras. All have captured images of grieving survivors and have relayed pictures of other situations which many readers, viewers, and critics felt might better have been left private. The fact that these scenes were photographed or taped in public places was of concern only because the public locale meant that no legal action was likely to succeed. But the raw emotion that was put on public display for a wide audience to see (and, often, to view repeatedly) still raises valid ethical concerns about the media's conduct as it affects individuals' right to be let alone (see also Chapter 15-G).

Privacy issues, and the closely related question of good taste, can also arise for the entertainment media. Producers of TV dramas or movies that focus on the lives of private individuals must either use materials entirely from the public record or get the individuals' permission to feature them this way, in order to avoid legal pitfalls. Nonetheless, the question of taste enters here as an ethical if not a legal concern. One wonders how much the public really needed to know about Amy Fisher, the "Long Island Lolita," who was the subject in 1993 of docudrama programming on all three major networks shortly after she was found guilty of trying to murder her lover's wife. Fisher may have desired this exposure, but others involved in the story might well have felt that personal aspects of their lives were exposed only to gratify public voyeurism. A detached assessment could reasonably conclude that these programs crossed the line separating good entertainment or useful information from out and out sensationalism.

■ POLITICAL CANDIDATES AND OTHER PRIVACY CONCERNS

Carol Reuss noted that the news media provide an important public service by scrutinizing the background of political candidates. She is correct in saying that this media role has become particularly important with the demise of the "political boss" system where candidates were screened and selected behind the scenes. Few people would argue that the "smoke-filled back rooms" were better than the more open political system that now exists, and today's news media have a role to play in helping to weed out candidates with problems in their background. But that media responsibility has arguably been abused at times in recent decades, and at a minimum has been exercised with a zeal that has sometimes drawn valid public criticism and concern.

Focusing specifically on facets of private life that may illuminate politicians' character, Lee Wilkins suggested that such private facts must "be linked to public, political behaviors before publication or broadcast becomes ethically justifiable" (Wilkins, 1994, p. 160). She added that revealing private information without establishing that link "is a form of tabloid journalism that casts doubt on journalistic motives and credibility" (p. 162).

Political candidates must accept the fact that they give up much of their right to claim areas where their lives should remain private. But, at the same time, they should retain the right to keep *some* aspects of their lives private, especially those that have no direct bearing on their public actions, and perhaps even some that do if the motivation to reveal details is based only on a desire to improve ratings or circulations or just to titillate the public.

In a sense, the news media are playing a gatekeeper role not just with regard to information, but in connection with the determination of which candidates are "validated" for presentation to the public. Thus, arguments that the media should be the sole judges of what to report may have some minimal validity in regard to candidates and others who have consciously chosen to enter the public sphere, where the news media have a responsibility to provide all necessary information on which citizens can make informed choices and decisions.

Although people who choose to become active in politics and government (or in business, or education, or other aspects of life in the public sphere) must therefore live with that concept, they do have a valid point when they insist that the media gatekeeping role be exercised responsibly and that private aspects of character or behavior must, as Wilkins suggested, be connected to public actions to justify their disclosure. Once again, on the basis of the overall media track record, definitions of *responsible* or of *appropriate connections* shouldn't be left entirely to the news media. Some mechanisms must be in place to check their excesses, or at the very least to call attention to them so they will be harder to repeat.

Media attention may be even harder to bear for people who become newsworthy through no conscious decision of their own, such as the survivors of people who have been killed in ways that make them newsworthy. For example—in the context of visual communication and privacy noted earlier—consider the feelings of the family of a boy whose drowning death was documented in a large picture of his family anguishing over his body shortly after its recovery. Was the portrayal of the family's grief—displayed as it was in a public location—really fair game for the newspaper photographer who snapped the picture (and for the editors who decided to run it)? Was it worth the impact on the victim's survivors to present a very dramatic picture and (as an editor claimed in this instance) to warn the general public to be more careful when swimming (Christians et al., 1998, pp. 119–122)?

In such circumstances, it seems highly appropriate for the media to consider more than just their own definitions of *news* (or even of *entertainment*), no matter what ethical theory is used for guidance. John Rawls's concern for protecting the weakest party in a situation would go further and give priority to the privacy needs of accident victims. But even stopping short of Rawls's approach, the reaction of the victims and their families, and questions of public sensibilities, should certainly be relevant factors. Concern for them might prevent such complaints as the one expressed in a letter to Ann Landers by a mother whose teenage son was killed in a traffic accident. She called media coverage of the tragedy "absolutely heartless" and noted that the boy's grandmother got the news of the accident from TV before the mother could notify her. "Is 'news' that important?," the mother asked. "Do people really enjoy tragedy that much? Where has compassion gone?" (Landers, 1994).

Perhaps the media need to ponder such questions in the abstract, and discuss them with people who have differing and detached viewpoints, in order to develop some reasonable guidelines without deadline pressures looming over the discussion. Somehow, the media ought to develop mechanisms through which they can be accountable when serious privacy concerns are at stake. Doing this only under deadline pressures, with no input from media critics or the public, is not a sensible approach.

■ SOME PRINCIPLES FOR DECISION MAKING

In considering such issues, Clifford Christians and his coauthors enunciated three moral principles that can serve as guidelines for the use or nonuse of material that may invade privacy. The first of these "promotes decency and basic fairness as nonnegotiable" and bans such things as innuendo and exaggeration. The second principle posits "redeeming social value"—specifically as opposed to "prurient interests"—as the basis for deciding what (private) information should be disclosed. The third principle holds that "the dignity of persons ought not be maligned in the name of press privilege. Whatever serves ordinary people best must take priority over some cause or slogan" (Christians et al., 1998, p. 111).

As Bok has noted, even the First Amendment's "*legal* right to free expression cannot do away with the need for *moral* scruples in choosing what to publish" (Bok, 1982, p. 255—italics in the original). The need to pay "special attention to individual privacy" is especially important, she said, when the media provide material that satisfies the public's curiosity rather than content that affects the public welfare (p. 258).

Parent's first four questions might also be used in determining whether information of a private nature should or shouldn't be revealed, regardless of whether its acquisition constitutes an ethical invasion of privacy. For instance, consider the question of whether a rape victim's identity should be revealed by the media, an issue that has become even more complex with the televising of trials on such channels as Court TV.

One might argue that the media should help society eliminate the traditional stigma attached to rape victims by publishing or broadcasting their names as they would the victims of other crimes. But that argument is flawed by the fact that identifying the rape victim against her will usually results in extreme pain and trauma for her, and discourages other victims from reporting rapes. Moreover, it appears to have little or no impact on reducing rape's societal stigma. Thus, printing the rape victim's name fails Parent's third test of relevance to the larger purpose, and probably the fourth test as well, because there have to be less harmful ways of pursuing the elimination of rape's stigma. Printing the victim's name—and also possibly publishing the accused's name—also fail to meet Christians' criteria of decency, fairness, and preservation of personal dignity.

Kant would require that rape victims be treated as individuals worthy of consideration rather than as vehicles to educate society that rape is not a stigma. He would probably agree with a guideline that victims' names could be made public only if they were willing—a middle position that Aristotle would undoubtedly support, as would many situational ethicists.

Utilitarians would argue for the greatest overall good, which might allow identification even of victims who object, *if* that really would lead to changes in societal attitudes. Rawls would support the protection of the weakest party in each situation, and that would almost certainly be a rape victim who did not want her name revealed.

In the case of rape victims, the Supreme Court in *Cox Broadcasting Corp.* v. *Cohn* (1975) held specifically that no invasion of privacy suit is possible if the name or other information is obtained by the news media from a public record or proceeding. Nonetheless, most media outlets still refrain from identifying living rape victims, even though they are legally protected in doing so. However, for media that do identify rape victims, this Supreme Court ruling means that the legal system can't act as an outside referee to establish the boundary between valid media coverage and incursions into areas where individual privacy deserves protection.

The courts, however, have on occasion provided such outside guidance to the media on the broader question of reporting the victims' names in crimes other than rape. The media have routinely reported such names, but this practice may well need further consideration and perhaps some guidelines developed by more than just the media gatekeepers. Some newspapers that used to print routine "police log" reports of crimes have modified or eliminated the practice after complaints that running names and addresses of burglary victims has set up the likelihood of repeated attempts. Similarly, printing names of those arrested may be prejudicial when cases come to trial. Other papers apparently take the utilitarian position that the overall benefits of running such details outweigh any harm that might come to individuals.

This issue gets even more complicated when news media make available personal details that can result in serious risk of bodily harm or death to an individual, and it is in this area that the courts have begun to step in. In one such case, a woman escaped from an abductor who briefly kidnapped her off the street, but became a further victim when the abductor began stalking her and terrorizing her with phone calls *after* he learned her name and address because a local paper had printed them!

The woman sued the city and the paper for releasing and using that information negligently, and the court held that regardless of the state's open records law, there were valid grounds to sue for negligence. Such a "foreseeable risk" of future harm should have led the paper to omit the woman's identity even if it was obtained from public records. (See *Hyde v. City of Columbia*, 1982, as discussed in Scott, 1993.) Although this precedent has been followed only in part by other courts, it nonetheless illustrates how outside forces are beginning to impinge on the media's ability to serve as the sole judges for their approaches to the limits of privacy.

It is worth noting that, over the years, the courts appear to get involved in mass media issues more often when they perceive that remedies are needed for media excesses. Thus, if the media want to retain the greatest possible control over such things as determining the appropriate boundaries for privacy, they would be very well-advised to exercise enough self-control that the public—and the judiciary—do not start to clamor about media excesses and begin to protect individuals by imposing monetary damages for such practices, or threaten the First Amendment's existence.

■ OTHER POSSIBLE SOURCES OF GUIDANCE

If not the courts, then what other sources might provide outside guidance? News councils and ombudsmen (a combination of inside and outside sources of guidance)—or journalism reviews (e.g., the "Darts and Laurels" column in the *Columbia Journalism Review*) and outside media critics—might serve this function. At the risk of being called slightly heretical, I'd also suggest that such criticism and guidance is something academics could do better than they have, especially if some of them were less dependent for support on some of the media companies that would be affected by such critiques. (For a discussion of other media accountability systems, see Bertrand, 1993.)

Classes in media criticism—or other efforts to educate media users about what they should and should not expect from their media—might be another step in this direction. So would increased media efforts to promote feedback from their audiences, through such devices as advisory boards or town meetings.

There are many other specific concerns that could be discussed in exploring whether the media need outside help in setting the boundaries within which individual privacy will be respected. Among them are the questions of naming juveniles accused of crime, naming "johns" arrested for patronizing prostitutes, identifying HIV victims, and many other situations where the media have to make decisions daily about an individual's privacy.

One of the most difficult and emotion-laden examples of such a decision occurred when a local paper learned that a very promising and talented young woman from Missoula, Montana, who had gone east to college, had been found dead on a Washington, D.C., street after turning to prostitution. The decision about whether to print the information was made more agonizing by the fact that the story was being distributed in the Missoula area by a regional paper using a very complete account distributed by *The Washington Post* news service. *The Missoulian* decided to publish much of the story, despite insistent requests from the victim's family not to do so. The decision brought down a firestorm of local criticism, as well as an editorial criticizing this decision *on its own editorial page* (Hart and Johnson, 1979; see also Christians et al., 1998, pp. 114–117).

The Missoula decision could well be argued either way, and at least it was made after considerable internal discussion and debate. But less responsible news and entertainment media are also faced with similar decisions on a regular basis, and they have on too many occasions shown too little concern for the individuals whose privacy was at stake. It therefore would seem, on balance, that concerns about individual privacy are too important a matter to be left solely to the discretion—or lack of it—of the news and entertainment media.

■ MERRILL: Commentary

The main problem with the controversy over privacy is that nobody really knows what *privacy* is. As is true of so many arguable topics in mass communication, *privacy* is extremely difficult to deal with. Carol Reuss and David Gordon have had a thoughtful fling at it, but the basic questions linger: What is privacy? Who has a right to it? How does it comport with the idea of the people's right to know? Is it in the public interest to know so much about other people's lives? Furthermore, when does a private person become a public figure?

In general, the media themselves determine when and how to focus attention on people, public and private. There are broad, fuzzy guidelines (such as not invading the sanctity of private homes), but such notions at best only moderate media behavior and at worst are completely ambiguous or meaningless (e.g., if you use a long lens from a public road). The right of privacy—the right of a person to be let alone—immediately comes in conflict with the First Amendment's press freedom clause. It also comes in conflict with the assumed right of the people to know.

If broadcasters were to leave people alone, to generally ignore them, where would television be today? Television is, even more than the print media, a leech, sucking every possible drop of personal dignity from the principals in their stories. An exaggeration? Watch the talk shows, the Oprah Winfreys, *A Current Affair*, *Inside Edition*, *Hard Copy*, and a number of lesser-lights among the "people exposure" shows. Watch even news magazine shows of the *60 Minutes* or *20/20* genre. Are people being let alone? They and all their human foibles are being held up for constant public gaze—warts and all, especially warts. Most of these people, by the way, are public figures only in the sense that they are being presented *to the public* and—surprising as it may seem—a large proportion of participants *ask* to appear on these shows.

Perhaps it would be helpful for the media person to include in a kind of unstated footnote to every story an exposé of the **justifications for that story and the tactics used in getting it.**

It is certainly true that most Americans today realize that they are fair game for the media if they, in any way, happen to get in the way of the sweeping media searchlight that constantly shifts around hoping to fall on some person caught in the unexpected grip of circumstance. Pity the poor mother who finds herself beside her wrecked car with her dead daughter lying beside her. Pity the parents of the American soldier in Somalia whose naked body is being stepped on and dragged through the streets of Mogadishu. Remember the pictures of the dead bodies in Oklahoma City? The crumpled Mercedes in which Princess Diana was killed? You can count on it: The cameras are there and they eagerly portray every detail. Do the people need to know such things? See such things? Will it help them be better citizens, more informed voters? Just what are the limits of the so-called right of privacy?

I suppose a basic ethical question revolves around the degree of, and limits of, media exposure of people, and also the *need* for audience members to have access to such information. This may well be the basis for violations of this amorphous right of privacy: audience need. But it is doubtful that many mass communicators predicate their digging into people's lives on the question of *need to know*. They (even journalists) see themselves as free agents in their determination of what is to be made public. After all, if you were to retain in the average daily newspaper only the news that the readers actually *needed*, you could probably get it all on the front page.

The main question usually asked by mass communicators of themselves (if they ask themselves *any* questions) is, What do I want to present to the public? If I think it is proper, then it is appropriate. This is, indeed, an egocentric test, but it is generally used, and it is consistent with the whole theory of editorial self-determination—a basic and traditional American concept of press freedom or freedom of speech. But what about the *ethics* of such publishing or broadcasting? If this question is asked at all, it is easily rationalized away by the media person who is skilled at justifying any action taken. The *ethical question* is usually sacrificed in the hurry-and-scurry of everyday media work to the more immediate and tangible *pragmatic questions:* Will it work? Will it accomplish my goal? Will it succeed? Or will it please some constituency—even a very callous one, a small one, or one with a need to have its prurient interest satisfied?

How would the media person like to have some observer or reporter digging into his or her own daily activities? How would it feel to have one's every action questioned, every motive analyzed, every statement dissected, every opinion interpreted? In essence, how would it feel to go behind Rawls's "veil of ignorance"? Perhaps it would be helpful for the media person to include in a kind of unstated footnote to every story *an exposé of the justifications for that story and the tactics used in getting it.* Actually, too many media people in America seem to see themselves as above the *moral law*, falling back on media rights and press freedom granted by the Constitution.

As was pointed out in the dialogues above, the invasion of privacy is often related to poor taste, especially in the use of pictures. Weeping parents, corpses beside the road, mutilated or starving children, suicidal people leaping to their deaths, couples involved in sexual intimacies, a former First Lady topless on a private beach, and on and on. Forgetting for a minute the *ethical* implications of such pictures, in most cases we can admit that they are in poor taste. Recognizing full well that many will reply that "poor taste" is relative and therefore not an appropriate determinant for publishing or not publishing information, there is no doubt but that most media people recognize poor taste when they see it. For economic or egoistical reasons, they simply desire to pass it on, to titillate, to entertain, to shock, to expose, to generate gossip, and to mock normal conventions. And their actions are contagious; other media follow suit, not to be outdone by their competitors.

In American society, the traditional and revered journalistic tendency is for the media people themselves to determine when privacy is invaded. Certainly that would be the ethical determination. Otherwise, the *legal* controllers or determiners come into the picture. The contending authors above take two polar positions: that the media determine privacy problems and that outside judges make the determinations.

Because this is a book on media *ethics*, I must come down on the media-determination side of the controversy, despite the example of the feeding frenzy in the almost *ad nauseam* coverage of the O.J. Simpson murder case in 1994 and 1995—and the ensuing civil trial. If we were talking *law* instead of ethics, I might feel otherwise. But ethics concerns freedom and voluntary decision making, not coercive legalism, and *media* ethics pertains to the media voluntarily making these decisions. In an ideal world, media ethics might well correspond to socially or judicially dictated solutions. But when the factor of *freedom* is considered as part of the ethical formula, the responsibility for such media decisions must fall squarely on the media decision makers themselves.

REFERENCES

Anderson, Jon. (March 6, 1979). "People's Five Big Years of All the Faces that Are Fit to Print." *Chicago Tribune*, sec. 2, pp. 1–2.

Benedict, Helen. (1992). *Virgin or Vamp: How the Press Covers Sex Crimes*. New York: Oxford University Press.

Bertrand, Claude-Jean. (Fall 1993). "Media Ethics in Europe: Media Accountability Systems." *Media Ethics* 6(1), pp. 7–9.

Bok, Sissela. (1982). *Secrets: On the Ethics of Concealment and Revelation*. New York: Pantheon.

Christians, Clifford G., Mark Fackler, Kim B. Rotzoll, and Kathy Brittain McKee. (1998). *Media Ethics: Cases and Moral Reasoning*, 5th ed. New York: Longman.

Cox Broadcasting Corp. v. Cohn, 420 U.S. 469 (1975).

Denniston, Lyle. (April 1994). "Going Too Far with the Hidden Camera?" *American Journalism Review*, p. 54.

Elliott, Deni. (Summer 1997). "Journalists' Con Games Can Backfire." *Montana Journalism Review* 26, pp. 3–6.

Hart, Jack, and Janis Johnson. (May 1979). "Fire Storm in Missoula: A Clash Between the Public's Right to Know and a Family's Need for Privacy." *Quill*, pp. 19–24.

Hyde v. *City of Columbia*, 637 S.W.2d 251 (Mo., 1982), cert. den., 459 U.S. 1226 (1983).

Lambeth, Edmund B. (1992). *Committed Journalism: An Ethic for the Profession*, 2nd ed. Bloomington: Indiana University Press.

Landers, Ann. (October 17, 1994). "Mourning Mother Resents TV News." *The Boston Globe*, p. 36.

Media Ethics 8(2). (Spring 1997). Includes seven articles on the Food Lion case.

Parent, W. A. (1992). "Privacy, Morality and the Law." In Elliott D. Cohen, ed., *Philosophical Issues in Journalism*. New York: Oxford University Press, pp. 92–109.

Scott, Sandra Davidson. (1993). "Blood Money: When Media Expose Others to Risk of Bodily Harm." Paper presented at the annual convention of the Association for Education in Journalism and Mass Communication, Kansas City, MO, August 11–14.

Warren, Samuel D., and Louis D. Brandeis. (December 15, 1890). "The Right to Privacy." *Harvard Law Review* 4(5), pp. 193–220.

Wilkins, Lee. (1994). "Journalists and the Character of Public Officials/Figures." *Journal of Mass Media Ethics* 9(3), pp. 157–168.

Witcover, Jules. (March/April 1998). "Where We Went Wrong." *Columbia Journalism Review*, pp. 18–25.

CHAPTER 9

DATA PRIVACY

A re there differences between the general notion of individual privacy and the privacy of personal data located in computerized databases? Can such data, often collected for important and beneficial social and government purposes, be reused—by the mass media, or by others—in ways that actually or potentially invade an individual's privacy?

This chapter focuses specifically on the potential for such abuses. One early expression of these concerns was a book by Arthur R. Miller, a law professor who foresaw more than 25 years ago some of the problems that could arise from "the computer, with its insatiable appetite for information, its image of infallibility, and its inability to forget anything that has been stored in it" (1971, p. 3).

The computer's ability to store data, and the inability of government and business to do without such data, have provided opportunities for the media to obtain computerized information for their own use. Recent developments, including the "information superhighway," have reinforced such concerns at the same time that they have provided new media and new contexts in which to discuss this topic. But we might still conclude, as Miller did in 1971, that

> not enough is being done to insure that computerized data, either in their stored form or while in transit, are any more immune from the intrusive activities of snoopers than private telephone conversations have been protected against the machinations of wire-tappers. (p. 20)

This chapter asks whether the technological revolutions in computers—and their impact on data storage and retrieval and on the distribution of electronic messages—pose new questions about the responsibility of the mass media (and various other societal institutions as well), or whether these technological changes merely call for an updating of some of the older and more familiar concerns about privacy in mass communication. These questions remain far from resolution, but are important to pose to a generation that grew up with computers and accepts them uncritically.

David Gordon maintains that there is a right of informational privacy that must be respected. John Michael Kittross thinks that the technology itself has gotten beyond us, and that trying to control its abuses—whether by the government and business or by the mass media—is merely spitting into the wind.

■ GORDON: The mass media—in their news, marketing, and similar activities—must respect informational privacy concerning personal information contained in private or government databases.

John Michael Kittross will make an interesting argument, in the second part of this chapter, against the need for special efforts by the mass media to avoid misusing personal information from databases. He says, logically enough, that the normal efforts to be fair, truthful, and accurate are all that's required in this area, as in others.

But this logic breaks down on at least two points. First, we must recognize that the huge and growing amount of personal information available from electronic databases poses the kinds of temptations that mass media communicators have rarely, if ever, had to face. Second, there is the ethical ambiguity Kittross notes in regard to using data collected for specific purposes in ways that were never intended.

The first point seems obvious, and doesn't require much elaboration (though it may well require some changes in the way we educate advertising and public relations practitioners, journalists, and others to deal with these temptations). With an increased ability to access expanding electronic databases comes an increased capacity to use this expanded storehouse of information for "good" or "valid" purposes (however those may be defined), but also to misuse it for less worthy goals.

A special concern here may be the need to find a way to distinguish ethically between information about public figures that should be made available to the public and computerized information about such people that should remain private. This problem poses increasing concerns as the amount of personal information about public figures increases, but it is essentially the same issue that was addressed more generally in Chapter 8.

A variant of this concern deals with the ethics of reporters browsing through electronic bulletin boards in search of an eye-catching quote from some useful source, to include in a story. Some chat rooms, listservs, and other Internet sites have their own rules but ethical—and legal—standards across the Internet are less clear. Reporters who use messages from Internet sources in their paper or on the air may well have some legal protection, whether or not they have the writer's permission to use the material. But the ethical questions posed are more complicated.

First of all, does it matter whether the message comes from a person in the public eye or from someone who is a totally private individual? Although neither public nor private users of electronic bulletin boards may expect their messages to show up in the news, can they validly complain about reprinting material that may already have been seen by thousands of people with access to the site (Resnick, 1994)? Does the situation differ when the source of the material is e-mail addressed to a specific person and is posted by the recipient?

In addition to the question of republishing material without obtaining permission, reporters also face the problem of knowing who the source really is. The dilemma was neatly illustrated by a cartoon in *The New Yorker* showing two pooches at a computer, with one noting, "On the Internet, nobody knows you're a dog" (Resnick, 1994, p. 11). It may well be that both ethics and the demands of careful journalism coincide here, to require that reporters confirm the author's identity before using quotes gleaned from the Internet along with other checks they should make. Taking that a step further, it might also be useful to develop ethical guidelines dealing with what kinds of electronic messages should be considered public and which should remain private unless the author's permission is obtained. In any case, the growth of e-mail and electronic bulletin boards, and the ability to tap into both, have created some new concerns about informational privacy that journalists must address, or run the risk of having others impose answers.

A more wide-ranging problem is the second one noted above: the concern about reusing data in ways that differ from the original purpose in collecting it. Personnel in the mass media field should be very much aware of this potential problem, lest they fall unwittingly into this ethical morass. Of course, this problem exists far more broadly than just in mass communication, but that makes it no less of a concern for mass media practitioners.

Mass communication education hasn't dealt with this concern extensively, in part because computerized databases are such a relatively new phenomenon. But the daily, perhaps hourly technological (and conceptual) advances in collecting and analyzing new kinds of data for widely varying purposes open up a steadily increasing number of opportunities to obtain and use that data for one's own particular purposes and benefit, regardless of the original intent in collecting it. Some of those individual purposes may well be beneficial to the society as a whole. The challenge is to sort out which ones are worthy and which should be avoided.

Journalists are far from the only mass media people affected by this issue. Advertising and public relations practitioners and direct marketers are (or will soon be) faced with many of the same dilemmas, as capabilities increase to obtain electronically stored data on individuals and to reuse those data to target a PR or advertising campaign more precisely. And what about advertisers who obtain lists of e-mail addresses and send them mass electronic advertising messages—the approach known as "spamming" the recipients?

In the abstract, there is not necessarily any problem with collecting and using data in these ways. But if the data use clearly differs from the purposes for which it was collected, there are informational privacy ethics issues well worth considering, perhaps especially because the ability to obtain and reuse computerized data "is washing away the traditional lines between public and private information" (Hausman, 1994, p. 139).

The temptations for such data reuse are likely to become particularly seductive with the growth of interactive cable systems and Internet service providers that will routinely collect various individually identifiable data as consumers use these new two-way capabilities. These data will be needed to keep the system running properly—for instance, to make sure that customers are billed properly for the different uses they make of the interactive system. But the data—if made available—would also be of considerable interest to advertisers, direct marketers, and others who want to target their ads or their sales pitches to the most likely prospects. Auletta (1994) offers this observation:

> With the set-top box digesting huge amounts of information about consumers, the box becomes a camera in the home. "When you put those powerful converter boxes in the home, they will know your habits," Viacom's president and C.E.O., Frank Biondi, Jr., says. "Marketers want to know your habits." To sell advertising, communications companies will naturally want to sell information that citizens would rather keep private. Who, if not government, would protect citizens from what has been called data rape? (pp. 52–53)

Indeed, if communications companies can't resist the temptation to commit "data rape," the government may well have to step in with strong control measures. In the absence of government safeguards on how databases can be used and on who can have access to them for what purpose, it remains risky ethically—and perhaps legally as well—for mass media practitioners to disclaim any responsibility in this area.

"Who, if not government, would protect citizens from what has been called data rape?"

It seems far more prudent, on both legal and ethical grounds, for communications industries to police themselves and to make sure that they respect citizens' informational privacy to some reasonable degree, rather than leaving this responsibility to the government. In this regard, direct marketers and others in the United States might well follow the example of their counterparts in the European Union, whose standards concerning data privacy are more stringent than those in effect here.

■ PRIVATE AND PUBLIC DATA BANKS

The data privacy concern relates to both information in government data banks and that held by private parties. For our purposes, much privately held data is material collected by mass media organizations such as cable companies, newspapers, TV networks, and advertising agencies. However, it also must extend to various private data banks—credit reporting companies are perhaps the outstanding example—that reporters or others may be able to tap into. For some data collected by the federal government, minimal safeguards do exist. These are outlined in the Privacy Act of 1974, which specifies that there must be public knowledge of government data banks and that citizens must have the right to correct any false or misleading information. This rather minimal approach might well be used—at least as a starting point—in regard to private data banks as well, either voluntarily by the mass media industries or through government action.

Such requirements do apply at least minimally to the cable industry, under the provisions of the Cable Franchise Policy and Communications Act of 1984. Cable systems must inform their customers that data are being collected and must obtain subscriber consent to release any individually identifiable data to third parties. But these regulations were written for the more traditional one-way cable systems that gather much less—and very different—data than may be collected by interactive systems. The regulations fail to mandate an opportunity for misleading data (such as information residing in a data bank without adequate context) to be corrected or reinterpreted.

Several states have also adopted similar legislation, aimed at protecting the informational privacy of cable consumers. These statutes are generally modeled after the code adopted by Warner Amex for its trial of the QUBE system in Columbus, Ohio, from 1977 to 1985 (Wilson, 1988, pp. 84–88).

These various regulations fail to deal adequately with the reuse of data under either government or private control without the consent of the individual concerned, particularly by media other than cable systems. For example, an on-line publication would not be barred from encouraging its audience to furnish demographic information as part of an interactive contest entry, and then selling that data to direct marketing firms. Nor would a newspaper be prohibited from requiring people to register when visiting its website, and then selling the names to a spam marketer.

As noted above, the 1984 cable legislation forbids system operators from marketing to outside firms any individual data gathered through interactive transactions with customers, unless they have those customers' permission. But this kind of information has tremendous potential economic value, and it is not far-fetched to worry that cable companies may argue strongly for the right to use it freely and persuade Congress to agree. This could involve selling it to the highest bidder, to help recoup the major financial investments necessary to develop the infrastructure for two-way cable systems, or simply using it without restriction to help market various products more efficiently (Wilson, 1988, p. 48).

Some formula will be needed—if not immediately, then before long—to balance individuals' privacy interests with the profit-making concerns of media corporations, or the reportorial needs of journalists. We certainly cannot ignore the considerable benefits investigative journalists derive from having access to all sorts of computer-based personal data and government records about individuals (such as police records—see Morgan, 1994, pp. 30–31). Journalism is rapidly learning what computer-assisted reporting can accomplish. In many cases, the retrieval and use of such data allows journalists to override any individual privacy concerns when they decide the information is important enough to the public.

But these capabilities also open up the temptation for uses that invade individuals' privacy for much less worthy purposes, and that's where care and caution must be exercised. The use of private data merely to entertain the public may well inflict such emotional distress on the subjects of that data as to make it ethically (and perhaps legally) unacceptable. The possibilities of tabloid TV shows such as *Hard Copy* tapping into computer databases to obtain titillating information is a scenario that necessitates the use of solid ethical criteria in drawing the line between acceptable and inappropriate uses of private data. So does the possibility of using such public databases as driver's license records for purposes ranging from target marketing to investigations by journalists—not to mention private investigators or other users "who frequently view our private lives as public commodities" (Hausman, 1994, p. 136).

Kittross will argue that the media need to have access to computerized databases maintained by the government. As a general principle, that works pretty well because "public information" should certainly be available to the public. However, this principle still raises ethical concerns about government databases of which the general public remains ignorant, or to which there is no access for corrections. Hausman argues for a redefinition of "public information," largely because the advent of powerful computers has produced "a fundamental ecological change in the nature of information" (Hausman, 1994, p. 140).

With regard to private databases, suggestions of total freedom for media retrieval and use of the information should set off ethical alarm bells. The reuse of data collected by commercial entities for some valid purpose, but used for very different purposes, rests on an extremely slippery ethical slope, one that requires important questions to be carefully framed and discussed.

It is at this point that Kittross's reliance on the media's "high ethical standards of truth, fairness, and accuracy" is most in danger of breaking down. It's true, as he notes, that most magazines regard their subscription lists as commodities to be sold. But to dismiss this as normal practice without asking whether it *should* be normal practice begs an ethical question that we shouldn't overlook. Ethicists concerned with protecting individuals and their dignity would argue that this normal practice disregards both, and therefore must be modified.

Part of the danger comes from the fact that we still aren't aware of all of the future technological wrinkles that will continue to provide new avenues for access to computerized databases, sometimes more quickly than we can frame questions about propriety. But a much greater danger is inherent—as with so many other ethical issues—in the clash of bottom-line economic interests (and opportunities) with the need to weigh competing concerns and values.

In regard to data privacy, these competing concerns and values should help us continue to focus on the degree to which individuals should be safeguarded from inappropriate dissemination of personal data. This focus seems especially important in light of the burgeoning growth in the amount of data available through computerized retrieval systems—not to mention the development of new means for such retrieval. The normal efforts Kittross would have us rely on are simply inadequate in the face of the rapid changes taking place in information technologies.

■ ETHICAL GUIDELINES

From a legal perspective, the amount of protection investigative journalists have regarding the use of such information isn't totally clear because the law dealing with issues posed by advancing technology is still evolving. From an ethical perspective, the answer is—if anything—murkier. But despite the fact that the technology seems to be changing constantly, there are some useful guidelines offered by several of the ethical theorists we've consulted on other issues.

Machiavelli would argue, of course, that the end justifies the means and that any appropriate end—from maximizing profit to providing useful information to the public—eliminates the need for concern over the use or reuse of database information. An ethical egoist would take a similar approach, arguing that it would be ethical to use personal data as long as his or her own interests were advanced. The act utilitarian would contend that doing the greatest amount of good for the largest number of people is the key, and would try to quantify the good at stake in any particular use and measure it against the good done by giving priority to the preservation of individuals' privacy.

At the other end of the spectrum, Kant would argue that individuals—and their right to keep some data private—must be respected rather than used as a means even to some worthy end. John Rawls, with his veil of ignorance approach, would emphasize the need to protect the weakest participant in the situation to an appropriate degree—in this case, to make sure that the potential user of the information could live comfortably with the results if she or he were to find the roles reversed and be the person whose data privacy might be violated.

Husselbee (1994) offers a five-part test to help determine when it is justified to invade individual privacy by obtaining and revealing information from databases. He suggests the obvious initial questions of whether the public has a legitimate need for the information and whether its release will "shield the majority from imminent harm" (p. 151). If so, he suggests that the following four questions must still be answered satisfactorily to justify the disclosure ethically:

- Can the same goal be reached without using the information?
- "What procedures will be used to verify the accuracy of the information . . . ?"
- What steps might be taken to minimize the potential harm?
- Would it be helpful to disclose the mechanics of obtaining the data and explain how it satisfies "socially redeeming needs and values?" (p. 152).

Verifying the accuracy of the material is especially important in light of the possibility—Husselbee and others have said the probability—of errors creeping into the material entered into databases. That problem exists for data in government as well as private databases, and further weakens Kittross's argument for unlimited access to "public information."

A 1982 survey (Vidmar and Flaherty, 1985) indicated that Canadian citizens overwhelmingly saw privacy concerns as a very important issue and felt that they needed more protection. Nearly 60% of the respondents said that selling magazine subscriber data was an invasion of privacy, and about 90% said that reuse of information collected by interactive cable systems should be forbidden. But 57% of the respondents were willing to trade off the right for such data to be reused if the cost of the cable service was cut in half. The authors also noted that their results showed considerable similarity with some fairly limited survey data about attitudes in the United States.

An economic approach to this problem could require payment to individuals when individually identifiable information is reused in some manner unrelated to the purpose for which it was collected, thus recognizing that individuals have a property interest "in the secondary use of their names, likenesses and other identifiers" (Laudon, 1986, p. 381). But even if such an economic approach were implemented, ethical issues would remain prominent.

One guideline that suggests itself would focus on who controls the reuse of personal data. If private individuals are given a reasonable opportunity to stop such reuse or to receive some compensation for it, the ethical issues are greatly reduced if not altogether eliminated. Such an approach might well be viewed as an Aristotelian middle ground, somewhere between an outright utilitarian formula and Rawls's concern that the weakest or most defenseless party in a situation (here, undoubtedly, the individuals whose personal data are at issue) must always be protected.

Building on the attitudes discovered in the Canadian survey noted above, it *might* even be argued that a significant payment for the reuse of some kinds of data should make them available even if the individual still disapproved of their reuse. Such a provision would at least begin to acknowledge some ethical concerns for privacy while not totally ignoring the free enterprise concerns of the companies that control the data, which may well have been collected originally for very legitimate purposes. This approach, of course, would be much closer to the utilitarian (or even the Machiavellian) end of the ethical spectrum than it would to Rawls's concern for the weakest parties in any situation.

But regardless of the specifics of any efforts to deal with these concerns, what seems clear is that the convergence of new technologies, new economic opportunities and needs, and concern for individual informational privacy have created a context that requires some new ways of thinking about the ethical issues involved, not just "ethics as usual."

As Miller said more than a quarter of a century ago, "self-regulation and self-examination by every organization that uses or handles personal information is imperative and is certain to play an important role in any serious attempt to guard informational privacy" (1971, p. 257). Much more recently, ethicist Jay Black wrote that "a sensitive balance must be struck between freedoms and responsibilities, and between unlimited and irresponsible access to and utilization of information" in what he saw as an emerging electronic marketplace of both ideas and data (1994, p. 134).

If the mass media don't deal adequately with these concerns internally, it seems certain that government regulation will become part of the picture. I believe that the media—and the society in which they function—will be better served if the media themselves take the necessary steps to resist the siren song of using databases for purposes that were never intended, even if that means giving up some potential income. I suspect that only if the media are willing to safeguard informational privacy can we keep the government camel's nose from poking into the electronic information tent.

■ KITTROSS: There is no need for the mass media to be concerned about using personal information from private or government databases, but we all should be concerned about its collection and abuse by others.

My position is pragmatic and perhaps paradoxical. In a nutshell, I believe that far too many data *are* being collected by government and business about each of us, and they are often used in ways that harm rather than help us. But, once the information has been collected, there is no particular reason that it shouldn't be used by the mass media.

Ethically, I find myself in an ambiguous position on this question. It is analogous to using what lawyers call the "fruit of the poisoned tree" or answering affirmatively the question "is it ethical, in order to save lives or for other worthwhile purposes, to use data (such as medical data generated by the inhuman Nazi experiments) that were collected by someone else in shameful or inappropriate ways?"

Indeed, it may be that resentment over the *publication* of personal information will lead the public to protest its *collection!* If this is sophistry, let's make the best of it.

■ PERSONAL DATA AND IMPERSONAL USES

I'm not arguing against the collection of personal but valuable data that can be used only in *impersonal* ways. Most of these data are used only in the aggregate. The telephone company needs to know usage patterns, to staff and plan for new capacity. The decennial census and its supplements supply the nation with quantitative data that allow valid planning to take place, ameliorate problems, and tell us where we, as a nation, stand. Even though these data are collected from individuals, thus far strict procedural safeguards have prevented a pattern of misuse. Such data have been extremely valuable to us all. As Bacon said, "knowledge is power." Clearly, I support the collection and use of such data, from whence may come knowledge, and hope that wisdom may evolve from that knowledge.

However, these aggregated data can be examined to determine individual behavior and characteristics. Every reporter—or public relations practitioner—has a file of telephone numbers of potential sources. Are the fruits of the labor in compiling such a file from public sources (such as the telephone book or business cards) to be discarded for ethical reasons? Does putting them on a computer and sorting them somehow change their intent or effect? Unlike David Gordon, I don't think it does. If aggregated public data are used for public purposes, it doesn't matter whether we call them an address book or a database. To a great extent, I follow the teleological approach—looking at goals rather than duty—in deciding whether or not using a database is ethical.

If aggregated public data are used for public purposes, it doesn't matter whether we call them an address book or a database.

But what about records of *individual* drug prescriptions, adoptions, video rentals, or telephone calls—information that the individuals almost certainly have no intention of making widely public? They obviously exist in data banks or in the sales records of various stores. Can we justify media (or government and business) access to them, for any reason other than direct benefit to the customer, or is their very existence an unreasonable intrusion into the individual's privacy?

I believe we should try to keep such types of information private, even though I'm aware that, because these data exist in the aggregate and businesses have legitimate uses for them, it is likely that an unscrupulous person with access would find it easy to tease out knowledge of individual status and habits for commercial or other reasons.

Gordon's particular concern about cable television operators who might inappropriately use the data they can collect has been answered by Congress. A 1984 amendment to the Communications Act of 1934 (47 U.S.C. 551) now makes it necessary for cable companies to secure subscriber approval before distributing most personally identifiable data. A similar law affects information about the video movie rental habits of individuals. I'm sorry to have to say that both laws were passed because of fear that the media could not forgo the deliciousness of reporting such material. Such fears, of course, did not stop the special prosecutor in the Whitewater case involving President Clinton from trying to subpoena Monica Lewinsky's bookstore records.

Somewhere in the middle of the continuum of available data are records for which there is a narrow public purpose. Such ambiguous data could come from arrest records, tax returns, records of psychiatric interventions, license plate assignments, and the like. It can be argued that vital statistics, such as individual records of marriages, divorces, births, and deaths should be available to all—but here the question is whether they should be available only as summary statistics or as records pertaining to individuals. For example, we may need to know how many people died of AIDS in our community last year, but it probably isn't necessary to know the cause of John Doe's death.

■ PRIVACY AS A LEGAL CONCEPT

The entire legal concept of privacy in the United States, as is discussed in part in Chapter 8, goes back little more than a century, to an article by Warren and Brandeis published in 1890 in the *Harvard Law Review*. Once articulated, it was easy to associate privacy with the Fourth Amendment "right of the people to be secure in their persons, houses, papers, and effects, against unreasonable searches and seizures . . . ." But it took decades for the tort of privacy, "the right to be let alone," to become established to the point where courts were willing to entertain arguments and render decisions based on it, particularly where private (rather than government) actions to breach it were involved. For the media, this tort (injury) usually is divided into four parts: unreasonable intrusion into another's seclusion while gathering information (often related to trespass), appropriation of another's name or likeness usually for commercial purposes (a form of theft), being placed in a "false light" (related to the "injury to reputation" of libel and slander, and important to all journalists and creative people in the entertainment media), and public disclosure of embarrassing private facts. Only the last of these is the subject of this chapter, although it could be argued that any use of a database—even without public disclosure of the results—is an intrusion into an area that one might reasonably expect to remain private (Ernst and Schwartz, 1962).

It may come as a surprise to realize that the development of large databases and the technology for mining and manipulating them efficiently also dates back to 1890, when machines first were used for tabulating census data. But those crude mechanical sorting and counting devices moved to a new plane of efficiency less than a half-century ago, with the development of the electronic computer. As recently as the early 1960s, many business and government agencies still kept records by hand and people hadn't yet started to blame all their errors (and troubles) on the computer.

■ CURRENT PRACTICES

Today, almost every bit of information anyone could ask for is on a computer somewhere. The networks or linkages between computers—the "information superhighway"—on a worldwide basis are so many that for most practical purposes they approach infinity. An endless array of data—financial, health, production and sales, school records, scientific information, news, real estate sales and valuations, personnel, utilities and thousands of other categories—are aggregated into accessible databases. Some are restricted; it is unlikely that a utility, manufacturing, or service company will release its customer list to a potential competitor. Others are open to anyone with a few dollars and a modem, including commercial services such as Lexis/Nexus, America On Line, and CompuServe. Yet others, such as the catalog of a university library, require special arrangements. Government data, once available only in rigid formats published by the Government Printing Office, are now often available on-line through the Internet, with politicians of both parties striving to achieve control—or, at least, acclaim—for instituting this practice (Shribman, 1995).

Less formally, chat rooms on the various computer networks attract those who have some information (or opinion) to give or receive. Gordon has expressed some worries over using these sites for news gathering: do the news media need permission to republish website information? Might those people interested in particular data prefer to get it directly from the Internet or other networks? How do we know what the source of the material really is?

But these various sites are different only in degree, not in kind, from listening to short-wave radio (which has served the news media well from the 1930s through the 1991 Gulf War), CB radio, amateur radio transmissions, and cellular phones. They, too, may be transmitting private information, have already reached the intended audience, and cannot be certified or verified as to source. All of them, for many years, have frequently been used by news gatherers, even though totalitarian states prevent listening to transmissions from other countries and there is a Federal Communications Commission regulation against using "ham" radio for news reporting in the United States. It is possible to eavesdrop on *any* radio transmission, even if it is intended to be point-to-point rather than broadcast—for example, the embarrassing cellular telephone calls from members of the British royal family intercepted and published in 1994. The fact that a computer's output enters a telephone cable doesn't mean that part of the circuit won't be carried on radio—usually microwave or space satellite relays.

Regardless of whether wire or radio is used, the ability of hackers to enter databases has been demonstrated many times. Such talents are made to order for reporters who believe that nothing should stand between them and the information they wish to acquire. An example was the pilfering of Tonya Harding's e-mail "box" during the 1994 Olympics.

Every high school—and probably every newsroom—has a resident "technoid" or six capable of simple technical miracles with a pocket screwdriver. Unless information is given a high level of encryption protection, there is *no* circuit free from the possibility of someone looking into it. Unfortunately, this abridgement of privacy is not limited to computer bulletin boards and databases. The unscrupulous reporter (or police officer, private detective, voyeur, or hobbyist) with a satellite dish and the proper receiving (and decryption) equipment may get sound and pictures as well as data from almost any location at any time.

■ THE LEGAL STRUCTURE

Laws are unlikely to stop privacy abridgements, just as they haven't stopped the use of radar detectors on the highway. Appropriate lines *can* be drawn—for example, a photographer cannot trespass on private property but can take a picture of private property from the public street. Similarly, a reporter can ethically make use of a computerized database but should not break into the files to isolate an individual's record from among the aggregated public data.

However, laws are unlikely to prevent a different kind of invasion of our privacy—the recorded sales message tying up our telephone at dinner time, the direct marketing materials (junk mail) advertising of goods and services on paper or on line, fundraising by political, social, and environmental causes to which the Postal Service seems to give priority. Obviously, advertisers and others wish to sell their goods, services, and causes and there should be no legal impediment against this. But if they are able to use databases to focus their sales efforts more narrowly, wouldn't those of us tired of too many poorly targeted sales messages actually benefit?

■ DATA PRIVACY: PAST, PRESENT, AND FUTURE

Are our new abilities to store, manipulate, and use data really so different from old ways of dealing with data? Gordon thinks so, and maintains that "normal efforts . . . are simply inadequate in the face of the rapid changes taking place in information technologies." I disagree. Human society has watched the government's insatiable demand for data grow for thousands of years—the only reason Joseph and Mary were in Bethlehem when Jesus was born was because Caesar Augustus decreed that all the Roman world should be counted, listed, and taxed. The biggest, most used, and most usable database is the ubiquitous telephone book. The demands of watershed events such as World War II on national and global economies and societies softened up the populace for the continuous increments in the collection of data by both government and business. The modern computer merely has made things technologically easier.

As late as the 1930s, it was possible for an individual in the United States to change his or her name and disappear. Today, this is almost impossible for a person without extraordinary and extralegal resources. The Social Security number, originally restricted to Social Security and unemployment insurance purposes, now is used everywhere from military serial numbers to drivers' licenses and student ID numbers. The much-closer-than-science-fiction hypothetical "national data bank" could remove our last vestiges of freedom from government supervision of our lives, finances, education, communications, travel, and health. Only a few years after the setting of George Orwell's *1984*, cash is suspect and credit card use may be traced anywhere. Bank records, despite the misnamed Bank Privacy Act, are almost wide open to police or other government agencies. Income tax forms call for more and more information of dubious relevance. "Free citizens" in the United States must show a "photo ID" when taking a plane ride, even if paying with cash. Democratic nations such as the United Kingdom were, in the mid-1990s, toying with the idea of requiring citizens to carry "smart card" ID packed with information the state might want to know ("Identity Crisis," 1994). Passports, which once merely asked other nations to "please take care of our citizen," now are used for exit control. With these and many other violations of our more than 200-year-old concepts of freedom, it is no wonder that to the government—any government—the idea of privacy for its citizens is a joke.

Gordon believes that recent technological and procedural changes require special consideration. He opines that "government regulation will become part of the picture" and "government may well have to step in with strong control measures" to prevent what he calls "data rape" by the media. But it is that same government that is collecting most of these data, and the government that often abuses them and their sources! Rather than proposing ethical standards and practices that the media (and others) may employ to prevent such abuse, Gordon seems to advocate putting the fox in charge of the henhouse.

Sometimes, though, government practices are inconsistent. For example, legislation prohibits using "insider data" in bidding on government contracts but, on the other hand, government has turned data obtained through the expenditure of taxpayer dollars over to private firms in the guise of privatization (which also forces taxpayers to pay for it twice!). Most extreme is the government's insistence that encryption systems to be used by private individuals and companies must be of the "public key" (accessible to law enforcement agencies) type that will permit the government to have access, regardless of the wishes of those sending and receiving messages. The government already restricts the export of strong encryption programs (Schwartz, 1997), and proposes to do the same within the country. Although I'm in favor of making information available to the citizens who need it to make rational decisions about their own government, finances, and lives, I'm not so naïve as to think that government and business feel the same way about data they have collected from the citizenry or have generated within the bureaucracy itself!

Once any data bank exists, it is possible for the media and others to abuse their access to it. Many police departments jealously guard their exclusive access to rap sheets—records of individuals' previous arrests—and point to abuses in the use of driver's license records by benign advertisers and predatory sexual stalkers. One of the most egregious abuses was Procter & Gamble's 1991 use of the courts to secure telephone records of some two million people in the Cincinnati area in an attempt to discover which of their employees had been leaking information to the press ("P&G Calls in the Law to Trace Leaks," 1991).

■ JOURNALISM AND DATA PRIVACY

If a news organization were to use privileged journalistic access to a database such as a list of library users as a means for marketing itself, it might be considered mildly wrong both by library users and by commercial competitors, such as book sellers—but similar acts are committed by all sorts of organizations, and there is no published legal or ethical standard to prevent them. Some people still are horrified to find that most magazines consider their subscription lists to be little more than another commodity to sell. But, whether we like it or not, this is normal practice. Examine the postal meter imprints and minor address variations on the direct mail you receive, and it becomes obvious that most of it originated in a database entry that was initiated by *your* order for some product, publication, or service. Sometimes these lists become very specialized—your name can be sold on the basis of geography (including the income level of those living in your census tract or ZIP code area), industry in which you work, or college attended, and this barely scratches the surface of the ability of computers to sort data.

But what about use without abuse? Obviously, journalists and those in advertising and public relations should have normal (presumably, paid) access to all commercial databases—making it likely that embryonic reporters will have to add classes in computerized information retrieval to their courses of study. If reporters Woodward and Bernstein, as recounted in their book *All the President's Men*, could go through thousands of charge slips in the Library of Congress in their investigation of President Nixon's coverup of the Watergate break-in, why can't they also go through the computerized equivalent? The media should continue their fight to have access in convenient form—i.e., direct access to the computerized database, on-line, or magnetic tape or other electronic storage medium—for any government (or available commercial) data that exist either on paper or in electronic form (Reporters Committee).

Such access troubles some government agencies—those that claim that providing the data in convenient form (together with the software that makes it possible to use the data) is too time-consuming, disruptive, expensive, or troublesome. So far, while there may be some truth to this side of the argument (although providing access to paper copies also may be time-consuming, disruptive, expensive, or troublesome—but of great public value), it also seems to be driven by a disinclination to have anyone from outside rummaging in the files. This is analogous to the prohibition against possession of pens and pencils when reviewing paper files—a fear that computer access might lead an unscrupulous person to make changes in the files themselves.

On a more mundane level, some agencies might take financial advantage of the needs of journalists and other public researchers, and supply access only at a very high monetary cost to the inquirer. Private firms also have information for sale: One advertises that it can supply, for a fixed price, all sorts of financial information about an individual such as employer, salary, pension, stock options, bank accounts, telephones, credit card account numbers and limits, home ownership and mortgage details, and the like (McConnell, 1994). One on-line service exhibited its services—personal demographics, past and present addresses, corporations and businesses, property, bankruptcies, liens and judgments, criminal histories, driving histories, phone numbers, neighbors, relatives, assets and more—at the 1997 RTNDA convention. Reporters should abjure such often unreliable (and even illegally obtained) data and fight this greed. Even more of a target are agencies (including the FBI) that use their legal right to recoup costs for commercial use of their data as a means of circumventing the Freedom of Information Act (5 U.S.C. 552) by raising prices so high as to discourage prospective users.

This leads to another series of questions: Is it wrong for a reporter to tap into an unauthorized database? The answer depends on whether the database should be restricted. Who decides? Hmmm. If one favors personal privacy and property rights as paramount, then the database should be restricted—and this might be considered a categorical imperative. On the other hand, a utilitarian approach would ask whether more people would benefit from seeing what is in the database. Obviously, the "it depends" means that we can't make use of Rawls's veil of ignorance.

The news business is a business. But taking anything—including information—from another person is theft. There are laws restricting "hacking" into computerized memories, and reporters are subject to these laws. Just as it is possible to prosecute for theft a reporter who, when invited into a home to interview its residents, steals a photograph that might be used to illustrate the story, so might criminal or civil prosecution be initiated against a reporter who takes improper advantage of access to a computer data bank. No special law is necessary.

Yet another restriction on the use of databases derives from a common—but alas, not universal—journalistic practice: focusing on a story of significance to readers or viewers, rather than merely conducting a dragnet for gossip with which to slander unwitting subjects or titillate some readers or viewers. Some restraint should be shown. In writing a story about a political campaigner, one shouldn't use journalistic access to computerized data as an excuse to drag out dirt that can be smeared over others who happen to be in the same database. Indeed, such a use may be tantamount to blackmail, and there have been unfortunate cases over the years where unscrupulous columnists and reporters have demanded money to keep names out of the paper or off the air.

By the same token, medical records on illnesses that could have no effect on a political candidate's ability to serve in office may become available to a reporter, but are hardly appropriate to air or publish unless voluntarily released by the subject. In this country, the onus caused by *any* knowledge of contact with the mental health system can destroy a candidate, but the willingness of a candidate to get professional mental health help in the past is unlikely to help us predict her or his future behavior. Is knowledge of a candidate's elementary school grades or family finances before entering public life going to help the electorate make its decisions?

Similarly, the histories of our presidents should give pause to those who say that *everything* in a candidate's earlier life is fair game, deserving of a full court press. Yes, prior events that involve the candidate's character *should* be explored by the press—but what an elected official actually *does* while in office should be far more important to all of us than previous activities of the official or his or her family. It is beside the point (and discussed in Chapter 8) that some public figures *want* their private lives disclosed, others are able to shrug it off, and still others—such as former presidential candidate Gary Hart—take the risk of daring the press to uncover verifiable proof of their peccadilloes and suffer the consequences.

With few exceptions, reporters and editors are not "hired" by their audiences to serve strictly as voyeurs. Nor can they escape their responsibility to draw the line between privacy and appropriate disclosure by deferring to the perhaps conflicting desires of their story's subjects in deciding what to publish. Nor should they assume it is their right, and even their duty, to make their pages and screens the place to see, hear, or read about ordinary neighbors and leaders alike in embarrassing situations. This has nothing to do with the reason why the press has the protection of the First Amendment. Instead, the media should carefully *balance* the public value of disclosure against the private harm to individuals, an Aristotelian Golden Mean approach. They should never forget the utilitarian notion that media's client is the public (Bates, 1994). When it comes to personal information and personal attacks, *fairness* and the *public interest* are the keys. Applying these criteria doesn't require a computer.

For example, the public needs to know how well its tax laws are working, and a newspaper's analysis of the proportion of income paid by the wealthiest individuals would be instructive. But is it necessary to know the names of the rich individuals in order to instruct our representatives to amend the tax law? What about corporate taxes? After all, corporations are "persons" only by virtue of a legal fiction. Suppose the argument is made that publicizing such corporate data would adversely affect the business climate in your state, thus reducing economic growth?

■ CONCLUSION

If the public interest—not merely "what the public is interested in"—is met by analyzing databases, then the practice is benign, at worst. If care is taken, as I argued in Chapter 4, to be fair to all—particularly the audience—then such practices are beneficial, and there is certainly no need for special efforts aimed to achieve informational privacy.

As an individual, I fight for my personal privacy whenever I can—to the annoyance of many telemarketers and bureaucrats. I hope that others will do the same because privacy is an increasingly rare condition in a world that is doubling its population every third of a century.

On the other hand, it is legitimate for media to distinguish between private and public lives. If I were voluntarily in the public eye as a candidate, business leader, or entertainer, I would legitimately be subject to scrutiny and *should* expect the media to examine the databases that contain information on my public persona, if not my private life.

Gordon's concern about using data in ways that were unintended at their collection is not, I believe, an ethical problem. To convert it into an ethical matter, he had to twist the question from how these data are *collected* to how they are *used* in the end.

In an interdependent society, our desire for privacy probably should not extend to the point where nobody can reach us, nobody can know anything about us—whether the information is used for our benefit, or for theirs, or for both.

. . . using data in ways that were unintended at their collection is not . . . an ethical problem.

The largest collectors of individual data (other than the government) are credit reporting firms. Their original purpose was to disseminate valid and reliable data received from merchants so that other merchants wouldn't be cheated, resulting in lower prices for all of us. Such firms have abused their responsibility by being careless and sloppy, and public outcry has led to remedial legislation—copies of records must now be made available to the citizen being examined, corrections must be made promptly, and limitations have been placed on the number of years that negative data may be used. The mass media are more like credit reporting bureaus than we may care to admit, often guilty of indiscriminate collection of data, sloppiness in reporting and editing, and unwillingness to admit error.

How can the media take warning from what happened to the credit reporting companies with respect to data privacy? The answer is simple and obvious: The news media must maintain the same high ethical standards of truth, fairness, and accuracy in dealing with data banks that they should maintain elsewhere, as discussed in Chapter 4. I hold that this is—or should be—normal practice in the newsroom, the sales department, and the marketing office, not an extraordinary special effort.

This is easy for me to say, but—and in this I agree with Gordon—hard for the working journalist to resist temptation and accomplish. Yet if our reputation, credibility and freedom are to be preserved, it must be. We can't turn back the clock. Databases are here to stay. Although we can—and should—work to limit the seemingly insatiable informational appetites of government and business, as long as these databases exist I maintain that journalists should have the right to use aggregated data from them for the public's benefit. This utilitarian approach is difficult to separate from merely satisfying the public's curiosity about its neighbors, but it is a defensible goal.

■ MERRILL: Commentary

This is a controversy that I don't feel strongly about one way or the other. David Gordon and John Michael Kittross have made their respective points and I am inclined to let it stand at that. But if I did, I would be neglecting my assignment to provide some kind of commentary. So I will make an attempt here, although I hope the reader will supply a hefty amount of compensating perspective.

I think that most people don't worry much about the use of personal information obtained by media from databases. Probably very few of them are concerned about preserving their informational privacy, a term that is alien to most people. What the term means, presumably, is keeping computer-held personal information in the hands of the person who put it there. One position would respect the people's right to such informational privacy; the other sees little to be concerned about. I tend to side more with the latter view, although I admit that I am somewhat confused about basic definitional problems and, of course, the degree to which such privacy is invaded.

Undoubtedly Gordon is correct in maintaining that electronic databases pose great temptations for mass communicators eager to obtain personal information for their stories. However, the question is just what data use constitutes an invasion of privacy; and, as we know, privacy is one of the most troublesome concepts facing the mass media worker. Gordon, taking the more hard-line communitarian approach, bemoans what he calls "data rape" and says that if this is not resisted by mass communicators, the government may have to step in with strong control measures. An ominous Orwellian prospect!

Although Kittross finds himself in an ambiguous position on this issue, he comes down on the side of the media using such data if they have been collected and stored. He takes the more libertarian approach and supports the use of personal data, believing that from it may come knowledge, and he hopes that wisdom may evolve from that knowledge.

After delving into many of the intricacies of databases and media temptations to use the data, both authors seem to have trouble coming to any firm conclusion as to the ethics of the matter. Gordon is more legalistic and, indeed, pessimistic about media and data. Kittross is more sanguine in his approach to data privacy, saying that the answer is simple: News media must have high ethical standards of truth, fairness, and accuracy. But does this "simple answer" solve the problem? I doubt it. Cannot truth prove to be an invasion of privacy? Cannot accuracy? Now, as to fairness, there is the rub. Perhaps this concept alone relates to the mass communicator's concern with ethics: Indeed, fairness may cancel out both truth and accuracy, both of which Kittross extols.

Following up on this seeming paradox would get us into areas dealt with elsewhere in this book, so I will forgo the temptation to elaborate here. But it is doubtful that a concern for truth (and accuracy) will solve the problem of privacy-invasion. Doesn't truth include the concept of thoroughness—of providing more than a partial or gap-filled story? Any reporter tapping into fact-filled databases knows that he or she is filling in the gaps and adding to the truth of the story.

Kittross hedges his support of available data banks at the very end of his essay. He maintains that journalists should use them for the *public's benefit*, and not merely to satisfy the *public's curiosity*. This has a good, wholesome ring to it, but why should we not say this, then, about *all* journalistic reporting? Everyone knows that journalism is a supplier of information that satisfies the public's curiosity all the time. Journalists have no qualms about using such material. So why should they feel differently about such information obtained from databases?

Perhaps the reader of this book can shed additional light on this increasingly important problem. Here we have the difficult clash of professional reportorial integrity with a more teleologically based ethical position: In short, should mass communicators *report truthfully and fully information available* or should they *ignore or tamper with the facts available* because of some consideration of possible consequences? That is basically the question we are left with.

REFERENCES

Auletta, Ken. (January 17, 1994). "Under the Wire." *The New Yorker*, pp. 49–53.

Bates, Stephen. (Fall 1994). "Who Is the Journalist's Client?" *Media Ethics* 7(1), p. 3.

Black, Jay. (1994). "Aereopagitica in the Information Age." *Journal of Mass Media Ethics* 9(3), pp. 131–134.

Ernst, Morris L., and Alan U. Schwartz. (1962). *Privacy: The Right to Be Let Alone.* New York: Macmillan.

Hausman, Carl. (1994). "Information Age Ethics: Privacy Ground Rules for Navigating in Cyberspace." *Journal of Mass Media Ethics* 9(3), pp. 135–144.

Husselbee, L. Paul. (1994). "Respecting Privacy in an Information Society: A Journalist's Dilemma." *Journal of Mass Media Ethics* 9(3), pp. 145–156.

"Identity Crisis." (October 14, 1994). Editorial in *The Times* (London), p. 21.

Laudon, Kenneth C. (1986). *Dossier Society: Value Choices in the Design of National Information Systems.* New York: Columbia University Press.

McConnell, Sara. (October 15, 1994). "No Financial Secrets Are Safe from Prying Eyes." *The Times* (London), p. 34.

Miller, Arthur. (1971). *The Assault on Privacy: Computers, Data Banks, and Dossiers.* Ann Arbor: University of Michigan Press.

Morgan, Hugh. (May 1994). "Doing It in Dayton." *Quill*, pp. 29–33.

"P & G Calls in the Law to Trace Leaks." (Fall 1991). *The News Media and the Law* 15(4), pp. 2–3.

The Reporters Committee for Freedom of the Press, "Access to Electronic Records," a "guide to reporting on state and local government in the computer age," published periodically, sometimes as part of *The News Media and The Law*.

Resnick, Rosalind. (April 1994). "Please Don't Quote Me: The Electronic Version." *American Journalism Review*, pp. 11–12.

Schwartz, Rachael E. (Fall 1997) "Prior Restraints and the First Amendment: From Press Licensing to Software Export Licensing." *Media Ethics*, 9(2), p. 6.

Shribman, David M. (January 23, 1995). "The Odd Trio: The Tofflers, Gingrich Look to Crest on the Third Wave." *The Boston Globe*, pp. 1, 4.

Vidmar, Neil, and David H. Flaherty. (Spring 1985). "Concern for Personal Privacy in an Electronic Age." *Journal of Communication*, 35(2), pp. 91–103.

Warren, Samuel D., and Louis D. Brandeis. (December 15, 1890). "The Right to Privacy." *Harvard Law Review* 4(5), pp. 193–220.

Wilson, Kevin G. (1988). *Technologies of Control: The New Interactive Media for the Home.* Madison: University of Wisconsin Press.

CHAPTER 10

VIOLENCE AND SEXUAL PORNOGRAPHY

How to deal with violent content in the mass media was a hot topic in the 1990s. And in the 1980s. And the 1970s. And the 1960s, and back about as far as there have been mass media. The dime novels of a century ago were criticized for portraying excessive violence in print. Since then, films, popular music recordings of various kinds, and television have each been blamed for fostering additional violence in society, including "copycat" violence. There were even Senate hearings in the mid-1950s on the dangers posed by violent comic books (see Twitchell, 1989).

Media portrayals of violence have been given renewed and heightened scrutiny in the past decade, perhaps reflecting concerns over more general violence in society at large. That's the crux of this issue: Does media violence contribute to societal violence, or merely reflect it? Or both? And what role should the media play in regard to this problem? That role might well be examined from both an *ethical* perspective—which is the one taken in the material that follows—and from a *political* point of view, which might well conclude that the media have already been found guilty of contributing to violence in society and ask what should be done about this.

Sexual content in print media and, more recently, in the electronic media, has been of concern to some segments of society for longer than the controversy over violence. Obscenity laws, regulation of "indecency" on the airwaves, the ill-considered Communications Decency Act of 1996, movie ratings, outright censorship, and various types of pressure group tactics have all been used in efforts to regulate sex in the mass media. This can be carried to extremes: a student of photography who took artistic pictures of her nude child for a class assignment was arrested as an aftermath of a commercial photo lab calling the police upon seeing the photo.

From the legal perspective, there have been relatively few efforts to regulate violent content. Several attempts to impose limits on alleged media incitement to violence through the award of monetary damages have failed, as the courts quite uniformly held that the First Amendment bars such restrictive penalties. That leaves it up to consumer and political pressure groups, or more direct government intervention—and to the ethical standards of media practitioners—to serve as checks on media violence.

When we discuss violent media content here, we're referring mainly to television (both entertainment and news) and film. Newspapers, magazines, and some records (particularly rap music, which has been a target of concerned parents and others) also figure into this discussion, but to a lesser degree. Such related topics as concerns over violent toys and especially violence in video games, although posing important ethical issues for society as a whole as sales increase rapidly, lie largely outside the scope of this discussion.

The authors are very far apart in the positions they take in this chapter. John Michael Kittross argues that outside efforts to control media violence would be a "cure" that is worse than the disease. David Gordon maintains that violent content must somehow be controlled if the media refuse to do it themselves.

■ KITTROSS: Violence and sexual pornography in the media, however regrettable, are merely reflections of the world, and government or group measures to control them would create a "cure" that is worse than the disease.

Let's ask some simple questions of those who blame most of the evils of the world on the mass media: Were there murders before television? Was there child abuse before the daily newspaper? Were sexual deviations known before the movies? The answers, obviously, are *yes*. As is the answer to the questions: Do violence and sexual relations exist in the world today—and are they portrayed in today's media?

But does this latter, absolute *yes* answer the implied questions about the *relationship* between these practices and the media, particularly the implication of causality: that the media (in their entertainment, persuasion, and informational functions) *cause* violence; and that hard- and softcore pornography in the same media functions *cause* sexual violence? And, are all these of equal importance?

Lee Loevinger, former associate justice of the Minnesota Supreme Court and former member of the Federal Communications Commission, wrote in 1968:

> [M]ass communications are best understood as mirrors of society that reflect an ambiguous image in which each observer projects or sees his own vision of himself and society. . . . However, broadcasting is . . . an electronic mirror that reflects a vague and ambiguous image of what is behind it, as well as of what is in front of it. While the mirror can pick out points and aspects of society, it cannot create a culture or project an image that does not reflect something already existing in some form in society.

Hence, as Loevinger goes on to say:

> A substantial element of violence in American television reflects a tolerance and taste for violence in American society. This is somewhat offensive to Europeans, who have a different attitude toward violence and there is less of violence in European broadcast programming. On the other hand, European television has fewer sex and religious taboos than American television and this corresponds to European attitudes, which are looser in these fields than American attitudes.

In this connection, a British visitor to the 1994 National Association of Broadcasters convention, when asked from the dais whether television content was a problem in the UK, drawled in response that "we enjoy rather more sex and rather less violence" than people in the United States.

Or, in the words of satirical songwriter Tom Lehrer, "when correctly viewed, everything is lewd . . . ."

Loevinger continued:

Basically all mass media are censored by the public since they lose their status as mass media if they become too offensive or uninteresting to a large segment of the public.

While the mass media reflect various images of society the audience is composed of individuals, each of whom views the media as an individual. The members of each audience project or see in the media their own visions or images. . . . (Loevinger, 1968, pp. 108–109)

■ APPORTIONING BLAME

Let's also not forget that the media are a very convenient whipping boy. Because most media generally depend on the goodwill of as many people as possible, in order to attract advertising, it is very difficult for the media to fight back, even with the First Amendment on their side. This has given rise to a virtual cottage industry of criticism against the media: When a member of Congress needs something to attack, the media are there. When psychologist Fredric Wertham needed to provide reasons for the apparent causes of juvenile dysfunction, he wrote accusatorily first about the movies, in the early 1950s about comic books, and later about television, blaming each medium in turn almost exclusively for the various faults identified in children.

When a child does something antisocial or an adult perpetrator blames his or her childhood upbringing for a crime, most of the public is glad to blame TV, the big baby-sitter and tutor.

Complaining about juvenile delinquency has been a practice for as long as there have been children. Juliet was only 14 when she and Romeo got together, *Oliver Twist* featured a subculture of young thieves, and for millennia there have been both tales and treatises of how children—including Beavis and Butthead—have acted immaturely. Our written culture doesn't go back more than a few thousand years, but both the Greeks and the Romans complained about this fact of life, and Socrates had to die as a result of it.

. . . the media are a very convenient whipping boy.

The saving grace is that very few children turn "bad," in the sense of being acute dangers to society. Most children grow into mature adults who are a functional part of society. Although there are more people jailed in the United States than in any other nation, a large proportion of them are incarcerated under the provisions of draconian anti-drug laws and other "mandatory sentencing" legislation. Although the number of gunshot deaths is reported to be approaching the number of motor vehicle deaths, the absolute numbers for both of these causes of violent death combined constitute less than one twenty-fifth of 1% of the total U.S. population, or less than 4% of all deaths. Neither law enforcement nor medical professionals can explain fully the drop-off in those with a heroin addiction after age 45. "Maturity" has many facets!

■ VIOLENCE

We still need much more research. The arguments by the Surgeon General and others about a cause-and-effect relationship between violence on television and violence in the home or on the street have something of a fallacious *post hoc, ergo propter hoc* (that which went before caused that which followed—regardless of any other possible relationship) ring to them, as does the even more simplistic "television's fictional violence is a catharsis that defuses and prevents real-life violence" argument adduced by the commercial media as far back as the (televised!) Senate hearings on juvenile delinquency chaired by Senator Estes Kefauver in the 1950s.

As an analogy, the fact that a large proportion of those occupying prison cells are dyslexic doesn't mean that their criminal behavior is caused by dyslexia, but rather that the often intelligent, motivated, and above all frustrated and misunderstood dyslexic may feel that he or she has nowhere to turn except to crime in order to make a living. Or perhaps there are other relationships.

Television isn't the only medium blamed for violence. Numerous police forces object to "gangsta rap" lyrics on records and the radio that seem to be advocating violence, particularly directed toward police officers. Almost since its origination, the motion picture industry has been blamed for antisocial actions of its viewers. Indeed, the conflict between self-expression and the potential for harm that might result from artistic expression has been going on for millennia.

Nobody is denying that the media have some effect—unspecified but almost certainly interactive with other causes—on violence in the society. Obviously, the media, including news programming, join many other factors—economic conditions, social changes (such as the role of the family, career-limiting effects of converting our economy from production to service, easier travel, and greater longevity), and even some claims of genetics. But these factors are complex and interactive, and don't make easy targets for those looking for simple solutions. It even is possible to blame the media for some of these contributing factors, such as parental abdication of responsibility.

David Gordon's claim that I am dismissing "the extensive research on TV violence" as "irrelevant" because it "doesn't clearly prove a cause-effect relationship" is flawed in two ways: First, much of the research in question is not very good research. Second, what standard of proof should be applied? Gordon apparently believes that whatever supports his argument is satisfactory because, on its face, it appears reasonable or even logical—at best the very weak "face validity" argument. Gordon's example of imprisoned males ignores both the possibility that those in jail for violent crimes will want to excuse themselves and con their jailers by blaming an outside agency (television this year, movies in the '30s, and "the devil" in previous centuries)—and that the causal relationship he implies is circular: People who are jailed for violent crimes might be of a type that is attracted to violent TV. Which comes first, the chicken or the egg? "Face validity" is not a good basis on which to judge research and, particularly, not a good basis on which to make policy decisions that will affect what information we make available to ourselves.

Even the data on "copycat" crimes are questionable. The person who shot at residents of a Midwestern town during the showing of a made-for-TV movie about a sniper turned out not to have known that *The Texas Tower Massacre* was on television that night. Research on psychological warfare illustrates the weakness in any cause → effect media model. There is inferential evidence that a few automobile crashes are really suicides by people affected by the news of the death of a movie star or political leader. But this does not mean that everyone will run out and mimic what is shown on television.

A 1996 federal law requires the installation of a "violence chip" in new television sets, with 2000 as the deadline for final implementation. On receipt of a warning signal from the station, this chip will prevent suitably equipped and adjusted sets from receiving violent programs. But what level of violence should trigger such a device? Should it be aimed at five-year-olds or teenagers? How do "children" learn how to handle adult fare as they grow up? Do all children of a given age think and react the same way? Suppose there are adults who will miss significant programming as a result of an arbitrary label, much as there are people who miss important films because they carry an "X" or even an "R" rating? Finally, should the station or network control the switch, or should individual parents be able to obtain receivers with electronic "lockout" devices that they can program in a manner suited to their own children's psychological health rather than assume that the "V-chip" will do their thinking? This device—called a "C-chip" by some advocates ("Choice!") and opponents ("Censorship!")—is a real can of worms, as witnessed by Gordon's touching trust or blinkered belief that programs will be "rated" in a valid and reliable fashion with enough information so that parents could block an undesired program.

Even the definition of violence is difficult to nail down. The periodic surveys by George Gerbner and others still have unanswered questions about their methodology; e.g., even small children can distinguish cartoons from reality (Comstock et al., 1978, pp. 64–70). Another study once tabulated a parent's goodnight kiss as an assault!

Bad research (even that whose conclusions are socially desirable) leads to bad decision making, and good research (even that whose conclusions are unpopular) tends to lead to good decisions. Some experimental studies on this topic, and some field studies, are useful mainly as bad examples in research methods classes. Gordon's reliance on what *Newsweek* thinks is adequate research—rather than on studies that demonstrably have been properly conducted and on carefully precise, rather than journalistic, reports on them—shows the weakness of his argument.

As Gordon intimates, it is silly to expect that the research results on any important social question will agree 100%. I never said it would, or that we should be paralyzed until it does. As in a civil court, all we need is the preponderance of the evidence on our side or, if the matter is important enough (i.e., if life or liberty are at stake), the criterion usually is the much stricter requirement for evidence "beyond a reasonable doubt." Both parents and media may wish to opt for the stricter criterion with regard to televised violence.

With respect to the effects of televised violence, the jury is still out. Far too much research on it does not meet generally accepted scientific standards for validity and reliability. In such a situation, until the weight of independently conducted research is unequivocal, we should be very careful not to use poor research as the justification for poor policy decisions—no matter how popular or trendy it would be.

We also need to be very careful as to how we interpret findings. For instance, although content analyses that compared the incidence of well-defined nonverbal violent behavior shown on television (e.g., a deliberate shooting or stabbing) with the incidence of such behavior in the nation's crime and death statistics show that American television is unquestionably violent, it *doesn't* prove a cause and effect relationship . . . in either direction. Correlation does *not* equal causality.

This is particularly true when we also consider bodily collisions in football and hockey to be violent, or when the evening news is full of war, murder, mayhem, and accidental death. And we certainly must include coverage of hurricanes and earthquakes in this litany!

■ PORNOGRAPHY

Media other than television have their own problems with violence and pornography. Radio is a "theater of the mind," with the ability to be both startling and frightening, particularly for children to whom euphemisms can be terribly frightening ("the dog was put to sleep" can make "go to sleep, Marsha" an awful injunction). The growth of 900-number "verbal sex" services shows the aural medium's abilities in this realm as well. The print media have similar textual abilities, particularly with regard to pornography.

Pornography, however, is even harder to define than violence. To many feminists, pornography is the precursor to violent acts directed against women, and thus should be considered a form of violence. Some fundamentalist Islamics maintain that *any* depiction of contact between male and female is obscene. Some fundamentalist Protestants have similar opinions about sexual practices outside of marriage and outside of conventional heterosexual behavior. There are many who are made uncomfortable by advertisements for condoms (even considering the AIDS epidemic), underwear, or menstrual products. Obscenity, indecency, profanity—all have their varied definitions.

■ BLASPHEMY, OBSCENITY, AND PROFANITY

Blasphemy charges can lead to assassination and threats of assassination, as in the case of Salman Rushdie, a British author whose book, *Satanic Verses*, has made him the worldwide target of Islamic extremists who claim that the book is blasphemous. But blasphemy, obscenity, and profanity are really outside the scope of this chapter. Two aphorisms reflect my feelings: "Sticks and stones may break my bones, but words will never hurt me" and, to sum up Heywood Broun's (1927) chapter on censorship, "Who ever heard of a woman who was ruined by a book?" But if—as has happened before and may happen again—religious or "moral" groups succeed in securing political power, formal or informal, then the media will have to concern themselves with such matters or accept the censorship that will result.

■ CENSORSHIP WAITING IN THE WINGS

Make no bones about it: Censorship *is* about to step into the limelight. Perhaps its establishment will be blatant, much as the Eighteenth Amendment established Prohibition in 1917. Perhaps it will be the result of a national consensus, much as public smoking of cigarettes became increasingly unacceptable in the 1990s. Perhaps it will be the result of fear of the effect of either legislation or consensus, and will take the form of self-censorship, as seen in the motion picture and television "codes of good practice" of bygone years and in today's rating systems. Sometimes it will be by government edict, as in 1997 when CompuServe had to pull the plug—worldwide, as it turned out—on any website that might violate German content laws.

Sometimes "voluntary" restrictions are the most pernicious, as when members of Congress called upon the FCC to chastise NBC for not adhering strictly to a *voluntary* content rating code, and might also suffer from unintended consequences. For example, these content labels, which are industry approved and awarded, may be used in an unintended manner. Since young people in their teens and 20s—prime audiences for movies—wouldn't be caught dead at a "G" rated film showing, some filmmakers will insert gratuitous sex, violence, or strong dialogue in a film in order to get an "R" rating, which makes the desired audience more likely to attend.

In any case, with or without legislative or executive mandates, there will be a tendency toward "the wholly inoffensive, the bland" (FCC, 1964, p. 179). If this tendency wins with respect to something like "violence," it is unlikely to be too long before various proselytizing or nonproselytizing religious or political dogmas become equally unacceptable. The First Amendment refers to Congress passing "no law" abridging freedom of speech and the press. The media should demand no less, no matter how much of a fight it takes, and how unpopular the causes that will benefit. Fairness to the citizens of the United States is at stake.

■ CONCLUSIONS AND SUGGESTIONS

The media may not be the *cause* of violence, but there is considerable evidence that real-life violence is more acceptable to more people as the result of violence in the media. Yet, as I wrote after President Kennedy's assassination:

> [H]ave the American people become inured to violence as a way of life through a constant diet of dramatic programs that seem to look at one type of personality warped by life and solving all his problems through violent action? Thankfully, the reaction of almost all of us to the senseless slaughter in Dallas gives the lie to this line of reasoning. Violence has not yet lost its power to horrify. . . .
>
> [H]ave we lost the capacity to feel deep emotion after a generation of viewing human lives summed up or torn apart in the 23½-minute framework of a dramatic program? No. Even though we felt, at the end of four days, that we were drained of all emotion, we were not. And neither are our children even after a dozen years glued to the television set or another dozen with transistor radios plastered to their ears. (Kittross, 1963, p. 284)

So, *can we*, as media practitioners, reduce the destructive cycle of violence in America, to prevent the Oswalds (and the Rubys) from developing as they did? Perhaps.

Should we? Do we have an ethical duty to try? I believe that the answer is "Of course!" Both the utilitarians and Kant demand no less. Although the sales department may argue that such a course of action would put the size of a media audience at risk, or an advertiser may want maximum shock value, if all media adopt the same moral standards, then nobody has an unfair advantage. True, *The National Enquirer, Hard Copy*, and their equivalent seem to be with us always. But although "good news" news services have shown little success, most people do not actively seek out violent themes. The most important argument in favor of trying to reduce violence is a personal one for media practitioners: Do we want our own children to be exposed to it? Are we personally comfortable with it—and why? Dare we have the arrogance to say that different standards should be applied to the masses than we apply to our own families? Far too many major figures in the communication industry restrict their own offspring's viewing for the rest of us to be complacent about the content of the media. If we want to sleep well, we need to do what we can to benefit humanity.

Must we? Ay, there's the rub. Morally and ethically, I believe that we should do what we can, as individuals. But the First Amendment is under enough stress in the current political climate to prompt me to say "No" to this question. I don't think it inconsistent with the preceding paragraph to argue that the mass media should fight against allowing any "outsiders" to determine what we broadcast and print. The end is commendable, the means unacceptable.

If, as Gordon maintains, "at this point in our history . . . violent content should be no more protected under the First Amendment than is libelous content," then we are a long way down the slippery slope to determining content on the basis of what Congress says it should be.

. . . we are a long way down the slippery slope to determining content on the basis of what Congress says it should be.

Would pictures of American fighting leading to American dead during the Vietnam "living room war" have been allowed under Gordon's formulation? These pictures were surely violent, but they also had a significant and, many would argue, beneficial political impact. It is arguable that the war—and the casualty lists—would have been longer if television hadn't shown this true violence.

The quick fix to this argument might be to allow journalistic but not fictional coverage of such violence. Another quick fix would be to have (as we do) special rules that apply to materials available to (or, in some cases, directed to) children. But at what age does one stop being a child? What about children secure and mature enough to accept such programming at an early age, or those who never achieve maturity? Can we really help children to grow by wrapping them in cotton wool? In protecting the most vulnerable, do we take away the liberty of everyone else? Would I, like Gordon, throw the First Amendment baby out with the bathwater? Obviously not. I look at the positive, rather than the negative potential of the media. Any news broadcast would still be supplying violent images to those who might be harmed by them. And to prevent dramatic coverage, in the form of documentaries or drama, of human activities that include violence such as war, crime, imprisonment, torture, and even medicine, would be a political act of the greatest significance. Of course, if such censorship were carried out, there soon might not be enough of the nonbrainwashed around to realize how significant this decision was.

■ GORDON: There is far more violence in today's mass media than is good for society, and that violent content must somehow be controlled.

Let me note at the outset that I am not going to deal with pornography as separate from sexual content or from violence in the media. Although pornography is certainly degrading to women, I can't buy the argument of feminists Andrea Dworkin and

Catherine MacKinnon that a clear link has been established between it and violence directed toward women. *Should* such a link be established, I'd argue that pornography ought to be regulated because of the violence it could provoke. In the meantime, because some legal controls are already in place regarding pornography and obscenity, I prefer to focus mainly on the ethical aspects of violent mass media content.

The key points in this argument are where the line should be drawn regarding how much violence is *too* much, and who should draw it. John Michael Kittross argues that wherever the line is drawn, it must be purely an internal decision within the media. And he seems to be saying that since there is no 100% satisfying solution to this dilemma—and new questions can always be raised—we must leave any palliative efforts to the same voluntary self-regulation that has underwhelmed the problem to this point.

I disagree! I start from the premise that this is an increasingly crucial issue for the American people, as the current plague of violence seems to escalate into all corners of the society. Experience has shown that dealing with the media portrayal of violence cannot be left solely to the media. I do find it slightly uncomfortable to be on the same side of this argument as Reverend Donald E. Wildmon's American Family Association (AFA), which took out full-page newspaper ads to proclaim that its members "are *FED UP* with the sex, violence and profanity on television" and to threaten boycotts against sponsors of offending programs.

The AFA appeared to be much more concerned with sexual content than with violence, although it also made very clear its concerns about the latter. By contrast, I believe that the concern in many European countries over violent media content, combined with a much more laissez-faire attitude about sex, is an approach that would benefit American society (although it would run into all sorts of opposition from the deeply ingrained streak of American Puritanism that persists regarding sex). I *don't* believe there is any need to control television's sexual content in any way other than by turning off a program if one is offended by it. But violence is far more dangerous to society than sex is.

As of 1998 (despite the adoption of a parental guidance rating system by all but one network), violence was still considerably less regulated than was sexual content, either by the media themselves or externally. NBC's refusal to go along with the second part of the rating system (content indicators), and the generality of the categories relating both to suitability by age and to content, left few people fully satisfied and provided little incentive to alter content rather than merely labeling it. Nor is this rating system an overwhelming success with viewers. A February, 1998 Associated Press poll indicated that while nearly two-thirds of parents "sometimes use the ratings to make viewing decisions" and 40% do so regularly, just over half of the parents surveyed said they pay little or no attention to the ratings in program listings or on-screen—as do 70% of all adults in the poll ("'TV-NU'", 1998, p. 6A). With violence still such a prominent part of the TV landscape, some limits on it must be established, with assistance from outside the media if self-regulation continues to prove inadequate.

Protesters are perfectly within their rights to oppose both sexual and violent content on television, to organize boycotts, and to urge sympathizers to turn off the offending programs. One might argue that such efforts to influence the medium's content are enough, and that the television industry should be left to deal with these concerns guided only by viewer and pressure group reactions. In regard to sexual content, I agree. But I believe violence poses greater threats and can't be left to the influence only of public pressure or industry self-regulation.

One place this problem *may* be showing up is in the area of spouse and child abuse, as children raised on TV violence grow up and marry. As in most media violence studies, researchers in this area have found some very suggestive correlations rather than any clear cause → effect relationships. (See, among other sources summarizing some of these studies, Plagens et al., 1991, p. 51, which notes a longitudinal study that followed a set of children for more than 20 years and concluded that "kids who watched significant amounts of TV violence at the age of 8 were consistently more likely to commit violent crimes or engage in child or spouse abuse at 30.") I'll return to the statistical validity question later, because I think Kittross has expressed some errant conclusions in that regard even though he is correct that we don't have definitive proof of a sole cause → effect relationship.

The argument that anything beyond consumer and pressure group activities violates the media's First Amendment freedoms just doesn't wash in today's context of violence on TV and in society. Rather than an absolutist approach to the concept of freedom for the media, I'd suggest a utilitarian perspective that concerns itself with the greatest good for the greatest number of people.

Another alternative from an ethical perspective might be to get more women into positions that gatekeep violent media content. If Carol Gilligan's approach to developmental ethics (1982) is correct, and females' moral and ethical maturation relies more on nurturing than on the legalistic or rule-oriented approach of males, then women who have the power to control content might naturally reduce the amount of violence simply because it conflicts with their nurturing ethical perspective. It may have been only coincidence, but the two top executives were women at KVUE-TV, Austin, Texas, when that station cut back its crime coverage in early 1996, to present a less sensational picture of local crime (Hardie, 1996; Gordon, 1996). By 1998, although the guidelines were no longer in place, the station was still largely adhering to them in practice.

One might argue, of course, that the "V-chip" control of TV violence would be sufficient, when implemented, especially if we can get past Kittross's almost endless series of "straw man" questions about it. This technological approach to screening out programming above a specified level of violence (or sex, language, and dialogue) relies on an electronic chip, built into TV sets, that could be programmed by parents (or any other responsible adult)—*not* by the originating station or network—to block the reception of programs whose content is rated above whatever level *they* desire. Such technology, together with more precise classification (by some as yet undetermined group) of the violence in each program and with viewers exercising choices, would certainly be a self-regulating step in the right direction. It would also be one response to the concern that "television is an 'open-admission' technology . . . [that] is largely free," is very easy to switch on, and requires no reading skills (Postman and Powers, 1992, p. 148).

Violence in American society seems to be an epidemic that is increasing, perhaps fueled in part by the apparent growth in its acceptability or "normality." Portrayals of violent incidents in both news and entertainment programming seem ever more prevalent, often shown as an acceptable solution to problems and too often failing to show any real consequences resulting from the violent acts. All of this tends to desensitize viewers, which may be as great a danger as the possibility of violent content promoting either short-run or long-term violent behavior.

■ GRATUITOUS VIOLENCE

In addition to showing that violence *does* have consequences, another approach might also be taken (or required). Various critics and researchers have called for the elimination (or at least the reduction) of *gratuitous* violence, especially in entertainment programming. When violence is necessary to the plot—and particularly when it simply reflects the violence in society—it is arguably more appropriate than when it is used for shock value. Meg Greenfield, in a *Newsweek* column, noted that Shakespeare's works, among others, contain violent episodes that are "every bit as shaking and horrible" as anything on TV. But she cited crucial differences in the better literature:

> . . . the violence in the story meant something; it was singular; it was committed by a particularly cruel character; it had some purpose beyond its mere power to titillate, frighten and repel. Nor do I think any age has seen anything comparable to our own unending, daily inundation of the home by filmed, superrealistic close-up portrayals of human violence, of maiming and mutilation and slaughter. (Greenfield, 1993, p. 72)

Or, as another *Newsweek* article put it two years earlier, "Our fascination with such material is older than Lizzie Borden. What's new is the obsessively detailed description of all 40 whacks, with their attendant shrieks and splatters" (Plagens et al., 1991, p. 49).

A similar perspective might be useful with regard to violence on the news. Where violent footage is needed to illustrate violent news—or sports—events, it is far more justifiable than when the story can be told just as well without what one news director called "'the graphic blood'" (Simmons, 1994). When news accounts include violent footage gratuitously—or when violent stories are hyped simply to promote interest in an upcoming newscast segment—there are ethical questions that cry out for answers and self-regulation may well be inadequate to deal with the problem.

This approach obviously leaves itself open for the criticism that one person's gratuitous violence is a necessary illustration for another person. It's easy to criticize efforts to eliminate "unnecessary" violence by arguing that it would require various individuals (or groups or institutions) to make value judgments affecting the content of the news or the entertainment program, and would give them undue power over media content.

With all due respect to those concerns, I suggest that this is no more of a problem in regard to violent content than it is in regard to any other aspect of media content. Media gatekeepers make value judgments all the time regarding the inclusion or exclusion of certain materials in their communications. What, after all, is "news judgment" if not a kind of value judgment? The Communications Act of 1934 mandate that broadcasters serve the "public interest, convenience and necessity" is a phrase that clearly requires some value judgments to be made. And ethics, by definition, is a series of judgments about values.

A few local news operations in the mid-1990s began to go against the general trend, by "playing down violent crime, eschewing graphic footage and trying to make their shows 'family sensitive'" (Zoglin, 1994, p. 55). The KVUE-TV experiment noted earlier set up five specific guidelines for responsible crime coverage, dealing with why a story should be reported at all, and how it should be done. If at least one guideline wasn't met, crime stories were not reported (Gordon, 1996). These are encouraging signs, but similar approaches are needed in many more news markets and generally in entertainment programming. There is really no reason to be afraid of applying value judgments—externally, if necessary—to reduce the gratuitous violence appearing in the news and the entertainment media.

■ EVIDENCE OF VARIOUS SORTS

It just doesn't work to argue, as Kittross has done, that because the extensive research on TV violence doesn't clearly prove a cause → effect relationship, it should all be dismissed as irrelevant. Although there have been some widely varying results from that research, and although some of the earlier research in particular can validly be questioned, there also seems to be a clear indication that televised violence—probably in combination with other factors—affects some people in ways that lead to antisocial behavior in the long run as well as the short term.

One such study compared a sample of men who were imprisoned for violent acts with a matched sample of men outside of prison. Some 80% of the prisoners reported both heavy childhood viewing of violent TV *and* in-home domestic violence. The comparable figure in the nonimprisoned population was 30% (Kruttschnitt et al., 1986). In fairness to Kittross's concern about such studies, it should be noted that the authors concluded that violent parental role models and weak attachments to family and schooling were at least as important as exposure to violent TV content as predictors of future violent behavior. However, contrary to Kittross's cavalier dismissal of these data, the jailers didn't do this study, and the respondents were providing information rather than "blaming" their behavior on any factors. This—or any other single study—certainly doesn't prove a cause → effect relationship, but the growing number of studies with similar results certainly suggests that the impact of TV violence on violent behavior can't be dismissed as just *post hoc, ergo propter hoc.*

There is also considerable anecdotal evidence. One of the more striking stories concerns a four-year-old girl who asked "who killed him?" when told by her parents that a playmate's father had just died:

> The parents were prepared to discuss the many concerns that a child might have about the death of a parent, but not the question that she asked. After explaining that her playmate's father had died of a disease, they asked why she thought someone had killed him. "Isn't that the way people die?" the girl asked. "That's the way people die on TV." (Slaby, 1994, p. B1)

Increasingly, though, there is more than just anecdotal evidence to link televised violence with violence in society. A 1992 article in the *Journal of the American Medical Association* noted that some 20 long-term field studies in recent years have shown a positive correlation between watching violence on TV and violent or aggressive behavior (Centerwall, 1992). Although the evidence is not completely unequivocal and the data are not conclusive in regard to cause and effect, there is enough smoke coming from the myriad of TV violence studies to make it unwise to claim that no fire has been scientifically proven. To paraphrase an old saw, if it looks like a fire, it smells like a fire, and if it smokes like a fire, it probably is a fire.

■ PORTRAYALS OF VIOLENCE

Some of the problem may stem from the way in which violence is shown on American television. George Gerbner, a research pioneer on the impact of televised violence, noted that a study comparing Japanese and American television "found that Japanese violence, unlike ours, is not happy violence. It's painful, it's awful, it teaches a very different lesson" ("The Experts Speak Out," 1992, p. 15).

A similar comment about violence on American TV (and in films) was offered nearly two decades earlier by author Tom Wolfe, who noted that it is usually shown from the perspective of the perpetrator (or from a third-person perspective). Rarely if ever is violence seen from the perspective of the victim, which would illustrate the consequences much more graphically and help to deglamorize it. Wolfe called the usual approach "porno-violence" because

> in almost every case the camera angle, therefore the viewer, is with the gun, the fist, the rock. The pornography of violence has no point of view in the old sense that novels do. . . . You live with the aggressor, whoever he may be. One moment you are the hero. The next you are the villain. No matter whose side you may be on consciously, you are in fact with the muscle and it is you who disintegrates all comers, villains, lawmen, women, anybody. (Wolfe, 1976, pp. 183–184)

This choice of perspectives, though perfectly logical, may be one further reason that violence portrayed in the media seemingly contributes to its acceptance in society.

Another concern focuses not on viewers whose aggressive actions might be stimulated by televised violence, but rather on the reactions of viewers who constantly see a violent video world portrayed. To quote Gerbner once again:

> [T]elevision trains us to be victims. Our studies, as confirmed by many independent investigators, show that the most pervasive, long-term consequence of growing up in a media cult of violence is a sense of pervasive insecurity, what we call "the mean-world syndrome." It's a sense of feeling vulnerable, of dependence, of needing protection. ("The Experts Speak Out," 1992, pp. 12–13)

Gerbner has been involved in a long-running study that has recorded at least 26 annual week-long samples of prime time and weekend programming, and coded and analyzed their violence content. While the methodology of this study is not infallible, it seems to me to be far better than Kittross is willing to admit, and provides a useful context within which to analyze violence trends. (Signorielli, 1995)

The exact number of people affected negatively by TV violence is certainly debatable. I'd suggest, however, that even if we can prevent—or discourage—"only" a few killings or a relative handful of assaults each month, or if we can alleviate that sense of insecurity for even a few people, it is well worth trying to do so even if it raises the potential risk of stepping on some First Amendment toes.

It's interesting to note that both the *Journal of the American Medical Association* and *TV Guide* called TV violence a public health problem in the early 1990s. In addition, "the American Academy of Pediatrics concluded that TV violence 'promotes a proclivity to violence and a passive response to its practice'" (Postman and Powers, 1992, p. 147). If there is *any* truth to such concerns, our society is facing—or is already in the midst of—a crisis that requires *some* entity to act regardless of whether such steps raise First Amendment concerns.

A major part of the problem is the sheer volume of violent acts shown on television during regular entertainment programming, especially in children's programs. A study of the 1991–1992 TV season showed that children's programs have far higher rates of violence than do prime-time programs—an average of 32 violent acts per hour in children's programs compared to four in prime time, and 79% of children's programs had characters who were involved in violence either as perpetrators or victims, compared with 47% of prime-time programs (Waters et al., 1993).

A study commissioned by *TV Guide* analyzed 18 hours (6 A.M. to midnight) of programming on April 2, 1992, on each of 10 channels (including four cable channels—HBO, WTBS, USA, and MTV) in Washington, D.C. In the 180 hours of programming, which included no exceptionally violent movies or news events that day, this study identified

> . . . 1,846 individual acts of violence; 175 scenes in which violence resulted in one or more fatalities; 389 scenes depicting serious assaults [without guns]; 362 scenes involving gunplay; 673 depictions of punching, pushing, slapping, dragging, and other physically hostile acts; 226 scenes of menacing threats with a weapon.
>
> Newer programming forms like music videos and reality shows . . . are significantly increasing the amount of violence on our screens. And commercials for violent theatrical movies and TV series have become a major source of televised violence. (Hickey, 1992, p. 10)

So have cartoons, which were found by the *TV Guide* study to be "the most violent program form, with 471 scenes," which may be particularly inadvisable for very young children (ages two to five) "who may not distinguish between animated violence and the real thing" (Hickey, 1992, p. 10). In all, critics have concluded, the average American child sees a huge amount of televised violence while growing up—by one estimate, "roughly thirteen thousand killings [and] 100,000 violent episodes" by the time of high school graduation (Postman and Powers, 1992, p. 146).

Films have also come in for their share of criticism regarding violent content, even though the top box office hits since 1980 include many more relatively nonviolent (often family-oriented) movies than "R" titles. Hollywood has been turning out an increasing number of "R"-rated movies in recent years—often over 60% of all releases. However, the median for box office receipts from films rated "R" or "PG-13"—usually for sexual and/or violent content—lagged well behind comparable figures for "G" and "PG" films between 1983 and 1989 (Medved, 1992, pp. 287–289).

Film and television are increasingly similar in some key ways, since most movies are available on home TV or videocassette. Film violence is at, or close to, an all-time high; one critic came up with body counts of 81 in *Robocop 2*, 106 in *Rambo III*, and 264 in *Die Hard 2* ("The Experts Speak Out," 1992, p. 17). Another study showed that "among *all* major releases in 1991—including PG- and G-rated 'family films'—62% featured violent fight scenes, and 39% showed 'graphic deaths'" (Medved, 1992, p. 187).

One critic has also lamented the increased violence in recent years in televised sports events, creating an audience that "has, because of TV, become accustomed to seeing [violent] displays. . . . Almost all technological advances in the [sports] broadcasting industry [e.g., super slow motion] have been concerned with transporting violent images more effectively" (Twitchell, 1989, p. 12).

Violent video games also have come in for criticism as one possible breeder of violent behavior. A former CBS vice president for program practices told the story of an erstwhile West Point psychology professor, paratrooper, ranger and Vietnam veteran who "has been particularly troubled by the coexistence of increasingly violent films and video games and the considerable rise in criminal assault." The former soldier drew a parallel to the training given to American infantrymen to increase their willingness to fire their weapons in battle—training that helped raise the rate from 15 to 20% in World War II to 95% in Vietnam—and the ways in which American children are influenced by violent cartoons and by what he calls the reflex training in violent video games. The ex-CBS executive suggested that— no matter how unlikely the connection might seem (and he added violent feature films to the mix)—we ignore the possibility at our societal peril (Dessart, 1996, p. 39–40).

Entertainment media are not the only sources for concern about portrayals of violence. Television news has also come in for criticism and these concerns cannot be dismissed merely by pleading First Amendment protection for the news media. Some of the problem is very clearly in the ethics realm, such as the decision by NBC to show the 1993 murder of a Florida woman by her ex-husband on its *Nightly News* program. The shooting occurred during an interview of the ex-husband by the tabloid Spanish-language news program *Ocurio Asi* ("The way it happened"). The man wanted the program to investigate the possibility that his ex-wife was involved in their pregnant teenage daughter's suicide; he was being interviewed at the cemetery where his daughter was buried when his ex-wife showed up unexpectedly. The camera continued to roll while he pulled a gun and shot her.

The tape was offered to the major networks by Telemundo, the Spanish-language network that produced the original program. Only NBC used it; among the reasons given by the other networks for declining was the fact that the story was a day old by the time the tape was made available to them. Some news directors at NBC affiliates questioned whether this incident had enough news value to warrant its use, or whether (in the words of one of them) it "'was thoughtless, irresponsible and shouldn't have been done'" (Winslow, 1993, p. 8). As another affiliate news director put it, in criticizing the use of this material, "'It was real, not the movies, not entertainment'" (p. 9).

There are other major ethical questions here as well—for instance, whether the whole shooting sequence should have been shown, if it were used at all, and whether the audience should have been cautioned much more fully about what was coming. Although NBC claimed that showing the video illustrated the horrors of domestic violence, which the network is committed to cover, one critic noted that the story was run without any references to the larger context of domestic violence (Winslow, 1993, p. 9). This after-the-fact, self-serving justification by the network serves as a pointed and forceful argument that some type of outside influence is not only helpful but necessary in setting limits on violent content. I am not suggesting direct censorship in regard to such portrayals of violence on the news, but it might well be appropriate to consider whether this kind of material truly serves the "public interest, convenience and necessity" when the FCC considers the license renewal applications of individual stations.

Another concern regarding violence in news programming is the so-called copycat syndrome in civil disturbances, where viewers see live televised violence occurring and take to the streets themselves. Ted Koppel, among others, blamed such "live, unedited telecasting of the [1992] Los Angeles riots [for spreading] the virus from one part of the city to another" ("The Experts Speak Out," 1992, p. 18).

Where entertainment programs and "copycat" crimes or suicides are concerned, Kittross may be right in questioning any direct relationship, though there is anecdotal evidence that this has happened. But Koppel's concern about imitative behavior produced by news accounts can't be dismissed as easily.

A related issue has surfaced in the controversy over attempts to televise the executions of convicted criminals, either live or on tape. Aside from the concerns over possible sensationalism and the arguments that the public should be able to witness executions as part of the ongoing debate over capital punishment, some critics of televised executions have argued that they might well wind up desensitizing viewers to the taking of human life, especially in view of studies that have found that violent films or TV programs may well lower viewers' sensitivity to violence in general (Linz et al., 1984; note also the comments by Meg Greenfield [1993], which follow shortly).

One key ethical question here is whether the entertainment media—ranging from TV and movies to the music industry—*should* be putting forth material that demonstrates different methods of violence, romanticizes teenage suicide, or focuses on the murder of policemen. Should there be some restrictions placed on television gatekeepers so as to keep some of the mindless violence off the airwaves, if they lack the responsibility or the good sense to excise it on their own? For example, should there be some type of outside control over the televising of four real-life killings, all made available by camcorders, on just the *premiere* episode of *I Witness Video* (Waters et al., 1993)? Should there be restrictions on films that provide models of violence that just a few people may copy-cat? When at least 14 accused murderers may be said to have emulated the film *Natural Born Killers* (Gibeaut, 1997, pp. 63–64), such restrictions seem overdue. Is this perhaps a public health issue—or, as novelist/lawyer John Grisham has suggested, a product liability issue—rather than a First Amendment issue (Gibeaut, pp. 64, 66)?

The social responsibility theory put forth by the Hutchins Commission in 1947 would argue that, one way or the other, the epidemic of media violence must be controlled (Commission on Freedom of the Press, 1947). As Greenfield noted:

> Most of this stuff has long since abandoned any pretense to what the Supreme Court once called, in the context of an obscenity ruling, "redeeming social value." It is gore for gore's sake, drama based on violence as a first and only resort in conflict. (Greenfield, 1993, p. 72)

Greenfield added her concern that TV's fictional violence "will dull our reactions to the kind that is filmed not on a set but from Bosnia or Liberia or places in this country."

Because the media have failed to exercise much self-restraint, some outside forces must be brought into play to help reduce the levels of violent media content. Pressure groups—such as the Parents Music Resource Center, organized by Tipper Gore to twist the recording industry's arm to label records that have violent content—are one possibility, with economic marketplace forces lurking in the background. But with violence continuing as a societal problem, it may be necessary for the government to intervene indirectly or even directly, despite the real concerns this would raise about First Amendment rights.

. . . violent content should be no more protected under the First Amendment than is libelous content.

First Amendment rights, though, have never been widely regarded as absolute. A reasonable argument can be made, at this point in our history, that violent content should be no more protected under the First Amendment than is libelous content. Libelous material is allowed when it deals with matters relating to public life, and such an approach might work very well as a guideline for government regulation of violence in the media. Certainly, it seems no harder to define *violence* than it has been to define *obscenity* over the decades, and the definitional difficulties haven't kept the courts from regulating the latter.

One thing appears increasingly clear—the media need to become part of the solution to the societal violence plague, rather than contributing to it. They need to remember that one of the major goals set out for them by the Hutchins Commission was to raise social conflict from the level of violence to the level of discussion. It would be best if the media would do this themselves. But, lacking that, society shouldn't shirk the responsibility of pressuring or compelling the media to take on this responsibility, with regard to the long-term effects of violent TV and its desensitizing aspects, if nothing else.

■ MERRILL: Commentary

Again we see in this controversy the perennial clash of freedom and responsibility. David Gordon's position judges control of media for the good of society as more important than informational freedom. John Michael Kittross has made the case for the naturalness of violent media content and believes that attempts to control it would be counterproductive.

This is a difficult one, even for the so-called pure media-libertarian. It is difficult for the very reason that a dedication to social responsibility (or media ethics) *is* always lurking in the mind of the media practitioner. This is true even for the individualistic and libertarian communicator. When ethics comes into the picture, freedom is forced to retreat at least a few steps backward. If we were sure—and many researchers insist that we are—that violence in the media adversely affects audience members (especially children), making them more callous and inhumane, then I think that any person concerned with media ethics would want to see such violent emphasis modified or even eliminated. But the jury, as Kittross reminds us, is really still out on this; there seems to be no consensus among serious researchers on the impact of violent media content, although the scales appear tipped toward some impact.

[T]here seems to be no consensus among serious researchers on the impact of violent media content . . .

One thing is rather obvious: There is more violent content (especially on television) than is necessary, even from an artistic or aesthetic point of view. Gratuitous violence is perhaps like gratuitous sex in the media. Much extreme violent behavior is almost unbelievably excessive, and maybe this word "unbelievably" is a key one. Defenders (or tolerators) of media violence would probably say that people realize that the exaggerated violence is not real, just as children do when they see a *Roadrunner* cartoon. It is simply not believable.

The wording of the controversial positions in this chapter defines the issue quite well. Gordon argues that there is more violence in the media "than is good for society" and that it "must somehow" be controlled. And Kittross calls such violence "regrettable" but says that it is natural, and that *outside* pressures to control it would be unwarranted. I can agree with both positions, and I'm sure the reader can also.

I would say that all the violence is obviously not *good* for society and that it should *somehow* be controlled. That "somehow" could very well be by the voluntary actions of media people who have gained an ethical sensitivity and a determination to moderate such violence. This is the kind of control we must be concerned with here: *ethical control*. It is consistent with freedom and does not imply any kind of retreat into authoritarianism that would usurp media autonomy.

Turning to the other position, argued above, that contends that media violence is regrettable but natural, I have to agree. It is, indeed, regrettable—from an ethical, if not from a pure entertainment, point of view—and it is "natural" in that if media reflect even superficially the "real world," they will naturally provide slices of the violent reality of such a world. But Kittross's warning that outside (nonmedia) forces might attempt to control violence and pornography might very well introduce something worse than the negative aspects of such violence, for instance, censorship.

In this chapter, Gordon is taking the more communitarian or absolute (legalistic) ethical position, whereas Kittross is defending the liberal or libertarian—some would call it permissive—position. I tend to agree with Kittross, although as I read, hear, and view the plethora of rubbish that assails me from the mass media every day, I am sorely tempted to slide over into a more absolutist communitarian position. Perhaps, as Gordon intimates, the government should go further than it does in protecting us from invasions that damage our minds and souls as well from those that endanger our property and lives.

REFERENCES

Broun, Heywood. (1927). "Censorship." In Heywood Broun and Margaret Leach, *Anthony Comstock: Roundsman of the Lord*. New York: Boni & Liveright.

Centerwall, Brandon. (June 10, 1992). "Television and Violence: The Scale of the Problem and Where to Go from Here." *Journal of the American Medical Association*, pp. 3059–3063.

Commission on Freedom of the Press. (1947). *A Free and Responsible Press*. Chicago: University of Chicago Press.

Comstock, George, Steven Chaffee, Natan Katzman, Maxwell McCombs, and Donald Roberts. (1978). *Television and Human Behavior*. New York: Columbia University Press.

Dessart, George. (1996). "Reflections on the V-Chip." *Television Quarterly* 28(3), pp. 37–40.

Dworkin, Andrea. (Spring 1985). "Against the Male Flood: Censorship, Pornography and Equality." *Harvard Women's Law Journal* 8, pp. 1–29.

Federal Communications Commission (FCC). (January 2, 1964). "Memorandum Opinion and Order In re Application of Pacifica Foundation for Renewal of Licenses KPFA–FM, . . . et al." Reprinted (Spring 1965) as "The 'Pacifica' Decision: Broadcasting and Free Expression." *Journal of Broadcasting* 9(2), pp. 177–182.

Gibeaut, John. (June 1997). "Deadly Inspiration." *ABA Journal*, pp. 62–67.

Gilligan, Carol. (1982). *In a Different Voice*. Cambridge, MA: Harvard University Press.

Gordon, David. (Fall 1996). "A Response to Beechner," *Media Ethics* 8(1), pp. 12–13.

Greenfield, Meg. (June 21, 1993). "TV's True Violence." *Newsweek*, p. 72.

Hardie, Mary. (May/June 1996). "KVUE-TV Takes a Bite Out of Crime Coverage." *Gannetteer*, p. 15.

Hickey, Neil. (August 22, 1992). "How Much Violence." *TV Guide*, pp. 10–11.

Kittross, John M. (Fall 1963). "Four Days" (editorial). *Journal of Broadcasting* 7(4), pp. 283–284.

Kruttschnitt, Candace, Linda Heath, and David A. Ward. (1986). "Family Violence, Television Viewing Habits, and Other Adolescent Experiences Related to Violent Criminal Behavior." *Criminology* 24(2), pp. 235–267.

Lehrer, Tom. (1981). "Smut." In *Too Many Songs by Tom Lehrer*. New York: Pantheon, pp. 100–105.

Linz, David, Edward Donnerstein, and Steven Penrod (Summer 1984). "The Effects of Multiple Exposures to Filmed Violence Against Women." *Journal of Communication* 34(3), pp. 130–147.

Loevinger, Lee. (Spring 1968). "The Ambiguous Mirror: The Reflective–Projective Theory of Broadcasting and Mass Communications." *Journal of Broadcasting* 12(2), pp. 97–116.

Medved, Michael. (1992). *Hollywood vs. America*. New York: HarperCollins.

Plagens, Peter, Mark Miller, Donna Foote, and Emily Yoffe. (April 1, 1991). "Violence in Our Culture." *Newsweek*, pp. 46–52.

Postman, Neil, and Steve Powers. (1992). *How to Watch TV News*. New York: Penguin.

Signorielli, Nancy, George Gerbner, and Michael Morgan. (Spring 1995). "Violence on Television: The Cultural Indicators Project." *Journal of Broadcasting and Electronic Media* 39(2), pp. 278–283.

Simmons, Bob. (July/August 1994). "Violence in the Air." *Columbia Journalism Review*, p. 12.

Slaby, Ronald G. (January 5, 1994). "Combating Television Violence." *The Chronicle of Higher Education*, pp. B1–B2.

Surgeon General's Scientific Advisory Committee on Television and Social Behavior. (1972). *Television and Growing Up: The Impact of Televised Violence*. Washington: U.S. Government Printing Office.

"The Experts Speak Out: *TV Guide's* Panel: 'The New Face of Violence on TV.'" (August 22, 1992). *TV Guide*, pp. 12–22.

"'TV-NU': poll gives ratings system new category: not used." (March 2, 1998). Eau Claire, WI *Leader-Telegram*, p. 6A.

Twitchell, James B. (1989). *Preposterous Violence: Fables of Aggression in Modern Culture.* New York: Oxford University Press.

Waters, Harry F., Daniel Glick, Caroline Friday, and Jeanne Gordon. (July 12, 1993). "Networks Under the Gun." *Newsweek*, pp. 64–66.

Winslow, C. Catherine. (March 1993). "Is It News?" RTNDA *Communicator*, pp. 8–9.

Wolfe, Tom. (1976). *Mauve Gloves and Madmen, Clutter and Vine: and Other Stories, Sketches and Essays.* New York: Farrar, Straus, and Giroux.

Zoglin, Richard. (June 20, 1994). "All the News That's Fit." *Time*, p. 55.

CHAPTER 11

MEDIA ETHICS AND THE ECONOMIC MARKETPLACE

S hould we be concerned about ethical behavior in a business that depends on bottom-line profits for its survival? That's the problem facing mass media practitioners who are concerned about ethics but who literally can't afford to ignore the economics of their calling. As long as the media are supported primarily by advertising, they will need to attract audiences they can deliver to the advertisers, and that need can clash seriously with the desire to "do the ethical thing."

The growth of conglomerate owners of mass media outlets has compounded this problem considerably. It has brought into top decision-making positions people who sometimes have little or no experience with the media channels they control and minimal understanding of ethical concerns that have arisen in a particular medium over the years. For example, might an owner with little journalism background be too willing to pull a column that offends a group of large advertisers? Might someone without ad agency background be unwilling to take economic risks that may accompany new approaches to creativity? Might an accountant who heads the parent company of a TV production firm be negative about proposed programming that breaks new ground, and prefer to rely on tried and true formulas?

One perspective on this controversy is the contention that economic realities make concerns for ethics more difficult, if not impossible, or perhaps superfluous. This is the position argued here by John Michael Kittross. Another approach (though certainly not the only alternative one) holds that economic considerations can be beneficial to the ethical climate in which the mass media operate. David Gordon espouses this position in the material that follows. The bottom-line questions here might well be whether the drive to maximize profits affects ethics; if so, what results from that impact; and, if there is an imbalance, what might be done to tilt it back toward ethics?

■ KITTROSS: The economic marketplace is at best superfluous, and at worst counterproductive, with regard to media ethics.

Every field of knowledge has its shibboleths. Every era has its aphorisms. Every political or social movement has its slogans. Sometimes, they are inappropriately applied to other fields—such as media ethics. My thesis for this chapter is simple: The magic word of applied economics, *marketplace*, has no useful function with respect to media ethics, either as an abstraction or as a euphemism for a quest for monetary gain.

There is no need to bring in formal economic theory, or to ask "What would be the alternative to a marketplace?" Pragmatically, I presume that both media ethics and economic marketplaces will continue to exist but should be thought of as separate concepts, and with separate criteria for evaluation. The purpose of the economic marketplace is generally to maximize profits of individuals and firms, nowadays usually in the short term. The purpose of media ethics is to improve the lives of both the general public and media practitioners, in the long (as well as short) term. Although most (but not all) mass media are businesses, I maintain that they are something else as well. An analogy would be the doctor, who collects large economic fees, yet has as her or his *primary* societal function the maintenance and improvement of the public's physical and mental health.

It is often possible to "do well by doing good" . . .

In a nutshell, economics and media ethics generally are independent or in opposition, unless one merely wants to find out one's price, or one's employer's price. Many sins have been committed by those who did evil while using the excuse, "Unless my business is profitable, I can't do *any* good." In the political arena, a similar approach is taken by politicians: "Unless I do whatever it takes to get reelected, I won't be in a position that empowers me to do good things for my constituents." I take a different position: It is often possible to "do well by doing good," and taking an ethical stand may often, serendipitously, bring the accolades and income that a weaker person hopes for—but rarely achieves—by selling his or her soul. To reverse this injunction—to do good by doing well—is, except to the spiritual descendants of the robber barons of a century ago, a logical impossibility.

A perhaps unintended sign of the difference between the power of economics over the daily newspaper, and the power of having a governmental agency looking over the shoulder of radio and television stations, is the fact that the former calls that part of the paper in which news is published "the news hole" (i.e., what is left over after the advertisements have been placed), and broadcasting stations refer to "commercial interruptions"—reflecting also the physical reality that, while additional pages can usually be printed in a newspaper, the broadcast day cannot be stretched beyond 24 hours.

In another example of how economics and performance interact, both newspaper and broadcast news operations, when the budget runs out, are unable to respond to unanticipated disasters (and good news as well). This is particularly true in units owned by large conglomerates or owners of multiple media outlets. No matter how important, with few exceptions, if the annual budget has been spent or if income projections are lower than expected, such news will be covered "on the cheap"—possibly by using wire service reports, stock footage, simple "stand up" or anchor-read formats—or just plain ignored.

If we look at the traditional ethicists—Aristotle, utilitarians such as Bentham and Mill, Kant, Rawls—we find that either their principles are irrelevant to the economic marketplace (or vice versa), or in opposition to the very concept. Kant, as well as the

Judeo-Christian ethic, would place the needs of the public (your neighbor) above the fiduciary responsibility and greed of the market.

■ ECONOMICS AND POLITICS

Each field of knowledge also has its own version of the assertion, "Don't confuse me with facts; my mind is made up!" Usually this happens so that one can avoid having to reason through every turn of the often-illogical road, but occasionally it is so one can free one's mind for other things.

In our era, some of the more consequential articles of faith are in the field of theoretical and applied economics. Theoretical economics has justifiably been called the dismal science, and it is noted for its inability to predict either the fat years or the lean. Applied economists' income levels reflect the same patterns as those of their less-knowledgeable fellow citizens. Yet, the financial world has evolved to being almost as important as sports and weather on the 6 o'clock news—and, conceptually, we have come a long and tortuous way from the condemnation of money lending in many major religions (including Christianity and Islam) to the present glorification of Wall Street. The global financial community is as aware of the power of the media to affect prices as it is of the growth of automation.

But when economics and politics join, very strong forces may be unleashed, as writers from John Stuart Mill to the greenest pundit who reinvented the opinion that "people vote their pocketbooks" have pointed out. Today, it would be silly to assume that government has no role in America's economy, no matter what the slogans say.

In the late 1970s and during the Reagan and Bush administrations, government was still in the picture even amid the sudden popularity of "deregulation," "marketplace solutions," and similar manifestations that the pendulum had swung to the laissez-faire side of economics. This was so even when it became fashionable to argue that government itself was the problem and should be reduced to an ever-smaller fraction of its present size—during the same administrations in which three-quarters of the national debt was being amassed.

Many conservatives, mostly in business, desire less government except when it can be used for their own benefit as a regulator (of competitors) or as a customer or source of research and development funding. Although this can be derided as the result of selfish motives, there are also a substantial number of those who might be called "right libertarians" who are philosophically and intellectually opposed to most or all current functions of government regardless of personal economic consequences. A former Speaker of the House of Representatives, "Uncle Joe" Cannon, maintained in the 45th Congress more than a century ago that "the function of the Federal government is to afford protection to life, liberty, and property. When that is done, then let every tub stand on its own bottom, let every citizen 'root hog or die'" (Weinberg and Weinberg, 1961, p. 96). Today's Speaker, Newt Gingrich, apparently holds similar views.

It is bureaucracy that is the enemy, not government as such. To use a health care example, big insurance company bureaucracies certainly are just as inefficient and uncaring as big government bureaucracies. They also want to make a profit and, in many instances where employers select insurance carriers on the basis of price and the employee cannot make a free choice, there is no equivalent of the ballot box as a feedback mechanism or control.

Even when the argument continued that the free marketplace or privatization would solve all problems of economic incentive and equitable (undefined!) distribution of wealth, and the myth of trickle-down economics held brief sway, the government was to be used to achieve these ends. Some have even imagined that the free market concept was enshrined in the U.S. Constitution.

It isn't part of the Constitution, of course, and never was. One can hardly be called un-American for supporting some economic view other than free enterprise, as many Americans did during the 1994 national debate over the funding of health care or the less salient debate over whether public broadcasting should continue to receive roughly 10% of its income from the federal government. Rather, market economics is only one view among many of how to make the world operate efficiently, but it is a very popular one. Now that state socialism, as practiced in the former Soviet Union, is no longer a goal or an exemplar, free enterprise may indeed be the only economic *weltanschauung*, or world outlook, for the 1990s.

■ THE MARKETPLACE

Today's "free market" isn't quite the same as the laissez-faire approach of the robber barons of the 19th century because now it is often noteworthy for efficient use of the government's powers to support the strategies and profits of "private" business, even if public resources—such as the national forests—are thereby harmed.

In this context, it is comforting to realize that the electromagnetic spectrum is infinitely renewable: If all stations (and sources of artificial electromagnetic interference) were shut down, the spectrum would be as large and pristine as it was before Marconi was born. However, strictly economic considerations—the value of all the transmission and reception equipment rendered useless—probably would prevail to prevent such a shutdown. On the other hand, if one is willing to exercise political power, one doesn't have to wait—for example, the 60 years or so that it takes a tree to grow to useful economic size—in order to make changes in use of the electromagnetic spectrum.

The free market approach certainly shows little resemblance to the populist and socialist views more prevalent (but certainly not universal) earlier in this century, and tends to be used for propagandistic and selfish purposes rather than more altruistically as a means of optimizing the U.S. (or world) economy. David Gordon even seems to argue that the live hand of government is a necessary backstop to the "dead hand" of classical economics. (In the interest of full disclosure: I adhere to Goethe's more balanced view: that government is best that governs *best*, not the one that governs least.)

There isn't only one marketplace, either. There are *many* economic, quasi-economic, and other markets in which communications in the United States operate. These are real enough. A sampling would include markets in which individual media organizations and groups compete for advertiser dollars; ideologies and political views compete for hearts and minds; various goods and services compete for customers; creators search for patrons; program producers and syndication services compete for selection by stations, newspapers, magazines, and other mass media distribution entities; employees of the media compete for jobs, pay, and perks; those seeking attention from the public compete for that attention; communication schools try to attract students; nonprofit entities (including colleges and public broadcasting stations) beg for contributions; politicians compete for votes; suppliers of equipment compete for its adoption by buyers; news reporters and producers compete for air time; providers of electromagnetic spectrum bandwidth—radiated or conducted—on which information travels compete for paying users; box offices, coin boxes, and games of chance compete for our "disposable" income; the "leisure time" of each person's 168 hours in the week is fought over by those who wish to claim it. And more!

Even though there is no single free market for communication, there are strong political tendencies to act as if one existed.

"Deregulation," in the 1981 words of former FCC Chairman Mark Fowler, was intended "to create, to the maximum extent possible, an unregulated, competitive marketplace environment for the development of telecommunications" (Kittross, 1989, p. 207). The evolution of technologies and the entrepreneurial urges of the 1990s have led to an even more fervent adoption of this principle.

But if it ain't broke, why change it? There is little evidence that this marketplace of communication is a good regulatory mechanism, that deregulation truly has provided a net benefit to the public interest even in areas of supposed success such as the airline industry, or that the increased competition in, for example, long-distance telephone communication should be transplanted to such other arenas as local telephone service. In particular, Gordon's point that it is good that the market may be causing us to "unite (our) computers, telephones and cable channels" makes me wonder if he has forgotten the common sense warning not to put all one's eggs in the same basket.

■ COMPETITION

The basic problem is that, according to both history and theory, uncontrolled economic competition generally leads, in the long run, to uncontrolled monopoly. The company that excels, with a differentiated product, will get the most customers. Weaker firms will go under until, eventually, only one (or an oligopolistic cartel) remains. In the media, it already is cheaper and easier for advertisers to deal with the largest stations, magazines, and newspapers than hassle with a large number of smaller or local outlets. In the 1980s, mergers of advertising agencies into giant companies became the rule. As long as advertisers want large numbers of people paying attention, the money will go with the numbers. The fear shown by smaller players— for example, the entire cable and broadcasting industries are very small compared to the computer industry or even the regional telephone companies—is quite justified.

Although we are discussing industries and institutions, we should note that from a *content* point of view—the marketplace of ideas, not economics—competition can be valuable. After all, ideas are inexhaustible, unlike most economic factors. Unfortunately, some of the best examples of competition in a given media operation—such as ABC Radio's two-hour block of news and commentary in the 1960s, in which commentary from both the right and the left was heard—have been eliminated in the interests of substituting more profitable programming and providing pabulum or oatmeal rather than raw meat in order to avoid offending any potential listeners or advertisers.

Not all of the major players or competitors in these interlocking economic markets or arenas think of them as zero-sum games, like poker, in which, if the game is played long enough, eventually most will lose all and one will win all (Morgenstern and Von Neumann, 1953). A non-zero-sum game, in which all could lose (as in a nuclear war) or all could win (as in a true "meeting of minds" contract) could appeal to some. Should one risk all one's eggs in one basket, no matter how carefully watched? Or should one adopt the strategy of John Malone, who built the largest cable television firm in the United States, of "wanting a piece of everyone's business"? Malone, CEO of Tele-Communications Inc., has been called "the most influential man in television." In 1994, he controlled one out of every five cable boxes in the country (one out of four in 1997), had an interest in 29 cable program services, and had just negotiated a several billion dollar merger with Bell Atlantic that later fell through (Auletta, 1994).

It is still possible to have a win-win non-zero-sum game, to "do well by doing good." An example would be the immensely popular and usually profitable Ben & Jerry's ice cream company, which embraces social responsibility in its business operations. Not only does Ben & Jerry's make a good product (if one isn't on a diet), provide excellent working conditions and benefits, and support the Vermont family farm and environmental protection, but it spends a significant proportion of its profits on other worthy causes. Ben Cohen and Jerry Greenfield even restricted their own income to seven times the salary of their lowest-paid employee—a policy and example they had to change in 1995 when selecting a new chief executive because few "outside" candidates would accept such a limit. But Ben & Jerry's is unusual, almost unique. In contrast, the CEOs of 11 media companies were paid an average of 48 times the $50,000 salary of a top print reporter, with Capital Cities/ABC leading the pack at 113:1 (Crystal, 1993). In early 1994, *The Guild Reporter* recalculated these figures to compare CEOs with average top reporters under American Newspaper Guild contracts; it found that the average ratio was 66 to 1 (Capital Cities/ABC = 154:1). Now that Cap Cities/ABC is owned by Disney, these ratios may be even wider.

The notion that being ethical can pay off and some ethical companies are *very* successful is not a contradiction of my generally pessimistic position because so few firms follow any ethic except that of improving payouts to managers and stockholders. These payments uphold one narrow ethic, fiduciary responsibility, which rarely does anything for customers or staff. One of the staunchest proponents of this sort of "bottom-line journalism," Mark H. Willes, publisher of the *Los Angeles Times* and chairman of the Times Mirror Company, maintained that the stockholder obligation is not optional—that it is "not a nice-to-do, it is a must-do." This was in response to being accused of being a person who "killed a great newspaper, but . . . raised the stock price," by a former employee of the closed-down *New York Newsday* (Peterson, 1998). In today's business climate and philosophy, it is unfortunate that one cannot draw the conclusion that being ethical leads to business success. I wish it did, because then this chapter would not be needed.

Folklore (or marketplace ideologues) may say otherwise, but we should be aware that there are fewer and fewer real players in any economic field, from automobiles to airlines, from banks to broadcasters. Economies of scale are valuable to the larger players, but thereby we lose the very real values of, for example, local or demographically specialized media. Although there are several thousand franchised cable systems in the United States, the top 50 (or even the top 10) multiple-system operators (MSOs) control the "boxes" in an ever-increasing majority of homes: According to *Television Digest*, the top 50 cable operators served roughly 97% of all U.S. basic cable subscribers in 1998. The 25 largest served 93.3% of these, the top ten 78.0%, and the top five 63.3%. Cable is *not* a Mom & Pop industry, although it does a good job of persuading Congress and the public that it is.

In another communication industry, the number of general-circulation daily newspapers in New York has shrunk more than two-thirds since World War II, and the number of dailies in the United States has generally shown a slight decline each decade during the past century. Newspapers or stations controlled by individuals or families are an endangered species. Although there are still several thousand book publishers, they too merge—as has the publisher of this book—and also are at the mercy of the ever-fewer giant bookstore chains. (Of course, authors are at the very bottom of this pecking order.) Although conglomerates consisting of firms with little in common except their ownership or control are not as popular on Wall Street as they were a decade ago, the concept of ever-larger organizations in a single industry, such as the broadly defined entertainment industry—built through buyouts, mergers, and forcing weaker competitors to the wall—remains the goal of many business leaders. Unfortunately, since many buyouts and mergers are "leveraged," with resulting huge loads of debt that must be paid off, it is not surprising that too few operating funds remain to support the quantity and quality of the staffs and operations that were the original reason for the acquisition.

Several megamergers in the 1990s, notably the merger of Warner Communications with Time, Inc., and the mid-1995 announcements of the CBS purchase by Westinghouse (which later sold its industrial businesses and adopted the CBS name) and the $19 billion buyout of Capital Cities/ABC by the Walt Disney Co., illustrate this trend. On a smaller scale, removal of restrictions on how many radio stations one firm may own has led to entities owning more than 100 stations, notably Westinghouse, and cities where one company controls a half-dozen or more. The older values of "localism" and "dispersal of ownership" disappeared within months of the leash being loosened.

It can be argued that the six most powerful communications companies—Microsoft, Disney/ABC, Time Warner, GE/NBC, TCI, and News Corp.—don't actually compete directly but, like the Japanese *keiretsu*, form an interlocked web of agreements, activities and joint ventures. All six engage in cable, television and film production, Internet technology, Internet content, home video/games/interactive programs, and sports teams and venues. From three to five of them also engage in satellite transmissions, newspapers, magazines and books, telephone and wireless communications, TV broadcasting and stations, music and records, and theme parks and stores. (Auletta, 1997). Whether all six will continue to compete (or cooperate) in these areas in years to come is doubtful in light of the many megamergers of the past decade. While *keiretsu*-like activities have many of the same advantages as sheer size, such as economies of scale, they can also lead just as easily to less attention being paid to customers, employees, the public interest, and the ethical standards of the industries and media involved.

■ THE PUBLIC INTEREST

As "Deep Throat" told Bob Woodward in *All the President's Men*, "Follow the money!" Without legal, enforceable requirements to operate in the public interest, most entrepreneurs have no commitment to anything other than a profitable bottom line. Fiduciary responsibility to stockholders (and ambitions of managers)—with little regard for workers, customers, or society at large—is a hallmark of today's "free enterprise" economic system.

The actual 20th-century economic system is not to be found in elementary text-books. For example, separation of ownership from "professional" management has become virtually complete in larger firms. Although management has a fiduciary re-sponsibility to stockholders (if not to employees, customers, or the public), it is obvi-ous that the desire of the typical M.B.A. is to maximize her or his *own* income. Hence, because managers often are given raises and stock options or cash bonuses on the ba-sis of short-term (one-year) profits, rather than long-term profitability, it is rare that the manager's horizon is for a longer period. This mindset, and short-sighted tax laws, have also led to a reduction in investment in research and development and produc-tion facilities, as well as praise and higher stock values on Wall Street when companies "downsize" or move to areas with cheaper labor (Vaillancourt, 1991).

This ethic, however, may not be in the best interests of society. A so-called free enterprise system generally is lively, but there is a major price—inefficiency, high cost, lack of real choice—for society to pay. This is as true of the communication media as it is of other fields of endeavor. Although cable television viewers have a growing number of TV channels from which to choose, real choice in content isn't growing much. Being a copycat is the easiest way to "succeed," except for a handful of creative programmers such as Pat Weaver, Ted Turner, Gordon McLendon, Brandon Tar-tikoff, and the like. As Bruce Springsteen wrote, one can find lots of channels and nothing on. In other words, the "marketplace of ideas" may be adversely affected by competition in the "marketplace of business." As I've said before:

> [S]ince the push toward deregulation is aimed only at government, we may find ourselves at the tender mercies of (monopoly) business. Since the loved and the rich don't really need much protection, only government can enable the minority and the mass publics to mobilize against economic power. While government doesn't always recognize or act for the "common good," who else is equipped or willing to even try on this role? Deregula-tion will be beneficial to some—but probably not to thee and me. (Kittross, 1989, p. 207)

Of course, each marketplace has a few restrictions, and some even require obliga-tions. Taxes affect most economic marketplaces and are a much truer reflection of public policy than the grand words of the First Amendment, the Communications Act of 1934, or the Telecommunications Act of 1996—and the current federal taxation framework looks more kindly on property than it does on creativity. Government *can* protect people. Cattle markets are more orderly when there is an inspector of brands around; after the 1929 "crash," the Securities and Exchange Commission was estab-lished to try to make it harder for those with predatory instincts and power to use them; and most cultures have restrictions of one sort or another against harming chil-dren. Sometimes these restrictions (proscriptive) or mandated requirements (pre-scriptive) are extremely explicit; for example, some proposals for political campaign financing reform included a somewhat selfish argument to give candidates free time on broadcast stations (not print media or cable) no matter how much this might ad-versely affect the station's performance in marketplaces that are concerned with the bottom-line profits of media entities. (Such proposals—like those of 1998—are un-likely to be supported by most incumbent members of the Congress.)

Ethics tend to arise from the internal needs of a group and aren't imposed from outside as are the laws and regulations applied to all of us. But when "competition" is the deontological holy grail, the group doesn't have much of a chance to get together to formalize a code of ethics. (Of course, if "competitors" did get together for this purpose, it probably would be considered a cartel under the antitrust laws.) Morality, arising from individual training, education, and experience within a culture, can direct individuals with power toward making this a better world in which to live. How does the marketplace concept apply to this dimension?

Our ethical obligations will not be satisfied by relying on the "dead hand" of economic competition—they require active, not passive, actions by individuals *in the communication industries.*

As I see it, the only advantage of the marketplace concept in the field of media ethics is that it promotes a form of cowardice: Do nothing that will make advertisers and the public (in that order) mad at you. Minority political or social views are rare in any truly mass medium. News has been cheapened to gossip, political commentary to scandal-mongering. Newspapers justify astrology columns in the name of the First Amendment. Programming on the national television networks is at best intended for the lowest common denominator in terms of taste and appeal, and rarely demonstrates itself as more than timid and intimidated with respect to political matters (Lashner, 1984).

Unless one accepts success in meeting simplistic fiduciary responsibilities (or greed) as sufficient evidence of ethical media behavior, faith in the benefits of the economic marketplace with respect to media ethics is misplaced and superfluous. Our ethical obligations will not be satisfied by relying on the "dead hand" of economic competition—they require active, not passive, actions by *individuals* in the communication industries.

■ THE INFORMATION SUPERHIGHWAY

There is no question that we now have the technical competency to establish an "information superhighway" with, among other attributes, hundreds of channels of digital television. It seems that we also have the financial resources, and probably the entrepreneurial zeal (Information Infrastructure Task Force, 1993). But will these innovations really lead to business or content competition? Would such business competition really provide the diversity and variety it advertises?

For example, when one looks at the limited amount of original programming produced by cable today, the promises of unlimited diversity in the future become illusory. If the *same* movie is shown on HBO, Cinemax, The Movie Channel, Bravo, Showtime, Movietime, and several "superstations" in the same week, or if there are dozens of home shopping channels selling much the same merchandise—analogous to a shopping center with all the stores carrying the same brands of the same products—does the viewer really have more choice by having 500 channels? Do cable systems have competition in their franchise areas, or are they natural monopolies? Once the telephone and cable industries have fought to the death or have disappeared through mergers, what real competition in the choice of channels or services will we have? If one entity decides the menu from which we may select, what real choice have we? Indeed, the mass medium that most meets the multiple specialized needs (not just wants) of the American public is the magazine, which—perhaps not by accident—is most removed from direct advertising "sponsorship" of specific content.

Let us assume that the information highway, laden with entertainment, information, sales pitches, computer bits, and a whiff from the barnyard, is in existence. Despite Vice President Gore's assurances that all Americans will have access to this
"highway," in the prevailing economic climate it certainly will be a toll road. This isn't
bad per se: It will cost a great deal to build, and as Ayn Rand and Robert Heinlein
have reminded us, TANSTAAFL—There Ain't No Such Thing As A Free Lunch.

But, as is discussed in Chapter 6, how many citizens will be able to afford access
to it? Would the nation be divided permanently into the information haves and have
nots? Will those who managed the funding control the content? Can the nation survive, to paraphrase the debate over slavery before the Civil War, half with and half
without? Gordon quotes H. L. Mencken's description of democracy as making sure
that the people get what they think is best for them as well as the consequences they
deserve, not necessarily what they need. I'd like to counterbalance this by paraphras-
ing Winston Churchill: Democracy is the recurring suspicion that more than half the
people are right more than half the time. What is "the public interest" in a nation and
world whose population growth, and consequent reduction of privacy and living
space, in the past century has made the allocation of scarce economic resources one of
murderous importance? People or nations lacking an important resource, such as
electrical/electronic communication, and with little hope of obtaining same, are unlikely to be civil—and many nations now have the ability to trigger the destruction of
life on our planet.

So it is no wonder that I consider the two most important economic conflicts in
the communication field also to be political and social matters: access versus fairness
(Barron, 1973) and the New World Information and Communication Order
(NWICO) debated in UNESCO (MacBride, 1980; A. Smith, 1980). Both of these
concepts have economic implications. The first argues that there is a choice: Either
professional communicators are scrupulous about being fair in allocation of resources,
or each group or person, no matter how obscure, should be entitled to unfettered
(and possibly unlimited) access to transmission and reception channels. I leave it to
the reader as to whether either approach describes the current communication system
in the United States. The second, the debate over the NWICO, in the international
arena, argues that nations—even the smallest and most impoverished—have the right
to control information imported into and exported from their country, should have
access to the international communication networks (now mostly consisting of space
communication satellites that pass over equatorial countries), and should receive help
in establishing and training personnel for internal electronic communication networks. Again, I leave it to the reader to decide the extent to which the NWICO is in
place and—because American tradition embraces concepts such as free press and freedom of information, without control or censorship of information flow—the extent to
which it *should* be.

■ CONCLUSION

In the newsroom, the marketplace concept often is detrimental to everyone but the
owner. As A. J. Liebling once wrote, "Freedom of the press is guaranteed only to
those who own one" (Liebling, 1961, p. 30). The wall that theoretically existed between the business and the editorial sides of a newspaper has been torn down in many

papers (Jurkowitz, 1998), and it is a rare media organization that will knowingly antagonize its advertisers. Some advertisers—such as Chrysler automobiles—have demanded pre-publication access to magazine content, which leads to further editorial timidity in a medium that used to be relatively independent (Baker, 1997). In this way, profits are maximized: In daily newspapers alone, the amount of money that can be spent for all editorial functions is rarely more than 10% of revenues, but often two to three times this proportion of income is paid out to stockholders every year; many broadcasting stations and cable systems have similar ratios. This reflects, once again, the short-term goals of the free enterprise system. Gordon is willing to mention some of the many ways of paying for the media—box office, hobby, ancillary enterprise, donations, tax revenues, license fees, etc.—but, as might be expected, falls back on the status quo of today's heavy reliance on advertising. Yet the existence of other ways of paying for the media may offer some guideposts to a system that need not always program for the lowest common denominator.

In another economic arena, reporters and editors are well aware of the disparity between their salaries and those of top management. Annual reports in *Journalism & Mass Communication Educator* show how the growing number of new graduates, all eager for jobs in the media, keep starting salaries depressed to the point where many of the best and brightest graduates switch to other industries. The newspaper industry has largely destroyed its most articulate union, the American Newspaper Guild. Because media now are being bought and sold as commodities and the antitrust laws and special provisions of the Communications Act have been weakened to permit even more rapid turnover, each sale tends to shake out the more expensive and experienced senior members of a creative or production staff. (Because many of these jobs are never refilled, such "downsizing" does not really help those trying to get their foot on the bottom rung of the ladder.)

This too is a function of making the marketplace a goal or end in itself, rather than merely a process: If someone will work more cheaply, hire them. Only the public will lose, because your competition will act according to the same economic principles. For years, it was obvious that the National Association of Broadcasters favored emphases in American education for careers in broadcasting that would provide them with a surfeit of candidates for jobs as technicians or disk jockeys, keeping—through competition—wages low. Each time communication scholars show an independent turn of mind, the media find ways to show their displeasure. Again, an obvious strategy—but hardly one that would improve the mass media content that we all need in order to make those rational decisions in a democracy. I believe—with Loevenger (1964, pp. 120–121)—that providing this content is the only indispensable purpose and function of American mass media.

If one considers the nitty-gritty aspects of media economics—profit, loss, wages—then I believe that the often-touted hypothetical free market rarely exists. If it does, it obviously isn't completely free. Certainly, it doesn't exist in media ethics, which are considered irrelevant by those who believe only in the greedy bottom lines of the strictly economic marketplace, or who consider the free market to be a God-given goal rather than merely one of many economic concepts to be considered and questioned.

It is fairly easy to bring Kant and the utilitarians into support of my separatist position on the economic marketplace and media ethics. I'll even throw in some political philosophies that are no longer in common use, such as Marxism, "left" libertarianism, and true conservatism. After many years in the academy, I support wholeheart-edly, but no longer quite have Gordon's faith in, his proposals for increased and im-proved education.

I continue to believe that, in the few instances where a free marketplace does ex-ist, and not merely as a grubbing for profits, it tends to work to the detriment of both those who work in the media and the publics they serve. Economics, like Mother Na-ture, really doesn't care about human beings. After all, as one astronaut said to an-other as they looked at the spacecraft they were about to board, "Just think—all of that was built by the lowest bidder."

■ GORDON: The "dead hand" of the economic marketplace, and more knowledgeable media consumers, are sufficient to hold the media fully accountable for their actions and are ethically beneficial to the media.

A respected media critic, voicing his concern in 1990 about the potential negative im-pact of conglomerates on the news media, noted:

> News organizations that are a part of big business are governed by market forces, and market research is said to determine what America (and the rest of the world) reads, hears and watches. . . .
>
> [W]e are confronted by economic movements on Wall Street and in board-rooms around the world that think of the media mostly as machines producing widgets. We are told by some critics that the media more than ever are driven by the greed of a market that values short-run profits over long-term investments. The results for networks and national newsmagazines, we are told, are shrinking staffs and depleted resources. The audience numbers that generate advertising rev-enues drive news organizations and, in a circular fashion, cause them to court audi-ences to whom their advertisers can sell their products and services. (Dennis, 1990, pp. 6–7)

All of that is certainly correct, as far as it goes. But as Everette Dennis noted in the same speech (perhaps a bit hyperbolically), these economic forces have not pre-cluded an "extraordinary performance by our journalists as they masterfully cover more of the globe than ever before" (Dennis, 1990, p. 7), albeit with fewer foreign correspondents.

Why this seeming paradox? Or is it only superficially a paradox?

It seems to me that we are often much too quick to dismiss the positive impact the marketplace can and, often, must have on ethics. Joseph Turow, for example, traced the origins of the concept of objectivity in news reporting to the need of the emerging "penny press" in the 1830s to appeal to readers of all ideological stripes (Turow, 1992, pp. 158–159). Others have pointed out that this objectivity concept was reinforced in the mid-nineteenth century by the fledgling Associated Press, which needed to put its news reports into a format that would satisfy clients at all points along the ideological and political spectrum. Those are clearly market-driven bases for objectivity, which, hard as it is to define, has remained central to journalistic ethics over the subsequent decades.

Much more recently, economic forces have led to developments such as cooperation between cable systems, TV stations, and newspapers. This might provide additional news and information for the public, but must make economic sense to the firms involved. The economic marketplace, using new technologies, may be increasingly headed toward encouraging audience members to unite their computers, telephones, and cable channels to send as well as receive increased amounts of information and entertainment. These are only two of many examples of how media economics—and the convergence of formerly separate media industries—are producing greater benefits for an increasing number of people. This could certainly be viewed as a utilitarian outgrowth of the economic forces affecting the mass media.

Commitments to high-quality news and entertainment content as a means of producing success in the economic marketplace are not uncommon (despite many examples to the contrary). One observer noted that such commitments may occur more readily if editors and news directors (and, by extension, creative people in the entertainment media) "learn to express their journalistic needs in counting-house language—" i.e., if they learn to argue persuasively that a high-quality product will have a positive effect on revenues (Fink, 1988, p. 110). Making that argument successfully will very likely require using market research to demonstrate that there is an audience for high quality.

Thus, despite Dennis's implied criticism of it, the use of market research to shape media content isn't necessarily bad. This is true even when it results in less than top-quality content. Such research contributes at a minimum to a product that serves the interests of the public (which, of course, are not always identical to the public interest). This certainly accords with the utilitarian approach of providing the greatest amount of good or happiness (or satisfaction) to the greatest number of people. And it is in line with the perspective that views "newsroom and corporate imperatives as synergistic—not conflicting—forces" (Fink, 1988, p. 113).

Before we condemn the economic marketplace as counterproductive to ethical concerns—or as irrelevant, as John Michael Kittross does—let's recall that there are essentially only three sources for the funding necessary to keep mass media systems operating: advertisers, consumers, and the government. This focus on operating funds ignores private investors who often provide start-up funding for media ventures, but that's a different area of concern. To simplify matters somewhat, this approach also ignores the possibility of conglomerate owners producing sufficient operating revenues from nonmedia sources to finance the operations of the media portions of the conglomerate if they wish to. In general, and especially for our purposes, unless one or more of the three basic sources provide an adequate revenue stream to cover operating costs and make *at least* a small profit, even a well-capitalized commercial media venture will sooner or later fail.

Relying on advertisers as the revenue sources, as most of the American media do, has its own sets of problems. But relying on consumers or on the government for funding would raise more serious concerns. Relying on government funding creates the likelihood of political or ideological control of the media content, and runs the danger of creating a much more repressive ethical climate than currently exists. One need only recall the vendetta against the National Endowment for the Arts carried on in the late 1980s and into the late 1990s by such political figures as Senator Jesse Helms (R-NC) to be aware that when the government pays the piper, it retains the power to call the tune.

Reliance on consumer fees to produce operating revenues runs the risk of creating economic barriers between the public and the media, a topic that is discussed in far more detail in Chapter 6. Although some portions of American mass media do use consumer payments to cover part of their operating expenses (e.g., newspaper sales and subscription revenues to a degree, and premium cable channels—or books and movies—at a much higher level), the vast majority of American media are financed mainly by revenues from advertising sales. And relying on advertising revenues and the economic marketplace is an alternative that seems to me to be much more likely than the other two approaches to produce media that have a concern for ethics.

The market-driven nature of most American media means that what the public wants must be taken into account. That's all to the good, unless one prefers to assume an elitist stance and determine media content (and practices) on the basis of what she or he thinks the public *should* want or need. Rather, the idea of the media providing content that the public wants certainly is appropriate to a democratic society in which ultimate power is vested in the people. That won't always result in choices that "the experts" believe to be in society's best interests, but that's one of the risks you run in a free society, with regard to entertainment no less than to political choices.

Kittross's contention that marketplace economics requires the media to do nothing to anger advertisers or the public isn't realistic because it takes much too monolithic a view of both groups, particularly the public. The fact is that there are widely varying interests, values, levels of taste, and concerns for what's "right" among both groups. Commercially supported media may well create far more serious economic problems for themselves if they try to achieve the impossible and offend *no* portions of their potential constituencies. The result is likely to be a bland product that doesn't succeed in either the economic or the qualitative sphere.

. . . the temptation to pander to the lower elements of the public's tastes regarding media products is a very real danger . . . .

Certainly, the temptation to pander to the lower elements of the public's tastes regarding media products is a very real danger, as has been reflected in both news and entertainment content over the years. If such a threat to responsible media performance is posed by the preferences of the actual (or desired) media audiences, we need to do more than merely decry the potential impact of the marketplace. Rather, we need to approach it positively and use the audience's influence (actual or potential) to encourage ethical rather than unethical media practices.

■ THE NEED FOR MEDIA "CONSUMER EDUCATION"

One way to do this would be to increase greatly the amount of "media consumer education" that is provided for members of the potential media audience. On this score, in general, the American educational system, and the media themselves, have both done poor jobs and have fallen far short of meeting the need for knowledgeable and critical media consumers. Surveys (such as those by the Times Mirror Company during the 1980s and early 1990s before it closed down the Center for Press and the Public to improve the parent company's already impressive profit margin) have shown that the public does have concerns for ethical behavior by the news media. But a sizable portion of the public doesn't fully understand how the media function, and therefore lacks guidance on how to go about producing more of the desired results.

James Carey has written eloquently of the need for informed and continuing public analysis and criticism of newspapers (and, by extension, the mass media more generally), which would "scrutinize the values upon which the institution is based" (Carey, 1978, p. 363). This would require a knowledgeable group of experts and ordinary citizens who would help "reconnect the newspaper to the community it serves." (p. 364):

> The basic critical act in journalism is public scrutiny of the methods by which journalists define and get what we call news and the conventions by which they deliver it to the public. (p. 367)

Dennis has suggested a novel approach to ensuring that the public has a better understanding of how the news media function. His prescription calls for news organizations to instruct their audiences

> . . . about (a) the operative theory of journalism with which any given news organization guides itself; (b) the resources it has devoted to newsgathering; (c) the ways in which the public ought to assess and evaluate the results; and finally, (d) how individual readers and viewers might "talk back" to or interact with editors and producers of the news. (Dennis, 1990, p. 8)

The opportunities for such interaction are increasing steadily as more and more newspapers provide and publicize ways for readers to contact their staffers by Internet or telephone. Building on Dennis's final item, there is a great need to educate media consumers to know what buttons to push in order to produce desired changes in media practices. Such approaches would complement the impact of economics on media ethics, and would help ensure that marketplace pressures are indeed beneficial to the media and, in general, to society as a whole. Specific instances where market influences unfortunately do lower the ethical level are perhaps the media counterpart of H. L. Mencken's somewhat cynical definition of democracy as "the theory that the common people know what they want, and deserve to get it good and hard" (Mencken, 1955, p. 232).

Kittross's discussion of the free enterprise marketplace notes briefly that even in the deregulated business climate of the Reagan and Bush years, government remained considerably involved in the economic marketplace. So when we refer to that marketplace as free, we're speaking relatively rather than absolutely. We appear to have, in regard to the economy in general, a situation that isn't too different from the social responsibility approach prescribed for the media after World War II by the Commission on Freedom of the Press. In essence, if business is not at least somewhat socially responsible, the government stands ready to step in to ensure responsibility—and has done so in a number of areas; minimum wage requirements and antitrust regulations are just two ongoing examples.

Certainly, we're not talking about the specter of "uncontrolled economic competition" that Kittross raised. The advent of many additional communication channels and the growth of smaller target audiences and niche marketing might encourage more players in the media marketplace, and open it up beneficially to economic as well as content competition. Additionally, as noted above, the continuing role of government also tends to provide buffers against Kittross's concern about the money always following the large numbers.

Thus, the business aspects of the mass media are already operating in an economic marketplace that has some economic, social, and political constraints on it. Those constraints have already had a variety of effects on the structure and operations of the mass media, including some aspects that relate to ethics. For example, consider the federal estate tax laws that have influenced the sale of many family-owned newspapers at the end of the third generation of that ownership. Depending on your perspective, these laws have either given such newspapers more resources as parts of chain operations and thereby enabled them to serve their readers better, or they have destroyed the papers' closeness to the communities they serve . . . or a little bit of both.

In some instances, economics have led chains to close down a newspaper and use its resources more profitably elsewhere, as happened in Holyoke, Massachusetts, in 1993. In the short run, that certainly hurt the audience that had depended on the paper for local news (Shanahan, 1994). Taking a longer-range view, it's possible that other news outlets will move into the vacuum, if a need really exists, and provide different—and perhaps better—coverage of the local scene. Utilitarians might well argue that closing one chain paper and directing resources elsewhere does in fact benefit the greater number of people in the chain's other markets, which will be served better by the reallocation of those resources. Rawls, of course, would disagree.

Similarly, mergers have raised ethical alarm bells in some quarters, but these may also benefit the ethical climate. For instance, joint ventures between cable and telephone companies might well provide improved technological and financial resources that will result in better service to a greater number of people—an approach that would warm the hearts of utilitarians.

All of this should be kept in mind when we talk about the impact of the economic marketplace on ethics in general, or on social responsibility more specifically. The mass media, by what they do *and don't do*, are going to impact the lives of individuals and groups in the society, and affect society as a whole. I believe that we are far better off if those impacts derive primarily from an advertiser-driven source of media revenues than from either government funding or charges to consumers. When I argue for the sufficiency and benefits of media accountability to the economic marketplace, though, I'm referring to the marketplace as we've come to know it, with government still involved directly in some ways and potentially involved in others.

■ ARE ECONOMIC FORCES SUFFICIENT?

Idealistic readers may justifiably ask whether these economic forces are really sufficient to result in ethical media behavior. Shouldn't there perhaps be some higher standard of ethical expectation that supplements if not supplants economic marketplace forces? A few firms—such as the Ben & Jerry's ice cream company, as Kittross noted—have adopted some ethical operating principles as part of their policy, along with the goal of making a profit. I certainly applaud that approach. But I don't really think it's realistic to expect this from the vast majority of profit-driven businesses. And, in regard to the mass media, I don't think it's really necessary because the economic marketplace has had various positive impacts on media ethics and might well be made to have more.

Note, for example, that *The New York Times,* shortly after it began accepting condom ads in 1987, "broke new journalistic ground with a lengthy article . . . describing in explicit detail how heterosexuals and homosexuals alike could use condoms to avoid sexually transmitted diseases" (Fink, 1988, p. 131). Although there may well have been no cause-and-effect relationship, the fact that the business side of the operation deemed the subject acceptable certainly complemented the willingness to deal with it on the editorial side. In the area of advertising acceptability, the *Times* has also indicated a relationship between business and ethical concerns. The long-time head of its Advertising Acceptability Department, noting that a newspaper's credibility can be damaged by misleading or offensive advertising as well as by its editorial content, wrote:

> [N]owhere is it written that concern for the welfare of the reader and sound business practice are mutually exclusive. On the contrary, self-regulation and discipline with regard to the acceptance of advertising is about as good an example as you will find to illustrate the profitability of principle. (R. Smith, 1984, p. 11)

Ethical standards, advertising acceptability codes, and general codes of ethics are fine as far as they go. But if ethical standards clash too sharply with economic realities, then either the economic realities are going to win out in the long run, or the media company is going to falter and perhaps go out of business. Over the years, I've found very few students who carry their idealism so far as to say that they're willing to work for a highly ethical mass medium that has too little revenue to pay their salary.

So if economics may indeed triumph over idealism, perhaps we need to return to the idea of educating mass media consumers better. Neil Postman and Steve Powers suggest eight relatively simple steps viewers can take to improve public understanding of television news. These steps include remembering that news programs are generally called "shows" and that commercials may tell us as much about our society as does the news content of the programs. The authors also suggest learning about the background and the political and economic outlooks of the people who run your friendly local TV station; and encouraging elementary and secondary schools to teach children about how to watch TV news (Postman and Powers, 1992, pp. 159–168).

Elizabeth Thoman of the Center for Media and Values has identified four general principles that would help audiences understand their media. Media, she explained, construct reality; secondly, they use

> . . . identifiable production codes and techniques which viewers can be taught to isolate and decode; third, media are businesses with commercial interests; and fourth, media contain ideologies that media literacy education can help identify. (Finn, 1993, p. 15, citing Gould, E., "Talking Back to Media." *Reflex* (May–June, 1993), p. 4)

Increased efforts toward media literacy could result in knowledgeable audiences whose interests in and demands on the media produce an economic marketplace where social responsibility, idealism, and ethical behavior carry economic rewards with them. The results would almost certainly fall well short of some utopian ideal, but on balance might improve the ethical fallout from our dependence on the economic marketplace. Educating media consumers to exert a positive ethical influence on the media, through their economic preferences, would be a middle-ground approach that derives from both utilitarianism and Aristotle's Golden Mean.

Another aspect of this issue needs some further mention here: the question of whether emerging patterns of media ownership and new technology bode well or ill for the ethical climate of the media and the overall good of society. There are major ethical as well as economic (and legal) concerns lurking in the late 1990s patterns of media ownership, and in many aspects of new media technologies, and these cannot be ignored now or in the coming decade.

Joseph Turow sees the future of the mass media industries as being linked to the concept of synergy, which he defines as coordinating the various parts of conglomerates so that the parent firm's offspring in different media are "worth more than the sum of its parts acting alone, without helping one another" (Turow, 1992, p. 235). Turow notes that the results of such synergy can be both good and bad, economically and ethically. And the increasing opportunities for such synergistic relationships pose many questions for the public and for the media industries.

As just one example of how this might play out in an ethical as well as a business dimension, Turow raises the question of how new synergistic relationships might "affect the way people are hired and trained by the conglomerates." He asks especially whether there might be changes in the way "members of minority groups have often tended to be pigeonholed in certain segments of certain industries" and how such changes might affect the content of media channels (Turow, 1992, p. 256).

■ CONCLUSION

It may well be that ethics (and high-quality performance) survive in part *because of* the pressures of the economic marketplace. Some research into newspaper ownership has found that "chain and monopoly newspapers place greater emphasis on product quality [than on profits] and can improve the quality of the product," though there are also data to the contrary (Demers, 1994, p. 2). Alvah Chapman, then chair of Knight Ridder, Inc., noted in 1985 that

> ". . . good journalism is good business. As an information company, our success depends on the excellence, reputation and usefulness of that information which is our product. We want our readers and viewers to have the highest possible confidence in what we produce. This is essential to maintaining our credibility and consequently the loyalty and following of our readers and viewers." (Fink, 1988, p. 105)

Such concerns are certainly part of what Edmund Lambeth calls the *stewardship principle* of media ethics—the need to "manage [the] resources of communication with due regard for the rights of others, the rights of the public, and the moral health" of the mass communication industries (Lambeth, 1992, p. 32). But beyond this perspective (and for media organizations that fail to see the economic advantages of high-quality products), it would seem that ethics and high quality will also survive to some extent *despite* the pressures of the economic marketplace, in part perhaps because the constant presence of those pressures might sharpen our awareness of the need for ethics as a countervailing force.

Potentially, ethical media behavior can also be enhanced by pressures from a more media-literate audience flexing its economic muscle. Failing that, though, if the boardrooms regard the media as widget-producers, it is up to media practitioners to be aware continually of ethics and other non-widgetary aspects of their calling. I suspect that Dennis was referring mostly to the news media in his descriptions, but these concerns, and the need to maintain a focus on ethics and on quality because (or in spite) of the bean-counters, are equally applicable to the entertainment media, to public relations, and to advertising.

Maintaining such a focus will mean that the hand of the economic marketplace need not be a dead one. It will allow that marketplace to continue to function as the basic source of media operating revenues while also contributing to an appropriate concern for ethical and societal responsibilities. If that can also be coupled with a more knowledgeable universe of media consumers, sufficient accountability will follow.

■ MERRILL: Commentary

I agree with the position in this controversy that the marketplace, in a purely survivalist way at least, does hold the media accountable. But it is with the second part of the stated position that I have trouble: that the marketplace is *ethically* beneficial.

It seems that to take such a position (as David Gordon does) about media ethics is pushing the benefits of the marketplace far beyond their limits. The implication here is that if large numbers of people *like* a medium's contents and its ethical standards and support that medium financially, then this will ensure *ethical* actions by that medium. This is a classic *non sequitur*. In fact, a good case perhaps could be made that the more popular a medium (or a specific story or TV program) is, the *less ethical* it will be. I will not make that case, for I have no empirical data to support it, but common sense might at least suggest it as a reasonable hypothesis to be investigated.

A possible objection to the position that the marketplace is ethically beneficial would be that many (perhaps most) people *do not know* when a medium is indulging in unethical activities, and what's more, they quite likely do not really care. Or, for some audience members it is quite likely that they are exposing themselves to a particular medium for a number of reasons unrelated to the ethics of the story content or the programming essence. For example, they may well *want* to be titillated by "far out" (questionable or unethical) content; they will not stop buying the tabloid *Star*, for example, because they think it misrepresents reality and even fictionalizes. In fact, this is probably the very reason they buy it. Many audience members, it should be recognized, do not base their reading, listening, and watching media on the credibility and ethical appeal those media have. Therefore, it is hard to see the marketplace having a direct linkage to a medium's ethical accountability.

It seems that John Michael Kittross goes to the other extreme in his contention that the marketplace is superfluous or even counterproductive in regard to media ethics. Most likely there are some cases where the level of ethics (especially in the areas of truthfulness, balance, lack of overt propaganda, and good taste) of certain media *very much affects* the audience's loyalty and financial support of those media. Especially among serious, ethically concerned segments of the public there is an appreciation of media that are thought to have an ethical motivation and a high moral sense, so I think it is somewhat disingenuous to say that the marketplace is superfluous.

As to Kittross's second contention (that the marketplace is counterproductive), I am still not quite sure just what that means. Perhaps it means no more than what I said a few paragraphs earlier—that reliance on the marketplace often leads to a kind of lowest-common-denominator ethical level, implying that many audience members actually seek content that is *unethical* (or nonethical) rather than *ethical*.

There is little more in the way of commentary that I can contribute to this issue. The reader who ponders the two opposing perspectives presented above, can, I'm sure, provide other arguments on both sides. It is an interesting—and I think, important—controversy, and one that will surely surface regularly in an open, free-market, competitive media system, especially as the economics of new communication technologies work themselves out. Such a controversial issue should be of vital importance to countries that are on the verge of embracing a market economy, but are uncertain about the harm or benefit—especially for media of mass communication—that might result from such an action.

If . . . we had real competition among media, the ethical benefits of the market might be more evident.

One other point: If, in America, we had real competition among media, the ethical benefits of the market might be more evident. But the fact is that most media indulge in unethical practices of some type, so the citizen who desires ethical media has little or no selective power. Of course, there is a matter of degree in the unethical nature of media, and a concerned citizen can take the best of several evils. But in many markets there is little real choice. Conglomerates, groups, and multimedia cooperative ventures are giving the American people little to choose from—at least from the perspective of *ethical* differences. For average Americans, it is not a choice among ethical levels found among media; some other factor determines their adherence to some media and avoidance of others.

REFERENCES

Auletta, Ken. (February 7, 1994). "John Malone: Flying Solo (Annals of Communications)." *The New Yorker*, pp. 52–67.
———. (October 20, 1997). "American Keiretsu." *The New Yorker*, pp. 225–227.
Baker, Russ. (September/October 1997). "The Squeeze." *Columbia Journalism Review*, pp. 30–34, 36.
Barron, Jerome A. (1973). *Freedom of the Press for Whom?* Bloomington: Indiana University Press.
Carey, James. (1978). "But Who Will Criticize the Critics?" In Everette E. Dennis, Arnold H. Ismach, and Donald M. Gillmor, eds., *Enduring Issues in Mass Communication*. St. Paul, MN: West, pp. 362–368. (Excerpted from James Carey, "Journalism and Criticism: The Case of an Undeveloped Profession." *The Review of Politics* (April 1974), pp. 227–249).

Commission on Freedom of the Press. (1947). *A Free and Responsible Press*. Chicago: University of Chicago Press.

Crystal, Graef. (November/December 1993). "Salary Survey: The C.E.O. Factor." *Columbia Journalism Review*, pp. 49–50.

Demers, David Pearce. (June 1994). "Structural Pluralism, Intermedia Competition, and the Growth of the Corporate Newspaper in the United States." *Journalism Monographs, No. 145*.

Dennis, Everette E. (1990). "In Allegiance to the Truth: News, Ethics and Split-Personality Journalism." New York: Gannett Center for Media Studies. Speech delivered March 6, Honolulu.

Fink, Conrad C. (1988). *Media Ethics: In the Newsroom and Beyond*. New York: McGraw-Hill.

Finn, Catherine L. (1993). "A (Current) Affair to Remember: Tabloid Television News and Its Impact on Network News Organizations." Paper presented at the annual convention of the Association for Education in Journalism and Mass Communication, Kansas City, MO, August 14.

Information Infrastructure Task Force. (September 15, 1993). *The National Information Infrastructure: Agenda for Action*. Washington: U.S. Department of Commerce.

Jurkowitz, Mark. (May 23, 1998). "Move by L.A. Times sparks industry debate." *The Boston Globe*, p. F1.

Kittross, John M. (1989). Commentary on "Deregulation." In Frederick Williams, *The New Communications*, 2nd ed. Belmont, CA: Wadsworth, pp. 206–207.

Lambeth, Edmund B. (1992). *Committed Journalism: An Ethic for the Profession*, 2nd ed. Bloomington: Indiana University Press.

Lashner, Marilyn A. (1984). *The Chilling Effect in TV News: Intimidation by the Nixon White House*. New York: Praeger.

Liebling, A. J. (1961). *The Press*. New York: Ballantine. (Chapter originally published as "Do You Belong in Journalism?," in *The New Yorker*, May 14, 1960.)

Loevenger, Lee. (Spring 1964). "The Role of Law in Broadcasting." *Journal of Broadcasting* 8(2), pp. 113–126.

MacBride, Sean. (1980). *Many Voices, One World*. London: Kogan Page; New York: Unipub; Paris: Unesco.

Mencken, H. L. (1955). *The Vintage Mencken*. New York: Vintage Books.

Morgenstern, Oskar, and John Von Neumann. (1953). *Theory of Games and Economic Behavior*. Princeton, NJ: Princeton University Press; see also J. D. Williams, *The Compleat Strategyst* (New York: McGraw-Hill, 1954); Martin Shubik, *Readings in Game Theory and Political Behavior* (Garden City, NY: Doubleday, 1954); and John McDonald, *Strategy in Poker, Business and War* (New York: Norton, 1950).

Peterson, Ivor. (March 9, 1998). "Media." *The New York Times*, p. D7

Postman, Neil, and Steve Powers. (1992). *How to Watch TV News*. New York: Penguin.

Shanahan, Edward K. (November 6, 1994). "'Read All About It!' But Read About It Where?: No News Is Not Good News." *The Boston Globe Magazine*, pp. 20–34.

Smith, Anthony. (1980). *The Geopolitics of Information*. New York: Oxford University Press.

Smith, Robert P. (June 1984). "Advertising Acceptability Policies Protect Newspaper's Credibility." *INAME News*, p. 11; quoted in Fink, 1988, p. 127.

Television Digest. (May 4, 1998). 38(18), pp. 2–3.

Turow, Joseph. (1992). *Media Systems in Society*. New York: Longman.

Vaillancourt, Meg. (June 15, 1991). "Labor Chief Blasts Quick Stock Gains." *The Boston Globe*, p. 91.

Weinberg, Arthur, and Lila Weinberg. (1961). *The Muckrakers*. New York: Putnam.

CHAPTER 12

INFOTAINMENT PROGRAMMING

While the number of media outlets has grown in recent years, some (especially those on television) have increasingly been filled with material that blends serious information with titillation. Some critics call the more extreme video versions "trash television" and decry its existence just as their predecessors condemned such print outlets as *The National Enquirer* and later supermarket tabloids.

Others, however, have noted that the public seems to have an almost insatiable appetite for such material and that the media are simply responding to this demand. So-called reality TV shows such as *Rescue 911* and *America's Most Wanted* are one manifestation of this. So was the strong audience response to the tabloid coverage of the 1994–1997 O.J. Simpson melodrama—on both the infotainment and the mainstream news programs—which went far beyond reporting just the hard news in that case. Coverage of the death and funeral of Princess Diana in 1997—in print and on TV, and in both mainstream and infotainment media—was another dramatic illustration of public appetite and media response . . . or perhaps it was the other way around. Some of the early Clinton/Lewinsky coverage was yet another.

The Simpson coverage also illustrated another aspect of this controversy. By following the courtroom drama, the argument went, the public learned far more about how the judicial system operates than was generally known before that exposure. This is the crux of the argument that follows—whether infotainment programs are just fluff, or whether they can serve a useful purpose in addition to their entertainment function. David Gordon takes the latter position in the following discussion, while Carol Reuss maintains that the entertainment and titillation aspects of these programs drive out much useful information that might benefit the audience more in their daily lives.

■ GORDON: Tabloid news programs, talk shows, scandal sheets, and other forms of infotainment provide needed information in formats that get through to citizens and help make democracy work.

It would be wonderful if most people wanted to watch the *NewsHour with Jim Lehrer*, read the op-ed pieces in their local newspapers, or otherwise make an effort to inform themselves in depth about issues that "should" be important to the citizens who make the ultimate decisions in a democracy. Such an abstract ideal is not at all realistic, however. It's doubtful that we could even come up with a consensus on the definition of what is important, not to mention the problem of who would decide what fits that definition. (The question of *who decides* could lead to a discussion of whether such decisions should be made by "average people" or by those who may appoint themselves to determine what's important to the public. That whole area goes beyond the scope of this topic, but merits much further thought.)

The fact is that the vast majority of people don't, and won't, spend much time watching in-depth news on PBS, reading the op-ed pages, or otherwise seeking out large amounts of detail or context on the complex issues that ultimately affect their lives. That doesn't mean the general public is uninterested in the issues. It's just that, with all the distractions of today's society, the public is selective about the time it devotes to what the news media deem important and is likely to pay the most attention to topics that appear to affect it directly or personally.

I believe that some important information can be conveyed to citizens if the mass media try to meet people where they are, rather than where the idealists or the elitists wish they were. Among other approaches, this means that so-called tabloid news programs and talk shows—perhaps especially the latter—can be excellent vehicles for focusing public attention on important current issues. These programs can provide information on a wide variety of topics in packages and in amounts that people will pay attention to amid the entertainment quotient of these shows.

I am *not* arguing in favor of the "Space Alien Romances Gwyneth Paltrow" approach of some of the supermarket tabloids or for the peepshow segments of some syndicated tabloid TV programs. Nor am I defending sensational television programs whose motto may well be "a scandal a day (or 'a freak of the week') keeps reality away." Rather, I'm suggesting that people *do* tune in to the talk and tabloid news shows, to escape or to be distracted or entertained. I believe that many of these programs can and do provide some useful and even important informational wheat amid the chaff that often fills up the air time.

For example, the 1994 efforts by Phil Donahue to televise an execution live—though perhaps motivated as much by a desire for ratings as by a desire to inform—nonetheless would have focused considerable public attention on the debate over capital punishment. There may well have been more informative ways to consider and debate that issue, but I strongly suspect that a *Donahue* telecast of an execution would have drawn a much larger audience, and greater public attention to the topic, than would any "more thoughtful"/less sensational alternative approaches.

Even the supermarket tabloids occasionally provide information that helps the democratic decision-making process. And programs such as *Larry King Live* on CNN do this with some regularity. A good example of this was King's hosting of the 1993 debate between Ross Perot and Vice President Al Gore on the North American Free Trade Agreement, while the agreement itself was awaiting a final Senate vote. This was a milestone of national debate and discussion of a major legislative issue while final action was still pending. It drew a very impressive audience—an 18.1 rating on cable and 11.9 nationally, according to the Nielsen tabulations.

Talk shows have made quite an impact on the electoral process, beginning with their major role in some state elections toward the end of the 1980s. By the 1992 presidential campaign, they played an important role in conveying both images and information to the voters. Some of these programs have served as forums for the exchange of information and opinion—and, sometimes, invective and humor—on various public issues since at least 1980 (Rehm, 1993). Their listenership—and resulting political power—has declined since 1994, but no political figure can overlook them.

. . . sensational publications and tabloid/"reality" programs and talk shows do enlighten as well as entertain.

Despite their excesses, the sensational publications and tabloid/"reality" programs and talk shows do enlighten as well as entertain. And this kind of sensationalism does attract audiences by appealing to viewers' "'insatiable appetite' to hear horrors, crimes, disasters, sex scandals, etc." (Tannenbaum and Lynch, 1960, p. 382, quoting from an unpublished preliminary study by Wayne A. Danielson et al., "Sensationalism and the Life History of Magazines"). At the same time, though, sensationalism tends to evoke emotional responses in the audience, often at the expense of reason or understanding (Gorney, 1992, p. 458). Because sensational material "limits experience as a source of knowledge in favor of emotional or sensory stimulation" (p. 455), too much of it could be a barrier to disseminating useful information to the public through these infotainment channels.

■ BLURRING LINES BETWEEN NEWS AND INFOTAINMENT MEDIA

In fact, the more traditional news media have realized the appeal of some techniques used by these infotainment media to attract audiences and have begun to use them as part of their more mainstream news coverage. Content, too, has been adapted to some degree from the tabloid to the traditional news outlets, including both an increase in feature stories on the network news and some stories that first surfaced on programs like *Hard Copy*, such as the William Kennedy Smith rape charge in 1991. At the same time, the tabloid news programs have themselves hired a number of former network and local journalists to produce, report, and anchor the shows, in part to appear more like traditional news programming. Some tabloids have received Emmy nominations in the news and documentary area (Finn, 1993).

Media critic Barbara Ehrenreich put it very well during a 1994 panel convened by *The New York Times* to discuss whether the news media were out of control:

> [T]he TV news magazines everybody likes to criticize so much are actually putting on more serious pieces every week than we've ever had before. Every news magazine has its tabloid piece, but also has its relatively serious piece that either relates to something people care about or goes out and does a foreign leader and watches its ratings go down. ("Talking About the Media Circus," 1994, p. 53)

Tabloid news shows have certainly had an influence on the local news programming of major stations. This was perhaps most notable on WSVN in Miami, which gained a great deal of notoriety in the late 1980s when it went to more than seven hours of daily news shortly after losing its network affiliation. Much of its daily news menu featured sex and violence, but the vice president for news of the station's parent corporation offered two demurrers to criticism on that score in a mid-1993 newspaper interview.

First, he noted, the station was operating in a market where crime had been high-profile and very much of concern to viewers. Second, he stressed that the station's approach to graphics and to the general presentation of news goes beyond what most local newscasts do and thereby draws more attention to crime and other emotion-laden stories. He saw this approach as retaining the core of sound journalistic standards while still adapting the presentation of news to attract viewers who are no longer "wowed by this little picture coming through the box" (Siegel, 1993, p. 52).

When the same corporation purchased a network affiliate in Boston in the early 1990s, it refocused the station's news coverage toward sex and violence. While it didn't do so to the same extent as in Miami, this competition nonetheless had a discernibly detrimental effect on the quality of the other, more popular, major Boston stations' news programming. Whether this sort of coverage of crime and violence *creates* rather than *reflects* a climate of fear is one of the major worries of thoughtful media observers.

Both Daniel Boorstin in the 1960s and Ken Auletta some 30 years later—and many others in between—have noted that American audiences want excitement and drama in their news and information programming. When the "real" world can't provide this, the news media have turned to coverage of celebrities or "pseudo-events" (Boorstin, 1962) and to TV's shock programming or "sock-em-in-the-nose novelty," which eroded the dividing line between news and entertainment while trapping additional viewers and thereby boosting news division revenues (Auletta, 1991, p. 459).

This narrowing of the gap between traditional and tabloid news programs shouldn't be surprising. *News*, after all, has always been defined to include material that departs from the expected or the norm, so we really need to focus on how much deviation is appropriate. If some use of tabloid techniques and some inclusion of tabloid content are indeed appropriate for the networks or for local stations or newspapers, then why should we condemn this approach wholesale? Rather, the discussion must deal with where to draw the line in regard both to techniques and to content, and perhaps with how to distinguish between news and infotainment programming. (The need for audiences to develop the ability to analyze media messages is discussed in the portion of Chapter 11 dealing with media "consumer education.")

A related concern is that tabloid news programs often refer to themselves as journalistic in orientation—or use sets similar to news programs—regardless of their subject matter. What would help in this regard is a bit more "truth in advertising" or in packaging, with both supporters and detractors of these programs acknowledging that they may well depart from higher journalistic norms while still providing some information that can be useful and even important to their audiences.

A striking example of tabloid television providing highly useful information that was overlooked by mainstream media came in the aftermath of the 1993 gang rape of a 14-year-old Minnesota girl and her father's fatal shooting of one of the assailants. Initial accounts of the situation, in the Bemidji and St. Paul papers, relied almost entirely on sources other than the rape victim and her family, and resulted in the young victim being "called a liar, a slut, and a murderer more times than she could count. She was spit upon at football games, received death threats . . . [and] finally dropped out of school" (Mengelkoch, 1994, p. 36).

With assistance from a local couple, the family eventually appeared on the *Sally Jessy Raphael* show, *Hard Copy*, and *Donahue*. This not only gave them a chance to tell their side of the story, but also helped pay for a lawyer to defend the father. Perhaps more important, these appearances gave the family "a sense of authority in their own community and legitimized their concerns and complaints." They also directed intense local and statewide scrutiny at the case "ever since the national [tabloid] media paid attention" (Mengelkoch, p. 38). One observer summarized the situation this way:

> The tabloids' greatest virtue . . . is exactly [what] makes people sneer at them—they're often foolish and not very selective. As gatekeepers they're lousy, and that's often fortunate for those who need them most. They will listen to your story when nobody else will, if it has the elements and the angles they're looking for. If we truly believe in access, that journalists should be dedicated to comforting the afflicted and afflicting the comfortable, the tabloids must be recognized as sharing that mission. (p. 38.)

One danger with this, as Bob Steele of the Poynter Institute noted in a panel discussion several years ago, is that journalistic ethics of the 1990s are being driven by the tabloid news approach—as news media graphics and, to some degree, news media content also seem to have been influenced. This concern certainly deserves attention, perhaps especially from the perspective of whether tabloid news adequately respects the human dignity of its subjects. But that's a totally different question from whether infotainment shows provide useful information in ways that in fact catch the public's attention.

■ PRODUCING AND PACKAGING THE PRODUCT

It therefore seems useful to focus not just on the content of the infotainment shows, but also on their packaging and production values. If the MTV approach gets across information or a concern with issues, then perhaps the norms of how news and information are presented must be reexamined. One new approach is seen in the "Rock the Vote" campaign originated in 1990 by people in the recording industry and aired on MTV in an effort to get more young people to register and vote in presidential elections. In mid-1998, this campaign was expanded to encourage not only voter registration but also activism by them in community affairs (Schultz, 1998).

What has worked almost since the infancy of television and its news operations may not be the most appropriate way to head into the 21st century. If news departments can learn from MTV's production techniques and from the packaging of infotainment programs, society may benefit from new and more successful ways to make all sorts of useful information available. Audiences may pay closer attention to mainstream news and information presented with new production techniques that are more attention-getting, stimulating, and familiar.

There are parallels in the newspaper world, where the arrival of *USA Today* in the early 1980s was greeted by criticism of its format, which many dubbed tabloid and superficial. It was fashionable then for more established papers to say that they were not being influenced by *USA Today*, at the same time that they were changing their weather sections and their graphics and adding various quickly read roundups of short news items.

Earlier newspaper practices related to the infotainment issue involve the sensational papers whose origins go back to the 19th century. Though justifiably criticized for much of their content, there is little question that these papers still provided some useful news and information for audiences that otherwise might *not* have been reading newspapers. Modern-day tabloids have also been criticized for condensing and oversimplifying the news as well as for sensationalizing it but they, too, mix in some worthwhile material amid the fluff and the sleaze. Coverage such as that given by these papers to the 1990 Donald/Ivana Trump marital scandals, which were not ignored in the more "respectable" print and broadcast news outlets either, may well have been spurred by competition from the tabloid electronic media—or vice versa.

> In their scramble to outdo local television news and tabloid television, columnists and editors at these papers seized on the Trump story and played it for all it was worth and more. And as a story it worked. All of the "buttons" that foster sensationalism lit up. We had celebrity, wealth, power, sex, a love triangle, even religion and Valentine's Day. (Dennis, 1990, p. 4)

We also had continuing coverage of major world, national, and local events in mainstream papers, albeit more of it inside the paper while front pages featured the Trumps.

Even a publication such as the old *Confidential* magazine—which author Tom Wolfe once called "the most scandalous scandal magazine in the history of the world"—claimed to provide some useful information along with its particular brand of sleaze. Wolfe quoted the magazine's publisher as saying that *Confidential* regularly ran stories exposing racketeering and other societal problems. "'But we had to have the other stuff, the gossip, to sell the magazine, or we could never have run these stories at all'" (Wolfe, 1965, pp. 180, 199).

TV's current tabloid news and infotainment shows are thus just following in some well-trodden paths blazed by the print media, and should be recognized both for what they are and for the information they do provide. As Van Gordon Sauter, former president of CBS News, noted in 1989:

> What these people do is a form of journalism. Not the capital J variety, that's for sure. But it's a journalism that would have been recognized and appreciated by some of the great editors and publishers of the popular press that thrived in this country before journalism became hopelessly corporate, upper-middle-class, complacent, and condescending. (p. 4)

It's worth noting, as well, that tabloid journalism also gets some subjects out in the open, where the more "responsible" media can provide fuller coverage, using perspectives that go beyond titillation. We've seen this repeatedly as mainstream media report on the coverage by tabloid and other sensation-seeking media of stories that otherwise would not be made public, such as some aspects of the Clinton-Lewinsky situation. It's happened, as well, in regard to some aspects of stories overlooked by the mainstream media, such as the Minnesota rape story noted above. This process can be carried to excess, of course, but it isn't necessarily a bad thing. Once again, a key question is where to draw the lines ethically.

■ ATTRACTING AND HOLDING THE AUDIENCE

Kant's approach here probably would be not to use the infotainment/MTV approach unless you're willing to make that the universal standard for news and information programming. That absolutist standard simply won't work for the current decade and its changing audiences. In fact, such an absolutist standard has never really worked in regard to the news. Both print and broadcast journalists have always been concerned with the need to attract and hold their audiences, and have used various techniques—going beyond unadorned presentation of news and information—to reach that goal. Sensational, scandal-mongering papers aside, think for a moment about the astrology columns, comics, and various "soft" news one finds in almost every daily *news*paper in the country.

To be sure, some comic strips have also served very well over the years as sources of information and ideas about current concerns in society. Walt Kelly's *Pogo* and its strong stand against McCarthyism in the 1950s will probably always be the benchmark for this genre. More recently, Garry Trudeau's *Doonesbury* has managed to work on some extremely short deadlines to remain topical on a variety of political subjects, to the point where some papers have either furloughed the strip or put it on the editorial pages during election seasons. Others run this strip—and, in some cases, *Mallard Fillmore* from the other end of the ideological spectrum—on the editorial pages at all times, viewing it more as social commentary than entertainment.

The early 1993 *For Better or For Worse* comic strip sequence dealing with one important character's homosexuality provided both information and differing perspectives for readers who may well not have gotten that exposure through more traditional news and information channels. It also led to a staff revolt at the *Macon Telegraph* in Georgia "led in part by two lesbian staffers upset by the paper's decision" not to run the strip (Shumate, 1995, p. 14); the result of the discussions that followed that decision was a four-day, 17-story series titled "Gay in Macon" and the addition of a lesbian to the paper's diversity committee. But when this strip returned to the same theme in 1997, at least 20 newspapers used syndicate-supplied reruns instead ("Some newspapers . . . ," 1997).

Movies can also provide important information for their audiences, and grist for the public's agenda on major topics, along with their primary entertainment focus. One excellent example was the 1993 depiction of a number of AIDS-related issues in *Philadelphia* and the way in which those issues were then considered in different segments of society.

Television news over the decades has been quite concerned with visuals and other production values as well as news content. In a visual medium, this is not inappropriate. The problem comes when visual values (or availability) overwhelm news judgment completely. For example, the use by NBC News of the Telemundo tape showing a Florida man shooting his ex-wife (discussed in more detail in Chapter 10) was criticized on the grounds that the tape's availability was the key factor in the decision to use it, and that news values and the need for context were ignored (Winslow, 1993). Many other examples might be cited of news coverage being blown out of proportion because a network or a station had compelling (or titillating) video footage that far exceeded the situation's real news value—once again an indication that the gap between traditional and tabloid news is often not really that great.

Just because there have been excesses in using the infotainment approach, the media shouldn't overlook the value of such techniques (in moderation) in reaching a larger audience than would otherwise be interested. If that larger audience can be attracted to useful information by packaging it in new and innovative ways, the net results will be positive rather than negative. Similarly, if infotainment programs can use human drama and emotion to unearth and present some worthwhile stories better than the conventional media can, that's probably good—on balance—for society.

This approach draws on Aristotle and utilitarianism. Using some infotainment techniques while maintaining a concern for news and information seeks a middle ground that will make that material available to a wider audience, thus benefiting a larger portion of the public and entertaining the viewers or readers in the process.

Talk shows ... are perhaps the late-20th-century equivalent of the colonial tavern, the ... Main Street barber shop....

Talk shows have often exemplified this combining of news, information, and entertainment to produce very useful results. These programs—which range from very good to awful—are perhaps the late-20th-century equivalent of the colonial tavern, the early-20th-century Main Street barber shop, the 1960s coffeehouse, or just the old backyard fence back when we were much more likely than now to talk to our neighbors and friends in such venues. Talk shows give us a chance to be heard and to talk (if somewhat indirectly and anonymously) with some of our fellow citizens. And they, too, can be a source of information on topics that are—or might be—of interest to us.

For people who want their news and information "unadulterated," the options are there. The two CNN all-news channels spend a considerable percentage of their broadcast day providing straight news, though some entertainment aspects creep into the programming. C-SPAN provides informative material with little concern for entertainment values, as do such specialized sources of information such as the Weather Channel. All-news radio stations and regional TV news operations such as New England Cable News don't ignore entertainment values, but their main focus is on news and information, as it is in *The New York Times* or *The Washington Post*, to single out only two prime examples in print journalism, or on *Nightline*, to note a TV counterpart. The emergence of online sources of news and information may provide even more opportunities for people to get as much straightforward information as they want.

But as we noted at the start, there are huge numbers of people for whom such news sources have only limited appeal. If this country is to have an *informed* democracy, those people must be reached through other channels. It's much too easy to dismiss tabloid news programs and talk shows as exercises in excess or fluff, but this isn't true across the board. Even where it may be largely true, the programs' entertainment value does attract audiences, and this is something the elitists or purists among us shouldn't overlook.

Rather than just criticizing or ignoring these programs, a more logical and beneficial idea would be a twofold Aristotelian approach. First, we might adapt the infotainment production techniques to make serious news more appealing. Second, we could strive to improve the content of these infotainment channels, recognizing that they will continue to reach a significant percentage of the potential audience. Developing ethical frameworks to provide guidance, or to help set reasonable expectations, for programs such as talk shows might accomplish more than condemning many of them out of hand. This truly is an area where the Golden Mean approach to media ethics can be valuable.

■ REUSS: Tabloid news publications and programs, talk shows, and other forms of infotainment confuse the public by offering entertainment at the expense of information.

Whether he intended to or not, in setting up his argument that infotainment media exert a necessary and positive influence on the democratic process, David Gordon suggested many of the negative aspects of infotainment media offerings. I must do the opposite. I must acknowledge that infotainment media can, indeed, positively influence the democratic process—but I then question how much or how well.

The infotainment media often appeal to audiences that give little, if any, attention to more serious media. In that respect, those that contain even minimal amounts of information *can* help these people make decisions—they can help make democracy work. But because infotainment media tend to overemphasize entertainment, to oversimplify, trivialize, and titillate, too often they confuse their audiences about important issues.

Infotainment epitomizes a media Gresham's Law: With limited time and space, popular, often simplistic programs, articles, or arguments prevail. This means that "hot" subjects and sources, entertainingly presented, can easily dominate the public agenda so other important topics don't get the attention they deserve. Thus, a topic such as abuse—child, spousal, substance, you-name-it—played out dramatically and convincingly day after day, even hour after hour, in a variety of media can become so imbedded in the public's mind that other important topics or issues are downplayed or even overlooked. It makes no difference whether the tantalizing presentations, in print or on-air, spotlight famous public figures or heretofore unknowns; they too often trivialize important news and information and drive it to oblivion.

Dramatic programs and articles about real and alleged crime can generate powerful negative stereotypes and unintended, unnecessary fears among the public. Boisterous, poorly reasoned arguments and impertinent questions, the lifeblood of popular talk shows and call-in programs, can set the style for listeners and viewers and spoil their own interpersonal relationships.

Media decision makers know that infotainment is profitable. So do supermarkets and other newsstand operators who stock the tabloids, and broadcast managers who schedule infotainment programs. Should they—indeed, can they—act as the consciences of media publics who choose to spend time and money on media that tend to distort reality? Do they care whether readers and viewers can differentiate between the entertainment and the information offered in infotainment media? Should they?

Advertising critics caution "Buyer beware" (*caveat emptor*). Infotainment audiences need a similar reminder—"Audience beware"—because entertainment often overpowers information in infotainment media. Neither of the words from which *infotainment* is derived—*information* and *entertainment*—demands truthfulness nor concern about others, but that does not excuse us from concern about the ethics of infotainment programs and articles. Or does it?

Some may argue that if infotainment media truly entertain, they offer pleasure and escape from our ordinary obligations. Thus they fulfill John Stuart Mill's concept of utilitarianism: They offer happiness to great numbers of people and thus are positive influences on society. Similarly, if infotainment prompts audiences to discuss the subjects presented in publications and broadcasts—even taboos that traditionally have been repressed—they fulfill Mill's concept of utilitarianism. Both of those perspectives stretch Mill's point.

I am more concerned that infotainment media too often stretch the truth and give false perceptions of reality. To entice audiences and to fit the constraints of media time and space, they rely heavily on stereotypes, exaggeration, half-truths, and innuendo that impressionable audiences accept as reality.

No news and information media are immune from such tactics, but infotainment media capitalize on them. Thus, in infotainment media, relatively complex problems are simplified to "we versus them," what rhetoricians would call a "straw man" technique. In these programs, there are also unnatural crescendos of emotional involvement that are either scripted, developed through audience participation, or created through editing.

■ ANGER AND ABUSE

Teachers know that lessons become more "real" and take hold more permanently when students participate in their classes. This is worrisome when we analyze some contemporary infotainment programs, particularly when on-air participants engage in shouting—or, in the case of Jerry Springer's show, punching—matches. It doesn't matter whether the participants are randomly selected members of a studio audience, telephone callers, or the bright, intelligent panelists on John McLaughlin's public television program. Such explosive incivility can carry over to the vicarious participants in the listening/viewing audiences. Society is the loser if this tactic becomes the norm, and verbal bouts become verbal and even deadly physical abuse, as witness recent media stories on "road rage" and school shootings.

"Media rage" is as big an ethical problem of some contemporary infotainment media as is their tendency to mock and distort the reputations of people, ideas, and ideologies they don't agree with. It is socially destructive. Refer back to John Merrill's commentaries about Kant and others in the Overview section of this book. With them, I believe that infotainment must be based on truth, not half-truths, and that it must not sacrifice information for the sake of entertainment. Infotainment producers should be concerned with the maturity and sensitivities of the audiences that watch or listen to them, but too often these programs focus only on audience size. Admittedly, the audiences are in control because they can choose whether or not to watch, read, or listen. But that is not an adequate response because audiences that do not have the ability to discern between what is and what is not personally and socially acceptable behavior can too easily be swayed by media offerings. Television, especially, is a powerful teaching tool—a dangerously powerful teaching tool when audiences learn antisocial behavior from it.

Concerns about infotainment have increased with television's voracious appetite for programs that attract and hold audiences. The networks and individual stations have found that infotainment does just that, and at reasonable cost. Scan your local TV schedule to see the proliferation of infotainment programs, many of them repeated time after time. Even the pace of stories on television is motivated by the desire to have crescendos that will "hold" the audience through the next commercial break.

The grandmère of contemporary TV infotainment programs is *60 Minutes*. Its format is well-established and has been copied widely. Each program includes several segments cast as news stories, each with a recognized reporter involved as interlocutor, interviewer, observer, interpreter of the situation or event under consideration. Although a range of staff assistance is given credit, the impression is that the reporter has investigated the situation under discussion and is giving the audience a balanced investigative report. The crescendo of promotional hype for the program and for individual segments begins hours and even days before airtime, peaks at the intro to each segment, and is recapped as the credits scroll at the end of the hour. "This *must* be important," the viewer is encouraged to believe. By the time each program segment gets center stage, audiences are to presume that the subject under scrutiny is very important, and the *60 Minutes* reporting team has *the* interpretation of it. For anyone who doubts this, visual highlights are often repeated as the program credits roll across the screen at the end of the hour.

I admit I am hooked on *60 Minutes*, and I have to remind myself regularly not to be seduced by its entertainment aspects and fail to scrutinize the information being presented. My ethical obligation, I have decided, is to have a healthy skepticism for information heavily laced with entertainment.

My ethical obligation . . . is to have a healthy skepticism for information heavily laced with entertainment.

CBS's profitable experience with *60 Minutes* has, as we know, spawned *48 Hours* and a number of other news-exposé shows on all the major networks, including *20/20*, *PrimeTime Live*, and *Dateline*. As long as the program costs balance favorably with audience demographics and size that bring in revenues, there will be more rather than fewer versions of these popular shows—nearly a fifth of major network prime-time programming in 1996–1997—and more opportunities for audiences to meet evil dragons that haunt society.

The studio talk shows that fill many radio and TV hours—and no doubt raise the blood pressure of many listeners and viewers—also deserve scrutiny as infotainment media. I am not against any of these because collectively they *do* have the potential for important discussion and some—notably on NPR—do not fit the stereotype. They also can *limit* discussion when the "talent" and the audiences are single-minded and closed to any but their own thoughts and opinions. Radio talk shows probably have more potential for such "tunnel vision" than televised programs because radio stations tend to appeal to smaller, more specialized audiences, particularly in larger markets. In a truly liberal spirit, this might be an example of democracy in action. Certainly, opinions are freely expressed. These programs cater to the inquisitive, and often to bombastic exhibitionists, who give the appearance that they represent the concerns of the nation. The networks now understand their appeal—and so, *Politically Incorrect* moved from the Comedy Channel to ABC in 1996.

These programs propose an "encounter" mentality—every situation is an encounter between good and evil, right and wrong (whose right and whose wrong?), my view and yours, often with the most outspoken—or the host, like Rush Limbaugh— the unofficial "winner." Audiences are encouraged to enter the fray. They are volunteers and cheap "talent" indeed. Such free-form treatment of sometimes important subject matter is manipulation at its worst. The media environment suggests that the material under discussion and the participants in the discussion carry the traditional credibility of the media form. They don't.

Television schedules are loaded with these programs because they draw audiences at comparatively small cost to stations. Every day, in my viewing area, I have the opportunity to view the world with Maury Povich, Jenny Jones, Sally Jessy Raphael, Oprah Winfrey, and a gaggle of other television performers who capitalize on people's willingness to share their traumas and troubles and sometimes their achievements and, more rarely, their assessments of serious subjects. The guests and members of the studio audiences vie for attention and the hosts and hostesses are skillful interlocutors. But, collectively, do they generate useful debate of important issues or do they skew attention and give sincere but false interpretations of potentially important topics?

Television is *the* dominant national communications medium. Single programs reach millions of people. Every program combines appealing sight and sound, action and color. All of those basic characteristics, combined with the number of television sets turned on at any given moment, mean that television can have tremendous impact on the people who watch as well as those who are affected by the watchers. Thus, we should be very concerned about the ethical lessons imbedded in television programs, including such popular syndicated infotainment programs as *The People's Court*, *Rescue 911*, and *Cops*. All of these programs are fact-based and some of the segments are inspiring. Too often, though, they give the false impression that complex problems can be resolved in minutes. For example, virtually all of those rescued on *Rescue 911* recover fully from their injuries. By program-end, the injured have survived, good is rewarded, and evil is punished.

A Current Affair, *Entertainment Tonight*, *Hard Copy*, and *Inside Edition* capitalize on reportorial style and hype. How well do their audiences distinguish between the two? Newsworthiness is often short-lived—unless the infotainment specialists keep it alive and embellished with continued reports, opinions, and questions. It is immaterial who offers new information or opinions or who asks the questions. It helps if they can be entwined in show-biz intrigue or hype. We have become accustomed to these programs—but have we considered the real value of the information disseminated, the effects on individuals and on society, the merits of energized "reporting"? Do these programs block the transmission—or reception—of information more vital to viewers' lives and to society? I don't have answers to the general questions but they are worthy of consideration as we experience the proliferation of infotainment in the mass media.

Cable television, which consumes programs faster than they can be developed, can become a haven for infotainment, especially for programs created by special-interest organizations, many of which aggressively attack people and ideas they disagree with. Argument and debate are one thing; vicious attacks clothed in righteousness, or in entertainment, are another. Especially when such programs encourage audiences to do likewise, society is often the loser.

■ GLOBAL IMPACT

In past decades, "inside" stories and hoaxes had limited effects in limited geographical areas. Now, with satellite transmission and the Internet allowing fast simultaneous transmission around the globe, an isolated story can burst into a major worldwide event. Information can be transmitted and repeated broadly and quickly, *ad hoc* staffers and expert (and inexpert) sources can be found and signed on easily. Like a virus, the fever of the "big one" can encourage both competition and continued attention to a subject that strikes the fancy of audiences. News begets infotainment, which begets more news and infotainment. In addition, home videos can bring life and emotion to scenes not yet reached by professional companies. Interestingly, home videos have spawned infotainment programs, although many critics probably classify some of these programs solely as entertainment. Home VCRs also encourage people to view programs at their own convenience—sometimes repeatedly, so the limitations of time slots do not deter audiences from viewing infotainment (or any other) programs.

Also on the home front, increasing numbers of children are left on their own with their TVs and increasing numbers of adults are alone with TV rather than interacting with others. For all of these, televised infotainment programs have the potential for setting frightening new standards of social or antisocial behavior. They can be personally and socially destructive.

Publications are not immune from the pitfalls of infotainment—the eagerness to entertain readers, even at the price of accuracy and veracity. I have concentrated on television because it has a much greater reach than any publication and because contemporary television is entertainment-based and has exceptional capability to attract audiences that can get its messages off-air—free.

Publication staffs, nevertheless, continually make value judgments about what is and is not included in their publications and how information is presented. Like their broadcast media counterparts, they can mislead readers, intentionally and unintentionally, especially when they let the entertainment aspect of their efforts overrun the information. They can confuse the adrenaline flowing from their own work with readers' interest in a story. They can resort to clever words, phrases or examples that only they, who have been working full-time on a story, fully understand. Reporters, editors, designers, and others who create publications must be wary of the nuances of language and display. They must be sensitive to audience interests and level of maturity.

It is difficult to assess definitively the ethics of the mass media, especially those that offer infotainment. The diversity of media, of potential subject matter, of sources and styles of presentation, the varied creative talent that produce the media, and even the diversity of the media audiences must be considered. Infotainment has a dual role:

to offer information and entertainment. It can be useful to society, but when it confuses the public, when it misleads or promotes antisocial actions, the gatekeepers need to take responsibility.

Unfortunately, no simple list of ethical rules can apply across the board to infotainment. Fortunately, there shouldn't be such a list in a nation blessed with the freedoms encompassed in the First Amendment.

Years ago, I assigned book reviews from a long and varied list. The books were not of equal value and they offered a range of opinions about the mass media. At least one was a popular, bombastic, iconoclastic criticism of media programs that contained some ludicrous statements about media effects, which most students realized when they read it. One student, who was usually very perceptive, selected that book and wrote a report that indicated total acceptance of the author's opinions. I was puzzled by his report so I talked to him about it. He had been trapped by the medium. He reasoned that as long as the information was in a book, it must be true. It was a good lesson for both of us: Beware of the trap of beguiling misinformation and the further trap of "mass media halo."

I am not such a spoilsport as to condemn combining information and entertainment. I do caution that we be careful to discern what is entertainment and what is the information that we and our neighbors need to function as citizens in a complex world.

■ MERRILL: Commentary

This seems to me to be an overblown controversy. However, I would not be surprised if there are many thoughtful and concerned media followers who see the infotainment/docudrama explosion in the media as quite significant. The contending authors of the above discussions are evidently among such concerned followers. It is unclear just when this hybrid entertainment-news emphasis began, but it is clear that it seems to be peaking toward the end of the century.

As David Gordon posits, infotainment and docudramas provide much useful information to the public. Just how much of it helps "make democracy work" is another question. But there is no doubt that much substantive information is spread through lively talk shows and so-called tabloid news programs and they are, indeed, "excellent vehicles for focusing public attention on important current issues." Carol Reuss sees it differently. She believes such entertainment-oriented material confuses the public and distracts people from serious attention to the news and its meaning. She is not so unrealistic as to believe that such "fluffy" material can be eliminated, but she is worried that it is dominating the media content and causing increasing public lethargy.

I believe the actual truth of the situation is somewhat different from either position. Chit-chat news anchors, the growing number of talk shows on radio, tabloid news programs on TV (such as *A Current Affair* or *Hard Copy*), more serious newsmagazines (such as *60 Minutes*), and personality-anchored semi-news shows (such as Oprah, Limbaugh, and Larry King)—all these and other hybrid entertainment-journalistic shows are proliferating and gaining popularity. The print media are sprucing up, livening their writing, using more catchy headlines, splashing color across their pages (even in *The New York Times*), and increasing their personality profiles and human interest features.

So infotainment is here to stay. The question is this: Does it harm the democratic process by stressing entertainment at the expense of information? And is it unethical for infotainment media or programs to pass themselves off as information outlets when they are in reality simply entertainment?

I don't consider this an either/or question. Perhaps it never has been. Quite likely, from the earliest days of journalism, readers and writers have considered the hybrid nature of their news and their entertainment features. The news writer has always wanted to catch the attention of the reader, to make the reader enjoy the experience of getting the news. And feature writers and editorialists have always managed to provide *information* in their pieces. After all, information—factual data, historical and geographical insights—has always been found in nonjournalistic media, even in novels.

And so it is today. Is Oprah an entertainer, a propagandist, an information purveyor—or what? What about Rush Limbaugh? Larry King? Bill Moyers? John McLaughlin? William Buckley? Dan Rather? And on and on. The answer, I think, is this: They are all *news purveyors, propagandists,* and *entertainers.*

Certainly I realize that there is a difference between a Montel Williams and a Dan Rather, between a Rush Limbaugh and a Bill Buckley. The difference is significant. Montel Williams is primarily an *entertainer* whereas Rather is primarily a *newsperson* or information-disseminator. And whereas Limbaugh sublimates his "information" under colorful entertainment wrappings, Buckley stresses information, analysis couched in interesting and attention-grabbing linguistic mannerisms.

But in all these cases there is at least a dual-dimensionality: information *and* entertainment. Often, propaganda is there, too. Both straight-news and straight-entertainment, it would seem, are helpful in an open, pluralistic, audience-focused society. Likewise, a hybridization of the two is also helpful. Democracy can tolerate all kinds of information, however packaged.

... the citizens ... think *they are getting the news when, in effect, they are getting somebody's propaganda or somebody's version of entertainment.*

Both Gordon and Reuss might well reply that it is the *ethical* issue they are mainly dealing with. And what might that be? Well, it would seem that the citizens (readers, listeners, and viewers) are having their media content *misrepresented* to them. They *think* they are getting the news when, in effect, they are getting somebody's propaganda or somebody's version of entertainment. This, many might say, is unethical. Evidently news should always be clearly identified as news and entertainment as entertainment. This, however, is impossible. Was the over-coverage of the O.J. Simpson case in California news or was it entertainment? Was it information or was it a continuing soap opera? Well, it obviously was *both.* In modern times, there has probably never been a better example of infotainment.

I recommend that the reader of this chapter take a good course in general semantics, a Korzybskian perspective that stresses a multivalued orientation rather than a two-valued (either/or) one. Another main emphasis of general semantics is likewise relevant to this "controversy": the basic concept of flux or change, that everything is in the state of *becoming* something else—news to entertainment, entertainment to news. This constant process philosophy of change, in which our labels are inadequate to keep up with reality, is an extremely important one for the person interested in communication. I recommend it heartily.

REFERENCES

Auletta, Ken. (1991). *Three Blind Mice: How the TV Networks Lost Their Way*. New York: Random House.

Boorstin, Daniel. (1962). *The Image*. New York: Athenaeum.

Dennis, Everette E. (1990). "In Allegiance to the Truth: News, Ethics and Split-Personality Journalism." New York: Gannett Center for Media Studies. Speech delivered March 6, Honolulu.

Finn, Catherine L. (1993). "A (Current) Affair to Remember: Tabloid Television News and Its Impact on Network News Organizations." Paper presented at a meeting of the Association for Education in Journalism and Mass Communication, Kansas City, MO, August 14.

Gorney, Carole. (Summer 1992). "Numbers Versus Pictures: Did Network Television Sensationalize Chernobyl Coverage?" *Journalism Quarterly* 69(2), pp. 455–465.

Korzybski, Alfred. (1933). *Science and Sanity: An Introduction to Non-Aristotelian Systems and General Semantics*. Lancaster, PA: Science Press.

Mengelkoch, Louise. (November/December 1994). "When Checkbook Journalism Does God's Work." *Columbia Journalism Review*, pp. 35–38.

Rehm, Diane. (Summer 1993). "Talking Over America's Electronic Backyard Fence." *Media Studies Journal* 7(3), pp. 63–69.

Sauter, Van Gordon. (August 5, 1989). "In Defense of Tabloid TV." *TV Guide*, pp. 2–4.

Schultz, Tom. (May 26, 1998). "Campaign promotes youthful activism." *Lansing* (MI) *State Journal*, p. 6A.

Shumate, Richard. (January/February 1995). "Discovering Central Georgia's Gay Community." *American Journalism Review*, p. 14.

Siegel, Ed. (August 21, 1993). "What Cheatwood Brings to Ch. 7: Miami-Style Glitz or Just Good TV?" *The Boston Globe*, pp. 41, 52.

"Some Newspapers Won't Run Comic Strip's Series on Gays." (August 14, 1997). Eau Claire, WI *Leader-Telegram*, p. 3A.

"Talking About the Media Circus." (June 26, 1994). *The New York Times Magazine*, pp. 26 ff.

Tannenbaum, Percy, and Mervin Lynch. (Summer 1960). "Sensationalism: The Content and Its Measurement," *Journalism Quarterly* 37(2), pp. 381–92.

Winslow, C. Katherine. (March 1993). "Is It News?" RTNDA *Communicator*, pp. 8–9.

Wolfe, Tom. (1965). "Purveyor of the Public Life." In *The Kandy-Kolored Tangerine-Flake Streamline Baby*. New York: Farrar, Straus and Giroux, pp. 180–203.

CHAPTER 13

ETHICS AND ADVERTISING

In contemporary capitalistic societies, the mass media are largely supported by commercial advertising; the major exceptions are film, much cable television, books, and some magazines. This is so common and so well-accepted that the few exceptions, such as *Consumer Reports* magazine, are noteworthy. Even public broadcasting, with its commercial underwriting and on-air "begathons," often seems similar to commercial stations and their paid ads.

Advertising ethics—a term that some see as an oxymoron—have been a source of controversy almost since advertising began. But some argue strongly that advertising practitioners should have no problems adhering to "appropriate" ethical standards.

The key point in this discussion is that advertising's purposes and goals differ greatly from those of the media that aim to present news and information, or offer entertainment, to the public. Answers to the question of whether advertising media are operating ethically must be sought within the context of what advertising *intends* to do and the role it plays in the American media system (and, along with the media, the advertisers, and the consuming public, in the capitalist economy more generally). Advertising *does* differ from both the news and the entertainment media, and its ethics must be evaluated with those differences in mind.

That doesn't mean that advertising shouldn't be socially responsible in the messages it brings to the public and how it brings them. But definitions of that term can vary widely, depending on one's perspective. There is also a fine line between standards of advertising acceptability and outright censorship. Keep in mind, too, that although we are referring here mainly to product or service advertising, the advertising of ideas, or of political candidates, are areas that also raise many important ethical issues. So does the question of advertising products by making sure they'll be visible in films or television programs, an issue discussed briefly in Chapter 15-C.

In the discussion that follows, Carol Reuss and David Gordon agree that there are *some* ethical standards that certainly *should* apply to advertising. But they disagree as to what those standards should be. Gordon argues that truth is *not* an appropriate ethical norm to apply to advertising, and Reuss maintains that honesty and a lack of deception or duplicity should be important ethical concerns for advertisers.

■ GORDON: Everyone understands that the function of advertising is to create images that sell products and services, and there is therefore no need for it to adhere to truth as an ethical standard.

Arguing that advertising is creative rather than factual, and persuasive more than informative, does not automatically mean that it should have absolutely *no* concerns for ethics. Rather, this ought to lead one to consider carefully which ethical standards should apply to advertising and how any such standards should differ from the ones applied to the news, information, and entertainment media.

This is especially important for advertising students to ponder because mass communication education too often fails to differentiate among its various subfields. Thus, when the talk turns to ethics, that discussion often is centered on what the standards should be for the news media—if for no other reason than that we are all news media consumers—with too little attention paid to the other parts of the wide-ranging mass communication field.

Dealing with this issue more generally will also lead to a careful consideration of what ethical standards should *not* apply to advertising communication. I believe that chief among such inapplicable standards is "truth"—an elusive enough concept when applied to the news media, but one that is both irrelevant and nearly impossible to define when applied to advertising.

Supreme Court justices, among others, have written that although the truth of factual statements may be ascertained, one cannot prove the "truth" of an opinion. The same might be said for persuasive communication such as advertising, where the validity of many claims is subject to opinion rather than to factual proof. The Federal Trade Commission (FTC) has had a great deal to say about outright deception in ads. That is a legal issue as well as an ethical one, and we'll proceed here on the assumption that advertisements must adhere to the requirement not to make false statements in an effort to deceive, for legal if not for ethical reasons.

Beyond that minimum requirement, however, there is no need for ads to be "truthful" in the same sense that the news must be accurate or truthful. News reporters are supposed to provide a fair, accurate, and complete account in the stories they present. Advertising practitioners have a responsibility to do the best job they can to persuade potential customers of the value of a product (or an idea) while avoiding the kind of deception the FTC has banned. Such persuasion usually requires that the advertising communicator emphasize the strong or appealing points of the product and omit or conceal the weaknesses. A full, fair, balanced picture is *not* what is intended.

I believe that the *public* has a responsibility to be aware of this, to understand the conventions of advertising, and to use advertising as it is intended—as an attempt at persuasion that often can and does provide useful information. To help produce this increased public awareness and understanding, the advertising profession might well commit *itself* to do a better job of explaining to the public just how it works and what might fairly be expected (and *not* expected) from it. (Such consumer education is also very much needed in regard to the news media, but that's a different argument, which I set forth in Chapter 11.)

The early 1990s use of greater realism in television advertising spots, particularly in regard to the people who appear in those commercials, illustrates strikingly that ads and advertisers can't be held to the same standards of "truth" that exist for news people. A 1993 article in *The New York Times* noted that this "so-called real people school of casting eschews the glamour and glitz of actors and models for the genuineness and imperfections of ordinary consumers" (Elliott, 1993).

This approach has its roots in the desire to persuade more effectively, rather than in concerns about ethics. It has to do with the ways in which the purveyors of the persuasive messages are perceived, not with the truth or completeness of the message itself. And this is appropriate for the advertising field. These "documercials" supposedly have "a more persuasive credibility, particularly among younger, more sales-resistant consumers. Such ads can then overcome the skepticism that so often results when professionals deliver paid pitches" (Elliott, 1993).

This phenomenon may reinforce the general notion that ethical practices and procedures can also be good business, in advertising as in other parts of the mass media world. But we must remember that the appeal of realism in TV ads has bottom-line rather than ethical roots. Its goal of presenting a bit of "purity amid a world of puffery" (Elliott, 1993) is driven by marketing forces, and would (and should) be abandoned if it proves ineffective. Here, also, it is the public's responsibility to provide the feedback that will determine whether this "realism" content should continue in advertising. Indeed, it also falls to the public to "regulate" advertising that goes beyond acceptable ethical limits simply by conveying its displeasure to the sponsor or the ad agency involved (directly, or by refusing to buy the product).

■ AN ARGUMENT FOR APPLYING ETHICAL STANDARDS

Richard Johannesen has made an interesting argument for the application of "ethical standards rooted in truthfulness and rationality" to advertising's efforts to argue "the actual nature or merit of a product." He suggests that "the evidence and reasoning supporting the claim [must be] clear, accurate, relevant, and sufficient in quantity," and that any emotional (or motivational) appeals must be directly relevant to the product being promoted (1996, pp. 129–130).

But advertising, as Johannesen notes, is inherently not necessarily an exercise in rational communication. Rather, it is persuasive communication, and I'd suggest that it should be given free rein as long as it remains within the legal boundaries regulating blatant deception. Indeed, Johannesen himself questions whether the truthfulness/rationality standards should still apply when advertising is aimed not at product quality, but simply seeks to get the attention of the reader or viewer in order to create awareness of the particular product (p. 130). This distinction between emphasis on product quality and "mere" attention-getting efforts seems to lack a clear dividing line, and strikes me as somewhat irrelevant when one considers the basic persuasive and pervasive nature of advertising.

Indeed, one observer argued more than two decades ago that advertising is a form of commercial poetry, and both advertisers and poets use "creative embellishment—a content which cannot be captured by literal description alone" (Levitt, 1970, p. 86). Accepting this approach would allow for some poetic license in the creation of advertising that, nonetheless, remained ethical.

Advertising and public relations have also been described as having "the goal of creating metaphors that resonate in the minds of the target publics: 'The Good Hands People,' 'The Friendly Skies,'" and so forth (Blewett, 1994, p. 42). Creating metaphors is clearly an approach to which standards of truth cannot and should not be applied in the usual ways.

The "commercial poetry" approach goes further, and sees advertisements as symbols of human aspirations that "are not the real things, nor are they intended to be, nor are they accepted as such by the public" (Levitt, 1970, p. 90.). If, indeed, this perception about the audience is correct, there is clearly no need to hold advertising to the same standards of truth and accuracy that are required for the news media. Alternatively, if the audience *does* see ads as reality, the advertising industry—and perhaps the educational system as well—should take steps to ensure that the public comes to understand better the role, practices, and "commercial poetry" of advertising.

[A]dvertising is a form of commercial poetry, and both advertisers and poets use "creative embellishment . . ."

Sissela Bok, though holding that truth is clearly preferable to lies except under very special circumstances, nonetheless suggests that it is better to focus on being "truthful" rather than on always telling the exact truth (Bok, 1979). Applying this to advertising could mean that literal truth is not required as long as outright deception is avoided, and it would seem to sanction the "poetry" concept of advertising copy.

Some people have seen political or ideological advertising as a special case, and therefore subject to a different set of ethical (and legal) expectations. Ads extolling or attacking political candidates serve a different purpose than do product ads, and may be more important to society. Critics in recent decades have often lamented the tendency of political ads to deal with images rather than substance, and at least one TV station has tried a short-lived experiment in which it refused to run political ads of less than five minutes. Although the goal of forcing political candidates to deal with serious issues rather than stressing only quick imagery and soundbites in their ads was a laudable one, opposition from both politicians and the public doomed the experiment.

And that's not necessarily bad. Political ads should no more be subject to standards of "truth" or "substance" than should the general rhetoric of political campaigns. It's a nice goal in the abstract, but both difficult and dangerous to try to implement.

The goal of advertising—perhaps especially political ads—is persuasion. If political ads sometimes stray from the truth, or concentrate on image rather than substance, then the best remedy is neither legal restrictions nor efforts to impose an ethical standard of truth. Rather, the remedy lies in further comment and discussion, either by opposing candidates or—as has been taking place increasingly in the 1990s—by news media materials that discuss the truthfulness, content, validity, and perceived effectiveness of political ads. Once more, it seems to be the responsibility of the public to sort out political as well as product ads and to send its own ballot-box signals about how effectively they persuade—a responsibility that may weigh more heavily as advertising, political and otherwise, spreads to the Internet.

In considering ideological ads, we can look at one of the most extreme cases imaginable in pondering whether such ads should be held to some standard of truth. Ads denying the existence of the Holocaust surfaced in many college and university newspapers in the late 1980s and into the 1990s. Arguments raged on every campus where this took place—and usually in the surrounding community as well—as to whether such ads should be accepted, or whether it was appropriate to reject them on the grounds that they were attempting to perpetrate a monstrous lie.

Some school newspapers wound up running these ads—often while attacking them editorially—and others refused them on various grounds, often including the fact that they distorted or perverted historical truths. Certainly, I have no sympathy whatever for the ideological position taken in these ads, and would much prefer that they never appeared. But I am uneasy with the position that they should be rejected because they fail to adhere to a standard of truth. If that stance is taken, we are opening ourselves up to an endless series of arguments as to just how "truthful" a political or ideological ad must be in order to be permitted to see the light of day. In these situations, as in so many others, I believe that we are better off worrying less about the truthfulness of an ad, and concentrating instead on somehow making sure that those who disagree with the contents have an ample opportunity to respond. More speech, rather than regulation of content (including the truth or falsity of the ad), seems to be a remedy far better suited to an open, democratic society—and this should be true for ideological and commercial ads as well as for other forms of communication in such a society. (For a thoughtful argument to the contrary, see the essay by Stephen Klaidman in Knowlton, 1997, pp. 167–169.)

■ ADS FOR HARMFUL PRODUCTS

Observers over the years have articulated ethical concerns about advertising for products that might be harmful in some way to the users. Indeed, some legal restrictions on that score are already in place, such as the prohibition since 1971 of cigarette ads on television, and the 1997 and 1998 tentative settlements under which the tobacco companies agreed to major restrictions on their advertising and marketing activities. Advertising acceptability standards and practices of individual media—and retail—outlets can also sharply curtail the freedom to advertise, quite aside from any legal restrictions, and this opens up a different set of ethical issues.

The question comes down to whether it is proper, in the name of ethics and social responsibility, to restrict or prevent advertising about products that may be legally sold but that some people regard as harmful to society or to potential users. Might it be better to make additional information about these products available to the public so people can make up their own minds? The late 1980s argument over whether radio and TV stations should run condom advertising illustrates both the acceptability issue and the impact that increasing public acceptance can have on such standards.

The acceptability problem is complicated immeasurably by the "commercial speech" doctrine under which the Supreme Court historically has excluded a considerable portion of advertising from First Amendment protection. In essence, what the Court has done under this doctrine is to equate the nonprotected parts of commercial communication with obscene communication, in that neither category is protected by the First Amendment. This seems to be unfair, unrealistic, and unwise because most if not all advertising conveys at least a kernel of potentially useful information (the "redeeming social value" of advertising, to carry the obscenity parallel just a small step further). Such restrictions also convey a very paternalistic view of an audience that is deemed to be incapable of making its own decisions or resisting advertising blandishments.

A much more pragmatic approach would hold that if a product is legal, it should be advertisable. That would appropriately shift the focus of any disagreements from the advertising sphere to the question of whether harmful products should be made illegal. As is, the opponents of particular products such as tobacco, alcohol, guns, and X-rated movies don't necessarily have to face up to the underlying issue of whether the use of that product should be allowed. Instead, they can shift the concern to the backs of the mass media and their advertisers, in the hope that by restricting or eliminating the ads, they can reduce product usage.

The 1990s flap over the successful use of the Joe Camel symbol by the R.J. Reynolds Tobacco Company illustrates the problem well. Attempts to ban the Joe Camel character, because of its reputed appeal to children, raised both legal and ethical issues. As *The Boston Globe* asked, "Are we to tell advertising firms that they can do their work as long as they are not too good or too successful?" The paper went on to note that this (laudable) attempt to protect children from being influenced to start smoking conceivably could be extended to some unlikely areas, such as banning the movie *Casablanca:*

> As John Banville wrote in *The New York Review of Books*, Humphrey Bogart, who died of throat cancer, was the "emblematic smoker" of his day. "No doubt many an adolescent boy bought his first pack of smokes after seeing a Bogart movie." ("Joe Camel's Rights," 1994)

As it happened, in 1997, "Joe Camel" was sent to pasture from RJR's ads as part of the tentative legal settlement between the tobacco industry and many states that had sued the industry over Medicaid costs.

On balance, it seems to me, the issues of advertising acceptability and the legality of ads for certain products pose far more serious ethical concerns for the advertising field than does the issue of adhering strictly to "truth."

Another area where advertising *should* be concerned about ethical standards has to do with its separation from the news portions of print and broadcast journalism. This is an ethical problem that applies as much to the news as to the business side of the enterprise. Although there is no need for advertising content to adhere to journalistic standards of truth, there is a clear need for news and information content to do so. The advertising side of the operation should remain completely separate from the news, and not try to water down or eliminate news content even if that material might induce advertisers to pull their ads. Aside from the highly questionable ethic of knuckling under, it often isn't good business because standing up to advertiser pressures can pay major dividends in the form of credibility and public trust and thereby produce a stronger audience base to sell to future advertisers. "Newspaper and television lore is burdened with examples of managers who caved in" to such pressures, but there are also examples where principle won out and produced long-run benefits even if there were short-term income losses (Fink, 1988, pp. 128–129).

One unusual example of caving in to advertiser pressure was a 1994 column written by the publisher of the *Mercury-News* in San Jose, California. His apology left the paper's automobile writer hanging out to dry in the face of strong complaints from area auto dealers (i.e., advertisers!) about an earlier story—fairly innocuous, by my standards—providing guidance to prospective auto buyers. After threats from the dealers to pull their ads, the publisher wrote a public apology for the original story, apparently fending off potential revenue loss but producing at least a few raised eyebrows among journalists.

A related concern is the so-called advertorial or infomercial, which should be clearly distinguished from news copy in printed publications or on the air, as Carol Reuss indicates. Unmistakable identification of the material as paid advertising is needed, in fairness to the readers, viewers, or listeners. But once that is ensured, the content can ethically be aimed at persuading the audience, without concern over news media standards of truth, objectivity, or fairness.

■ ETHICAL FRAMEWORKS REGARDING ADVERTISING

Edmund Lambeth (1992) has set forth a framework of five principles that he recommends as the basis for news media ethics. One of these—humaneness—might be argued as a principle that should also apply to advertising communication. This seems to require that ads avoid exploitation, that they not degrade individuals or groups, and, in general, "do no direct, intentional harm to others" (p. 30). But as Lambeth points out, the idea of avoiding direct harm to others is more of a universal *human* ethical principle than one that applies particularly to journalists or to advertisers. As for the balance of the humaneness principle, if advertising does not adhere to it, that's perhaps unfortunate, but (*possibly* with the single exception of ads that exploit young children) no more so—and no more preventable—than such occurrences are in the news and entertainment media.

It can be argued that it is up to parents rather than the advertising industry to control what their children watch. If, as Reuss says, children are in the "line of fire" of ads aimed at different and more mature audiences, that's unfortunate but it's hardly the fault of the advertisers. The sponsors, in fact, would unquestionably prefer that their ads reach the target audiences they're paying the media to reach, rather than being seen by children and others who are not potential customers for the advertised products or services.

In addition to humaneness, and to truth—which has been discussed previously at length—Lambeth discussed freedom, justice, and stewardship. These other three principles don't seem directly applicable to advertising, although Reuss appears to favor considerable stewardship on the part of advertisers. There are also a number of other ethical standards that don't apply here. For instance, Aristotle's Golden Mean, by definition, is not going to be useful concerning persuasive communication that is trying to achieve a nonbalanced goal.

Given the role advertising plays in the media and society as a whole, a utilitarian argument for wide-open advertising might be mounted. This argument would posit that both in economic terms and in terms of helping people to fill their needs and gratify their desires, the greatest good is achieved by giving considerable latitude to advertisements, particularly if the public is knowledgeable about the conventions of advertising. But this approach must also contend with the nagging question of how one judges what advertising practices or restraints produce the greatest good (or the most plea-sure) for the largest portion of society, and that question seemingly defies a conclusive rational answer and therefore weakens the utilitarian approach to this topic.

Kantian absolutes seem inappropriate formulations to apply to advertising con-cerns. Rawls's concern for the most vulnerable members of society appears to be a less applicable approach (again, with the possible exception of ads aimed at young chil-dren, which he would likely regard as inherently unfair) than the goal of educating the public to understand advertising and to take it for what it really is: an effort to make them aware of products and services and to persuade them to buy.

The special case of television advertising directed at young children is one where arguing the need for ethical concerns may be valid. However, the Children's Televi-sion Act of 1990 seems to have preempted the ethical perspective on this by establish-ing some minimum legal requirements aimed at preventing advertisers from exploit-ing young viewers. It therefore seems sensible to treat this area of concern similarly to the way the FTC dealt legally with deception in advertising and just accept those rules as a given rather than arguing about their ethical dimensions.

The controversy over the appropriateness of exposing school children to ads beamed into their classrooms over Channel One raises some of the same ethical (and economic) questions. This venture, launched in 1990 by Whittle Communications, may have reached as many as 40% of American high school students before running into serious financial problems originating largely in other parts of Whittle's holdings and resulting in its sale in 1994 (Stewart, 1994).

Channel One was criticized on the grounds that the students were a captive audi-ence and that it was unfair to expose them to ads in a school setting. The counter-arguments were that the 12-minute news and informational program (including 2 minutes of advertising) on Channel One provided more exposure to news than the students would otherwise receive, and that Channel One's donation of TV sets, VCRs, and satellite dishes to the schools receiving its broadcasts enhanced the oppor-tunities for improved educational experiences for all their students.

I'd suggest that for students living in a society where advertising is so prominent, exposure to ads in a school setting is not appreciably more of a problem than such ex-posure in the rest of their lives. It has also been argued that Channel One provided an excellent opportunity for teachers to discuss with their students advertising's role in the economy and to help educate the students to have an increased understanding of advertising. All in all, taking a utilitarian approach to this specific problem, one might conclude that on balance, Channel One produced greater benefits for more people than its absence would have done.

The same can be said for the general role played by advertising even if it is not held to ethical standards of truth. One can certainly argue cogently, as Reuss does, that it is *better* for the society as a whole if advertising adheres to certain overall ethi-cal standards concerned primarily with the welfare of society. One can even argue for the benefits of advertising codes of ethics, bland and unenforceable as they often are, or for the plausibility that Reuss supports.

Although I don't disagree with these positions in the abstract, I much prefer to let the audience determine whether ads are plausible. I find it totally unrealistic to think about requiring (or even advocating) an ethical stance that focuses on truth as long as advertising serves the purposes it does in our society—namely, as a provider of important commercial information and as the economic engine that drives (or "drive$") the media. That engine must be free to attempt to persuade and to serve the needs of the clients who are paying for that persuasion, subject to the basic legal standards acknowledged previously.

Any other approach runs the risk of making advertising less effective in the name of imposing such ethical standards as plausibility or literal truthfulness. Such results would diminish not only the effectiveness of the advertising-driven economy but also the economic viability and the independence of the American mass media. Advertising, after all, is the major alternative to having the media financed (and controlled) by the government, or to placing the entire burden of paying for the media on the shoulders of the consumers. Although advertising arguably should not be beyond the reach of some ethical principles, it certainly should not be saddled with such excess ethical baggage as concerns for truth, which are really not relevant to its function in society.

■ REUSS: Advertising, no less than news or public relations, should be held to standards of honesty and other ethical principles.

With few exceptions, mass media in capitalistic societies are entwined with advertising—paid messages that promote products, services, and causes. Among the notable exceptions are the renewed *Ms.* magazine and public broadcasting, both of which actively solicit individuals and organizations for financial support. The New York tabloid *PM* was founded as an advertising-free newspaper in 1940, but changed that policy in 1946.

There are many strong arguments for advertising in mass media. At the top of the list is the fact that advertisers pay roughly $90 billion a year for media time and space. Those dollars support most broadcasting and augment the newsstand and subscription dollars that print readers pay. Until audiences are willing to pay directly the total costs of the media they use, advertising will remain the fiscal foundation for U.S. mass media, even those that aggressively and critically cover advertisers and advertising.

Not everyone agrees that advertising is useful to society. Critics such as former ad man Jerry Mander, who proposes that advertising be eliminated, often cite its negative aspects. They overlook the positive effects of advertising, especially the fact that advertising dollars support the mass media. Mander's "Four Arguments for the Elimination of Advertising" makes a direct attack:

All advertising is a gross invasion of privacy.

All advertising is political propaganda representing the rich to the detriment of everyone else.

Advertising is dependent upon economic growth, which further concentrates wealth and power while destroying the planet.

All advertising encourages the centralization of feeling, destroys diversity of experience, and corrupts human interaction. (1993, p. 125)

Other critics of advertising, before and after Mander, are a shade more accepting. Typically, they recognize that people need *some* advertising—from information about "good" books and book stores and job openings to necessities such as health and plumbing services.

Directly opposed to Mander's broad attack against advertising is the libertarian view that there should be no limits on advertising. That view pushes the concept of *caveat emptor*—let the buyer beware—to an untenable extreme. It should not be an excuse for advertiser irresponsibility, nor should it excuse advertisers, the mass media, *and* the public from responsibilities related to advertising. If advertisers and the mass media that accept advertising cannot be socially responsible, individuals, groups, and even government should be prepared to intervene.

I agree with David Gordon that people have to learn how to interpret advertising, but I do not agree that the public bears all responsibility for interpreting the appropriateness, honesty, and accuracy of advertisements. The advertising industry should be the first guardian against the pitfalls of the three Ds: dishonesty, deception, and duplicity.

The advertising industry should be the first guardian against the pitfalls of the three Ds: dishonesty, deception, and duplicity.

When we look at the ethics of advertising from two perspectives, the advertisers' and the mass media's, by implication we include a third—audiences, both targeted audiences and all others who might be affected by advertising. The latter might include underage teens who are influenced by advertisements for alcoholic products and find ways to get them, or people of any age who are frustrated by the desire for products they cannot possibly afford. Advertisers, the media, and the public share responsibilities for all of these people.

■ DISHONESTY, DECEPTION, AND DUPLICITY IN ADS

Advertisements are created for one purpose: to persuade audiences to do something— to buy a product, for example, or to like or dislike a person or concept or to support a cause. The appeals vary, and so do media, ad sizes, designs, words, and illustrations, as well as the opportunities for dishonesty, deception, and duplicity. For example, I believe that advertisements targeted to students and offering "term paper services" are dishonest. The purpose of assigning term papers and similar reports is to get students involved in the research and writing process. This is subverted when students buy papers and turn them in as their own work. Students who succumb to buying the advertised products are as dishonest as the service offered—and do not receive the education for which they are paying tuition.

Gullible people can be caught with other kinds of dishonest advertisements. Ads that offer to help a person who has been a poor credit risk get a credit card, or buy "government surplus" property, or get a government job are often scams. They usually require either a deposit or credit card payment in advance. There is no guarantee that the buyer will get the help or the product offered or that the credit card information will not be misused. These ads capitalize on half-truths, at best. People who have been cheated by them are often too embarrassed to admit their gullibility and seek redress, or decide that the amount they have lost is not worth the cost of pursuing the advertisers.

Unethical deception in advertisements can take many forms, including basing sales messages on incomplete evidence or engaging in bait-and-switch tactics—whereby the product or service advertised grabs people's attention, but when they ask, they are told it isn't available and they are steered toward a more expensive version or product.

Other potentially deceptive practices are the use of "enhanced" illustrations and testimonials. Any illustration can now be altered by a computer, making this a much easier form of deception (see Chapter 15-F). Some deceptive testimonials were produced at a time when there was little or no concern about the health hazards connected with smoking, and capitalized on testimonials by opera stars and athletes to promote the pleasure of smoking. Some "pseudotestimonials" used actors, dressed in lab coats to imply that they were medical professionals, to recommend the pain-killing or other beneficial properties of over-the-counter remedies. Pseudotestimonials are getting more sophisticated; it takes very careful analysis before one realizes that a "slice of life" commercial, or a newspaper ad may be featuring, for example, actors or models and an invented company rather than the CEO of a small firm that supposedly is benefiting from a bank's services. More prevalent today are advertising messages presented in the guise of news or entertainment, advertisements that show violence or demeaning behavior as acceptable behavior, product promotions disguised as teaching aids, and obvious displays of brand-name products in movies and television programs. The list could go on and on.

There are so many products and services advertised in so many ways that it is impractical to make any definitive list of the advertising practices that are ethical or not ethical. The first consideration for advertisers and media should be whether the product or service under consideration is legal. Then, is the appeal legitimate, or even plausible?

Look at the clothing and cosmetics ads in contemporary fashion magazines. Jeans and other apparel are sold by the millions, but how many in the sprite-sizes depicted in so many of the ads? Or ask the time-worn question: How many women fret aloud about rings around the collar or in the toilet bowl? Granted, the models and the poses are intended to grab attention and create the mystique for the merchandise, but how honest—indeed, how plausible—are such depictions?

Pay attention to ads on TV, radio, in newspapers and magazines and evaluate them yourself. Are the sales pitches for beverages, autos, appliances—you-name-it—honest and appropriate for the wide variety of audiences who watch TV, listen to radio, read publications? Do the media in which the ads appear promote social responsibility one minute, or on one page, and then allow depiction of antisocial behavior in the remaining time or space?

Advertisers need to evaluate message content and placement and anticipate the potential effects on audiences, including audiences the advertiser doesn't really want to reach but who might well be in the line of fire—children and immature adults, for example, or people who cannot afford the products being advertised. Persistent and persuasive messages about the *need* to have brand-name clothing or to drink alcoholic beverages are two examples. At best they ignite family arguments, at worst they spark criminal activities, including vicious thefts.

Some may argue that "creative" advertising might well be misinterpreted by vulnerable people; others might say that part of the intrigue of ads is the potential for double-meanings, which appeal to audiences. I agree, to a point; the point is when impressionable audiences suspend reality. Ads can be powerful teachers. The fear is that the lessons are not always appropriate to the audiences watching or reading or listening to the ads. "Miller time" is not an entitlement for everyone, nor are expensive cars, clothing, or jewelry. Advertisers, and the media that carry the ads, are duplicitous when they hypocritically tout concern about the poor and then pitch appealing messages that tempt poor men and women to live well beyond their means. Although they are not their brother's keepers, they should have concern for the social implications of how their messages are received.

Advertisers can become involved in many other potentially unethical situations. Some, for example, pressure the mass media for special treatment, including favorable mentions in editorial sections or on-air. Some threaten television program content by canceling or avoiding advertising before, during, or even after programs that special-interest groups criticize. It matters little whether the interest group has previewed the program in question; the threat of dissatisfaction with a pending program can be enough to prompt advertisers to cancel contracts. The staff of *Ms.* magazine has said often that advertiser pressure was a major reason the magazine went ad-free, putting the burden of paying for the magazine on subscribers and organizations that are willing to pay the magazine's costs. The question here is whether it is right that only very strong and very determined media can withstand advertiser pressures.

■ THE MASS MEDIA AND ADVERTISING ETHICS

Dishonesty, deception, and duplicity are not limited to advertisers and advertising. Look at some situations that advertising-supported media face—situations that can spell the life or death of media and of content presented in the media.

The mass media that accept advertising are tightrope performers. They have a big stake in the advertising they accept and they cannot be casual about accepting any that might be inappropriate, offensive, or unacceptable to major groups within the audiences they serve—the same audiences that attract advertisers.

Some media try to appear to be open and editorially independent. They accept advertisements for products and services but reserve the right to criticize the use of those products and services. Few advertisers take kindly to such policies, however, unless the particular medium offers them superb demographics—audiences composed of people who respond favorably to the advertised products and services. Here, again, very strong media can be critical of advertised products and services, but few are.

Questions that need to be asked regularly of the mass media and of advertisers include the following: Can a mass medium accept all advertising? Advertising that its own staff members condemn or criticize because they believe the products or services are contrary to their audience's needs or interests? Can an advertised product be acceptable for one audience and not another? For one time slot and not another? Is such accommodation honest or fair, or deceptive to advertisers, audiences, or both?

Although public radio and public television do not accept paid advertising, they do accept underwriting and carry out extensive fundraising activities. Their acknowledgment of these donations has become more obtrusive, prompting at least one question: Are credits for sponsorship really advertisements supporting stations that profess to be ad-free?

The few publications that are reader-supported have big subscription prices and they usually make appeals to individuals and organizations for memberships or underwriting funds. These publications do not want to alienate their readers, so they establish sponsor-acceptability standards.

There are other ethical pitfalls facing the mass media. For example, is it honest to undersell the published advertising rates? To "sell off the rate card?" To lower ad rates selectively for one advertiser or another? Is it ethical for advertising sales people to coerce editorial staff to trade editorial or program space and time for ad contracts? To promise "puffs" in exchange for advertising contracts? Is it ethical to inflate audience numbers or to give false audience demographics to potential advertisers? I hope you will answer "No" to all of those questions—or have convincing arguments to defend questionable and unethical business practices.

Advertising rates are based on the audiences that the media draw. The media must give honest numbers to advertisers and potential advertisers and they must also have honest tactics for generating and retaining audiences. Circulation audits and audience studies help guard against misstatements. Circulation auditing services, such as the Audit Bureau of Circulation (ABC) for print and A. C. Nielsen for television, are retained by media to verify these numbers. These services are costly but advertisers and ad agencies want independent assurances that the media they pay offer the audiences they want to reach. Experience has convinced major advertisers that unaudited, unverified media don't deserve their serious attention—and dollars.

Few media people like to admit how advertising can directly affect mass media content. But television and radio networks and stations are very conscious of the fact that advertisers don't want their products to be connected with controversy, so broadcasters may refuse to air potentially controversial programs or ask producers to modify the content to make the programs less controversial. Publications are more specialized than network television but they are not immune from advertiser pressures. Audiences can be deprived of significant ideas when the media that pretend to be open arenas are not, and when advertisers assume the prerogatives of media content decision makers.

The mass media need to monitor and keep their own business and advertising activities ethical, and to guard against offending their audiences. To this end, they have practices and procedures for evaluating advertising before they accept it for publication or broadcast. Years ago, many newspapers prohibited advertising for alcoholic beverages. Some also prohibited advertisements for patent medicines, abortion clinics, and tobacco products. Some newspapers and magazines currently prohibit ads for guns, X-rated films, "gentlemen's clubs," products made from or tested by animals, personal care products, and controversial political and social organizations such as the Ku Klux Klan and neo-Nazi groups. Some media reject advertisements for foods and beauty products with ingredients they believe are unhealthy, or abortion clinics or pro-life counselors, or even term paper "consultants." To date, none of these prohibitions—except those against some controversial groups or ideas—has sparked serious complaints that an advertiser's freedom of the press has been infringed, at least not complaints that the public was willing to support. Some other media companies accept any and all advertising because they just want the revenues or because they believe in the letter and spirit of the First Amendment. A few even editorialize against advertisements they carry, assured that their viewpoints are equally protected by the First Amendment but not, of course, from ad cancellations.

Television broadcasters, on the other hand, have been required by the government to reject cigarette advertising and to limit advertising, particularly during Saturday morning children's programs. Network advertising for other products and services is scrutinized for acceptability before it is allowed to be broadcast. Television and radio stations have their own standards for acceptability, usually based on whether the advertisement will violate viewers' or listeners' tastes—and those tastes vary by region, channel, and time of day. Anyone in doubt should analyze the ads on early-morning, daytime, early-evening, prime-time, and late-night television.

Standards of advertising acceptability have become more complicated than lists of products to be avoided. The men and women in charge of advertising acceptability must judge advertising messages as well as products, and they often have to negotiate on deadline. They fear last-minute contracts and late arrival (or withdrawal) of ad copy as much as they fear ads that mislead or misinform. They work to protect the reputations of the publications, networks, and stations they work for and to minimize controversy that might affect circulations or ratings. It would be nice to be able to say that standards of advertising acceptability are based on more virtuous foundations, but most are not. Libertarians equate acceptability standards with censorship. But considering the impact of advertising messages on the specific audiences of specific media, carefully developed acceptability standards are a mark of social responsibility and a way for media to describe clearly, to advertisers and audiences alike, what they stand for.

An advertising technique that concerns the media is the "advertorial," paid advertising that is prepared to look like editorial copy, entertainment, or feature programming. Although advertisers usually make sure that advertorials are labeled as such, many of them copy the newspaper or magazine's type and editorial format so thoroughly that readers find it hard to distinguish the advertising copy from the publications' editorial offerings. Magazine publishers have become especially concerned about advertorials that visually mimic their magazines' editorial pages, thus confusing readers; the Magazine Publishers Association (MPA) has issued guidelines for advertorials. The MPA is a voluntary organization, however; not all magazines belong to it and observance of the MPA guidelines thus is limited.

Veteran journalist Gilbert Cranberg has expressed fear that if the difference between advertising and editorial blurs further, especially if the advertising sections are prepared by a newspaper's editorial staff members, the traditional protections of the First Amendment may become eroded (Stein, 1993). His concern is probably welcomed by newspaper staff members who dislike being asked to write promotional copy for advertising sections. One solution to both problems is to assign special advertising supplements or sections to a department and staff clearly separated from the paper's editorial department.

A natural question arises from this discussion: how obvious must the separation of editorial and advertising be? Both large and small mass media, because they are market-driven, often create departments and features that parallel advertising interests, such as travel or food sections. A magazine's editorial staff may regularly brief the advertising sales staff about pending editorial contents so that the latter can solicit advertising that matches editorial subjects. Many readers appreciate finding advertisements that complement the information contained in the articles they read. Others, however, may distrust the editorial content *because* of its association with the advertisement. Ethically, are editorial briefings good business practice because they eventually serve readers, or unethical conflicts of interest?

The television version of advertorials has begun to proliferate on cable channels and a few over-the-air stations. There is no reason to believe that other TV channels will be immune to them. The most deceptive among them, prepared by advertisers, appear to be interviews, demonstrations, or discussions. The production quality competes with network- and station-produced programs. However, they are prepared for one purpose—to promote or sell specific products and services, especially health and beauty products, home improvement products and tools, and food-processing equipment—and they are one-sided. Some of the programs are offered in videocassettes, too, in an attempt to increase direct sales.

Although the products and the program contents may not raise serious ethical questions, there is one problem: viewers might not realize that the programs they are watching have as their sole purpose the sale of a product or service. Video News Releases (VNRs) are common, and present many of the same problems.

The potential for deception increases with every new publication or channel. Cable television operators have added many channels in recent years, and will no doubt add more as will satellite delivery services. Viewers increasingly need to be informed when they are watching programs that are totally advertising, produced only to sell a specific manufacturer's product or a specific organization's services.

Advertising is important to the social, cultural, and economic life of the nation, to individuals as well as to groups, and to the mass media. If advertising and advertisers do not uphold high ethical standards, they and the nation suffer.

■ MERRILL: Commentary

Here we have the ends-means problem. Because the purpose (end) of advertising is to create images and sell products, there (is? is not?) a need for it to be truthful. The deontologist on this issue (Carol Reuss) would say that there is a need for truth because truth is *per se* an ethical principle; David Gordon, taking the teleological position, contends that because advertising needs to create good images and make sales, and because people understand this, it can be excused from telling the truth.

This seems a rather strange "controversy" for an ethics book, but here it is and we must deal with it. One would think the teleological position is really pragmatics, not ethics, and that Machiavellian considerations dominate instead of more ethical ones. But, of course, there are other times in ethical discourse where truth is set aside because of possible consequences, so it could be that this is what we find here.

For example, it might be contended that people *need* to accept some advertising messages, such as the warnings that smoking is dangerous to one's health. Is it, then, not ethical to stretch the truth somewhat, or to hide certain peripheral facts, in order to accomplish your purpose? Such a case *can* be made, weak though I think it is. Does a beneficial end justify the means (even when the means may be unethical)? I agree with Immanuel Kant that it does not. But this kind of rationalization is used in political advertising all the time. In order to keep "that scoundrel out of office" where he might be destructive to the people's best interest, it is justifiable to paint him as more villainous than he really is. If truth were the criterion for political advertising, there would be very little such advertising.

So we can see that, in a very broadly interpreted altruistic sense, advertising that is less than truthful *can* be considered ethical if we are thinking pragmatically or teleologically. The purpose of advertising is to sell, we are often told; therefore, if tampering with the truth helps us to sell, then what is wrong with that? Of course, what is wrong is that it ignores the normal ethical consideration of truth-telling; it contributes to misrepresentation, to providing false images, to exaggerated expectations, to unwarranted expenditure of money, and often to getting something that does not live up to promises.

Again we hear the voice of Kant: *Just tell the truth*. Be principled; feel a duty to truth-telling, without worrying about possible consequences. But then, from somewhere inside our rationality, comes the voice of the consequence-oriented ethicist: Think of the expectations of your employer. Think about the purpose of your work. Think about the good that selling this product (or this candidate) may do for others.

The perennial question arises: truth or consequences?

Advertising—at least certain kinds—can lead to obvious benefits to others and to society as a whole. But advertising can also result in overspending, conspicuous consumption, and the inculcation of unrealistic and frustrating expectations. Should truth play a key role in such advertising? Machiavelli would have said "Yes"—*if* your purposes can be secured by telling the truth. If not, then it would be permissible—even wise—to tamper with the truth to the extent necessary to achieve your ends.

If truth were the criterion for political advertising, there would be very little such advertising.

It seems to be all right with Gordon that advertising can play fast and loose with the truth; after all, he might say it is no more than a form of "commercial poetry" and that departing from the truth is simply creative embellishment. I believe that audiences of advertising *expect* and *desire* truth even though they may recognize that they seldom get it. It is regretful that Reuss does not take a firmer position against untruthful advertising in her arguments. She does, I think quite effectively, point out other potential problem areas in advertising ethics (such as the use of advertorials). But her position on truth in advertising is somewhat puzzling. For example, she says that "[u]nethical deception in advertisements can take many forms." Is she implying that *some* deception is ethical? I would think that *all* deception is unethical. But, then, maybe not in today's permissive moral climate.

Gordon is taking the Machiavellian view—at least a modified version of it. Reuss does seem to try to keep truth at the core of her ethical posture—agreeing, although at times half-heartedly, with Kant that truth-telling is a categorical imperative. Just who is correct? Who has the right ethical perspective on this truth-in-advertising question? I can't give an answer. Both perspectives may well be correct (ethical), depending on which megatheory of ethics one accepts. I prefer the Kantian view that *never* in advertising should the advertiser resort to untruths. Perhaps the reader will be able to cut his or her way through the thickets of ethical confusion and find a comfortable and satisfying clearing in which to find a moral resting place. But I doubt it. As with all the controversies in this book, there is simply no clear and completely satisfying answer. But there is no reason for us to discontinue the search.

REFERENCES

Blewett, Steve. (Winter 1994). "Poetry and Public Relations: Reality in a Waterball of Glass." *Journalism Educator* 48(4), pp. 39–46.

Bok, Sissela. (1979). *Lying: Moral Choice in Public and Private Life.* New York: Vintage Books.

Elliott, Stuart. (November 26, 1993). "Advertising: In Creating a Spot, Many Say There's Nothing Like the Real Thing." *The New York Times*, p. D15.

Fink, Conrad C. (1988). *Media Ethics: In the Newsroom and Beyond.* New York: McGraw-Hill.

"Joe Camel's Rights." (February 26, 1994). Editorial, *The Boston Globe*, p. 16.

Johannesen, Richard L. (1996). *Ethics in Human Communication*, 4th ed. Prospect Heights, IL: Waveland Press.

Knowlton, Steven R. (1997). *Moral Reasoning for Journalists: Cases and Comments.* Westport, CT: Praeger.

Lambeth, Edmund B. (1992). *Committed Journalism: An Ethic for the Profession*, 2nd ed. Bloomington: Indiana University Press.

Levitt, Theodore. (July–August 1970). "The Morality (?) of Advertising." *Harvard Business Review*, pp. 84–92.

Mander, Jerry. (1993). "Four Arguments for the Elimination of Advertising." In Edd Applegate, Sharon Brock, Joseph Pisani, and Eric Zanot, eds., *Advertising: Concepts, Strategies, and Issues.* Dubuque, IA: Kendall/Hunt.

Stein, M. L. (September 18, 1993). "Advertorials and the First Amendment." *Editor & Publisher*, p. 24.

Stewart, James B. (October 31, 1994). "Grand Illusion." *The New Yorker*, pp. 64–81.

CHAPTER 14

CONFLICTS OF INTEREST

Although Caesar's wife was required to be above suspicion, the need for journalists' reputations to be that high is more problematic.

The craft, and possible profession, of journalism does require *credibility*, a reputation for honesty—whether or not truth (as discussed in Chapter 4) is attainable.

It is public trust in the media, engendered by its credibility, that is essential for the media to serve *any* of its public functions. In Harold Lasswell's (1948) formulation, they are: surveillance of the environment, correlation or helping society make policy, and cultural transmission and socialization, to which we might add advertising and entertainment. The journalist *must* be credible if he or she is to be successful. Those involved in persuasive or entertainment communication—copywriters, filmmakers, editors, artists—in any of the mass media may also need to keep an eye on their credibility, but the profession and craft of journalism absolutely depends on it.

But this doesn't mean that the journalist must be a eunuch, an abstainer, or a saint. Communicators are human beings, and enjoy the rights of other citizens, including the right to privacy—even though journalists often are accused of invading the privacy of others (see Chapter 8).

But that right to do what one chooses ends where the journalist's credibility is seriously and validly called into question.

The debate in this chapter is really over where to draw the line. What ethical and practical limitations should be placed on communicators that will enable them to retain their credibility, do their job—and live their lives?

David Gordon takes the position that the journalist must be completely above suspicion, while John Michael Kittross asks that readers, viewers, and listeners trust media practitioners until or unless they are proven unreliable in the messages they construct.

But, unlike other chapters where extreme positions are taken, both Kittross and Gordon agree on *some* points about conflicts of interest:

• There is no excuse for extortion or prostitution, for lying to the audience about something in exchange for money or other favors. This is cheating the public. For example, the now-illegal practice of "payola," where disk jockeys accepted money (and sometimes drugs and sex partners) from record companies in exchange for playing certain records, violated the public trust that disk jockeys use only professional judgement and consider only the public interest in choosing records.

• Any restrictions on practitioners should apply as well to publishers, general managers, and owners.

In other words, we both reject true conflicts of interest—but this chapter actually is dealing with the *perception* of such conflict, not the reality.

■ KITTROSS: The credibility of the mass media will not be lost if honest practitioners are left unrestricted in their roles as citizens and humans.

Because this chapter is engaged in drawing a line, rather than in supporting an extreme position, my part of this chapter will look briefly, and in an interwoven rather than outlined text, at the broadcast or print journalist's involvement in the following:

- partisan political activity
- other social, religious, or economic movements
- presenting ideas
- political leanings or other biases of publishers and licensees
- civic journalism
- acceptance of gifts
- the "revolving door" between government and journalism
- reporting on matters affecting the reporter on the way to what might be a general rule about conflicts of interest.

First, let's make sure that we understand what is meant by "conflict of interest." The primary interest of the journalist should be to inform the public. Every other goal—money, fame, associations—might well lead to a conflict. For example, a business reporter who provides the audience with information that might result in a rise or fall in the price of a particular security is doing her job. But if that reporter engages in "insider trading," buying or selling the stock for his own account before publishing the story, that is a clear conflict of interest—as well as being illegal.

Further, merely being familiar—or even emotionally involved—with some of the "players" in a story is not necessarily a conflict of interest. True professionals can always keep the public interest in mind—or step down if they can't. When the passenger liner *Andrea Doria* sank in 1956 after colliding with another vessel, radio newsman and commentator Edward P. Morgan ad libbed a superb detailed report on the disaster and on the arrival of survivors in New York. It wasn't until the next day, when he reported calmly on a miracle, that his listeners realized that the rescued 14-year old girl he had reported missing and presumably dead the day before was his own daughter. In no way was his audience shortchanged. (Morgan, 1963, pp. 238–249).

With respect to engaging in partisan political activity, the rights of American citizens should not be abridged by others. If a citizen who happens to be a media practitioner wishes to vote in a partisan election, there should be no objection or hindrance.

Yet there are those who look at the results of somewhat invalid and unreliable surveys of Washington reporters, see that a majority of those few who answered the question claimed to have voted Democratic in the last election, and use that as "evidence" that "the press" is biased against Republicans.

While a bit more scientific than the claim that anchors used "raised eyebrows" to get across their "liberal" ideas, the use of such so-called research really has a hidden motive: to reduce the ability of the press to function. Once the idea is accepted that neutrality is the same as ignorance or not caring, then only those who don't care, or don't know anything about a story, will be acceptable reporters. The remaining question is whether brainwashed humans or computers will be used as reporters in the future.

A handful of newspeople do refuse to exercise their ballot, because of fear that their choice might become known—or that it might subconsciously affect their reporting, writing, or editing. However, I believe that this extreme act probably separates the reporter, editor, columnist, or commentator so far from the political life of the nation and the community that it actually precludes them from acting as objective communicators.

So, voting is "in."

But what about contributing funds to a political candidate? Writing promotional copy for a campaign? Conducting surveys? Pushing doorbells? Running for office? Being a member of a candidate's entourage—and then writing about the candidate (favorably or unfavorably) without letting the public know of your commitment?

And would the rules be different if one were, for example, a sports reporter or other communicator who wasn't professionally involved in the political arena?

The appropriate ethical line can be found, but not easily. In law as in practice, the giving of financial contributions is protected by the First Amendment. On the other hand, some election laws require the names of contributors and the amount they give to be published. This could affect the reputation for impartiality of the media person (including the publisher or general manager), who shouldn't ignore this factor when contributing to political campaigns. Permission for freelance writing of campaign literature and similar activity should be obtained in advance from one's editor—or whoever is the custodian of credibility for the paper or station. Other political activity that puts the journalist in the public eye, even as part of an anonymous crowd, may well affect the credibility of the journalist and the medium. But even that kind of behavior isn't a clear "no-no." Shouldn't a statehouse reporter be able to run for office in her child's PTA, or a reporter on the police beat become a trustee of the town library?

Shouldn't a statehouse reporter be able to run for office in her child's PTA . . . ?

A black newspaper editor who took part in the "Million Man March" of 1996, and a female reporter who participated in a pro-choice rally, were equally engaged in legal and moral activity that often isn't partisan or electoral politics.

But there are those who say "no" to any such First Amendment activity, on the grounds that it precludes writing objectively about the topic. Reporters have been transferred, or fired, for participating as a member of a mass of people who are concerned about a particular matter—even though the courts usually have overturned such transfers or dismissals.

Why does it preclude them from writing objectively? The short answer is that it needn't do so. I believe that there are few who enter the profession of journalism who aren't capable of placing their own feelings and opinions on the back burner, and writing about subjects dispassionately and objectively. As an editor, I often edit articles with which I disagree—but I've never been accused of doing anything other than improving the article in question, strengthening and sharpening its author's ideas, and sprucing up its English. While I might want to argue with the author—and sometimes do, in a separate editorial—I would never use my position as editor to disadvantage the writer's expression of his or her ideas. And I would hope that no reporter would use that position to unfairly misrepresent sources or subjects and their ideas. The public needs to be informed of this standard.

I do not wish to disparage the need to retain credibility. Yet, some of the very licensees and publishers who object most strongly to reporters and editors' involvement in civic and political activity are willing to use their station or newspaper to ride their own hobbyhorses, such as "unfair taxation," "development," or "the environment." Sometimes they are blatant, as William Randolph Hearst was; sometimes they are more subtle, as is today's *Wall Street Journal;* and sometimes they hide their biases under the guise of "civic journalism." True, what is sauce for the goose should be sauce for the gander, and all involvement by an owner shouldn't be condemned out of hand—after all, it is their candy store and, as quoted in Chapter 11, A. J. Liebling once reminded us that "freedom of the press is guaranteed only to those who own one" (1961).

A philosopher considering the "public sphere" concept of Jurgen Habermas might say that civic journalism is merely a cynical and Machiavellian attempt by the press to regain the moral ground and public function it lost when it became commodified with the advent of the Penny Press in the 19th century, after the heyday of the coffeehouse where discourse on economics, politics, literature, and the events of the day reigned.

There might need to be some special safeguards for the public when the media are using civic journalism. For example, *if* the staff collectively agrees that the topic is a significant one, and *if* the public is aware of the publisher's or licensee's own financial, social, or other stake in the matter, and *if* a multiplicity of viewpoints are available to the audience, then the boss's pet project does no harm.

A pernicious belief on the part of the public is that journalists are prostitutes, and cheap ones at that. A look at the newer editions of the codes of the Society of Professional Journalists and the Radio-Television News Directors Association (see Chapter 3) shows that this idea has taken hold. More and more attention is being paid to how reporters should avoid the appearance of impropriety—many media organizations even forbid the acceptance of a cup of coffee or a beer from a potential news source, or a key ring from an exhibitor at a professional convention.

At one time, in government as in the media, there were reasonable limits to the offering and acceptance of gifts or services. Yes, there were excesses, thinly disguised bribes. Now, however, even the smallest gift is considered to be an unacceptable gratuity. This adherence to a "no tolerance" standard means that the friendly, accepting, or sharing reporter or editor is being accused of weakness at best and venality at worst. So, journalists are expected to pay their own admission to events, avoid barroom or dinner sessions at which they might learn something from a source, learn not to relate to their subjects and sources as human beings, and forgo "freebies" ranging from coffee cups to White House "Air Force One" jackets.

It used to be that the definition of honest politicians was that they "stayed bought" if bribed. Today's definition of honest journalists is that they *avoid any appearance* of obligation to anyone. It isn't actual bribery or relationships that are important, but the possibility that paranoid readers or viewers might dismiss everything of value in a story or program because of some minor connection that could be interpreted as being "bought."

While we might dismiss this definition on practical grounds—it really does take much more than a meal or a friendly word to bribe a reporter—domestic paranoia, fed by the media ever since Watergate, and the low wages and slender expense accounts "enjoyed" by media practitioners place vulnerable media in an uncomfortable limelight.

Almost every White House press officer and many other government officials were once working journalists—and many of them return to journalism (including stars such as Bill Moyers and Diane Sawyer). The ritual is common enough to have its own label: "the revolving door." Some, like Pat Buchanan and Pierre Salinger, have made the trip in both directions—more than once. Here, for a change, common sense usually prevails: when the revolving door propels a person from the political world "inside the Beltway" to the media, political analyses by those who change their collars tend to be ignored by both the media and the public, at least during the remaining days of the administration in which they served . . . or until they have proven themselves again as journalists.

This is not a Kantian "categorical imperative" situation. The journalist should strive for a pragmatic Aristotelian Golden Mean. A few political activities—such as voting—should not worry anyone; many others require judgement; and only a few—such as secretly using one's media organization for partisan political content—should be condemned. The public, as well as the media, also needs to make these distinctions.

Sometimes what goes on in a reporter's "real world" is beneficial to her role in the media world. For example, many stories start when an alert reporter notices something out of the ordinary in his daily life, or makes a mental connection that hasn't been made before. The origin can be close to home—award-winning medical or environmental reporting often involves covering an illness or other problem of a close friend or relative. Reporting on a restricted event in which one is involved may be the only way in which the larger public can learn about the event, since those managing such events often exclude the press and other outsiders. Yet, those editors who believe that the ideal reporter is 100% dispassionate and aloof might reject such stories out of hand—to the detriment of their viewers and readers.

The status of the television station or newspaper involved in "civic" or "public journalism"—a movement to use the mobilizing power of the media to work with citizens on the solutions to public problems—should be no different than participation by a reporter in a political, economic, or social movement. (Patterson, 1997; Gade, 1997)

Utilitarianism reminds us of the ethical goal of "the most good for the most people"—and supporters of civic journalism maintain that, if the media are an interoperative part of the society, then the use of media resources to solve and not merely to report problems is appropriate. (Those opposed to the civic journalism movement believe that it is destructive to all of the goals of journalism. This is an on-going debate of journalistic philosophy, not applied ethics.)

The entire argument calling for not just neutrality and objectivity, but the *appearance* of neutrality and objectivity, may have a hidden motive: to reduce both the *ability* and the *power* of the media. The legal profession has similarly attempted to neuter juries by demanding that they be *ignorant* rather than merely *impartial*.

Ignorance, on the part of reporters, is never to the benefit of their audience. And learning a great deal about a subject (particularly politics) tends to allow a person—including reporters, editors and readers—to make the valid decisions that any citizen in a democracy should be making.

The real problem is that it takes a lot of work to analyze what someone is writing or presenting in order to detect either conscious or unconscious bias. And then it takes judgment to decide if that bias is significant. It requires knowledge of the subject matter and its context, a willingness to listen to other points of view, and an effort to go beyond the slogans and soundbites.

We ask this, sometimes, of our viewers, listeners, and readers. Why shouldn't we demand it of our editors?

The obvious answer, like so many other things, isn't conspiracy or dishonesty. It is that it is so much easier merely to neuter the press, and toss out anything that shows a reasoned point of view—from anyone who knows something, has thought about the matter, and come to a conclusion.

Obviously, I believe we should not encourage media ignorance and emasculation. I don't want *my* information to come from people who don't give a hoot about anything. I believe that we should educate and train media professionals—and, to the extent possible, their audiences—to preserve their professional purposes and responsibilities as well as their credibility, never losing sight of their place in both their profession and their society.

So, if some reporter or editor is aware of a real conflict of interest, it must be avoided. If that something *might* be thought of by the public as a potential conflict of interest, it is the job of the reporter or editor to evaluate his or her actions in the light of possible damage to the credibility of the media organization that hired them. Let's trust the reporter or editor to be professional. If a financial, social, or psychological bribe is reflected in content produced by a media person, there should be some means of removing such a person from their beat—or the profession. In any case, the public should be informed—in the same program or publication—of all significant relationships, including the possibility of such conflicts. This is done today in *Columbia Journalism Review*, *American Journalism Review*, *Quill*, and those newspapers and television news programs that are concerned about their real as contrasted to their surface reputations.

Thus, while we need guideposts, we certainly do not want our media professionals to be separated from society or treated like Calpurnia—Julius Caesar's wife.

■ GORDON: Journalists and public relations practitioners must abstain from any "private" activities that might be seen as creating conflicts of interest in their professional endeavors.

This is a very difficult argument for me to make, especially since I felt very strongly on the other side of the question as a young reporter a decade or four ago. But my opinion then was wrong!

John Michael Kittross has outlined well the wide range of potential conflicts of interest that journalists may encounter. But he seems to gloss over one that is among the greatest dangers in this area . . . the difficulty of maintaining an outsider's perspective when one has become friends (sometimes good friends) with some of the "'players' in a story."

If you socialize regularly with some of those players, it is obviously going to be difficult to report a story that makes them look bad, and "step(ping) down" from the beat isn't going to get the story written in a timely fashion. For this reason, many newspapers rotate their beat reporters every few years. This has the disadvantage of moving people around just about the time that they are really learning their beats, but it also means that they are no longer covering the same "players" with whom they may have become friendly.

One of the most egregious cases of reporter-source friendship was the one between Ben Bradlee, then a *Newsweek* bureau reporter in Washington, and John F.

Kennedy. The friendship began in the late 1950s and continued through Kennedy's presidency. It gave Bradlee far more access to major stories than was enjoyed by other reporters, but it made him far less of a detached reporter than were many other journalists. (Bradlee, 1995; Remnick, 1995, especially at p. 79)

I don't carry my conflict of interest concerns to the extreme of suggesting that reporters shouldn't vote in partisan (or other) elections. The ballot, after all, is secret and the public isn't going to know for whom an individual journalist's ballot was cast. But I would certainly argue that reporters (and editors . . . and publishers) who have *any* connection with public affairs in their professional capacities absolutely cannot be active in political circles (partisan or nonpartisan).

The key concern here—as Kittross points out—is the journalist's credibility. But Kittross's discussion doesn't begin to come to grips with the enormous potential that many "civic" or "outside professional" activities have for destroying not just an individual journalist's credibility, but that of his or her own news medium and of the media more broadly.

First Amendment rights are a spurious issue here.

For example, I'm appalled that he even suggests that "[p]ermission for freelance writing of campaign literature . . . should be obtained in advance from one's editor—or [the medium's] custodian of credibility." This type of political activity, by any news people regardless of their specific assignment, can too easily be misinterpreted by the public and result in a wide-ranging loss of confidence. Any editor who would give permission for that kind of activity shouldn't occupy such a position of responsibility. For once, Kant's categorical imperative emphasis on a universal rule makes very good sense as a guideline.

And so does a utilitarian approach. The media person's freedom to participate fully in societal activities may well have to be curtailed. But the loss to those individuals (and perhaps to society, as well) is far outweighed by the benefits to society of having news and information media that retain credibility with their audiences. Without that, the media's ability to provide the information needed to make the society work well will be seriously impaired.

In the process of protecting credibility, the media will also be improving the likelihood that their employees will abstain from activities that conceivably might produce actual (conscious or unconscious) bias in their coverage. Such activities will, in most cases, include a ban on taking part in entertainment-related activities, as Daniel Schorr did in 1995 when he appeared in the movie *The Net*, a development that raised much broader questions for one newspaper ombudsman:

> . . . at a time when Disney is buying the leading network news operation, when *Hard Copy* is the hottest source of O.J. trial tidbits and when *New York Newsday* is shut down like a sitcom with bad ratings, some media observers worry about the larger problem that Schorr's cameo reflects: a confusing and dangerous commingling—*journotainment*. (Jurkowitz, 1995, p. 70)

First Amendment rights are a spurious issue here. Of course, such rights are retained by mass media employees, and if push comes to shove, the courts *should* uphold those rights. But push should never have to come to shove in this area. The issue here is ethics, not legal rights. Mass media people should recognize that, in regard to real *or* perceived conflicts of interest, what matters is not the legal protections that they can make use of (or hide behind), but how far short of those legal limits they *ought* to stop.

This concern should also apply to media companies, which could be harming their own credibility by allowing their names and copies of their news sets to be used in feature films such as *Deep Impact* (MSNBC) or *Contact* (CNN).

Perhaps Kittross is correct that most media people can remain impartial despite their strong feelings on a subject, but I'm much less sanguine about that. Even if he's right, though, the problem is whether the public perception will recognize and acknowledge that impartiality. I don't think this is likely, partly because the public has been conditioned by the media to believe that scandal and gossip are among the highest forms of news—and that *everyone* might have a skeleton in the closet.

Among the situations that raise serious conflict of interest concerns is the practice of some journalists—including ABC's Sam Donaldson, among others—of accepting fees for speaking to groups that they sometimes have to cover. Donaldson has argued that he is being paid more for his celebrity status than for his journalistic reputation, and perhaps he's right (Knowlton, 1997, pp. 172–175). But even if he is correct, the *appearance* of a possible conflict of interest produces a serious risk of lowered credibility.

The question might also be asked as to whether the *size* of the fee makes any difference. Is it a conflict of interest to accept a four- or five-digit speaking fee, but acceptable to take a lesser honorarium? Does speaking for no fee prevent any taint or appearance of taint? What about speaking for a minimal fee to nonprofit organizations (which may well be involved in newsmaking themselves)? There are no easy answers here, and Kant's insistence on an absolute standard makes even more sense in these cases.

Similar strictures, it seems to me, are even more appropriate in regard to media owners. The many polls that reveal the public's concerns about media partiality/unfairness testify to a wide-ranging problem involving owners every bit as much as those concerns reflect on working journalists.

If media owners are serious about establishing credibility with their audiences, they need to hold both their employees *and* themselves to standards of conduct that will enhance rather than damage the public's attitude toward their media. That means, among other things, not only avoiding truly biased content but also the appearance of partiality that their activities may produce.

Using this standard, it was wrong for Alvah Chapman, publisher of *The Miami Herald,* to take a leading role in the opposition to South Florida casino gambling in the late 1970s, no matter how virtuous he may have thought that cause to be. His activism raised questions both within his newsroom and in the community at large, despite almost universal agreement that Chapman was not attempting to influence his newspaper's coverage of the issue.

This standard raises serious questions about the roles played by publishers in civic life, particularly in smaller communities. Meyer (1983) found that publishers belong to an average of seven local civic groups, far more than the number of memberships of their staffers. That can easily lead to the same kind of coziness with the community power structure that can come to exist between beat reporters and their sources. In fairness, it must also be noted that there is a danger that if journalists belong to fewer groups than do their readers, they run the danger of losing touch with (and perhaps diminishing their acceptance by) those readers. (Gaziano and McGrath, 1987).

Perhaps, in this regard, there needs to be an Aristotelian middle ground that would allow passive membership rather than active participation, but only in groups that do not overlap into areas covered by a reporter.

Kittross *is* on target when he discusses the way in which owners' biases have been advanced over the decades by the media they own. He's *way* off target when he uses "civic journalism" as a whipping boy to attack the subtle disguising of some of those biases. There can be some serious and valid arguments made in opposition to civic journalism, but masking owners' biases or stakes or pet projects isn't one of them. Civic or communitarian journalism is far more than the simplistic—or monolithic—process that Kittross described as the media working "with citizens on the solutions to public problems." As David Craig has pointed out, there are several varieties of civic/public journalism, and

> . . . communitarian journalism is no more a single entity than is communitarianism in the broader realm of social theory. It is not always as radical a departure from current press theory and practice as the single term might suggest. (1996, p. 116)

The so-called "revolving door" problem is one that is even broader than Kittross portrays it, and involves more than just going back and forth between government and the news media. In addition, increasingly, it now involves news and public relations people moving back and forth across the divide that used to separate them.

It used to be that once you crossed the line from journalism to public relations, you had a hard time getting back into journalism if you chose to do so. It took many years for CBS' Mike Wallace to regain credibility after appearing on entertainment programs and in commercials. Today, that seems to be an almost nonexistent problem, and there is considerable two-way traffic between news and PR slots. That's probably a good thing in the sense that it helps establish public relations as a potential source of information rather than flackery, and helps to cement the symbiotic relationship that enhances both good journalism and good public relations.

But it does set up the more general credibility problem that Kittross noted in regard to political figures becoming news analysts. That's less of a perceived issue if the person has been doing PR behind the scenes, rather than having a lot of public visibility. Either way, though, there is the potential for bias to creep into the work of the ex-PR person, simply because of familiarity with one side of the issue. (The same dangers exist for any mass communicator, just because we're each most familiar with the context in which we grew up—but that's a different discussion; see Chapter 7.) These dangers are, of course, an argument for careful editing—and responsible oversight by editors—in all situations.

A thoughtful essay on ethical standards in public relations concludes that ethical practices should take into account the overall good of society, not just "enlightened self-interest" (Martinson, 1994). But, since the ethical public relations practitioner is also supposed to demonstrate loyalty to the client, there is a different kind of conflict of interest at the core of the PR business for those who accept both of those standards. This conflict goes beyond either credibility or the possible direct public benefits of public relations activity, and its resolution will not be a simple task.

I *do* agree with Kittross's contention that conflict of interest concerns can be carried to ridiculous extremes when they are applied with zero tolerance to even the smallest of gifts. A very pragmatic city alderman once said that he solved this problem for himself by accepting nothing that couldn't be disposed of at one sitting—i.e., a cup of coffee or even dinner was okay but a full bottle of liquor wasn't.

I'd suggest that if there are concerns about the dinner, that's easily solved by paying for it yourself. And I believe that rules against gifts, like the one at the old Chicago *Daily News*, can take these concerns to ludicrous levels. As the story was related to me, a guard in the lobby one December afternoon turned away the proverbial "little old lady" from somewhere in Chicago's northern suburbs, who had trekked downtown to deliver a couple of boxes of Christmas cookies to acquaintances among the paper's reporters and editors. I suspect that even Kant could have formulated a universal principle that would have allowed those cookies to be delivered . . . and consumed.

It's important to remember that journalism as an institution—civic, public, traditional, or whatever--should be viewed through a different lens than the one used to scrutinize individuals' potential conflicts of interest. As Kittross notes, when the media institution as a whole is involved, it becomes a question of basic philosophy rather than one of individual ethics. The problems still exist, though, as the Gannett chain has discovered. That chain's guidelines require its journalists to report any *appearance* of a conflict, and to refrain from covering any activity where a *real* conflict exists. This creates a tension with the Gannett goal of stressing closer ties between journalists and their communities (Hardie, 1995, p. 17; see also Hardie, 1996).

Kittross, however, manages to oversimplify just what's at issue here. There is no real need to focus on resisting the neutering of the press or the elimination of input from informed journalists—or public relations practitioners. No responsible person is suggesting that reporters or PR people should be uninformed about their topics. I fail to see how "ignorance" by a reporter could possibly be equated to abstinence from overt participation in an activity or cause, as Kittross seems to do. And a journalist's personal experiences are not the same thing as his or her participation in some organized activity or cause, Kittross's argument to the contrary.

There are also better solutions for this whole concern than relying on some vague formula that calls on media people to evaluate their actions on the basis of potential damage to credibility. Such an approach smacks far too much of situational ethics to be a useful guideline, unless "credibility" is elevated to the status of a Kantian standard. It wouldn't be helpful even if human nature were more inclined to weigh things impartially, rather than looking—perhaps subconsciously—for the result that will allow one to take part in the desired activity.

The need for impartiality, and for the incontrovertible *appearance* of fairness, does indeed require journalists to remove themselves from many aspects of society and to adopt the "Caesar's wife" approach. To a somewhat lesser degree, public relations practitioners face many of the same constraints, since their activities in the public sphere should not undermine their dedication—or their perceived dedication—to the causes they have espoused and the clients they represent.

In some ways, these strictures may be unfair to the journalists and public relations people. But this is a price they should be willing to pay, in return for the credibility that both types of mass communicators need to have. Their only justifiable complaint would be if their bosses—the publishers, broadcast station owners, PR agency heads—refuse to live by the same standards.

■ MERRILL: Commentary

John Michael Kittross and David Gordon have just slyly slipped in several problems in journalism, subsuming them under the rubric of "conflict of interest." What seems to be the real issue with both debaters is the journalist's credibility. And credibility goes far, far beyond a so-called conflict of interest. Does the journalist participate in politics, and if so, to what degree? Does the journalist accept gifts, and if so, what kinds (and from whom)? Does the journalist fraternize with sources of information, and if so, to what degree? Does a book reviewer accept free books from a publisher? Does a reporter moonlight as a speechwriter for a politician? Does the journalist hide his/her biases under the guise of civic journalism? Does an honest journalist "avoid any appearance" of obligation to anyone—*even his/her editor?* And there are many other such questions that Kittross and Gordon bring up and discuss.

Kittross is somewhat sanguine about the journalist's need to worry about any conflicts of interest. Gordon seems to be more worried. But both are far from legalistic in the Kantian sense. Don't be too strict in all this, they both seem to say—just don't go over some imaginary line. Kittross takes a slightly more Machiavellian position, it seems to me. The reporter's job is to report, and she or he must be left alone to do it. After all, journalism is a "human" activity, and one must expect a journalist to be human—i.e., not to be perfect.

I once knew a city alderman who could drink a full bottle of liquor at one sitting.

If only journalists could be "objective," perhaps this debate would abate. Even if there is a conflict of interest (or a perceived one), objectivity would right all wrongs, and the public could have faith in those who are objective. But, alas, a journalist's credibility with the public will always be less than desired, for there is no objectivity. And this can be attributed not to some "conflict of interest," but rather to a far more natural factor—the subjectivity of the human being. Conflicts of interest that impinge on journalistic objectivity, like beauty, are in the eye of the beholder. Kittross says that if a reporter is aware of a real conflict of interest, it must be avoided. Just be professional, Kittross admonishes, and the problem will take care of itself. But Gordon doubts it, and so do I. My reason is somewhat different from Gordon's. I feel that two editors who are both "professionals" can come to different conclusions about a so-called conflict of interest, one avoiding it and the other embracing it.

Gordon informs us that he is not an extremist, that, for instance, he doesn't believe that a reporter should forgo voting. Would he, one wonders, shun friendship with political figures? Probably. For Gordon takes the high road, the almost ideal journalistic road of perfection. But "perfection" easily evolves into a kind of authoritarianism, and that should be anathema to the libertarian journalist. Listen to Gordon: "The media person's freedom to participate fully in societal activities may well have to be curtailed." But, he says, such a loss is "far outweighed by the benefits to society of having news and information media that retain credibility with their audiences." The assumption is that a journalist who avoids conflicts of interest will thereby retain credibility. But, sadly, there are too many other factors constantly denuding credibility.

Both disputants get into the subject of civic journalism. Kittross sees it as a danger, a subtle way of disguising media biases. Gordon is more supportive, which is somewhat strange, since in my view civic journalism represents a classic case of conflict of interest: *the conflict between editorial self-determination and public-determination of media content.* But press freedom is being misused and may be socially harmful, says the civic journalist and Gordon, and therefore freedom must be further curtailed or limited in the name of social responsibility. Freedom is becoming an increasingly bad word.

I feel the disputants have said about all that can be said about this ethical problem. Neither wins the debate, for such a debate is unwinnable. It is so wrapped up in vague terminology and intrinsic contradictions that real meaning seldom rises to the surface. A final example: Gordon quotes an unnamed "practical" city alderman as saying that the problem of gifts could be solved by accepting nothing that couldn't be disposed of at one sitting. A cup of coffee or even dinner was okay, but a full bottle of hard liquor wasn't. I once knew a city alderman who could drink a full bottle of liquor at one sitting. But that's not really the point. One must ask if a small gift cannot be a conflict of interest and just as compromising as a large gift. Is it not the *principle* of gift-receiving that is potentially dangerous, rather than the size of the gift?

As long as we leave such questions open-ended and to be decided individually by the journalist, such questions will continue to cause us trouble. Maybe we need to be more legalistic and Kantian; having an *a priori* maxim such as this: *Never accept gifts of any kind from anyone you might have to write about in your journalism.* It will be hoped that, if you accept such a maxim in the area of conflict of interest, you will never have to write about your family members.

REFERENCES

Bradlee, Ben. (1995). *A Good Life: Newspapering and Other Adventures.* New York: Simon & Schuster.

Craig, David A. (1996). "Communitarian Journalism(s): Clearing Conceptual Landscapes." *Journal of Mass Media Ethics* 11:2, pp. 107–118.

Gade, Peter. (Fall 1997). "A Response to Patterson." *Media Ethics* 9(1), pp. 5ff.

Gaziano, Cecilie, and Kristin McGrath. (Summer/Autumn, 1987). "Newspaper Credibility and Relationships of Newspaper Journalists to Communities." *Journalism Quarterly* 64:2/3, pp. 317–328, 345.

Hardie, Mary. (October 1995). "Activism: Taboo for journalists?" *Gannetteer* pp. 17–19.

———. (March/April 1996). "TV stations plug into communities." *Gannetteer*, pp. 20–21.

Jurkowitz, Mark. (August 13, 1995). "What's Their Line? Journo-tainment." *The Boston Sunday Globe*, pp. 69–70.

Knowlton, Steven R. (1997). *Moral Reasoning for Journalists: Cases and Commentary.* Westport, CT: Praeger.

Lasswell, Harold D. (1948). "The structure and function of communication in society." In Lyman Bryson (ed.), *The Communication of Ideas: A series of addresses.* New York: Harper.

Liebling, A. J. (1961). *The Press.* New York: Ballantine. (Chapter originally published as "Do You Belong in Journalism?" in *The New Yorker,* May 14, 1960.)

Martinson, David L. (1994). "Enlightened Self-Interest Fails as an Ethical Baseline in Public Relations." *Journal of Mass Media Ethics* 9:2, pp. 100–108.

Meyer, Philip. (1983). *Editors, Publishers, and Newspaper Ethics: A Report to the American Society of Newspaper Editors.* Washington, DC: ASNE Newspaper Center.

Morgan, Edward P. (1963). *Clearing the Air.* Washington: Robert B. Luce.

Patterson, Maggie. (Fall 1997). "An Open Letter to a Concerned Colleague." *Media Ethics* 9(1), pp. 4ff.

Remnick, David. (September 18, 1995). "Last of the Red Hots." *The New Yorker,* pp. 76–83.

CHAPTER 15

MORE TOPICS IN THE ETHICAL DEBATE

Paying even minimal attention on a daily basis to the media of mass communication immediately shows the complexity of the ethical controversies facing all media practitioners today. They include topics that the preceding 14 chapters cannot pretend to cover fully.

To write this book, we chose the areas of controversy we deemed most important. None of us was satisfied that all of our pet concerns had been covered, and other matters rose to prominence during the time it took to produce the first edition of *Controversies in Media Ethics*—and even more while we were producing the second edition.

To deal with this foreseeable problem at the start, we reserved Chapter 15 for the presentation—if not the full argument—of some *other* ethical controversies facing the media. We call these presentations mini-chapters, and publish them more or less in order of the amount of attention we have devoted to them. The first few mini-chapters are given several pages each; for the others we merely present one point of view, allowing *you* to look at the problem with an argumentative eye.

We hope you will!

■ CONTENTS

15-A. Checkbook Journalism: The Final Marketplace   **p. 270**

One Point of View (*John Michael Kittross*): Treating news as a commodity eventually will destroy journalism as a public benefit.

Another Point of View (*David Gordon*): News is a commodity, and journalism is surviving very well, thank you.

Your Point of View:

15-B. Co-option   **p. 273**

One Point of View (*Kittross*): The media not only can be bought, but are.

Another Point of View (*Gordon*): The media do a better job of remaining independent than almost any other institution in society.

Your Point of View:

15-C. Product Placement   p. 275

One Point of View (*Gordon*): Product placement in films and television is a perfectly acceptable part of the capitalist system under which the entertainment media operate.

Another Point of View (*Kittross*): The plugging of products in a film or television program could mislead the public and should be exposed to the light.

Your Point of View:

15-D. Is Public Relations Part of Journalism?   p. 276

One Point of View (*Gordon*): Public relations and journalism will both benefit when they are taught in the same school or department, and ethics in both fields have no relationship to this issue.

Another Point of View (*Kittross*): Teaching public relations and journalism in the same department is detrimental to the ethics of both fields.

Your Point of View:

15-E. Arrogance and Credibility   p. 279

One Point of View (*Kittross*): The arrogance of journalists who accept speaking fees, while holding news subjects to higher standards than they themselves are willing to meet, is unethical.

Your Point of View:

15-F. Digital Manipulation of Pictures   p. 281

One Point of View (*Kittross*): The ability to "doctor" pictures digitally and undetectably won't go away, so we have to find ethical ways to live with the technique.

Your Point of View:

15-G. Pack Journalism   p. 285

One Point of View (*Kittross*): The news media's current practice of pack journalism is not only inefficient but unethical as well.

Your Point of View:

15-H. Civility, "Dirty" Language, and Religion   p. 287

One Point of View (*Kittross*): The right to swing one's fist ends where someone else's nose begins.

Your Point of View:

15-I. Interviews   p. 291

One Point of View (*Kittross*): The interview is an unreliable, often invalid, and even harmful way of obtaining information for the media.

Your Point of View:

15-J. Honesty in Reporting   **p. 293**

One Point of View (*Kittross*): To lie to get access to the news may be justified, especially if it is the only way the public can get the information it needs.

Your Point of View:

■ 15-A: CHECKBOOK JOURNALISM: THE FINAL MARKETPLACE

■ KITTROSS: Treating news as a commodity eventually will destroy journalism as a public benefit.

In theory, it is very simple. The reporter digs out news (sometimes against the wishes of those who prefer to keep it hidden) and it gets edited and transmitted to the audience. Never mind that the public's interests seem tipped toward titillation rather than edification, or that there are sometimes legitimate privacy interests (which we discuss in Chapters 8 and 9)—journalistic theory and traditional standards say that there is nothing other than dogged legwork and luck (or serendipity) for the reporter to be concerned about.

In practice, there is something else: greed. And that which feeds it: checkbook journalism. We seem to be converting newsgathering into a buy-and-sell business, and members of the public who have information (eyewitnesses, record keepers, people with cameras at the right time and right place) now think that they have something to sell that the media want to buy. If the media keep pandering to this commodification of the news, there will be precious little remaining for the reporter to find or dig out ("Simpson Case . . . ," 1994)!

It is easy to claim blandly that checkbook journalism—the buying for cash of information that one can print or air—is the province only of yellow journalism, supermarket checkout-stand scandal sheets, gossip gazettes, and "flying saucers stole my Pomeranian" periodicals. But, unfortunately, it isn't true.

Today, it almost seems as though the only media organizations that do not engage in checkbook journalism are those that don't have enough money to enter the bidding!

. . . checkbook journalism destroys the credibility of all journalism.

The amount of money one must now ante up is impressive. When O. J. Simpson was arrested on charges of murdering his ex-wife and Ron Goldman, it was reported that one of Simpson's friends was offered up to one million dollars (which he turned down) for his story. The owners and a salesman at a cutlery store where Simpson bought a knife shared $12,500. ("Simpson Case . . . ," 1994). Checkbook journalism also can lead to disruption of the legal process: A friend of the woman who claimed to have been raped by William Kennedy Smith reportedly invented testimony, in part to earn $40,000 from television's *A Current Affair.*

One might ask why anyone should raise an objection over a "willing buyer/willing seller" transaction, even if the checkbook journalists engage in ruinous bidding wars for gossip, scandal, and the like. How can this affect "real" news, hard news, important news—what the public needs in order to make rational decisions in a democracy? There are two simple answers.

First, the person who sells a story may lose credibility. In the Simpson case, the Los Angeles district attorney's office decided to drop a witness after she was interviewed on *Hard Copy*. In the Michael Jackson child molestation case, two witnesses reportedly sold stories to tabloid television shows that contradicted (and were more sensational than) what they said in sworn depositions, which may have played a part in keeping them off the stand before an eventual out-of-court settlement.

More importantly, checkbook journalism destroys the credibility of all journalism.

Sure, there are precedents for checkbook journalism. All reporters are familiar with the long-standing practice of providing sources with a cup of coffee, a beer, a meal, $10 or $20 or $100 to those who need it or who need to feel that the reporter is a fellow human being. Even the prestige press often buys not the news (or so it claims), but a picture, diary or some other commodity for $1000 or more—but both parties obviously are well aware that there is a quid pro quo with sums that high.

The visual media issue large checks for photographs and videotape, ranging from pictures as significant as the Zapruder film of President Kennedy's assassination to the wedding picture of a run-of-the-mill murder victim. Such payments also are made for life stories or first-person accounts; the first astronauts, government employees all, made particularly advantageous "exclusive" deals with *Life* magazine. Are such payments different in any significant way from the cup of coffee or meal? Yes, because the cup of coffee would never be thought of as conveying *exclusive* rights to the part of the story that the source is telling the reporter between refills.

But in exchange for hundreds or thousands of dollars, the bean counters in media management insist on written contracts and exclusivity—the ability to prevent other media organizations and, consequently, the public, from using the story. How can there be a marketplace of ideas when there are early and preemptive purchases in the marketplace of news-as-a-commodity?

There is nothing illegal about selling news and information, nor is it illegal to buy news and information. But the buyers—the media—have the power to refuse to buy, in order to protect their most essential attribute, their stock-in-trade: their credibility.

Most of the news media are profit-making, and some of the rest would like to make a profit. If media organizations really want to spend money for news, they can always hire more reporters, pay them better, and give them more newsgathering resources.

If the current trend leads to the condition where all important news (not just scandal) is bought from greedy sources or (conversely but with similar effect) "given" to the news media by self-serving PR practitioners or advertisers—a case where the source's checkbook buys the news medium!—bias will be more likely and we will all lose. "All" doesn't refer merely to media organizations that lose in the bidding and become roadkill on the information superhighway. It also refers to the "winners" in the checkbook journalism bidding wars, who become ever-larger and ever-more monopolistic—and less able or willing to compete in traditional journalistic digging. Most important is the loss suffered by the public, which will get its news on the basis of price, not quality.

If media professionals don't show restraint in using checkbook journalism, then they (we) lose credibility—hardly a utilitarian approach. If the news media have lost credibility, not only are they dead in the water, but their practitioners don't sleep well. Checkbook journalism isn't merely economic. It is also both an ethical (with respect to the professional group and its clients, the body politic) and a moral matter.

Regardless of David Gordon's interpretation, a clear Kantian or "universal law" view would also reject checkbook journalism. After all, if we believe that information is only a commodity to be bought and sold, how long will it be before we, ourselves, also are on the block? What will be our price? Who will pimp for us?

■ GORDON: News is a commodity, and journalism is surviving very well, thank you.

This argument is really an offshoot of our economic marketplace discussion back in Chapter 11. News has always been an economic commodity, at least since the advent of movable type. Paying sources for information may well be somewhat different from the ways in which various news items were gathered in prior decades, but it isn't automatically any less ethical.

This issue must be considered within the context of news that concerns private areas of individuals' lives. If one refers to material that is (or should be) in the public realm, freedom of information laws should make unnecessary the purchase of information. Certainly, no one can argue that a public official has any right to demand payment for releasing information over which she or he has jurisdiction—although friendships, as well as the coffee, beer, or dinner noted by John Michael Kittross, clearly have influenced decisions about which media are favored with the initial release of such information.

But with private individuals or the private portions of the lives of public parties (perhaps especially people who are thrust unwillingly or unwittingly into the public spotlight), it's a very different situation. It shows more respect for privacy, or for individual dignity, to pay for a picture that the media want to run than it would to palm the picture from the home of its owner. This practice of lifting pictures (especially of disaster victims) was not unheard of through the early decades of this century (and, perhaps, even more recently than that). Such actions were nothing more or less than theft, justified by citing the "public's right to know" (and perhaps the newspaper's need to attract circulation by any means). In offering to pay for such pictures or videotapes, the media are at least giving the owners both an option to refuse to release them and an opportunity to be compensated if they agree to their use.

Kittross is correct when he says that paying for information will reduce the amount of material that reporters will need to dig out on their own. But that digging has too often resulted in considerable incursions on individuals' privacy, with no opportunity for those individuals to control what becomes public and no compensation for it.

Potential news sources who are offered money for such material can always say "No," as Al Cowlings did in the O. J. Simpson case—a point that Kittross noted but then ignored. I also think Kittross is far too alarmist in his concern for what happens when information is purchased for exclusive use by one media outlet. Although this certainly might keep some specific presentations of this material from other outlets, there's simply no way that it will keep the public from learning about the story.

Competition between news and infotainment outlets will ensure that at least one version of the material reaches the public. It's absurd to say that exclusivity diminishes the availability of that information to the audience at large. The actual live interview may well be the property of the outlet that paid for it, but the information (or the titillation) contained in it can freely be picked up by any and all other outlets and thereby spread as widely through the marketplace as is warranted.

It's not inconceivable that there may be some impact on the media's credibility from widespread use of checkbook journalism. But that's speculative, at best, and not really worth worrying about at this point, in view of all the more likely problems that also might diminish the media's credibility.

Before we condemn checkbook journalism out of hand, let's refer back to my Chapter 12 example, where the tabloid/checkbook journalism route was the only one available for a gang rape victim's family to tell its side of the story (Mengelkoch, 1994). In sum, one might argue that checkbook journalism is a utilitarian approach: It provides benefits to most people in the society (i.e., information for the public, and both control and cash for the people selling the information). One might also argue that it follows the Kantian ideal of treating private individuals who have become newsworthy as ends in themselves rather than merely as means to be exploited toward the end of providing information or titillation for the public. And this combination of Kant and utilitarianism—rather rare in our survey of ethical concerns in the media—should be fostered rather than condemned.

REFERENCES

Mengelkoch, Louise. (November/December 1994). "When Checkbook Journalism Does God's Work." *Columbia Journalism Review*, pp. 35–38.
"Simpson Case Puts Checkbook Journalism on Trial." (July 3, 1994). *The Boston Sunday Globe*, p. 4.

■ 15-B: CO-OPTION

■ KITTROSS: The media not only can be bought, but are.

What makes this prostitution even worse is that the price often is set very, very low.

Although reporters used to be taught that the only way to look at politicians is down their nose, those in the media are as susceptible to flattery and other ego-stroking as everyone else.

It is this that leads to "creampuff" interviews; maneuvering for social invitations; the proud wearing of a prestigious source's "freebies" (from a lapel pin to a warm-up jacket); a network anchor fawning over the president; acceptance of hospitality that might lead both parties to assume there is a reciprocal obligation to provide something in return; the idea that the most important need of the reporter is to keep on the good side of sources, editors, and publishers; and many other demonstrations of lack of independent judgment, all of which can damage both the reporters' stories and media credibility.

For example, the White House Office of Media Affairs finds it easy to decide which stations or papers to target for political advantage (Garcia, 1994). The selected media will drop everything to be able to say pridefully "He chose us!" It is very rare, even in the most blatant cases of political maneuvering, for the media to turn down the opportunity to brag about being so important that they have been selected as a sounding board by the White House, regardless of what this might do to their credibility.

Is this substitution of ego satisfaction for journalistic judgment desirable? Is the co-option of network and studio chiefs, producers, and writers to concentrate on the "social ill of the year" (drug taking, spouse beating, etc.) through invitations to the seats of government power really the best way to enlarge public debate over major problems—or even to get original ideas for programs? Are all "public service" campaigns run by print and broadcast media really in the public interest?

If any of the answers to these questions is "No," and I think that is very likely, then perhaps, in a Kantian way, the media would best serve their own sense of self-esteem as well as the public interest by returning to the "looking down the nose" standard.

■ GORDON: The media do a better job of remaining independent than almost any other institution in society.

If John Michael Kittross is arguing that people in the mass media are human, and subject to human failings, then I have to agree. But when he generalizes about media "prostitution," I have to disagree strongly.

It is highly unrealistic to expect media people to live up to a Kantian standard that requires complete selflessness 100% of the time. Wearing a lapel pin or even a warm-up jacket is not likely to influence news content very much.

There certainly are some potential dangers inherent in journalists becoming too cozy with sources or allowing themselves to be manipulated because the White House and other news sources can appeal to their egos. But by and large, journalists and their editors are aware of those dangers and do a pretty good job of either avoiding them or recognizing them soon enough to prevent the news coverage from becoming tainted. Most journalists, I suspect, try hard—and with considerable success—to follow the utilitarian prescription of having their work benefit the greatest number of people.

There will always be exceptions, because journalists are human and humans aren't perfect. But as advertisers have often learned, and as most public relations practitioners recognize, journalists are not all that easy to buy.

That doesn't mean that journalists and public relations people don't work together. They do, and they should, because at their best, these two fields are quite symbiotic. Public relations practitioners need to use the mass media to do what their clients hire them to do. Journalists can and do benefit from information, press and video releases, tips, suggestions, and guidance that public relations people or government press contacts provide.

Although a dash of skepticism is important for journalists, looking down one's nose, at politicians or anyone else, is definitely not the recipe for successful reporting! As long as journalists remember why public relations personnel are cooperating with them, and as long as PR people remember that the journalists must make the final decisions about whether and how to use the material provided to them, their symbiosis will benefit the media's audience and the society as a whole.

REFERENCE

Garcia, Robert. (November 1994). "Hey Mom, the President's on the Radio!" *Radio Reporting* (RTNDA) 1, p. 2.

■ 15-C: PRODUCT PLACEMENT

■ GORDON: Product placement in films and television is a perfectly acceptable part of the capitalist system under which the entertainment media operate.

There is no logical reason to be concerned about the highly visible use of specific brand-name products in films and television programs in return for payments to the producers by the purveyors of those products. This situation benefits many people without doing appreciable harm, and the utilitarians would be pleased.

This practice is not hidden from public knowledge. In no way does it even begin to compare to subliminal advertising. Entertainment programming requires the use of various types of props, and there is no real argument to be made that these should be limited to generic or unrecognizable brands. And the money received by the producers in these situations either adds to the profits of the enterprise—not a bad thing in a capitalist economy—or it decreases the amount that other sponsors, or the public, would be expected to provide.

All this amounts to is a very clever way of advertising that deceives or harms no one and provides some tangible economic benefits to the producers, among others. So what's the problem? (Note, however, that I made a contrasting argument on this point in Chapter 5 . . . yet another illustration of the different perspectives that can be brought to bear on any ethical issue.)

■ KITTROSS: The plugging of products in a film or television program could mislead the public and should be exposed to the light.

David Gordon's knee-jerk faith in the flimsy argument that we are in a "capitalist" system (rather than a "managerial" one) obscures the fact that what he advocates might well be illegal unless the public is notified.

Section 317 of the Communications Act of 1934 states that:

All matter broadcast by any radio [a term that includes television] station for which any money, service or other valuable consideration is directly or indirectly paid, or promised to . . . the station . . . shall, at the time the same is so broadcast, be announced as paid for or furnished . . . .

It is because of this section that many programs acknowledge, in their closing credits, that "promotional consideration has been supplied by" an airline or other purveyor. Strictly speaking, it may not be necessary to acknowledge "any service or property furnished without charge or at a nominal charge . . . unless it is so furnished in consideration for an identification . . . beyond [that] which is reasonably related to the use of such service or property on the broadcast."

But broadcasters are nothing if not cautious, and frequently lean over backward to avoid transgressing Section 317 (or Section 507, dealing with the practice of "payola").

Although identification of program sponsors has been in the Communications Act since it was written, some of the current language was inserted in 1960 as a result of the "payola" and "plugola" scandals of the late 1950s. ("Payola" is slipping money—or liquor, drugs, or women—to a disc jockey in exchange for playing particular records, thus defrauding the public, which is entitled to expect impartial selection. "Plugola" involves programmers or show hosts deliberately showing or mentioning the name of a product or service and expecting something in return, thus defrauding the station, which loses out on the possibility of selling commercial time to the plugola payer).

Although the Communications Act applies only to stations, and not to film studios, independent program packagers, newspapers, or magazines, there is a clear precedent for identifying the reason that a particular product is featured.

I'm not advocating a return to the days when the movie industry carefully showed only generic products—even constructing fake automobiles, particularly for those used by villains, that didn't resemble anything on the market. But I do think the public deserves to know why a particular brand of car, beer, refrigerator, airline, or other good or service is featured. If they just happen to be there, well and good. If they are selected so as to benefit those who place plugs and those who accept money for that placement, then it is certainly possible that the public is being coaxed or misled into an artificial preference.

Anything that causes the audience to pay close attention to the details is, I believe, the right thing to do.

■ 15-D: IS PUBLIC RELATIONS PART OF JOURNALISM?

■ GORDON: Public relations and journalism will both benefit when they are taught in the same school or department, and ethics in both fields have no relationship to this issue.

Public relations is obviously separate from journalism, but the two fields have a symbiotic relationship and practitioners in each have a great need to understand the other. Journalists these days couldn't function well without the availability of public relations people to answer questions and provide various kinds of information. In turn, public relations people must rely on journalists to provide the channels through which PR messages—often in altered form—reach many of the various publics at which they're aimed.

Separating the teaching of the two fields will just raise further barriers to their understanding of each other. If public relations students aren't involved in some journalism classes, they will lose opportunities to learn about what they should and shouldn't expect in their professional dealings with the field. If journalism students don't have the opportunity to learn about public relations—ideally, by taking a public relations course or two—they will know less about both the opportunities and the pitfalls that the PR field holds for them as working journalists. They will also be less well prepared when some of them want to make midcareer switches from journalism to a better-paying or less stressful public relations position.

I'm not sure I see what the separation of the two fields' curricula has to do with ethics in the first place. But if Stanley Harrison's concern—as noted in John Michael Kittross's argument—is indeed correct, then there appears to be considerable benefit to be derived from discussing this "intangible sphere" of ethics in classes where both journalism and public relations students can consider together some of the issues that affect their fields.

Kittross's notion that journalists owe their allegiance only to truth and the needs of society is a bit quaint in view of the increasing impact of bottom-line concerns on newsroom practices. And his contention that public relations and business schools owe no ethical duty to society at large is disputed both by many public relations teachers and practitioners, and by the increasing concern in business schools for the teaching of ethics courses. He also ignores the pragmatic PR function of providing straightforward material that the media might otherwise overlook.

At best, separating public relations and journalism students will have no effect on the ethics of both fields while decreasing the opportunities for both types of students to get to know each other. At worst, it will reduce the concern paid to the ethical issues in both fields, and will thereby weaken the ethical framework for both journalism and public relations.

■ KITTROSS: Teaching public relations and journalism in the same department is detrimental to the ethics of both fields.

When Willie Sutton, a famous bank robber, was arrested yet again after knocking over a bank, he was asked by a reporter, "Willie, why do you keep robbing banks?" Willie, without missing a beat, came back with the obvious answer: "Because that's where the money is."

As an erstwhile academic administrator in communication, I'm well aware of the appetite for constantly increasing enrollments fostered by bean-counting cost accountants imposing an inappropriate financial model on American higher education: quantity, often at the expense of quality. For the past decade or more, the proportion of communication students graduating in public relations and advertising has hovered just below 40%. (Kosicki and Becker, 1996, p. 10). No dean, director, or chair of an academic unit cares to contemplate the dire effect on budget and prestige of losing a fifth to two-fifths of their enrollment!

Other statistics support the desirability of public relations as a cash cow for schools of communication and journalism: 42% of institutions offering master's programs have PR majors (Briggs and Fleming, 1994), nearly a quarter of advertising executives took degrees in journalism/advertising (Donnelly, 1992), colleges get good publicity from the large proportion of PR majors (and some others) who find work in the field (Becker, 1992), and so on. (Of course, it may not be fair to lead students in any field into the belief that there are post-graduation jobs just waiting to be plucked; when Becker's data are looked at closely, it is apparent that public relations majors have just as difficult a time in getting a first job as do graduates in other communications specializations.)

Yet the question remains: Is it appropriate for public relations and journalism to be in bed together?

I think not. Journalism's goal is supplying the public with the information needed to make rational decisions in a democracy. Public relations, on the other hand, rarely pretends to be more than the handmaiden of commerce and the servant of those who, for political and social reasons, need to present a more attractive face for themselves (or their firms) than their behavior and nature have supplied—or, at least, to make their good points known. Journalism must serve the public interest and public relations must serve the client, regardless of what the codes of various public relations trade and professional associations say.

I believe that the entire field of public relations—whether defined as "relations with various publics" by those who can afford counsel or the time and energy to engage in it, or as "social imagistics" ("the selection, creation, projection of suitable public images" [Priestly, 1968, p. 39])—has such different goals from those of journalism that they should be separated in the classroom.

A recent survey of the contents of public relations textbooks concludes in part that "[m]any texts fall short of what should be covered for public relations ethics. At minimum, the burden for beyond-the-text preparation is staggering. An intangible sphere, like ethics, is more than likely to be swept aside in the need to cover necessary skills for the business world" (Harrison, 1990, pp. 36–37).

Those "necessary skills" clearly are thought important by PR students. Public relations majors in American colleges identify more with business than with journalism: In one study, 13.2% of PR majors have business administration minors, another 9.0% have marketing minors, 4.2% management minors, 3.4% advertising minors, and 2.4% economics minors. (Another 9.8% have political science minors, probably reflecting the attractiveness of political campaign spin doctors and managers.) These business-oriented minors constitute roughly one-third of all minors taken by PR students, whereas journalism, mass communication, broadcast communication, oral communication, and theater/drama constitute only 9.9% between them (McInerny, 1995, p. 32). Of course, other communication fields are "built in" to many PR curricula, and accreditation requirements impose severe limits on taking other communication courses.

Perhaps as a reflection of the difference between PR practitioners and journalists, practitioners are significantly more willing to believe that they are acting ethically when giving evasive answers to reporters seeking information intrinsically important for people to understand a story, and also significantly more willing to believe that they are acting ethically when they withhold information about an organization (Ryan and Martinson, 1994, pp. 208–209). This shaping of public opinion about an organization, candidate, or other individual doesn't have to involve categorical overt lying. All it needs is to warp or spin the story or image. That can be done by evasion or holding back information, through all sorts of techniques from military "security" classification of embarrassing facts to Price Waterhouse and the U.S. Postal Service skewing data by making sure that nobody connected with the media—one of the largest postal clients—participated in a program supposedly intended to obtain feedback about the service. Promoting a "good" image and eliminating or hiding a "bad" image accomplish the same ends: keeping from the public the truth, the whole truth, and nothing but the truth.

My position is identical to that of many public relations practitioners and educators, although my goals are different: Let public relations students affiliate with business schools, not with journalism schools. Not only is that where the money is, but ethical standards are much easier to articulate: the PR practitioner owes fiduciary responsibility only to the client, not to society at large. The journalist has the much more difficult row to hoe of having to consider the public interest as the primary goal, which requires difficult and complex attention to the truth and to the needs of society.

REFERENCES

Becker, Lee B. (Summer 1992). "Finding Work Was More Difficult for Graduates in 1990." *Journalism Educator* 47(2), pp. 65–73.

Briggs, Jean E., and Charles A. Fleming. (Summer 1994). "A Survey of Master's Programs Documents Diversity." *Journalism Educator* 49(2), pp. 12–17.

Donnelly, William J. (Spring 1992). "Correlating Top Agency Success with Educational Background." *Journalism Educator* 47(1), pp. 67–73.

Harrison, Stanley L. (Autumn 1990). "Ethics and Moral Issues in Public Relations Curricula." *Journalism Educator* 45(3), pp. 32–38.

Kosicki, Gerald M., and Lee B. Becker. (Autumn 1996). "Annual Survey of Enrollments and Degrees Awarded." *Journalism & Mass Communication Educator* 51(3), pp. 4–14. (Annual surveys of these communication enrollment and graduation statistics were conducted by Paul V. Peterson (1967–1988), Lee B. Becker (1988–1991), and Kosicki and Becker (1991–1996), and published in *Journalism Educator* [now *Journalism & Mass Communication Educator*] under various titles.)

McInerny, Paul M. (Winter 1995). "The Public Relations Curriculum and the Academic Minor." *Journalism Educator* 49(4), pp. 31–35.

Priestley, J. B. (1968). *The Image Men*. Boston: Little, Brown.

Ryan, Michael, and David L. Martinson. (Spring 1994). "Public Relations Practitioners, Journalists View Lying Similarly." *Journalism Quarterly* 71(1), pp. 199–211.

■ 15-E: ARROGANCE AND CREDIBILITY

■ KITTROSS: The arrogance of journalists who accept speaking fees, while holding news subjects to higher standards than they themselves are willing to meet, is unethical.

In 1994, ABC's *PrimeTime Live*, co-anchored by correspondent Sam Donaldson, attacked a junket that some congressional staff members had taken at the expense of the Independent Insurance Agents of America. Only a few months earlier, the same insurance group had paid Donaldson a large lecture fee (Auletta, 1994).

Arrogant.

Journalists often demand that their sources have perfect memories—"where were you on the night of January 14th?"—even though the questioners would be equally unable to recall such chronological details were they so queried without access to their diaries or datebooks.

Arrogant.

That is the best description of news people who keep an eagle eye on politicians and others while ignoring how they look themselves, or would look if subject to the same degree of scrutiny.

It is unfortunately true that, except at the top, few journalists are paid well. But those at the top, particularly in television, are also invited to give well-paid speeches to groups that might have good reason to want journalists to be on their side.

Does he who pays the piper call the tune? Maybe not, but if the public believes such a cause-effect relationship exists, the independence of the piper certainly can be questioned.

Of course, most journalists are honest—it may be that the insurance group realized too late that Donaldson apparently hadn't understood the unspoken definition of being honest in business: someone who will stay bought. (For Donaldson's rebuttal, see Chapter 14.) Yet this situation still would puzzle an objective observer: here is someone who accepts money to speak on a controversial topic, however dispassionately, and yet refuses to admit that there might be a reduction of his objectivity when reporting on this topic or a loss of credibility and reputation in the eyes of those who find out about these payments. Even worse, the same journalist attacks those in other professions—expert witnesses, researchers funded by drug or tobacco firms, government officials, and so on—who also claim that they can maintain objective standards while taking the Queen's shilling.

It doesn't take actual dishonesty for such an arrogant exercise of conflict of interest to be harmful to journalism, to those who need to rely on journalism, and to the public at large. When one says, "Trust me," then—like Caesar's wife—he or she must appear to be above suspicion. Journalists, even more than most other professionals, must retain their credibility.

I'm against the practice of journalists who make tens—possibly hundreds—of thousands of dollars giving frequent paid lectures or allowing themselves to be part of the window dressing of large business gatherings. My opposition isn't just jealousy fueled by the fact that I've never received more than a token fee and expenses. Many journalists refuse all "outside" or freelance work on principle, may speak rarely, and then accept only token fees or expenses. Those who speak to journalism associations or in communications classrooms may do so for free, but some still charge the school, student government, or association a great deal of money. About all that can be proven about such work is that those no longer on the air can no longer command such large fees.

Since American universities also need to lobby for funding, wouldn't the support of major news figures be useful in their lobbying? Isn't the thought of a university post attractive to a burnt-out journalist? Isn't there a potential conflict of interest on both sides? Yet, at the same time, aren't there benefits to journalism if students in communications schools "hear it like it is" from practicing journalists?

I think we need to find some solution to the problem of what Auletta calls "fee speech" other than strict abstinence.

The obvious solution is to be found in the basic principle of informative journalism: shedding enough light on situations and events that the public may learn enough to make rational decisions. I propose that the following practices be mandated in every newsroom, and that the public be educated to be very wary of any journalist who doesn't follow them:

- All news personnel must get approval from a high-level supervisor before accepting any money—fees or expenses—for giving a talk or appearance of any sort.
- All news personnel must periodically provide their supervisors with a list of any nonpaid talks or other participation in activities in any way connected with present or future news stories.
- These lists and approvals should be a matter of public record.

Will such practices reduce the take-home income of top-ranking journalists? Unfortunately, yes—which may lead to a salutary examination of the pay scales in all media. Will these practices infringe on the freedom of association that is the right of every American? Possibly, by a small fraction, which may cause working journalists to advocate openly some desirable control over the credibility-destroying activity of many publishers, licensees, and media entrepreneurs (See Chapter 14).

The most important question of all is "Will these proposed practices go far to reduce the reputation for arrogance that is seriously weakening the credibility of all news media?" Definitely yes!

REFERENCE

Auletta, Ken. (September 12, 1994). "Fee Speech." *The New Yorker,* pp. 40–47.

■ 15-F: DIGITAL MANIPULATION OF PICTURES

■ KITTROSS: The ability to "doctor" pictures digitally and undetectably won't go away, so we have to find ethical ways to live with the technique.

"Pictures don't lie."

If you believe the preceding sentence, I've got a Brooklyn Bridge I'd like to sell you.

Of course pictures lie, and always have! And we've learned how to live with that fact, although the situation may be changing.

■ THE HISTORICAL RECORD

Since the first artist or sculptor picked up a primitive brush or chisel, artists have been in control of the appearance of their subjects, although the person paying for a portrait or other picture may have something to say about it. Photographers may keep (or airbrush out) anachronisms or embarrassing contradictions. (For example, in his famous documentary *Man of Aran* [1934], Robert Flaherty carefully selected camera angles to make sure that no power lines showed in "primitive village" scenes).

Makeup and costumes have covered flaws and drawn attention to good points for centuries. Press photographers always have been on the alert for an opportunity to snap a subject with a compromising or misleading facial expression or gesture, regardless of whether the picture will be an accurate reflection of the event or person. File footage might be broadcast or printed without attribution or with a dishonest provenance (for example, during the Vietnam War, a New York television station pretended to be providing daily pictorial coverage but was merely using stock footage). For generations, any visual recorder or artist has been able to do amazing things with selection, focus, enlargement or reduction, contrast, cropping, and other tricks of the trade.

In the 1920s, the New York *Graphic* achieved notoriety by cutting out pictures of the faces of people in the news and pasting them over posed bodies or scenes that were believed to reflect more accurately or more entertainingly the underlying story (Mallen, 1954). More seriously, during wartime many pictures were doctored for propaganda purposes; domestically, nearly half a century ago the campaign against the reelection of Maryland Senator Millard Tydings carefully cropped two pictures to produce a composite that showed him "listening" to a communist.

The use of traditional cinematographic technologies for "faking" has been demonstrated in feature films such as *Forrest Gump* and Woody Allen's *Zelig*, where the hero was inserted into a variety of historical newsreels through the use of optical mattes. In television, the use of an electronic matte technique (such as Chromakey), which allows an actor or reporter to be inserted into another location, is an everyday practice, although it is condemned if used to make the public see an in-studio anchor as an on-the-scene reporter. In countries where former leaders can become "nonpersons" overnight, it now is as easy for pictures to be modified to eliminate a person as it was for writings to be manipulated in the same way and for the same political purposes as in George Orwell's *1984*. Closer to home, one can find in many shopping malls a growing business in electronically removing ex-spouses from family pictures.

Advertising pictures—whether drawings or photographs—since the days of woodcuts have used artistic license to make the product or service being advertised look better. During the 1960s, a variety of techniques were adapted for television: plain glass marbles were placed in soup so that the advertised contents floated at the top; easily "shaved" plexiglass sheets were used instead of sandpaper in a shaving cream commercial; an open window was used to demonstrate the clarity of automobile glass; and so on. Although the most blatant deceptions were later banned, many—particularly those dealing with food products that could not stand up to the photographer's lights—remain.

While many photojournalists of today (and yesterday) are concerned about the ethics of their field, the instant availability of technology may be even more tempting to them than to other media practitioners. (For an introduction, see Lester, 1991).

■ DIGITALIZATION WITHOUT DETECTION

Why am I talking about this as a new ethical dilemma? Recently, the ability to perform such technical miracles of manipulation has shown a quantum increase. Today, once a picture has been reduced to electronic form—whether by video, scanning, or direct computer generation—it can easily be modified. The results go far beyond the crude forgeries, editing, or composites of earlier times.

Most importantly, it can be changed without detection. That is why this minichapter calls it a "new" dilemma. Until the last decade, a faked picture could be detected by careful analysis of each generation of negative, and one might try to warn or inform viewers of the deception. But today it is possible to alter a picture digitally so that the change is impossible to detect (Phelan, 1992). This is a new, and disturbing, situation.

Let's repeat that. Today, anyone with the ability to digitize a picture and insert it into a computer can adjust the picture at will, and turn out a changed "original," with nobody being the wiser. With digitization, the picture—original or modified—is merely a string of zeros and ones, which means that there is no surefire way to tell what is original or what has been changed.

Although such techniques could be used in most media—film, television, newspapers, radio, recordings—I've chosen to provide examples from the field of magazines. The cover of the largest-circulation magazine in the United States, *TV Guide*, once published on its cover the face of Oprah Winfrey attached to the body of Ann-Margret. Another top-circulation magazine, *National Geographic*, once "moved" one of the Egyptian pyramids in order to compose a better-looking cover. In yet another case, *Time*'s cover photograph of murder suspect O. J. Simpson in June 1994 was darkened in order to produce a somber mood. It is unlikely that many would have noticed, except that *Newsweek* ran the same picture on its cover that week, unretouched.

In these cases, it so happened that there were enough people who were familiar with how the picture should have looked to object loudly. But how often will there be people as familiar with a run-of-the-mill scene or person? Not very often! How many who see a doctored picture will also be exposed to a correction? Not very many! Hence, although it might be difficult to revise a scene or individual face familiar to millions without someone noticing, it is probable that all but a tiny handful of news photos could be modified without anyone being the wiser. All it takes is a few thousand dollars worth of equipment, and somebody—a source, an enemy of the subject who has the ear of or control over the media, a publisher, a news director, an editor, a photographer, a technician—who wants to do so.

This prospect is dismaying. The possibility of doing harm to individuals and to society is large, yet the public may benefit from pictures that have been modified to clarify a situation or to prevent individuals from being shocked or unjustly revealed. More than any other ethical controversy I've written about in this book, digital manipulation of pictures shows fewest opportunities for an ethical solution that is, at the same time, practical.

Digital technology exists, and we will have to find ways to live with it. We've done so before, with technologies such as firearms or automobiles, both of which could be used for good or for evil. We can't stuff it back into the laboratory—or Pandora's Box.

If we must accept it, is there an ethical way to deal with digital manipulation? I know only of one practical fix that has been seriously proposed: that the copyright laws be changed to give permanent control over an image (but not necessarily its use) to the creator of the image (the camera operator or the artist) and require this creator to certify the authenticity of the picture. If the creator won't or can't so certify, then the publisher or station licensee is rendered vulnerable to legal action brought by anyone affected by the doctored picture, and the public may be trained to dismiss the unacknowledged image. An already developed form of "electronic watermark" used primarily to ensure the copyright status of still photographs might further identify the image as "original"—until someone finds a way to circumvent this technology.

However, video and film cameras are now ubiquitous. Few, if any, Americans are without a nonprofessional photographic life record such as family pictures. Trying to restrict publication of pictures to those that are certified isn't practical. Many pictures are many decades old; a photographer can die and not be available to give a certification; a picture may not have an attributable source, something that often happens when pack journalism or family pictures are involved; and the photographer may not even be aware precisely of what he or she has shot because many photographers today shoot dozens of pictures in a few seconds with a motorized still camera, or are involved in a half-dozen video assignments a day. For example, one photographer who took a picture of himself with a self-timer in front of the Berlin Wall was shocked to find, when the picture was developed, an unnoticed East German border guard a few feet away with an automatic rifle pointing in his direction.

Nevertheless, it certainly is possible to develop a system whereby special digital "copyright" versions of any picture to be published or broadcast would be certified under oath by the photographer and filed immediately, in an untampered form, at some governmental or other repository. Anyone questioning the picture could compare the master file print with the published version. The "electronic watermark" mentioned earlier could benefit this system.

But it isn't probable. Pictures taken by amateurs are a growing part of the pictorial record, and few of these would be certified. It would be far too expensive and the process outlined is very unwieldy and hardly foolproof. More importantly, what would make someone suspect that the picture had been modified or manipulated? Without such suspicion, there would be no reason to check the archival copy!

That leaves only two other possibilities. One is the personal moral and professional ethical standards of photographers, artists, editors, retouchers, computer graphics artists, and the like. But because communicators have used whatever technology was available to manipulate pictures for so many years that it is accepted practice, it hasn't been thought of as wrong by most people in the field, even though digital manipulation can be undetectable.

At the same time, unfortunately, because most of the public has accepted the "pictures don't lie" aphorism as truth, these practices have a definite value for advertisers and propagandists. Hence, although the individual communicator still has a utilitarian obligation to be as truthful as possible with pictorial matter, it would be sticking one's head in the sand to believe that an ethical approach is likely to be universal. The temptation, combined with the rapidly falling prices of the equipment that makes manipulation possible, may be too much for many otherwise-moral picture editors.

The last potential solution is to make it possible to use these techniques without harm to the public. Here I join David Gordon, who proposed education of the public as the solution for another problem in Chapter 11. The public should not trust pictures. They should look at all pictures through a veil of suspicion, without any presumption that they are truthful. That is the bottom line. If no picture is trusted, then the public shouldn't easily be harmed by a doctored one. True, this would reduce the communication value of pictures to the public and lower the photographer, artist, or editor in terms of public esteem, but it may be the price we have to pay. (Wheeler, 1995)

I advocate that we take a Kantian position: The public should categorically never, never, never trust a picture. By treating the problem in this way, advocating teaching of ethical as well as perceptual standards of "visual literacy," we may defuse digital technology's potential for harm.

Let me restate the simple ethical solution: Each of us working in or studying the visual mass media needs to make sure that our fellow citizens know that pictures do lie, and that every picture should be looked at with the same suspicion and caution that we've learned to employ when reading or hearing words that may be self-serving, wrong, or manipulative. In other words, don't trust anyone—including me—without first independently checking the truth of our verbal *and* our visual assertions.

REFERENCES

Lester, Paul Martin. (1991). *Photojournalism: An Ethical Approach*. Mahwah, NJ: Lawrence Erlbaum Associates.

Mallen, Frank. (1954). *Sauce for the Gander*. White Plains, NY: Baldwin Books.

Phelan, John M. (Spring 1992). "The Pseudo Context of the Processed Image." *Media Ethics* 4(2), pp. 9–10.

Wheeler, Tom. (August 1995). "Public Perceptions of Photographic Credibility in the Age of Digital Manipulation." Paper presented at a meeting of the Association for Education in Journalism and Mass Communication, Washington, DC.

■ 15-G: PACK JOURNALISM

■ KITTROSS: The news media's current practice of pack journalism is not only inefficient but unethical as well.

The so-called newsworthy event draws so-called journalists as honey—or manure—draws flies. A visit by a potentate, a major political or sporting event, an airplane crash, a juicy court trial, all attract the pack: hundreds of reporters whose words and pictures will be presented to readers and viewers as soon as modern technologies can carry them. When in full bay, the very size of the pack often—in a travesty of what "news coverage" is all about—becomes a story in itself, or the subject of a *Doonesbury* or *Bloom County* comic strip.

Although one might blame reporters, photographers, videographers, and sound recordists for the mob scenes that have cast disrepute on the news media and made public life much less attractive, the blame really should fall on the assignment or city editors who send out these reporters and photographers. This process was disturbingly illustrated in the case of the death of Princess Diana in 1997. The paparazzi pursuing her were mostly freelance but were nevertheless assured of cash rewards and promises of publication from both the tabloids and the mainstream press for any pictures they could take of her. Despite general revulsion with the paparazzi in this case, leading to calls for stricter British privacy laws, some publishers showed no shame. Press magnate Rupert Murdoch was quoted on the BBC as saying that "privacy laws are for the protection of people already privileged" and that his only problem was that he had been paying too much to the paparazzi.

Why must each station or newspaper have its own people report an event that often is of very limited intrinsic importance? Why do editors, publishers, and news directors reject the possibilities of pool coverage or the use of wire services or free-lancers? Why do we need to see dozens of ballpoint pens, throats, lenses, and microphones thrust at the accused, the victim, or the innocent bystander? For example, why was it necessary for any network to send its anchor to Los Angeles for the opening of the O. J. Simpson criminal trial? Did every photo outlet in New England have to get its own shot of the horror on the faces of Christa McAuliffe's class when the spacecraft *Challenger*, with her aboard, exploded on live TV in 1986?

The usual argument is that only with their own staff reporting the story can newspapers or broadcasters be confident of the validity and reliability of their content. But when one thinks about the stories that *aren't* covered because limited resources are devoted to being one of the pack, and of all media's reliance on the wire services, freelancers, CNN, or Court TV, this excuse falls flat.

. . . it may well be that the worst result of pack journalism is the loss of independent reporting.

Indeed, it may well be that the worst result of pack journalism is the loss of independent reporting. Every newsroom has tales of reporters whose stories are killed by overly cautious editors because the competition carried a story with a different slant. At the reporter's level, as Timothy Crouse pointed out in *The Boys on the Bus* (1973), those on the scene keep asking one another what their—and the television networks'—leads were.

Stories are covered with the resources available. If a volcano erupts, it is covered by those fortunate enough (from a career point of view) to have been on the scene; the carpetbaggers who swarm off the first available jets rarely add to the accounts that already have been made available to readers or viewers. During wartime, pool coverage is used to ensure that all members of the audience, regardless of what source they watch, read, or listen to, have access to the same important news. If news-gathering resources are left over, then human interest or sidebar stories are covered uniquely by each reporter—but this is merely frosting on the cake for most of the audience.

Remember, just because the same reportage is available to each media outlet, there needn't be only one way to present it. As has been true in the past, each editor can place a particular spin or emphasis on any story.

The economic inefficiency of pack journalism is easy to demonstrate. If a substantial fraction of the nation's reporters are tied up covering the O. J. Simpson trials (and, to those who have read the U.S. Department of Labor's media employment statistics, "substantial fraction" isn't hyperbole), then other news—possibly of equal or greater importance and interest—doesn't get covered. If budgets are drawn down through the rental of aircraft or tying up of satellite trucks, then all news coverage for the rest of that fiscal year will be diminished.

But what about the ethics of the time-honored journalistic practice of making sure that the competition isn't given a free ride with a story, story element, or angle? My opinion is that this practice results in both short-term and long-term harm to the public (see Bates, 1994). And if a news media practice harms readers and viewers, then I believe that practice is unethical from all points of view.

In the short term, pack journalism uses scarce human, technological, and fiscal resources inefficiently. In the long term, pack journalism reduces all news values to "let's make sure the competition doesn't get too far ahead of us." The desirability of searching for stories to cover, or the benefits of uncovering something new and significant to the audience, are lost when the assignment editor is worried more about what the publisher or news director will say about falling behind than about the possibility of being out in front.

Furthermore, the constant badgering of people "in the news" that is the obvious corollary to pack journalism goes a long way toward reducing the number of people who would be willing to put themselves in the public eye—a fact that may be reflected in the number of show-biz celebrities who have entered politics. Not everyone is willing to have every action of every moment of their (and their family's) lives scrutinized by a horde of yapping journalists and lose the modicum of privacy to which everyone should be entitled.

If news is defined as "what everyone is chasing," then newsgathering becomes a sports event rather than an essential part of our social and political life. I don't think it should be.

REFERENCES

Bates, Stephen. (Fall 1994). "Who Is the Journalist's Client?" *Media Ethics* 7(1), p. 3.
Crouse, Timothy. (1973). *The Boys on the Bus*. New York: Random House.

■ 15-H: CIVILITY, "DIRTY" LANGUAGE, AND RELIGION
■ KITTROSS: The right to swing one's fist ends where someone else's nose begins.

The points I'm trying to make in this mini-chapter reflect some of what my nonmedia friends and relatives often ask—even hector—me about. These matters are amorphous enough that arguing them is difficult, and in any given case I'm not sure on which side I'd land. However, I believe they reflect some important principles that bring up questions that must be answered in any discussion of controversies in media ethics. Each of the three topics listed in the title above—civility, language, and religion—has gratuitous injury, however major or minor, as a factor, and they are more related than they are separate.

■ THE CIVIL USE OF HONORIFICS

The road to hell can be paved with the best of intentions. For example, in an effort to eliminate the prejudicial practice of using applicable titles and honorifics (Mrs., Mr., Ms., Rev., Dr., etc.) of whites but omitting them when reporting on members of other races (or sometimes, as in England, other classes), the stylebooks in American newsrooms now suggest that all honorifics be omitted whenever possible. This has the further advantage of eliminating the need to ask every woman whether she uses Ms., Mrs., or Miss—a reflection of the discussion in Chapter 7.

But are all the results of this practice beneficial? Hardly! In the first place, even when it is an integral part of the story, the gender of an individual being reported on can be obscured because first names often are ambiguous.

Much more importantly, the omission of honorifics and titles is a further march down the road to increased daily incivility. Some titles are a function of gender, others are assumed, but many are granted only after major achievement. The paths to a professorship or to the privileges and responsibilities of a medical doctor or priest are long and difficult, and it is denigrating these achievements to ignore them. In some professions, such as the military, rank is the label for level of authority and responsibility. Why do the media now insult individuals of all classes, all occupations, and all conditions by omitting their earned titles and reducing legitimate individual accomplishments and status to naught?

Rudeness, whether on the part of a tough on the street or a reporter, should not be accepted. It makes the society in which we live a meaner one. It does not eliminate class barriers and promote equality, except at the meanest level. It reduces the impetus to excel in any field, particularly the traditional learned professions.

■ LANGUAGE

Here we deal with what our grandparents might have called "filthy language." Of course, generally speaking, words—or pictures—by themselves can't cause harm. As children, we learned that "sticks and stones will break your bones, but words will never hurt you." But their denotations and connotations may harm people, intentionally or unintentionally.

The prudery of earlier times, which ignored the fact that every living thing excretes, gave rise to the use of euphemisms, many of which had excretory or sexual connotations. Social barriers have risen against using some of these common terms. "To pee" is no less useful than "to urinate," and has been in use centuries longer. There no longer are any good reasons for not calling bullshit "bullshit," despite the fact that there are still regions of the United States where "cow brute" is said rather than "bull." We've come a long way since homosexuality was "the crime that had no name." Yet we—and the publishers of this book—still have some taboos in common with the major media, such as full frontal nudity and the common four-letter words for intercourse, penis, and vagina.

Is this because these banned words and pictures are inherently evil, or is it because there is no need to offend and disturb those who are bothered by such words—another aspect of civility? Or, as has occurred in some political campaigns, in both paid advertising and in public relations, does the public tune out when the language gets too rough?

It may be clever to title the best book on how to start a radio station *Sex and Broadcasting* (Milam 1975) but at what point does shock lose its value? Do pictures of nude women on page 3 of some popular British tabloid newspapers, or partially clothed models in the Victoria's Secret catalog, or gratuitous (not necessary to plot or character development) simulated or real sex acts in motion pictures really add to our understanding of the purposes or aesthetics of art, the human body, or human sexual or excretory functions? Do advertisers really sell more goods using ads with semi-nude models?

On the one hand, there was a saying in the Victorian era that one could do as one wished as long as he or she didn't disturb the horses. What I consider the best essay on censorship (Broun, 1927) reminds us that no woman was ever "ruined" by a book; humans act, and are responsible for their actions, regardless of whether they are moral or immoral.

On the other hand, to claim that sniggering titillation reflects human sexuality, or that a litany of four-letter words is a bold literary device reflects at best laziness as well as a willingness to pander to what earlier generations would call our baser instincts. Those in the mass media are responsible for their actions, regardless of whether they are moral or immoral.

■ RELIGION AND THE MEDIA

Finally, there are the relationships of the media, public relations, and advertising to the traditional repository of morality: organized religion. These relationships are the most problematic of all because faith—the unreasoning suspension of disbelief—is something with which it is difficult to compromise, and what is perceived as an attack on one's religion often is considered an attack on one's very being.

Yet, the mass media are often faced with pragmatic ethical questions that involve religion. For example, is it ethical to publish something that others consider an attack on their religion, regardless of intent (such as Salman Rushdie's *Satanic Verses*, greeted by some Islamics with death threats)? Should the media operate on religious holidays? (Journalists working on the Sabbath in Israel have been assaulted by Orthodox Jews with stones.) Is an account of a real or fictional religious leader's peccadilloes justifiable (as in the movie *Elmer Gantry*)? How about religious practices that cause revulsion in those not of that religion (such as snake-handling by a sect in the American south or scenes from the television program *Death of a Princess*, a broadcast that also raised Islamic ire)? Should misbehavior involving sexual assaults on young people by priests be covered in the press, or should the church be allowed to deal with such matters in private? Are conflicts over succession, theology, and liturgy public or private matters? Are ministers, priests, and rabbis fair game as butts for comedy programs or movies? Was Dan Quayle right in attacking Murphy Brown—a fictional character in a television situation comedy!—for the moral lapse of bearing a child out of wedlock?

More generally, should one's own moral standards be subject to religious doctrinal discipline? Should organized religion be sacrosanct—immune from coverage that might lead to criticism for its actions? What is blasphemy—and is it acceptable? Is religion somehow different from all other societal institutions?

These aren't easy questions to answer. Not only do they have ethical and moral implications, but there may be significant pragmatic consequences no matter which course is chosen. Organized religion, in almost every nation or culture, can show wrath in many ways—from death threats and boycotts to diplomatic ruptures—for transgressions that might be deemed acceptable or unimportant in another country, at another time, by a different sect or faith, or by those for whom religion is relatively unimportant or who are truly open-minded.

The media always have been the target of religions that are arrogant enough to believe that they have the right to control what the entire citizenry—not just adherents to that faith—sees and hears. One can go back hundreds of years and find the same pattern: a rejection of lay-produced morality plays here, and a condemnation of the commercial theater there; an index of banned publications here, and a ceremonial burning of offending literature there.

[I]ndividual human beings are in their most vulnerable and limited condition when a monolith imposes its will—with sword, sacrament, or soundbite.

Is this conflict, one-sided or not, real or imagined, to continue? I hope not, because religion is too important either to ignore or genuflect to without sound reason. Religion still plays a large part in domestic and international politics. The possibility of violent conflict between religions, on the order of Hindu versus Moslem in India after independence and partition, is always with us. It isn't only in developing countries that such violence may occur; some fundamentalist sects in the United States are willing to fight for the Lord with clubs and guns as well as with words. Sometimes, as in the former Yugoslavia, ethnic as well as religious issues are at stake. If the state becomes a religious one, then the media will be subject to religious law, as in Afghanistan. Fortunately for those living in the United States, the First Amendment to the Constitution prohibits both the establishment of religion and governmental barriers to its free exercise. It is where the law is silent that the conflicts between media and minister, between doctrine and entertainment, and between news and sin are most important.

Normally I believe that the separation between church and state should be reflected in separation between secular media and church because individual human beings are in their most vulnerable and limited condition when a monolith imposes its will—with sword, sacrament, or soundbite.

When there are various countervailing forces—such as church and state—individual human beings can find ways to exist around the edges. When church and state (and, today, business) cooperate or conspire to control and milk parishioners, subjects, and customers, then the media (until their suppression?) may be the only voices for freedom. Through their ability to stimulate public action or reaction, the media are the only major countervailing force in a world where multinational and even global firms control the economy, religions increasingly control government, and government claims the right to control movement and freedom, sanctions violence (all is fair in war) and often attempts to control what we think, even in the United States.

As usual, easy answers are not good ones, and vice versa. The values of civility should make it incumbent on the media not to insult gratuitously the followers of any religion—not merely the ones that a particular society or the employees of the media find "legitimate." The 1993 Branch Davidian disaster in Waco, Texas, tells us what can happen if we do. After all, can anyone who accepts Mill or Kant as a guide accept the forcible removal of someone's belief structure? Is brainwashing of *any* sort "good"?

By the same token, the media in general should neither ignore nor be co-opted by any particular religion; they have obligations to everyone in their audience as well as to the truth (as argued in Chapter 4). A special case would be the media now owned by religious organizations which, as long as competing secular media are available to the same audiences, should not adversely affect a diverse society.

■ CONCLUSION

Why do many of those in the mass media today take the easy way out in these three areas of civility, language, and religion? Laziness, arrogance, and immaturity are the only answers I can think of. Too much emphasis on and experience with the uncivil side of life—chicanery, scandal, disaster—may make it far too easy for the press to sneer at the rest of humanity. Repeated use can desensitize people's reaction to language. The institution of religion is certainly as important as, though different from, mass communication. The essential question is: are journalists part of society or separate from it? I believe that the media are a very important part of our society, and it would be sad if they enshrined laziness and arrogance as their goals.

REFERENCES

Broun, Heywood. (1927). "Censorship." In Heywood Broun and Margaret Leach, *Anthony Comstock: Roundsman of the Lord*. New York: Boni & Liveright.
Milam, Lorenzo. (1975). *Sex and Broadcasting*. Los Gatos, CA: Dildo Press.

■ 15-I: INTERVIEWS

■ KITTROSS: The interview is an unreliable, often invalid, and even harmful way of obtaining information for the media.

There is an old—and sick—joke that has a reporter asking the widow of an assassinated president, "Apart from that, Mrs. Lincoln, how did you like the play?"

Such a stereotypical, vapid, and insensitive question may reflect the reporter's ineptitude or inability to focus on the real story, but it may also reflect an unreasoned faith in the efficacy and significance of journalistic interviewing—one of the most basic journalism tools.

Unfortunately, there are only a few ways through which reporters can gather news, and social scientists warn us about unreliability of eyewitness accounts—even when a trained reporter is the observer or the interviewer. It is my opinion that the best, if not the most common, reporting is in the form of reasoned essays providing an analysis of myriad often-undocumented sources rather than merely repeating another's words and others' data. Woodward and Bernstein, in *All the President's Men*, illustrated the technique of using official and unofficial documents. But many reporters need to validate their work by using someone else's statements rather than their own brains, and find it easier to allow someone else to filter the wheat from the chaff of complex documents.

It can be argued that interviews give people a chance to tell their own stories, that they are a more valid, more reliable, and even more ethical way of gathering information than using jaded, possibly biased reporters' or documentarians' direct observations or analyses. Certainly, one form of interview—the testimonial—has played a major role in the history of advertising. But I believe that the mass media's practices of interviewing actually are much less ethical than journalists, documentarians, advertising researchers, and others claim, and that the ethics of interviewing may be confused with often selfish and ineffective practices.

What we really need is to use the interview as a way of getting at the truth, not as a way of touching all bases or transferring the contents of the reporter's brain into someone else's mouth or vice versa. People can be mistaken, or they can lie or misspeak themselves, but you'd never know it from most of the media. In court, there is the opportunity to test the probity—the truthfulness and reliability—of testimony. In the media, perhaps due to reporter gratitude to the interviewee for allowing the interview to take place, almost every utterance is taken and presented to the audience at face value.

Certainly, there are a few interviewers—Ted Koppel on *Nightline*, for example, or Studs Terkel—who allow the audience to draw its own conclusions about whether to believe the questioned person. More often, particularly in an "ambush" interview, the intent of a questioner is not to elicit answers, but to show the public how the interviewee reacted. It is very easy to make someone look stupid or guilty—more so in television because the print media's willingness to clean up grammar and syntax disappears when a taped interview is broadcast.

I have three major objections to current standards of interviewing. First, much ambush and similar interviewing, particularly in the aftermath of a disaster, is an unconscionable invasion of well-deserved and much needed privacy. The media's habit of "doorstepping" the relatives of the recently deceased—asking how a person "felt" when a loved one is killed—is ghoulish and adds little to our understanding of the tragedy.

Second, the media have taken the Edward R. Murrow/Fred Friendly "law" ("there is no substitute for someone with a fire in the belly") and turned it from being a way of informing into a way of titillating the public with the juiciest soundbite.

Third, the media often use interviews—sometimes with mythical or invented "people on the street"—merely as a way of justifying preconceived (and often stereotypical) stories.

With respect to the last of these complaints, there also seems to be an unreasoning belief that just because someone is quoted as saying something, it necessarily is true or important. For example, a televised "vox populi" may provide significant insights once in a blue moon. But a trivial or obvious bit of information—for example, "It's the first warm day of spring"—doesn't need an interview to validate it.

Yet another belief of some editors (and readers, viewers, and listeners) is that all sins are forgiven if we merely present "both sides of the matter." Are there only two sides? Do we really need carefully balanced political opinions if one candidate really has something to say and the other doesn't? Must we balance every interview with a victim of a crime by an interview with the accused or the accused's attorney? Do we know what the "person on the street" is thinking from the no-brainer triplet—soundbite interviews that say, "I like X," "I dislike X," and "What's X?"?

For some reason, there are few separate college courses in journalistic interviewing, although sociologists, clinical psychologists, and anthropologists all accept the need for specialized training in this delicate skill. What interviewing courses we have tend to deal with topics—how to cover the courthouse, how to cover a fire—rather than with the basic question of how valid and reliable our interviewing practices might be.

Because the editing of an interview—whether soundbite or lengthy discourse—is in the hands of the media, there is no reason to expect that an interview is more valid than information garnered elsewhere or in other ways. The advertising testimonial, which can be considered selective use of a form of interview, although under some control by the Federal Trade Commission or state agencies, certainly is susceptible to the same sort of manipulation.

In general, I believe that the interviews and advertising testimonials we read and see and hear rarely give us useful information. The practice helps neither interviewer nor interviewee nor the ultimate user, the public. Hence, from a utilitarian point of view, they are ethically useless. Typically, interviews give the appearance of objectivity without the reality, and they take the reporter off the hook of having to justify her or his reportage.

Of course, I'm generalizing. And it has been justly said that all generalizations are false—including this one. But suppose you were Mrs. Lincoln? Or you were made to look foolish by an interviewer? (Remember how Connie Chung made speaker Newt Gingrich and his mother appear on CBS early in 1995?) Or you were misled because an interview was cut off in the editing room for dramatic, rather than informative, purposes?

Aren't there better, more utilitarian ways of procuring less biased information?

■ 15-J: HONESTY IN REPORTING

■ KITTROSS: To lie to get access to the news may be justified, especially if it is the only way the public can get the information it needs.

In the spring of 1997, a North Carolina jury decision was rendered in the case of *Food Lion v. ABC*. ABC was on the losing side of a $5.5 million decision—not (according to jurors) because of what was said or shown in the program, or because of "hidden cameras" or investigative reporting per se. It was not a libel case. The reasons given for the punitive damages were that the two ABC producers who actually collected footage of unsanitary meat packaging conditions with hidden cameras had lied about their background in job applications, had been paid (a pittance) by Food Lion during time they actually were taping for ABC, and had shown disloyalty to their North Carolina employer.

Although the award has since been reduced to $315,000 and may or may not be upheld on appeal, it has caused many journalists to reconsider what had become fairly normal practice—misleading sources as to the reporter's identity in order to get a story. This story was particularly interesting to journalists, because it followed directly in the tradition of Upton Sinclair, who had written on the terrible conditions of meat slaughter and packing houses a century before in his book, *The Jungle*.

A vocal minority of members of the public, and some members of the journalistic profession (mostly print journalists, perhaps out of jealousy), hold that reporters should *always* identify themselves honestly. Ben Bradlee, *Washington Post* editor for many years, who fought so hard (and successfully) against giving a Pulitzer prize to the *Chicago Sun-Times* after the newspaper and a civic group had bought the "Mirage Bar" and waited (with cameras) for city inspectors to ask for payoffs, still argues this way.

But is this really practical? And, in many instances, does it matter if the person interviewing you is John Jones, nosey neighbor, or Sally Smith, reporter?

Stealing documents or pieces of tainted food is one thing, but turning on a camera hidden on one's person is another. Even though our society is asking for "ID" more and more frequently, almost anyone—mail carriers, fire inspectors, electricians, cleaners—could be coming through almost any commercial or governmental "non-public" space at any time, which mitigates against any real expectation of privacy.

I've experienced too many examples—trespass (through my back yard), applications for graduate school or for jobs that played fast and loose with the truth, and disloyalty to the aims of the institution someone is asking to join—to think that ABC has been the only transgressor of note. I ignore the trespass, reject the dishonest applications, and try to instill loyalty in the disloyal.

As it happens, perhaps ABC should have looked harder for other ways to report the story. It might not have been necessary to hide a camera in a wig—Upton Sinclair didn't need one. Perhaps there were ways to fill out the job application that didn't lie or rhapsodize over the meat industry—they truthfully could have said they had been working for Disney, which now owns ABC.

But these are small points, less heinous than the rule that permits members of the Internal Revenue Service to use false identities when dealing with taxpayers. As Louis Hodges (1997) reminds us, the real issue, a utilitarian one, was tainted meat. The story and the potential benefits of that story to the public, and not what fibs may have been told to get it, is what is important. For example, if ABC's undercover people didn't do the job for which Food Lion had hired them—to detect bad meat and get rid of it, rather than film it—then they are harming the public, and all appeals to the First Amendment will be of no avail if someone dies through eating the bad meat.

What will be best for the public? A rigid rule that only allows every potential interviewee or subject of a story to be sure that he or she is *not* talking to a reporter? Or a flexible rule that permits the reporter to serve the public by covering something that needs to be covered—in this instance, the packaging and sale of tainted meat, and in other cases, "snake pit" mental hospitals, quack physicians, dishonest office holders, police officers "on the take," and others to whom we need to be alerted.

Unlike the police, who must gather evidence within the doctrine of the "fruit of the poisoned tree," the reporter is not in a position to jail someone. If there is no penalty attached to using a nickname or a false identity in situations where there is no intent to defraud, then it is no big step to permitting reporters—when it is necessary to get the story—to omit their journalistic affiliation. Since the public—as represented by the *Food Lion* jury—disapproves of such practices, they should be used only when necessary and justifiable to a reasonable person.

The news media are a major part of the self-correcting mechanism of our society, and we should not allow Bradlee's iron-clad rule of "always identifying yourself" to make it impossible—in those few cases where concealing identity is necessary—to serve that function.

If this is saying that "the end justifies the means"—so be it.

REFERENCE

Hodges, Louis W. (Spring 1997). "The Real Issue Is Tainted Food." *Media Ethics* 8(2), p. 4. Hodges was an expert witness for the defense in the Food Lion case. This issue of *Media Ethics* contained several articles exploring *Food Lion* v. *ABC* from various viewpoints.

BIBLIOGRAPHY

This bibliography includes the most important and useful citations appearing at the end of each chapter. In addition, it presents a number of sources relevant to the issues discussed in this book but not specifically cited in any of the chapters.

Altschull, J. Herbert. (1996). *From Milton to McLuhan: The Ideas Behind American Journalism.* New York: Longman.

Andison, F. Scott. (Fall 1977). "TV Violence and Viewer Aggression: A Cumulation of Study Results 1956–1976." *Public Opinion Quarterly* 41(3), pp. 314–331.

Argyris, Chris. (1974). *Behind the Front Page.* San Francisco: Jossey-Bass.

Aristotle. (Many editions). *Nicomachean Ethics.*

Baker, Lee W. (1993). *The Credibility Factor, Putting Ethics to Work in Public Relations.* Homewood, IL: Business One Irwin.

Barbour, William, ed. (1994). *Mass Media: Opposing Viewpoints.* San Diego: Greenhaven Press.

Barnes, Hazel. (1978). *An Existentialist Ethics.* Chicago: University of Chicago Press.

Barron, Jerome A. (1973). *Freedom of the Press for Whom?* Bloomington: Indiana University Press.

Benedict, Helen. (1992). *Virgin or Vamp: How the Press Covers Sex Crimes.* New York: Oxford University Press.

Bentham, Jeremy. (1823). *An Introduction to the Principles of Morals and Legislation.* Oxford: Clarendon Press.

Bertrand, Claude-Jean. (1997). "Media Ethics and Media Accountability Systems," in C. J. Bertrand, *Les Medias Et L'Information aux Etats-Unis Depuis 1945.* Paris: Ellipses.

Bivins, Thomas H. (Summer 1993). "A Worksheet for Ethics Instruction and Exercises in Reason." *Journalism Educator* 48(2), pp. 4–16.

Black, Jay. (Summer, 1995). "Commentary: Rethinking the naming of sex crime victims." *Newspaper Research Journal* 16(3), pp. 96–112.

———, ed. (1997). *Mixed News: The Public/Civic/Communitarian Journalism Debate.* Mahwah, NJ: Lawrence Erlbaum Associates.

Black, Jay, and Ralph Barney. (Fall-Winter, 1985–1986). "The Case Against Mass Media Codes of Ethics." *Journal of Mass Media Ethics* 1(1), pp. 27–36.

————. (Fall 1992/Winter 1993). "Commentary: Journalism Ethics since Janet Cooke." *Newspaper Research Journal* 13(4)/14(1), pp. 2–16.

Black, Jay, Bob Steele, and Ralph Barney. (1995). *Doing Ethics in Journalism: A Handbook with Case Studies*, 2nd ed. Boston: Allyn & Bacon.

Boeyink, David. (Winter, 1994). "How Effective are Codes of Ethics? A Look at Three Newsrooms." *Journalism Quarterly* 71(4), pp. 893–904.

Bok, Sissela. (1978). *Lying: Moral Choice in Public and Private Life*. New York: Random House.

————. (1982). *Secrets: On the Ethics of Concealment and Revelation*. New York: Pantheon.

Boorstin, Daniel J. (1961). *The Image: A Guide to Pseudo-Events in America*. New York: Harper & Row.

Breed, Warren. (1955). "Social Control in the Newsroom." *Social Forces* 33(4), pp. 326–335.

Brewer, Marcus, and Maxwell McCombs. (Spring, 1996). "Setting the Community Agenda." *Journalism & Mass Communication Quarterly* 73(1), pp. 7–16.

Bryant, Jennings. (1993). "Will Traditional Media Research Paradigms Be Obsolete in the Era of Intelligent Communication Networks?" In Philip Gaunt, ed., *Beyond Agendas: New Directions in Communication Research*. Westport, CT: Greenwood Press, pp. 149–167

Bugeja, Michael J. (1996). *Living Ethics: Developing Values in Mass Communication*. Boston: Allyn & Bacon.

Byrd, Joann. (Fall 1992). "Fair's Fair—Unless It Isn't." *Media Studies Journal*, pp. 103–112; see also the rest of this issue devoted to "The Fairness Factor."

Christians, Clifford G., John P. Ferré, and P. Mark Fackler. (1993). *Good News: Social Ethics and the Press*. New York: Oxford University Press.

Christians, Clifford G., Mark Fackler, Kim B. Rotzoll, and Kathy Brittain McKee. (1998). *Media Ethics: Cases and Moral Reasoning*, 5th ed. New York: Longman.

Cohen, Elliot D., ed. (1992). *Philosophical Issues in Journalism*. New York: Oxford University Press.

Commission on Freedom of the Press. (1947). *A Free and Responsible Press*. Chicago: University of Chicago Press.

Comstock, George, Steven Chaffee, Natan Katzman, Maxwell McCombs, and Donald Roberts. (1978). *Television and Human Behavior*. New York: Columbia University Press.

Console, Stephen. (1983). "Cable Television Privacy Act: Protecting Privacy Interests from Emerging Cable TV Technology." *Federal Communications Law Journal* 35, pp. 71–94.

Cooper, Thomas W., Clifford G. Christians, Frances Forde Plude, and Robert A. White. (1989). *Communication Ethics and Global Change*. White Plains, NY: Longman.

Davenport, Lucinda D., and Ralph S. Izard. (Fall-Winter 1985–1986). "Restrictive Policies of the Mass Media." *Journal of Mass Media Ethics* 1(1), pp. 4–9.

Davies, Simon. (November-December, 1997). "Time for a Byte of Privacy Please." *Index on Censorship* 26(6), pp. 45–48.

Day, Louis A. (1997). *Ethics in Modern Communications: Cases and Controversies*, 2nd ed. Belmont, CA: Wadsworth.

Dennis, Everette E., Arnold H. Ismach, and Donald M. Gillmor. (1978). *Enduring Issues in Mass Communication.* St. Paul, MN: West Publishing.

Dennis, Everette E., and John C. Merrill. (1996). *Media Debates: Issues in Mass Communication,* 2nd ed. White Plains, NY: Longman.

Diamond, Edwin, and Robert A. Silverman. (1995). *White House to Your House: Media and Politics in Virtual America.* Cambridge, MA: MIT Press.

Duska, Ronald, and Mariellen Whelan. (1975). *Moral Development: A Guide to Piaget and Kohlberg.* New York: Paulist Press.

Dworkin, Andrea. (Spring, 1985). "Against the Male Flood: Censorship, Pornography and Equality." *Harvard Women's Law Journal* 8, pp. 1–29.

Dworkin, Andrea, and Catharine A. MacKinnon. (1988). *Pornography and Civil Rights: A New Day for Women's Equality.* Minneapolis: Organizing Against Pornography.

Edwards, Audrey. (Winter-Spring 1993). "From Aunt Jemima to Anita Hill: Media's Split Image of Black Women." *Media Studies Journal* 7(2), pp. 215–222.

Elliott, Deni, ed. (1986). *Responsible Journalism.* Newbury Park, CA: Sage.

———. (Fall, 1987). "Creating Conditions for Ethical Journalism." *Mass Communication Review* 14(3), pp. 6–10.

Etzioni, Amitai. (1993). *The Spirit of Community: Rights, Responsibilities, and the Communitarian Agenda.* New York: Crown.

Federal Communications Commission. (Spring 1965). "Memorandum Opinion and Order In re Application of Pacifica Foundation for Renewal of Licenses of Station KPFA-FM and KPFB (January 2, 1964)," reprinted as "The 'Pacifica' Decision: Broadcasting and Free Expression." *Journal of Broadcasting* 9(2), pp. 177–182.

Fink, Conrad C. (1988). *Media Ethics: In the Newsroom and Beyond.* New York: McGraw-Hill.

Fletcher, Joseph. (1966). *Situation Ethics: The New Morality.* Philadelphia: Westminster Press.

Gilligan, Carol (1982). *In a Different Voice.* Cambridge, MA: Harvard University Press.

Glazer, Nathan, and Daniel Patrick Moynihan. (1963). *Beyond the Melting Pot.* Cambridge, MA: MIT Press.

Goodwin, H. E., and Ron F. Smith. (1996). *Groping for Ethics in Journalism,* 3rd ed. Ames: Iowa State University Press.

Greenberg, Karen Joy, ed. (1991). *Conversations on Communication Ethics.* Norwood, NJ: Ablex Publishing.

Griffiths, Philip Jones. (November-December 1997) "No Di, no pix." *Index on Censorship* 26(6), pp. 26–31.

Hart, H.L.A. (1963). *Law, Liberty and Morality.* New York: Vintage Books.

Hausman, Carl. (1992). *Crisis of Conscience: Perspectives on Journalism Ethics.* New York: HarperCollins.

Henry, William A. III. (1994). *In Defense of Elitism.* New York: Doubleday.

Hobbes, Thomas. (1950). *Leviathan.* New York: E. P. Dutton.

Hodges, Louis. (1994). "The Journalist and Privacy." *Journal of Mass Media Ethics* 9(4), pp. 235–242.

Hoff, Kenneth M. H. (1984). "Two-Way Cable Television and Informational Privacy." *Comm/Ent Law Journal* 6, pp. 797–836.

Hulteng, John L. (1985). *The Messenger's Motives*. Englewood Cliffs, NJ: Prentice-Hall.

Johannesen, Richard L. (1996). *Ethics in Human Communication*, 4th ed. Prospect Heights, IL: Waveland Press.

Johnstone, J. W. C., E. J. Slawski, and W. W. Bowman. (1976). *The News People: A Sociological Portrait of American Journalists*. Urbana: University of Illinois Press.

Journal of Mass Media Ethics. (Fall-Winter 1985–1986). 1(1). (The entire issue is devoted to discussions of media ethics codes.)

Kant, Immanuel. (1959). *Foundations of the Metaphysics of Morals*. Indianapolis: Bobbs-Merrill.

Kapor, Mitchell. (July-August 1993). "Where is the Digital Highway Really Heading?" *Wired*, pp. 53–59.

Kieran, Matthew. (1997). *Media Ethics: A Philosophical Approach*. Westport, CT: Praeger.

Kittross, John M. (Spring 1988). "New, Improved RTNDA Ethics Code?" *Media Ethics Update* 1(1), pp. 5, 10.

———. (Spring 1989). "Round Three: Response to Marks." *Media Ethics Update* 2(1), pp. 7, 16–17.

Kohlberg, Lawrence. (1981). *The Philosophy of Moral Development: Moral Stages and the Idea of Justice*. New York: Harper & Row.

Knowlton, Steven R. (1997). *Moral Reasoning for Journalists: Cases and Comments*. Westport, CT: Praeger.

Knowlton, Steven R., and Patrick R. Parsons. (1995). *The Journalist's Moral Compass: Basic Principles*. Westport, CT: Praeger.

Korzybski, Alfred. (1933). *Science and Sanity: An Introduction to Non-Aristotelian Systems and General Semantics*. Lancaster, PA: Science Press Printing Co.

Kubey, Robert, ed. (1997). *Media Literacy in the Information Age: Current Perspectives*. New Brunswick, NJ: Transaction Publishers.

Lambeth, Edmund B. (1992). *Committed Journalism: An Ethic for the Profession*, 2nd ed. Bloomington: Indiana University Press.

Lashner, Marilyn A. (1984). *The Chilling Effect in TV News: Intimidation by the Nixon White House*. New York: Praeger.

Lebacqz, Karen. (1985). *Professional Ethics: Power and Paradox*. Nashville, TN: Abingdon Press.

Lester, Paul Martin, ed. (1996). *Images That Injure: pictorial stereotypes in the media*. Westport, CT: Praeger.

Levitt, Theodore. (July-August 1970). "The Morality (?) of Advertising." *Harvard Business Review*, pp. 84–92.

Lieberman, David. (February 22, 1992). "Fake News." *TV Guide*, pp. 10–26.

Limburg, Val E. (1994). *Electronic Media Ethics*. Boston: Focal Press.

Linz, David, Edward Donnerstein, and Steven Penrod. (Summer, 1984). "The Effects of Multiple Exposures to Filmed Violence Against Women." *Journal of Communication* 34(3), pp. 130–147.

Lippmann, Walter. (1922). *Public Opinion*. New York: Macmillan.

Machiavelli, Niccolo. (Many editions). *The Prince*.

MacIntyre, Alasdair. (1966). *A Short History of Ethics*. New York: Random House.

MacKinnon, Catherine A. (1993). *Only Words*. Cambridge, MA: Harvard University Press.

Makau, Josina M., and Ronald C. Arnett., eds. (1997). *Communication Ethics in an Age of Diversity*. Urbana and Chicago: University of Illinois Press.

Marks, Jeffrey. (Spring, 1989). "New Improved RTNDA Ethics Code!" *Media Ethics Update* 2(1), p. 6.

Martindale, Carolyn. (Summer 1990). "Coverage of Black Americans in Four Major Newspapers, 1950–1989." *Newspaper Research Journal* 11(2), pp. 96–112.

Matelski, Marilyn. (1991). *TV News Ethics*. Boston: Focal Press.

McCulloch, Frank, ed. (1984). *Drawing the Line: How 31 Editors Solved Their Toughest Ethics Dilemmas*. Washington: American Society of Newspaper Editors Foundation.

McElreath, Mark P. (1993). *Managing Systematic and Ethical Public Relations*. Dubuque, IA: Brown & Benchmark.

Meeske, Mike, and Fred Fedler. (1993). "Checkbook Journalism in the Electronic Media: Alive and Flourishing." Paper presented at the annual convention of the Association for Education in Journalism and Mass Communication, Kansas City, MO, August 11–14.

Merrill, John C. (1974). *The Imperative of Freedom: A Philosophy of Journalistic Autonomy*. New York: Hastings House.

———. (1993). *The Dialectic in Journalism: Toward a Responsible Use of Press Freedom*. Baton Rouge: Louisiana State University Press.

———. (1994). *Legacy of Wisdom: Great Thinkers and Journalism*. Ames: Iowa State University Press.

———. (1995) *Existential Journalism*, rev. ed. Ames: Iowa State University Press.

———. (1997). *Journalism Ethics: Philosophical Foundations for News Media*. New York: St. Martin's Press.

———. (1998). *The Princely Press: Machiavelli on American Journalism*. Lanham, MD: University Press of America.

Meyer, Philip. (1983). *Editors, Publishers, and Newspaper Ethics*. Washington, DC: American Society of Newspaper Editors.

———. (1991). *Ethical Journalism: A Guide for Students, Practitioners, and Consumers*. Lanham, MD: University Press of America.

Mill, John Stuart. (Many editions). *On Liberty*.

———. (Many editions). *Utilitarianism*.

Miller, Arthur. (1971). *The Assault on Privacy: Computers, Data Banks, and Dossiers*. Ann Arbor: University of Michigan Press.

Modern Media Institute. (1983). *The Adversary Press*. St. Petersburg, FL: Modern Media Institute.

Moore, Melvin M., Jr. (1980). "Blackface in Prime Time." In Bernard Rubin, ed., *Small Voices and Great Trumpets: Minorities and the Media*. New York: Praeger, pp. 117–140.

Newman, Jay. (1989). *The Journalist in Plato's Cave*. Cranbury, NJ: Associated University Presses.

Nietzsche, Freiderich. (Many editions). *Beyond Good and Evil*.

Packard, Vance. (1981). *The Hidden Persuaders*. New York: Pocket Books.

Parenti, Michael. (1992). *Make-Believe Media: The Politics of Entertainment*. New York: St. Martin's Press.

Pecora, Norma. (September, 1995). "Children and Television Advertising from a Social Science Perspective." *Critical Studies in Mass Communication*, 12(3) pp. 354–364.

Peikoff, Leonard. (1983). *Ominous Parallels*. Briarcliff Manor, NY: Stein & Day.

Pember, Don. (1972). *Privacy and the Press*. Seattle: University of Washington Press.

Phillips, David P., and John E. Hensley. (Summer 1984). "When Violence Is Rewarded or Punished: The Impact of Mass Media Stories on Homicide." *Journal of Communication* 34(3), pp. 101–116.

Piaget, Jean. (1932). *The Moral Judgment of the Child*. Glencoe, IL: Free Press.

Postman, Neil. (1985). *Amusing Ourselves to Death*. New York: Viking.

Postman, Neil, and Steve Powers. (1992). *How to Watch TV News*. New York: Penguin.

Rand, Ayn. (1964). *The Virtue of Selfishness*. New York: New American Library.

Rawls, John. (1971). *A Theory of Justice*. Cambridge, MA: Belknap.

Reaves, Shiela. (Fall 1992/Winter 1993). "What's Wrong with This Picture?: Daily Newspaper Photo Editors' Attitudes and Their Tolerance Toward Digital Manipulation." *Newspaper Research Journal* 13(4)/14(1), pp. 131–155.

Rivers, William L., and Cleve Mathews. (1988). *Ethics for the Media*. Englewood Cliffs, NJ: Prentice Hall.

Ritchin, Fred. (1990). *In Our Own Image: The Coming Revolution in Photography*. New York: Aperture Foundation, Inc.

Rosen, Jay, and Davis Merritt Jr. (1994). "Public Journalism: Theory and Practice," an occasional paper of the Kettering Foundation, Dayton, OH.

Rubin, Bernard, ed. (1978). *Questioning Media Ethics*. New York: Praeger.

Sartre, Jean-Paul. (1957). *Existentialism and Human Emotions*. New York: Philosophical Library.

Sauter, Van Gordon, (August 5, 1989). "In Defense of Tabloid TV." *TV Guide*, pp. 2–4.

Schreiner, Tim. (April 1992). "You Can't Ignore News . . . and Those Tabs Aren't All from Mars Any Longer." *Washington Journalism Review*, pp. 33–35.

Schudson, Michael. (1984). *Advertising: The Uneasy Persuasion*. New York: Basic Books.

Seib, Philip. (1994). *Campaigns and Conscience: The Ethics of Political Journalism*. Westport, CT: Praeger.

Serafini, Anthony. (1989). *Ethics and Social Concern*. New York: Paragon Press.

Shepard, Alicia C. (January-February 1994). "Legislating Ethics." *American Journalism Review*, pp. 37–41.

Siebert, Fred S., Theodore Peterson, and Wilbur Schramm. (1956). *Four Theories of the Press*. Urbana: University of Illinois Press.

Silha Center for the Study of Media Ethics and Law. (1998). *Media Ethics & Law Conference Book*. Minneapolis: Silha Center, University of Minnesota.

Smith, Robert E. (Spring 1969). "They Still Write it White." *Columbia Journalism Review*, pp. 36–38.

Speckman, Karon Reinboth. (1994). "Using Data Bases to Serve Justice and Maintain the Public's Trust." *Journal of Mass Media Ethics* 9(4), pp. 235–242.

Surgeon General's Scientific Advisory Committee on Television and Social Behavior. (1972). *Television and Growing Up: The Impact of Televised Violence.* Washington: U.S. Government Printing Office.

Tannenbaum, Percy, and Mervin Lynch. (Summer, 1960). "Sensationalism: The Content and its Measurement." *Journalism Quarterly* 37(2), pp. 381–392.

Twitchell, James B. (1989). *Preposterous Violence: Fables of Aggression in Modern Culture.* New York: Oxford University Press.

Tye, Larry. (September 5, 1993). "Privacy Lost in High-Tech Era." *The Boston Globe,* pp. 1, 3.

Warren, Samuel D., and Louis D. Brandeis. (December 15, 1890). "The Right to Privacy." *Harvard Law Review* 4(5), pp. 193–220.

Weaver, David H., and G. Cleveland Wilhoit. (1996). *The American Journalist in the 1990s: U.S. News People at the End of an Era.* Mahwah, NJ: Lawrence Erlbaum Associates.

Wicker, Tom. (May/June 1971). "The Greening of the Press." *Columbia Journalism Review,* pp. 7–12.

Williams, Frederick, and John V. Pavlik, eds. (1994). *The People's Right to Know: Media, Democracy and the Information Highway.* Hillsdale, NJ: Lawrence Erlbaum Associates.

Willis, W. J. (Jim). (1990). *Journalism: State of the Art.* New York: Praeger.

———. (1991). *The Shadow World: Life Between the News Media and Reality.* New York: Praeger.

Wilson, James Q. (1993). *The Moral Sense.* New York: Free Press.

■ PERIODICALS FOCUSING ON MEDIA ETHICS

Many organizations active in the field of mass media ethics publish newsletters; a list of some of them can be found in *Media Ethics* 8(1), Spring 1996, pp. 24–25.

American Journalism Review, 8701 Adelphi Road, Adelphi, MD 20783-1716.

Columbia Journalism Review, 700 Journalism Building, Columbia University, New York, NY 10027.

Journal of Mass Media Ethics, Lawrence Erlbaum Associates, 10 Industrial Avenue, Mahwah, NJ 07430-2262.

Media Ethics, c/o Department of Visual and Media Arts, Emerson College, 100 Beacon Street, Boston, MA 02116.

Media & Values, Center for Media Values, 1962 S. Shenandoah Street, Los Angeles, CA 90034.

The News Media and The Law, The Reporters Committee for Freedom of the Press, Suite 1910, 1101 Wilson Boulevard, Arlington, VA 22209.

Quill, Society of Professional Journalists, 16 S. Jackson Street, Greencastle, IN 46135-0077.

RTNDA *Communicator,* Radio-Television News Directors Association, Suite 615, 1000 Connecticut Avenue, N.W., Washington, DC 20036.

INDEX

ABC, 36, 51, 154, 155, 206, 234, 263, 279, 293, 294. *See also* Capital Cities/ABC
Absolutism, ethical, 7, 17–18
Abuse, spouse/child, 191, 193
Access to media (by sources), 37, 96, 99, 108, 116–117, 211
Accident victims and privacy, 152, 157–158, 161
Accountability, 160, 217. *See also* Responsibility
Accuracy, 72, 80, 85–86, 87, 88, 169, 179, 180
Accuracy in Media, 96
A. C. Nielsen, 251
Acquired-virtue ethics, 10–12
ACT-UP, 96
Adversarial relationship (press-government), 102–103, 107
Advertisers, 108, 188, 210, 214, 215, 217, 239, 271, 274, 284, 288
  and content control, 212
  and controversial content, 250, 251, 252
  and data bases, 166, 176
  and information access, 111–112, 114, 118
  and large audiences, 206
  specialized audiences, 113, 137–138, 213.
    See also Target audiences
  and Super Bowl, 104
Advertising, 15, 99, 113, 184, 202, 212, 215, 220, 232, 239–241, 247–248, 256, 288, 289, 291
  acceptability standards, 218, 239, 243, 244, 250, 251, 252
  and children, 129, 244, 245, 246, 249, 252
  as "commercial poetry," 241, 254
  condom, 218, 243
  and databases, 165, 166, 167, 174
  deception techniques, 249, 282, 284
  ethics, 239, 240–241, 242, 246–247, 248, 250–251, 254
  and freedom of the press, 251
  gender portrayal, 129
  for harmful products, 243–244
  honesty/dishonesty, 248, 249
  Internet, 174, 242

  political and ideological, 239, 242–243, 253
  and product placement, 275
  and realism, 240–241
  separation from news, 244, 245
  and social responsibility, 239, 248, 249
  and specialized media, 137–138
  and student enrollments, 277
  and Super Bowl, 104
  tobacco products, 102, 118, 243, 244, 251, 252, 253
  and truth, 81, 226, 239, 240–243, 244, 245, 246–247, 253, 254
  violent commercials, 195, 249
  women in, 128–129
Advertising rates, 251
Advertising revenues, 205, 213, 247
Advertorials, 245, 252–253, 254
Affirmative action, 136, 141, 144
Agape ethics, 8, 18–19
Agnew, Spiro, 103
AIDS, 80, 88, 98, 132, 172, 187, 229
Alabama Information Age Task Force, 114, 115, 121
Albert, Marv, 151
Allen, Woody, 282
Allen, Eric W., 63
All the President's Men, 176, 208, 291
Alternative media, 118, 119. *See also*
    Special-interest media
Altruism and media people, 47–48
Altruistic ethics, 7, 15, 16, 53
Ambush journalism, 156, 292
America Oggi (New York), 137
America Online, 173
American Academy of Pediatrics, 195
American Advertising Federation, 58
American Association of Advertising Agencies, 58, 138
American Family Association, 47, 190
American Journalism Review, 261
American Indian nicknames, 133
American Newspaper Guild, 207, 212

American Society of Newspaper Editors (ASNE),
    34, 56, 58–59, 66–67, 130
America's Funniest Home Videos, 95
America's Most Wanted, 233
Amos 'n' Andy, 127
Amsterdam News (New York), 137
Amusing Ourselves to Death, 121
Anchorage Daily News, 36
Andrea Doria, 257
Ann-Margret, 283
Antinomian ethics, 18
Aristotle, 20
    and economic marketplace, 203
    individualistic ethics, 7
    virtue ethics, 10–11
Aristotle's Golden Mean, 11
    and advertising, 245
    and autonomy, 50
    and codes of ethics, 64
    and conflicts of interest, 260, 263
    and diversity, 131
    and economic marketplace, 219
    and freedom/responsibility, 32, 36
    and media manipulation, 100, 101, 104
    and personal data reuse, 170
    and privacy, 158, 170, 178
    and public relations, 104
    and tabloid news programming, 230, 231
    and truth, 81
Arnett, Peter, 88
Associated Press, 213
Associated Press Managing Editors (APME), 58
Associated Press Sports Editors Association, 58
Audiences, 221
    and access, 116–117
    and moral values, 45, 48, 95
    participation, 37, 45, 94–96, 101
    responsibilities, 116, 118, 119, 120, 122
Audit Bureau of Circulation, 251
Auletta, Ken, 166, 226, 280
Autonomy, individual, 101
    and conglomerates, 48–50
    and organizational pressures, 49–50
Ayer, A. J., 18

Bagdikian, Ben, 50, 51
Bank Privacy Act, 175
Banville, John, 244
Barnes, Hazel, 22
Barney, Ralph, 74, 76, 77, 131
BBC, 285
Beavis and Butthead, 184
Becker, Lee B., 278
Bellah, Robert N., 11
Bell Atlantic, 207
Bell Curve, The, 136

Ben & Jerry's, 207, 217
Benedict, Helen, 129, 152
Benedict, Ruth, 12–13
Bentham, Jeremy, 8, 16, 203
Bernays, Edward, 65
Bernstein, Carl, 176, 291
Bertrand, Claude-Jean, 160
Better Government Association, 15
Biondi, Frank, Jr., 166
Black Entertainment Network (BET), 137
Black, Hugo, 28
Black, Jay, 74, 76, 77, 171
Blake, Eugene Carson, 63
Blasphemy, 187, 289
Bloom County, 285
Bogart, Humphrey, 244
Bohn, Thomas W., 115
Bok, Sissela, 73, 74, 155, 158, 242
Bonhoeffer, Dietrich, 19
Books, 239
    publishers, 208
    sales, 215
Bookstore chains, 208
Boorstin, Daniel, 104, 226
Borden, Lizzie, 192
Borgers, Edward, 140
Boston Globe, 244
Boys on the Bus, The, 286
Bozell, L. Brent, 96
Bradlee, Ben, 261–262, 293, 294
Branch Davidian conflict, 290
Brandeis, Louis D., 148, 172
Brand-name products in films, 92, 95, 102,
    275–276
Bravo network, 210
Breed, Warren, 48
British Press Council, 97
Broadcasters' code of ethics, 59, 64
Brotman, Barbara, 41, 44, 45
Broun, Heywood, 187
Brown, Murphy, 289
Brunner, Emil, 13
Buchanan, Pat, 260
Buckley, William, 237
Buddha, 54
Budiansky, Stephen, 2, 16
Bultmann, Rudolf, 19
Burger, Warren, 26, 27
Bush, President George, 47, 204, 216
Bylines and news releases, 94, 97

Cable Franchise Policy and Communications Act,
    167, 168
Cable television, 206, 208, 209, 210, 214, 239
    and access to information, 113
    content choice, 209, 210

industry, 207
and infotainment programming, 235
interactive systems, 166, 170
mergers, 207, 208, 217
premium channels, 215
and privacy, 166, 167–168, 172
programming, 210, 235
regulation, 47
tiers of service, 112
Caesar's wife (Calpurnia), 88, 256, 261, 265, 280
Cameras, hidden, 15, 74, 151, 154, 155, 156, 293–294
Campaign finance reform, 209
Canada, privacy concerns, 170
Cannon, "Uncle Joe," 204
Canons of Journalism, 58–59
Capen, Richard, Jr., 76
Capital Cities/ABC, 207, 208. *See also* ABC
Capital Times (Madison, WI), 81
Carey, James, 216
Cartoons (TV), 195, 199
Casablanca, 244
Casey, Ginger, 36
Categorical imperative, 17, 53, 64, 74, 78, 79, 141. *See also* Kant, Immanuel
    and advertising, 246, 254
    and affirmative action, 141
    and codes of ethics, 64
    and conflicts of interest, 260
    and digital manipulation of photographs, 284
    and freedom of expression, 31
    and gifts, 265, 267
    and infotainment, 229
    and media manipulation, 100, 104
    and political activity, 262
    and truth (in advertising), 254
CBS, 89, 156, 196, 208, 228, 233, 264, 293
Censorship, 30, 106, 184, 211, 239, 289
    and violence in media, 182, 186, 187, 189
Census data (U.S.), 139, 173
Center for Media and Public Affairs, 96, 127
Center for Media and Values, 218
Center for Press and the Public, 216
"Central Park jogger" case, 129
Challenger explosion, 84, 286
Channel One, 246
Chapman, Alvah, 219, 263
Chat rooms, 165, 173
Checkbook journalism, 270–273
Chicago Sun-Times, 15, 293
Chicago Tribune, 36, 41, 49, 50
Children
    access to adult media, 118
    and advertising, 129, 244, 245, 246, 249
    juvenile delinquency, 184, 185

and violent programming, 188, 189, 191, 193, 195, 196
Children's Television Act, 246
"Chilling effect," 28
China Press (New York), 137
Christian morality, 18–19, 22
Christians, Clifford, 3, 121, 131, 158
Chrysler Corporation, 212
Chung, Connie, 89, 293
Churchill, Winston, 211
Cigarette advertising, 243, 244, 252
Cinemax, 210
Civic journalism, 257, 259, 260, 264, 266
Civility, 143, 144, 145, 287–288, 290, 291
Clinton, Hillary Rodham, 89
Clinton, President Bill, 35, 44, 84, 121, 153, 172, 223, 228
CNN, 36, 113, 224, 230, 263, 286
Codes of ethics, 68, 146, 209
    advertising, 246
    benefits, 63–64, 68–69
    broadcasters' codes, 59, 64
    company codes, 58, 59–60, 66–67
    enforcement, 58, 61, 64, 66
    goals, 67–68
    and government, 58
    history, 56–58, 63
    internalized, 12
    international, 65
    interpretations, 60, 68
    and new technologies, 65
    professional organization codes, 56, 58–60, 64, 259
    public relations, 56–57, 61, 65
    violations, 66–67
"Codes of good practice" (film/TV), 187
Cohen, Ben, 207
Cohen, Jeff, 96
Cohen v. *Cowles Media Co.*, 66
Columbia Journalism Review, 160, 261
Comedy Channel, 234
Comics, 229, 285
Commercial speech doctrine, 28, 243–244
Commission on Freedom of the Press, 38, 97, 125, 131, 135, 145, 197, 198, 216
Committed Journalism, 43
Common-sense ethics. *See* Intuitive ethics
Communications Act, 28, 172, 192, 209, 212, 275–276
Communications Decency Act, 30–31, 47, 182
Communitarian ethics, 3, 4, 5, 38, 52, 54, 121, 131, 264
    and codes of ethics, 70
    and privacy, 180
    and violent content, 199
Community, 145

sense of, 137
Community media, 118
Company codes of ethics, 58, 59–60, 66–67
CompuServe, 173, 187
Computer-assisted reporting, 79, 168
Computerized databases. *See* Database
    information
Computers, 85, 164, 173, 174, 206, 214, 283
Condom advertising. *See* Advertising, condom
Confidentiality (sources), 66
Confidential magazine, 228
Conflicts of interest, 43, 65, 256–257, 261,
    265–267, 280
Confucius, 10, 11–12, 20
Conglomerates, 48, 50, 51, 208, 219
    and media, 202, 203, 213, 221
    and synergy, 219
Conscience and ethics, 6–7, 8, 15, 19
Consequence-related ethics. *See* Teleological
    theories
Conservative political theory, 213
Consumer education, 45, 160, 213, 215–216,
    218–220, 226, 240, 246, 261, 284. *See also*
    Media literacy
Consumer Reports, 239
Consumers as revenue source, 214, 215, 217
Contact, 263
Contextual ethics. *See* Situation ethics
Convergence of media, 214
Cops, 95, 234
Copycat crimes, 185, 197
Copyright protection of images, 283–284
Courier-Journal (Louisville), 111
Court TV, 158, 286
Cowlings, Al, 272
Cox Broadcasting Corp. v. *Cohn*, 159
Craig, David, 264
Cranberg, Gilbert, 252
Credibility, 43, 56, 77, 78, 81, 86, 87–88, 155, 179,
    218, 219, 220, 234, 244, 256, 258, 259, 261,
    262, 263, 264, 265, 266, 271, 272, 273, 280,
    281
Credit reporting, 167, 179
Creedon, Pamela, 133
Crime victims and privacy, 152, 158–159, 160,
    161
Crouse, Timothy, 286
C-SPAN, 113, 230
Cultural relativism, 12–13
Curran, John Philpot, 84
Current Affair, A, 161, 234, 236, 270
Custer, George Armstrong, 75
Custom and ethics, 6–7

Daily News (Chicago), 264–265
Dallas Morning News, 31

Databanks, government and private, 167,
    168, 170, 171–172, 175, 176, 179
Database information, 154, 164, 171–172, 173,
    179–180
    disclosure justification, 169, 171
    errors in, 167, 171, 179
    and governmental control, 167, 171, 180
    and media, 165–169, 171, 174, 176–178, 179,
        180
    and public figures, 165, 178
    reuse of, 165, 166, 167–169, 170, 171, 172,
        178–179
    sale of, 177
"Data rape," 166–167, 175, 180
Dateline NBC, 45, 233
Death of a Princess, 289
Deceptive advertising, 240, 242, 248–249, 254.
    See also Advertising, deception techniques
Deceptive information gathering, 15, 16, 43,
    44–45, 74–75, 151, 154, 155, 293, 294
Deep Impact, 263
"Deep Throat," 208
de Maistre, Joseph, 3
Dennis, Everette E., 16, 74, 76, 80, 109–110, 213,
    214, 216, 219
Denniston, Lyle, 155
Deontological theories, 7, 17, 209
    and advertising, 253
    and economic competition, 209
    and truth, 81, 89–90
Department of Labor (U.S.) statistics, 286
Deregulation, 28, 46, 204, 206, 209, 216
Dershowitz, Alan, 65, 70
De Tocqueville, Alexis, 11
Diana, Princess of Wales, 35, 36, 148, 161, 223,
    285
Die Hard 2, 195
Digital manipulation of photographs, 74, 84–85,
    249, 281–285
Dime novels, 182
Direct marketing
    and databases, 166, 167, 168
    online, 174
Directors Guild of America, 129
Disney Corporation, 51, 102, 207, 208, 262, 294
Divine command theory, 13
Docudramas, 72, 76, 149, 236
Donahue, Phil, 224, 227
Donaldson, Sam, 263, 279, 280
Doonesbury, 229, 285
Drudge Report, 36
Dworkin, Andrea, 189

Economic barriers to media, 215. *See also*
    Information access equity
Economic competition, 205, 206, 208, 212, 217

Economic marketplace and media, 52, 202–208, 209–210, 212–215, 217–221, 272, 277
and new technologies, 214, 219, 221
Economics, theoretical and applied, 203, 204
Egoism, ethical, 14–15, 20
and autonomy, 50
and privacy, 162, 169
Ehrenreich, Barbara, 225
Eighteenth Amendment, 187
Elbot, Eric, 110
Elderly characters portrayed in media, 127, 142
El Diario-La Prensa (New York), 137
Electronic bulletin boards, 154, 165, 166, 174
Electronic newsgathering (ENG), 48
Elitism, 4, 77, 114, 122, 215, 224, 230
Elliott, Deni, 31, 154
Elmer Gantry, 289
E-mail, 151, 154, 165, 166, 174
Emotivism, 13
Employees. *See also* Salaries, media
and company codes, 59–60, 66–67, 265
and freedom of expression, 5–6, 258, 262
Employment statistics, media, 129–130
Encryption
protection, 174
systems, 175–176
Endres, Fred F., 41–42
Entertainment media, 98, 208, 214, 220, 275
and pressure groups, 46–48, 98
and privacy, 156
and stereotypes, 126–128
and truth, 72, 73, 75–76
and violence, 182, 191, 192, 196, 197, 199
women in, 129–130
Entertainment Tonight, 234
Estate tax laws, 217
Ethical subjectivism, 13
Etzioni, Amitai, 3, 54, 121
European Union and data privacy, 167
Execution of criminals, 197, 224
Existentialist ethical theory, 21–23, 70

Fact-checking, 86
Fairness, 31, 37, 44, 46, 72, 73, 74, 80, 81, 86–87, 88, 89, 105, 124, 143, 144, 145, 146, 158, 169, 178, 179, 180, 188, 211, 240, 245, 265
Fairness & Accuracy in Reporting, 96
Fairness Doctrine, 28, 31, 46, 86
Fanning, Katherine, 36
Federal Communications Commission (FCC), 28, 46, 174, 183, 187, 197, 206
Federal Trade Commission (FTC), 240, 246, 293
Feminists, 142, 144, 187
Films, 50, 102, 127, 208, 215, 229, 239, 244, 251, 263, 282, 288
and AIDS, 229

anti-Communist, 46–47
brand-name products in, 92, 95, 102, 239, 275–276
code of ethics, 59
historical, 72, 75–76
rating systems. *See* Rating systems (TV and film)
technologies for faking, 282
and violence, 182, 185, 195–196
First Amendment, 209, 210, 294
and advertising, 251, 252. *See also* Commercial speech doctrine
and censorship, 188
and codes of ethics, 58, 70
and commercial speech doctrine, 28, 243–244
and conflicts of interest, 262–263
and ethical standards, 65
and financial contributions, 258
and freedom of expression, 32, 34, 37, 44, 96
and individual rights, 34–35
and information access, 109, 110–111, 113, 115, 121
and infotainment, 236
and libel, 198
and media content, 108
and privacy, 35, 159, 161, 162, 178
and religion, 290
and violent content, 182, 184, 188, 189, 191, 194, 195, 196, 197, 198
Fisher, Amy, 102, 156
Flaherty, Robert, 281
Fletcher, Joseph, 8, 18–19
Food Lion v. *ABC*, 74, 154, 155, 293, 294
For Better or For Worse, 229
Forrest Gump, 282
48 Hours, 233
Four Theories of the Press, 131
Fourth Amendment and privacy, 172
Fowler, H. W., 140
Fowler, Mark, 206
Fox network, 127
France-Amerique (New York), 137
Frank, Barney, 29
Freedom (of expression), 43, 266
and employees, 5–6, 258, 262
and privacy, 162, 171
regulation, 27–28, 29–30, 31
and responsibility, 26–29, 30–32, 34–35, 37, 38–39, 171, 198
Freedom of information, 211
Freedom of Information Act, 177
Freedom principle, 43, 73, 245
"Free marketplace of ideas." *See* "Marketplace of ideas"
Freud, Sigmund, 18, 19
Friendly, Fred, 292

Gannett, 265
Gannett 2000, 114
Gartner, Michael, 45
Gender-based ethics, 8–9, 191
General Electric, 208
General Motors, 45
General semantics, 237–238
Gerbner, George, 127, 128, 186, 194
Gifts to media people, 259, 264–265, 267
Gilligan, Carol, 8–9, 191
Gilmore, Gary, 36
Gingrich, Newt, 89, 204, 293
Glasser, Theodore, 31, 113, 121
Goethe, Johann Wolfgang von, 205
Golden Mean. *See* Aristotle's Golden Mean
Golden Rule, 14
Goldman, Ron, 270
Goldstein, Tom, 16
Gore, Vice President Al, 211, 224
Gore, Tipper, 198
Government, 216, 217. *See also* Regulation,
    government
    and codes of ethics, 58
    funding of media, 214, 217, 247
    public relations, 99, 102, 103, 107
    "revolving door" with journalism, 257, 260,
        264
Government Printing Office, 173
Graphic (New York), 282
Greatest Happiness Principle, 16–17, 79. *See also*
    Utilitarianism
Greene, Bob, 36
Greenfield, Jerry, 207
Greenfield, Meg, 192, 197–198
Gresham's Law (media), 231
Griffith, Thomas, 96
Griffiths, David, 82
Grisham, John, 197
Group W (former), 31, 46
Guild Reporter, 207
Gulf War, The, 88, 102, 133, 142, 173

Habermas, Jurgen, 259
Hall, Stuart, 140
Hannaford, Ivan, 136, 138, 140
Hard Copy, 148, 161, 168, 188, 225, 227, 234,
    236, 262, 271
Harding, Tonya, 174
Harmon, Mark, 30
Harrison, Stanley L., 277, 278
Hart, Gary, 178
Hart, H. L. A., 31, 32
Harvard Law Review, 148, 172
Hausman, Carl, 168
Hazlitt, Henry, 12
HBO, 210

Health care, 204–205
Hearst, William Randolf, 259
Hegel, Georg W. F., 11, 54
Heidegger, Martin, 70
Heinlein, Robert, 135, 211
Hellenic Times (New York), 137
Helms, Jesse, 214
Henry, William A., III, 4–5, 122
Hermann, Jean-Maurice, 63
Hewitt, Don, 15, 75
Hidden cameras. *See* Cameras, hidden
Hiebert, Ray Eldon, 115
Hill & Knowlton, 102
Hillerman, Tony, 139–140
Hippocratic Oath, 56
Historical films, 72, 75–76
Hobbes, Thomas, 14, 20
Hodges, Louis, 294
Holmes, Oliver Wendell, 29
Holmes, Stephen, 3
Holocaust denial, 243
Honesty, 44, 89
Honorifics, 143, 144, 287–288
House Un-American Activities Committee
    (HUAC), 46–47
How to Lie With Statistics, 85
Huff, Darryl, 85
Humaneness principle, 43, 73, 245
Humanistic perspective, 10
Hume, David, 8, 16, 30
Husselbee, L. Paul, 169–170
Hutchins Commission. *See* Commission on
    Freedom of the Press
Hyde v. City of Columbia, 159

Ice-T, 50
Image alteration, 249. *See also* Photographs,
    altering
In Defense of Elitism, 122, 187
"Indecency," 182, 187
Independent Insurance Agents of America, 279
Individual ethics. *See* Personal ethics
Infomercials, 245, 249
Information access equity, 109–117, 119–122, 211
    and media responsibility, 110–115, 119–122
Information(al) apartheid, 109, 117
Information superhighway, 109, 164, 173,
    210–211, 271
Information technologies
    and databases, 174–175
    and information access equity, 109–110, 112,
        114, 115, 120, 121
    and privacy, 167–169, 170
Infotainment
    media, 223, 225, 229, 231–232, 233, 237
    in print media, 225, 228, 235

programs, 223, 226, 227, 228, 230, 231–237
Inside Edition, 161, 170, 234
Instinct and ethics, 6–7
Institute for Media Analysis, 96
Interactive cable systems, 167, 170
Internal Revenue Service, 294
International Association of Business
     Communicators (IABC), 58, 88
International Organization of Journalists, 63
Internet, 30, 47, 103, 112, 113, 114, 115, 165, 173,
     208, 216, 235, 242
   service providers, 166
   sources, 165–166
Interviews, 101, 107, 273, 291–293
Intuitive ethics, 19–20
Investigative Reporters and Editors (IRE), 85
IQ controversy, 136
Irvine, Reed, 96
Irwin, Will, 57–58
I Witness Video, 197

Jackson, Michael, 137, 271
Jamieson, Kathleen Hall, 2
Jaspers, Karl, 12, 54
Jefferson, Thomas, 111, 116
Jerry McGuire, 95
Jesus, 12, 54, 175
Jewell, Richard, 153
Jewish Forward (New York), 137, 139
Jewish War Veterans, 29
Joe Camel, 244
Johannesen, Richard L., 62, 65, 241
Jones, Jenny, 234
Jones, Paula, 153
Josephson Institute of Ethics, 41
Journal-Constitution (Atlanta), 132
Journalism, 2, 11, 39, 69, 106, 228
   and public relations, 93–94, 98–101, 264,
      274–275, 276–279
   and violence, 182, 186, 189, 191, 192–193
Journalism & Mass Communication Educator, 212
Journalism Values Institute, 59
Journalists, 1, 2, 10, 11, 13, 15, 16, 17–18, 44, 52,
      53, 68, 70, 77, 78, 106, 107
   and altruism, 42, 47–48
   and co-option, 273–275, 290
   and data privacy, 168, 171–172, 176–177, 180
   and friendships, 257, 261–262
   paid lectures by, 263, 279, 280, 281
   studies of, 41–44, 48, 49, 60
Journal of the American Medical Association, 193,
     195
"Journotainment," 262
Judeo-Christian ethic, 203
Jung, Carl, 54
Jungle, The, 293

Justice principle, 43, 73, 245
Juvenile delinquency, 184, 185

Kalb, Marvin, 2
Kant, Immanuel, 7, 17, 20, 21, 52, 53, 73, 78, 212,
     265, 266, 274. *See also* Categorical
     imperative
   and advertising, 253, 254
   and checkbook journalism, 272, 273
   and diversity, 141
   and economic marketplace, 203
   and existential ethics, 22
   and infotainment, 229, 232
   and privacy, 158, 169
   and public relations, 104
   and religion, 290
   and speakers' fees, 263
   and truth, 73, 75, 78, 254
   and violent content, 188
Kaplan, Richard, 15
Kefauver, Sen. Estes, 185
Keiretsu (Japan), 208
Kelly, Walt, 229
Kennedy, Jacqueline. *See* Onassis, Jacqueline
     Kennedy
Kennedy, John F., 152, 261–262
   assassination, 188
   assassination footage, 94, 271
Kerner Commission, 130
Kierkegaard, Soren, 8, 22, 53, 54
King, Larry, 237. *See also Larry King Live*
King, The Rev. Martin Luther, Jr., 144
King, Rodney, 94
Klaidman, Stephen, 243
Knight Ridder, 25–43, 219
   project, 114
Kohlberg, Lawrence, 24
Koppel, Ted, 197, 292
Korea Central Daily News (New York), 137
Korzybski, Alfred, 237
Ku Klux Klan, 30
KVUE-TV (Austin, TX), 191, 193

Lambeth, Edmund B., 43, 50, 73, 101, 154, 219,
     245
Landers, Ann, 157–158
Language. *See also* Politically correct language
   "dirty," 287, 288–289, 291
   sexist/racist, 132–133
Larry King Live, 224, 236
Lasch, Christopher, 3, 99
Lasswell, Harold, 256
Lebacqz, Karen, 65, 67
Lehrer, Tom, 183
LePiere, Richard, 18
Lewinsky, Monica, 35, 44, 153, 172, 223, 228

Lewis, C. S., 8, 19
Lexis/Nexis, 173
Libel
  and accuracy, 86
  and company codes, 59
  and fairness, 87
  plaintiffs' concerns, 28
Liberal ethics. *See* Libertarian ethics
Libertarian ethics, 3–5, 212–213
Libertarian views on
  advertising, 248, 252
  economics and ethics, 212–213
  freedom of expression, 32, 28, 39
  privacy, 180
  violent content, 198, 199
Library of Congress, 176
Lichter, Linda, 96
Lichter, S. Robert, 96
Liebling, A. J., 211, 259
Life magazine, 94, 112, 271
Lillie, William, 6
Limbaugh, Rush, 234, 236, 237
Lippmann, Walter, 73, 82, 127
Listserv, 165
Live action, coverage of, 35
Locke, John, 3, 30
Loevinger, Lee, 183–184, 212
"Long Island Lolita." *See* Fisher, Amy
Los Angeles earthquake, 84
Los Angeles Times, 136, 140, 207
Lying, 41, 52, 73, 74, 75, 76, 81, 83, 256, 278, 292, 293, 294

McAuliffe, Christa, 84, 286
McCarthyism, 229
Machiavelli, Niccolo, 15, 50, 52, 77, 169
Machiavellian ethics, 10, 15–16, 50, 259, 266, 294
  and advertising, 253, 254
  and deception and truth, 75, 89, 253
  and media manipulators, 100–101
  and privacy, 169, 170
  and public relations, 104
MacIntyre, Alasdair, 3
McLaughlin, John, 232, 237
McLendon, Gordon, 209
McManus, John, 58
McMasters, Paul, 86
MacKinnon, Catherine, 190
Macon Telegraph, 229
McVeigh, Timothy, 31
Magazine Publishers Association (MPA), 252
Magazines, 50, 205, 208, 210, 213, 283
  and advertising, 239, 252
  subscription lists and privacy, 169, 170, 176
  subscription selectivity, 112

Mallard Fillmore, 229
Mallery, John, 112
Malone, John, 207
Management, media, 209, 212
Mander, Jerry, 247–248
Man of Aran, 281
Marconi, Gugielmo, 205
Marketplace and media. *See* Economic
  marketplace and media
"Marketplace of ideas," 5, 30, 111, 120, 206, 209, 271
  and data, 171
Market research, 213, 214
Markey, Edward, 109
Marks, Jeffrey, 64
Marx, Karl, 54
Marxist theory, 5, 20–21, 212
Maryland Internet access system, 114
Mass communication education, 165, 166
"Mayflower" case, 46
Media advisory boards, 160
Media consumers. *See* Consumers as
  revenue source
Media co-option, 273–275
Media events. *See* pseudo-events
Media, family owned, 208, 217
Media functions, 256
Media literacy, 119, 218, 220. *See also*
  Consumer education
Media ownership and ethics, 219
Media people and political activity, 257–258, 262, 265, 266
"Media rage," 232–233
Media Research Center, 96
Medical records, 177
Mencken, H. L. 211, 216
Mercer, Lucy, 153
Mercury-News (San Jose), 245
Meritocracy, 4. *See also* Elitism
Meyer, Philip, 34, 61, 68
Miami Herald, 27, 76, 263
Miami Herald Publishing Co. v. *Tornillo*, 26–27
Milkovich v. *Lorain Journal Co.*, 87
Mill, James, 3
Mill, John Stuart, 3, 8, 16, 30, 31, 53, 203, 204, 290
Miller, Arthur R., 164, 171
"Million Man March," 258
Milton, John, 30
Minnesota News Council, 62–63, 97
Minorities
  communications students, 143–144
  employed by news media, 129–130, 133, 134–135, 142, 143, 219, 229
  news coverage of, 125, 128–129
  numbers in population, 128, 138–139

portrayed by media, 125, 126–129, 132–133, 134–135, 144, 287

Minow, Newton M., 2–3

Mirage bar, 15, 293

Miranda warning, 152

Mississippi Burning, 75

Missoulian, 160

Modern Maturity, 134

Mondale, Walter, 76

Moral Majority, 96

Morgan, Edward P., 257

Morgan, George, 5

Mother Theresa, 35

Mothers Against Drunk Driving, 96

Motivation ethics, 53–54

Movie Channel, The, 210

Movies. *See* Films

Movietime, 210

Moyers, Bill, 237, 260

Ms. magazine, 129, 247, 250

MSNBC, 263

MTV, 227, 229

Murdoch, Rupert, 36, 49, 285

Murrow, Edward, R., 292

Mutualistic ethics, 15

Nation, 129

National Association of Broadcasters (NAB), 56, 212

National Conference of Editorial Writers, 58

National Dairy Council, 96

National data bank, 175

National Endowment for the Arts, 214

National Enquirer, 148, 188, 223

National Geographic, 134, 283

National News Council, 97

National Press Photographers Association (NPPA), 56, 58

National Rifle Association, 96

Natural Born Killers, 197

Natural law theory, 13–14

Nazi Party, American, 29

NBC, 45, 187, 190, 196–197, 208, 229

NBC Nightly News, 196–197, 229–230

Near v. *Minnesota,* 28

Negative Golden Rule, 12

Net, The, 262

New England Cable News, 230

News Corp., 208

News councils, 37, 62, 97, 160

NewsHour with Jim Lehrer, 223

Newspaper Guild. *See* American Newspaper Guild

Newspapers, 21, 114–115, 205, 208, 210, 214

campus, 243

chain-owned, 217, 219

decline in numbers, 208, 217

distribution in low-income or high crime neighborhoods, 109, 111–112, 113, 117, 132

ethnic, 137

and privacy, 167, 168

profits, 49, 50–51, 212

sensationalism, 56, 228, 288. *See also* Supermarket tabloids

News releases, 98

bylines, 94, 97, 99–100

evaluating, 93–94, 97, 100, 101, 106–107

labeling in stories, 100

video news releases, 93, 94, 98, 100, 103, 253

Newsweek magazine, 74, 186, 192, 261, 283

Newsworthy people and privacy, 148, 149, 150–151, 153–154, 157, 178, 287, 292

New World Information and Communication Order (NWICO), 211

New Yorker, 165

New Yorker Staats-Zeitung, 137

New York Newsday, 207, 262

New York Review of Books, 244

New York Times, 36, 48, 88, 98, 99, 218, 225, 230, 236, 241

New York Times Co. v. *United States. See Pentagon Papers*

Nicomachean Ethics, 10

Nietzsche, Friedrich, 22–23, 54

Nightline, 230, 292

1984, 175, 282

Nixon, Richard, 84, 117, 176

North American Free Trade Agreement, 224

Nothing Sacred, 95

Novoye, Russoye Slovo (New York), 137

Nozick, Robert, 54

NPR (National Public Radio), 233

Objectivity, 44, 72, 74, 80, 81, 83–85, 87, 88, 89, 105, 146, 213, 245, 260, 266, 293

Obscenity, 182, 187, 190, 198, 243–244

Ocurio Asi, 196

Oliver Twist, 184

Ombudsmen, 160

Onassis, Jacqueline Kennedy, 152

Oregonian (Portland), 133

Orwell, George, 175, 180, 282

Oswald, Lee Harvey, 188

Pack journalism, 36, 41, 284, 285–287

Paparazzi, 148, 285

Parent, W. A., 155, 158

Parents Music Resource Center, 198

Payola, 256, 276

PBS (Public Broadcasting System), 224

Peikoff, Leonard, 14, 19

Penny press, 213, 259
Pentagon Papers, 28
People magazine, 153
People's Court, The, 234
Perot, Ross, 224
Personal ethics, 3, 7, 8–9
Personalist theories. *See* Personal ethics
Philadelphia, 229
Photographs, altering, 74, 84–85, 249, 281–284
Piaget, Jean, 24
Pittsburgh Courier, 127
Plagens, Peter, 191
Plato, 7, 21
Plugola, 276
Pluralism, social and journalistic, 124–125, 131, 138
PM (newspaper), 247
Pogo, 229
Political advertising, 239, 242, 253
Political campaign finance reform, 209
Political candidates and privacy, 77, 149–150, 156–157, 177–178
Political correctness and diversity, 142, 144, 145
Politically correct language, 135, 136, 139–140, 144, 145–146
Politically Incorrect, 234
Political party conventions, 104, 105
Political public relations, 102–103, 104–105, 288
Pool coverage, 285, 286
Pornography, 183, 187, 189, 199. *See also* Sexual content of media
and violence, 187, 190
Posse, 132
Postman, Neil, 121–122, 218
Povich, Maury, 234
Powers, Steve, 218
Pragmatic egoism. *See* Machiavellian ethics
President, U. S. and privacy, 35, 44, 153, 178
Press councils. *See* News councils
Press releases. *See* News releases
Pressure groups, 47, 96, 97, 190–191, 198
Price Waterhouse, 278–279
PrimeTime Live, 15, 233, 279
Privacy, 14, 87, 148, 152–153, 211, 256, 270, 294. *See also* Database information
and accident victims, 152, 157–158, 161, 272
British law, 285
and cable television, 166, 167–168
and checkbook journalism, 272
and courts, 159
and crime victims, 152, 158–159, 160, 161
criteria for obtaining/using information, 151, 152, 153–154, 155, 157, 158
defined, 148, 172–173
and entertainment media, 156
and fairness, 87, 169, 178, 179, 180

and First Amendment, 159, 161, 162
and Fourth Amendment, 172
and good taste, 151, 156, 162
and Internet sites, 165
and involuntary public figures, 149, 151, 152, 153, 156, 157, 161, 272, 292
and media, 148, 149–150, 151, 157–158, 168–169, 176–179
and media people, 151, 162, 256
and methods of newsgathering, 154
and newsworthy people, 148, 149, 150–151, 153–154, 157, 178, 272, 287
and political figures, 149–150, 153, 156–157, 177–178
and truth, 77–78
and visual communication, 156, 157, 162, 174
Privacy Act of 1974, 167
Privacy laws, 149, 167–168, 174
Proctor & Gamble, 176
Product placement in films and television, 92, 95, 102, 239, 275–276
Profanity, 187
Professional organization codes, 56, 58–60, 64, 259
Professional perspective, 10, 17
Profits, 203, 212. *See also* Economic marketplace and media
and ethics, 202, 203
and individual autonomy, 49–51, 52
Prohibition, 187
Proposition 209, 141
Psuedo-events, 104–105, 226
"Psuedo-testimonials," 249
Public broadcasting, 113, 205–206. *See also* PBS
Public interest, 161, 178, 214, 274, 278, 279
"Public interest, convenience and necessity," 28, 192, 197
Public journalism. *See* Civic journalism
Public Opinion, 73
Public participation in media activities. *See* Audiences, participation
Public relations, 15, 93, 99, 108, 220, 242, 271, 274–275, 289
code of ethics, 56–57, 61, 65, 278
and databases, 165, 166, 171–172
and ethical standards, 104, 107, 264, 277, 278, 279
government, 99, 102, 103, 107
and journalism, 93–94, 98–101, 264, 274–275, 276–279
political, 103, 104–105, 288
student enrollment, 277–278
textbooks, 278
and truth, 72, 73, 74, 76–77, 81, 87–88, 89–90, 102
wire services, 98

Public Relations Society of America (PRSA), 56–57, 58, 61, 63, 65, 88
Public responsibility (for access to information), 116, 120, 122

Quayle, Vice President Dan, 289
QUBE, 167
Quill, 261
Quotas, 133, 141–143
Racism, 32, 50, 126, 132–133, 136
Radio–Television News Director Association (RTNDA), 56, 58, 64, 130, 177, 259
Rambo III, 195
Ramsey, JonBenet, 101
Rand, Ayn, 8, 14, 15, 211
Rape victims, 10, 86, 90, 129, 158, 226–227, 273
Raphael, Sally Jessy, 234. *See also Sally Jessy Raphael* show
Rashomon, 82
Rather, Dan, 237
Rating systems (TV and film), 47, 96, 118, 182, 186, 187–188, 190, 191, 195
Rawls, John, 20, 30, 54, 83, 88, 100, 104, 113, 131–132, 157, 159, 162, 169, 170, 177, 203, 217, 246
Ray, Ellen, 96
Read All About It!, 49
Reader's Digest, 134
Reagan, President Ronald, 76, 204, 216
Recorded music and violence, 50, 182, 198
    "gangsta rap," 185
Recording industry, 208
"Redeeming social value," 158, 244
Redlining, media, 37, 111–112, 117
Red Lion Broadcasting Co. v. FCC, 28
Reebok, 95
Regulation, government, 46, 47
    control of media, 113, 214
    data privacy regulation, 167, 175, 180
    and freedom of expression, 27–28, 29–30, 31
    and marketplace, 204, 216, 217
Relativism, new, 19
Religion and media, 183, 289–291
Religious ethical theory, 8, 13–14, 18–19
Rescue 911, 95, 223, 234
Research on violence, 184–186, 191, 193–194, 195–196, 197, 199
Responsibility
    and access to personal data, 171
    and First Amendment, 26–27, 31, 113, 121
    and freedom of expression, 28–29, 30–32, 34–35, 38–39, 171, 198
    and information access equity, 109, 110, 113–115, 120, 121
    and the public, 113–114, 120, 135
"Revolving door" between journalism

and government, 257, 260, 264
and public relations, 264
"Right to know," 10, 69, 108, 154, 161, 272
R. J. Reynolds Tobacco Co., 244
Road Runner cartoon, 199
Robocop 2, 195
Rockefeller, Nelson, 153
"Rock the Vote" campaign, 227
Roosevelt, Franklin D., 44, 153
Rousseau, Jean-Jacques, 20
Rowe, Chip, 96
Rumor dissemination, 82
Rushdie, Salman, 187, 289

Salaries, media, 42, 207, 212, 280–281
Salinger, Pierre, 260
Sally Jessy Raphael show, 226, 227. *See also* Raphael, Sally Jessy
Sandel, Michael, 3
Sarajevo, 137
Sartre, Jean-Paul, 21–22
Satanic Verses, 187, 289
Sauter, Van Gordon, 228
Sawyer, Diane, 260
Schaap, William, 96
Schindler's List, 82
Schmalz, Jeffrey, 88, 98
Schopenhauer, Arthur, 54
Schorr, Daniel, 262
Schramm, Wilbur, 139
Screen Actors Guild, 130
Section 315, 86
Securities and Exchange Commission, 209
Seib, Charles B., 61
Seidenbaum, Art, 136
Semantics, general *See* General semantics
Sensational stories/media, 225, 228, 235, 270, 288. *See also* Infotainment, in print media; Newspapers, sensationalism; Supermarket tabloids; Tabloid media; Tabloid news programs; "Trash television"
Sentinel (Orlando), 50
Serafini, Anthony, 2, 11
Sex and Broadcasting, 288
Sexism, 126, 132–133. *See also* Women
Sexual content of media, 182, 183, 189, 190–191, 288–289
Sheepherder's Gazette, 142
Shortwave radio, 173
Showtime, 210
Sidgwick, Henry, 8
Simpson, O. J., 35, 74, 150–151, 162, 223, 237, 262, 270, 271, 272, 283, 286
Sinclair, Upton, 293, 294
Situation ethics, 8, 12, 13, 18–19, 33, 103, 265
    and privacy, 78, 155, 158

60 Minutes, 15, 75, 156, 161, 232, 236
Skokie (IL) march, 29, 32
Smith, Adam, 3, 19
Smith, William Kennedy, 225, 270
Soap operas, 98, 142
Social contract theory, 20–21, 30
Social ethics. *See* Communitarian ethics
Social responsibility (theory), 21, 30, 38, 100, 113, 114, 131, 197, 198, 216, 217, 218, 248, 249, 252, 266. *See also* "Marketplace of ideas"
Socialist theory, 20–21
Socialization by media, 124
Social Security numbers, 175
Social Security tax payments, 41
Society of American Travel Writers, 58
Society of Professional Journalists (SPJ), 56, 58, 60, 64, 68, 69–70, 86, 259
Socrates, 184
Southern Public Relations Federation, 88
"Spamming" 166, 168
Spanish Information Network (SIN), 137
Special interest groups, 96, 97, 99. *See also* Pressure groups
Special-interest media, 116, 137–138, 139
Speech, hateful, 29–30, 32
Spin doctors, 93, 103, 107
Sports events and violence, 186, 196
Springer, Jerry, 232
Springsteen, Bruce, 209
Squires, James, 49, 50, 52
Star, 220
Star Trek, 126, 136
Star Tribune (Minneapolis), 133
State of the Union address, 104–105
Statistical Abstract of the United States, 139
Statistics and accuracy, 85–86
Steele, Bob, 74, 76, 77, 155, 227
Stereotypes, 82, 126–128, 136, 232, 233, 292
    of mass media, 138
    media portrayal of minorities, 126–128, 139, 142
    and rumor dissemination, 82
Stewardship principle, 43, 73, 219, 245
Stolley, Richard, 153
Stone, I. F., 101
Stossel, John, 85
Stuart, Carol DiMaiti, 80
Stuart, Charles, 80
Subjective ethics. *See* Personal ethics
Subjectivism, 13
Subliminal advertising, 275
Super Bowl, 104–105
Supermarket tabloids, 223, 224. *See also* *National Enquirer*, and *Star*
Supreme Court rulings, 26–27, 28, 29, 31, 47, 66, 87, 159

Surgeon General, report on violence, 184
Sutton, Willie, 277
Synergy, 219

Tabloid media, 227–228, 230, 271. *See also* Infotainment media; Sensational stories/ media
Tabloid news programs, 224, 225–227, 228, 236
Talk shows, 95–96, 98, 161, 224–225, 230, 231, 233–234, 236
Tannen, Deborah, 128
Target audiences, 114, 217, 248. *See also* Advertisers, specialized audiences
Tartikoff, Brandon, 209
Telecommunications Act (1996), 209
Tele-Communications, Inc. (TCI), 207, 208
Telemundo, 196, 229
Teleological theories, 7–8, 16, 17, 180. *See also* Machiavellian ethics; Utilitarianism
    and advertising, 153, 154
    and privacy, 149, 172, 180
    and truth, 81, 88, 89–90
Telephone(s), 206, 216
    cellular, 173
    industry, 208, 210, 214, 217
    service, 206
Television. *See also* Cable television programming
    channels, 209, 210
    networks and privacy, 167
    and political campaign finance reform, 209
    programming, 210
    stations, 214, 234
    and violence, 182, 183, 184–186, 187, 189, 190–198
    violence effects, 184–185, 186
Television Digest, 207
Terkel, Studs, 292
Term paper services, 248
Testimonials, 249, 291, 292–293
Texas Tower Massacre, The, 185
Thoman, Elizabeth, 218
Thomas the Tank Engine, 140
Thrasymachus, 23
Tillich, Paul, 19
Time magazine, 74, 122, 283, 298
Times Mirror Company, 207, 216
Time-Warner, 49–50
Title IX, 126
Tobacco industry, lawsuits against, 102, 244
Tobacco Institute, 96
Tornillo, Pat, 27
Total Recall, 102
"Trash television," 223
Trespass, 174
Trudeau, Garry, 229
Trump, Donald and Ivana, 228

Truth, 43, 72, 77–78, 80–83, 87, 88, 89–90, 220, 256, 277, 279, 290, 292
   absolutist view, arguments against, 82–83
   and advertising, 81, 226, 239, 240–243, 244, 245, 246–247, 253, 254
   and computer-assisted reporting, 79
   deontological standard, 81, 89–90
   as first principle, 73–74
   and privacy, 77–78, 169, 179, 180
   and public relations, 72, 73, 74, 76–77, 81, 87–88, 89–90, 102
   teleological theories, 81, 88, 89–90
Truth-telling principle, 73
Turner, Ted, 209
Turow, Joseph, 213, 219
TV Guide, 134, 195, 283
20/20, 161, 233
2 Live Crew, 50
Tydings, Millard, 282

Undercover reporting, 15, 74, 151, 154, 155, 293, 294
UNESCO, 211
Ungurait, Donald F., 115
United Paramount Network (UPN), 127
United States Postal Service, 278–279
United States v. *Schwimmer*, 29
USA Today, 227–228
Utilitarianism, 8, 11, 16–17, 79, 274
Utilitarianism, Rule, 31, 78–79
Utilitarian views on
   advertising, 245–246
   altering images, 284
   autonomy, 53
   checkbook journalism, 272, 273
   civic journalism, 260
   diversity, 131, 141
   economic marketplace, 203, 212, 214, 217, 219
   freedom of expression, 30, 31
   information access equity, 110, 114, 118
   infotainment programming, 230, 232
   interviews and testimonials, 293
   media manipulators, 100, 101, 104, 274
   media workers' activities, 262
   privacy, 154, 159, 169, 170, 177, 178, 179
   product placement, 275
   public relations, 87, 104
   truth, 78–79
   undercover reporting, 294
   violent content, 188, 191

Van Peebles, Mario, 132
VCRs, 235, 246
Veil of ignorance (Rawls), 20, 83, 88, 131, 162, 169, 177
Viacom, 166

Victoria's Secret, 288
Video and audio news releases, 93, 94, 98, 100, 103, 253
Video games, 183, 196, 208
Videotape, amateur, 94, 95, 101, 235
Videotape rentals, information on, 172
Vietnam, pictures of, 189, 282
Village Voice, 129
Violence. *See also* Entertainment media, and violence
   causality, 183, 186, 188, 191, 193, 194, 195
   censorship, 182, 187, 189, 199
   and children's programming, 188, 189, 191, 193, 195, 196. *See also* Children and violent programming
   and films, 182, 185, 195–196
   gratuitous, 192–193, 199
   legal regulation of, 182
   "mean world syndrome," 194
   and media, 182–183, 184, 185, 187, 189, 190, 191–192, 194–198
   and music videos, 195
   and news, 182, 186, 189, 191, 192–193, 196–197
   "porno-violence," 194
   and product liability, 197
   as public health problem, 195, 197
   research on, 184–186, 191, 193–194, 195–196, 197, 199
   and self-regulation, 187, 190, 191, 192, 199
   and society, 182, 183, 185, 188, 190, 191, 192, 194, 198, 199
   and sports, 186, 192, 196
   and spouse/child abuse, 191, 193
   and television, 182, 183, 184–186, 187, 189, 190–198
   and toys, 183
   and video games. *See* Video games
Violence chips in TV sets (V-chips), 185–186, 191
Virtue ethics. *See* Acquired-virtue ethics
Voltaire, F.M.A., de, 3

Wallace, George, 126
Wallace, Mike, 16, 264
Wall Street Journal, 94, 259
Warner Amex, 167
Warner Brothers Network (WNB), 127
Warner Communications, 208
Warren, Samuel D., 148, 172
Washington Post, 36, 61, 117, 160, 230, 293
Washington Star, 61
Watch-dog groups, 96
Watergate, 84, 117, 176, 259
Weather Channel, 230
Weaver, David H., 42–44, 48, 49, 60
Weaver, Pat, 209
Websites, 115, 173

Wertham, Fredric, 184
Westinghouse, 31, 46, 208. *See also* Group W (former)
White House Office of Media Affairs, 274
Whitewater investigation, 84, 172
Whittle Communications, 246
Wicker, Tom, 99
Wildmon, The Rev. Donald E., 47, 190
Wilhoit, G. Cleveland, 42–44, 48, 49, 60
Wilkins, Lee, 157
Willes, Mark H., 207
Williams, Montel, 237
Willis, Jim, 73
Wilson, James Q., 6, 8, 11, 19
Winfrey, Oprah, 161, 234, 236, 237, 283
Wolfe, Tom, 194, 228
Women
  in advertising, 128–129
  and control of media content, 126–127, 129–130, 191
  employed in media, 129–130, 143
  news coverage of, 129
  roles on television, 127, 128–129
Woods, Tiger, 135, 137
Woodward, Robert, 176, 208, 291
WSVN, Miami, 225–226

Yeats, William Butler, 134

Zapruder, Abraham. *See* Kennedy, John F., assassination footage
Zelig, 282
Zero-sum games, 206-207